SBN 684-12814-4

HOBBES
Selections

HOBBES
SELECTIONS

EDITED BY

FREDERICK J. E. WOO

CHARLES SCRIBNER'S S

NEW YORK

CONTENTS

                                                              PAGE
INTRODUCTION—FREDERICK J. E. WOODBRIDGE   ix
BIBLIOGRAPHY xxvii
ELEMENTS OF PHILOSOPHY CONCERNING BODY (Selections)
Chapter   I. Of Philosophy   1
Chapter   II. Of Names   12
             Supplement from Human Nature, Chapter
             V.   18
Chapter   III. Of Proposition   25
Chapter   IV. Of Syllogism   34
Chapter   V. Of Erring, Falsity, and Captions 37
Chapter   VI. Of Method   42
Chapter   VII. Of Place and Time   68
Chapter   VIII. Of Body and Accident   76
Chapter   IX. Of Cause and Effect   93
Chapter   X. Of Power and Act   99
Chapter   XXV. Of Sense and Animal Motion   104
Chapter XXVI. Of the World and of the Stars 124
LEVIATHAN (Selections)
The Epistle Dedicatory   134
The Introduction   136
Chapter   I. Of Sense   138
             Supplement from Human Nature, Chapter
             II.   141
Chapter   II. Of Imagination   146
Chapter   III. Of the Consequence or Train of Imagi-
             nations   157
Chapter   IV. Of Speech   164
Chapter   V. Of Reason and Science   174
Chapter   VI. Of the Interior Beginnings of Voluntary
             Motions, commonly called the Passions;
             and the Speeches by which they are ex-
             pressed   185
             Supplement from Liberty and Necessity .   205

viii CONTENTS

Chapter VII. Of the Ends or Resolutions of Discourse . 211

Chapter VIII. Of the Virtues commonly called Intellectual;
and their contrary Defects 217

Chapter IX. Of the several Subjects of Knowledge . . 234

Chapter XII. Of Religion 235

Chapter XIII. Of the Natural Condition of Mankind as
concerning their Felicity and Misery . . 249

Parallel Chapter from Philosophical Rudiments concerning Government: Of the
State of Men without Civil Society . . 257

Chapter XIV. Of the First and Second Natural Laws, and
of Contracts 268

Parallel Chapter from Philosophical Rudiments: Of the Law of Nature concerning
Contracts 286

Chapter XV. Of other Laws of Nature 295

Parallel Chapter from Philosophical Rudiments: Of the other Laws of Nature . . 312

Chapter XVI. Of Persons, Authors, and Things Personated 330

Chapter XVII. Of the Causes, Generation, and Definition of
a Commonwealth 335

Chapter XVIII. Of the Rights of Sovereigns by Institution 340

Chapter XIX. Of the several Kinds of Commonwealth by
Institution, and of Succession to the
Sovereign Power 357

Chapter XXI. Of the Liberty of Subjects 369

Chapter XXXI. Of the Kingdom of God by Nature . . . 381

Chapter XLIII. Of what is Necessary for a Man's Reception into the Kingdom of Heaven . . . 395

A Review and Conclusion 406

INTRODUCTION

THOMAS HOBBES, by publishing in London, in 1651, a book with the title, *Leviathan, or the Matter, Form, and Power of a Commonwealth Ecclesiastical and Civil*, made a place for himself among those writers on social and political subjects who find many readers in lands and times besides their own. The book can be read with profit without any knowledge of its author. There are in it, to be sure, quaintnesses and allusions which require an understanding of the conditions under which it was written, and of the man who wrote it, if they themselves are to be understood. These, however, affect so little what we call the philosophy of the book, that a reader can find that philosophy for himself, and find in it a vigorous challenge to his own thinking about man, society, and government. This is because Hobbes has asked and answered questions which are neither local nor temporary. They are questions men repeatedly ask when they become curious about human institutions. What are rights and obligations? How do they arise? How reasonable are they? On what basis do they rest? What are good and evil? What are justice and injustice? What is law? What authority is back of it? What respect and obedience are due it? What is liberty? Why should personal liberty be surrendered? What is government? Why do men submit to it? Questions like these Hobbes asks and answers. They are recurring questions. They are still asked. His answers are his own, but they are made in a way which makes the reader consider them as possible answers to be sifted and weighed. The reader may find fault with them. He is pretty sure, in this day, to find fault with that picture "of the natural condition of mankind as concerning their felicity and misery"—that war of every man against every man—which Hobbes paints with vividness and power, but of which no anthropologist has as yet been able to find the suitable original. But the attentive reader will not miss Hobbes's own comment on the matter. He will find himself driven to ask why then are locked doors, police, courts, armies, navies; why nations, "because of their independency, are in continual jealousies and in the state and position of gladiators; having their weapons pointing and their eyes fixed on one another?" Why do men seek to protect peace? As long as peace is an armistice, Hobbes might have said, there is ample evidence of the natural condition of mankind. He compels the reader to think in terms of peace and war, and to remember the lock on the door and the battleship in the harbor. He wanted peace passionately and was ready to pay an extravagant price for it. The reader has to make his own estimate of the cost.

The *Leviathan* is, then, a book which can be read by the student of politics immediately, without an introduction and without a commentary. This fact and the book's power, keep it in the select library of masterpieces in government. For an understanding of Hobbes, the man, it is not, however, the book with which to begin. I have mentioned it at the beginning of this introduction to the selections from Hobbes's writings which follow, because I think there is profit in distinguishing between men and their books. When an author produces a book which history takes out of his place and his time, and puts into the library of great intellectual possessions, it has ceased to be his book and become ours, ours to read, ponder, and enjoy in the realm of our own thinking, to be worked with and played with, not for an understanding of the author but for a clarification of our own ideas. This is what great books are for. They are companions for the mind. As we walk and talk with them, we may see things their authors never saw, and find things they never intended. These consequences are the tests of the greatness of the books. It proves that they are not dead, but living, even if their authors are forgotten, or belonged to ages long ago and lived amid institutions long disused. There is at least one book of Hobbes like that.

It was, however, his book when he made it. Thinking of this, we turn to the man and ask questions we would not otherwise ask. Who was he and what was he like? What else did he write, and how did this book, in which we can forget him, fit into his own life and his own time? We pass out of the realm of our own reflective ideas and enter the realm of history. We experience a radical change of attitude. Now our thinking is controlled by the facts we find. We become observers of a personality, and are curious about the forces which worked upon him and made him what he was. As we succeed in finding these out, we become more and more conscious of the difference there can be between men and books, and how men may work for one end and their books for another; how they die while their books live. And this consciousness is no small part of what philosophy is—an attempt genuinely to appreciate the interplay between the world of ideas and that world of the body in which we respond to circumstances and forces which we try to control.

"Thomas Hobbes," to quote from the interesting life

of him by his friend, John Aubrey,[1] "was second son of
Mr. Thomas Hobbes, vicar of Charlton and Westport,
juxta Malmesbury.—Thomas, the father, was one of
the ignorant Sr. Johns of Q. Elizabeth's time, could
only read the prayers of the church, and the homilies;
and valued not learning, as not knowing the sweetness
of it. He had an elder brother whose name was Francis,
a wealthy man, and alderman of the borough; by profession a glover, which is a great trade here, and in
times past much greater. Having no child, he contributed much to, or rather altogether maintained, his
nephew Thomas, at Magdalen-hall, in Oxon; and when
he dyed gave him *agellum*, a pasture, called Gasten-
ground, lying neer to the horse-faire, worth 16 or 18
poundes per annum." His ancestry was not conspicuous, but, as Aubrey remarks, "his renowne has and will
give brightness to his name and familie." He was born
in Westport, that English village with the glovers'
trade, on April 5, 1588, while the Spanish Armada was
off the coast of England bringing terror to the hearts
of English men and women. Hobbes thought that this
terror had influenced his life. In an autobiography
written in Latin verse late in his life he says:

> Atque metum tantum concepit tunc mea mater,
> Ut pareret geminos, meque metumque simul.

He and fear, like twins, were born together. His birth
and life were shadowed by war. He died on December
4, 1679. Those ninety-one years of his life were coincident with a very important period of English history
—the reigns of Elizabeth and James I, the trouble with
the Stuarts, the Civil War, Cromwell, the Restoration.
The "glorious revolution" of 1688, which put William,

---

[1] *Lives of Eminent Men,* the London edition of 1813. There
is a later edition of this interesting book: J. Aubrey, *Brief
Lives,* ed. A. Clarke, Oxford, 1898.

prince of Orange, and Mary, daughter of Charles I of England, on the throne on February 13, 1689, Hobbes did not live to see. He liked to think of himself as a scholar, a philosopher, a man of science and letters, temperamentally aloof from turbulent scenes, but the troubles of his country would not let his mind be at peace to compose, in orderly fashion, the system he had planned. Its order was interrupted. He tells us in a comment on his *De Cive*—a forerunner of the *Leviathan*: "I was studying philosophy for my mind's sake, and I had gathered together its first elements in all kinds; and having digested them into three sections by degrees, I thought to have written them, so as in the first I would have treated of *body* and its general properties; in the second of *man* and his special faculties and affections; in the third, of *civil government* and the duties of subjects. Wherefore the first section would have contained *the first philosophy*, and certain elements of physic; in it we would have considered the reasons of *time, place, cause, power, relation, proportion, quantity, figure*, and *motion*. In the second, we would have been conversant about *imagination, memory, intellect, ratiocination, appetite, will, good* and *evil, honest* and *dishonest*, and the like. What this last section handles, I have now already showed you. Whilst I contrive, order, pensively and slowly compose these matters; (for I only do reason, I dispute not;) it so happened in the interim, that my country, some few years before the civil wars did rage, was boiling hot with questions concerning the rights of dominion and the obedience due from subjects, the true forerunners of an approaching war; and was the cause which, all those other matters deferred, ripened and plucked from me this third part. Therefore it happens, that what was last in order, is yet come forth first in time. (English Works, Molesworth ed., vol. ii, p. xix.) Thus his controlling interest in stable government and established peace was like an offspring of that dread of war in which he was born.

He seems to have been a precocious child, "playsome enough," but with a "contemplative melancholinesse; he would get him into a corner, and learn his lesson by heart presently. His haire was black, and the boys, his schoolfellows, were wont to call him Crowe." Aubrey tells us that he went to school in Westport when four years old, and could, at that time, read well, and number four figures. With the help of his teachers, and particularly of a Mr. Latimer, "a good Grecian, and the best that came into our parts since the Reformation," he was ready to go to Magdalen Hall, Oxford, at the age of fourteen, having already, if we can believe the story, "turned Euripides' Medea out of Greek into Latin Iambiques." The teaching at Oxford bored him after a while. Aristotelian logic amused him and Aristotelian physics bewildered him. Apparently he did nothing with mathematics, a subject which later much occupied his mind, and led him into a bitter controversy with the Oxford professors over such problems as squaring the circle and duplicating the cube. Aubrey tells us: "He was forty years old before he looked on geometry, w'ch happened accidentally." He found, in a gentleman's study, a copy of Euclid open at Bk. I, Prop. 47. "So he reads the proposition, 'By G—,' says he, 'this is impossible!' So he reads the demonstration of it, w'ch referred him back to another, w'ch he also read, et sic deinceps, that at last he was demonstratively convinced of that truth. This made him in love with geometry." It was not from the teaching of Oxford that he seems to have profited, but from its book-stores, where he read about men and the world, and would gaze for hours at maps, feeding his mind on pictures of the globe and the stars. Yet he was admitted as a bachelor in 1608, and was well enough thought of by the University to be recommended as tutor to the son of William Cavendish, later the second Earl of Devonshire.

With this family he formed a life-long intimacy. Their social position and political fortunes carried him into the turmoil of public life in which his opinions were formed. The travels, incident to this connection, enlarged his mind and made him acquainted with the work of such men as Galileo, Kepler, and Descartes. His imagination was fired by the "new learning" which was producing men of such evident genius. He would be of their number. In Francis Bacon he saw a man to admire and emulate. So in teaching, travelling, meeting the leaders in thought and action, reading, now at home in the thick of political strife, now abroad in the interest of personal safety or public affairs, his project of a system of philosophy which would embrace the principles of all knowledge, was conceived. It is no small wonder that he succeeded in rounding it out in terms of the outline which he made—*De Corpore, De Homine, De Cive.* And it is a greater wonder that he wrote so much besides.

In 1675 he left London, *cum animo nunquam revertendi,* and spent the remainder of his days with the Earl of Devonshire at Chatsworth and Hardwick in contemplation and study. In the latter place he died after an illness lingering through October to December, 1679. Hobbes is described by his friend and contemporary, John Aubrey, as six feet high and something better; with a good eye of hazel colour; with a head of mallet form approved by the physiologers, and with a temperament "sanguineo-melancholicus," similarly ap-

proved; of temperate and regular habits; as an har-
monical soul and not a woman-hater, although never
married; of a sharp wit which was also sure and
steady; as one who contemplated more than he read,
and who remarked "that if he had read as much as
other men, he should have been as ignorant as they";
and as a man who "would have the worship of God
performed with musique."

Hobbes may have spoken contemptuously of those
who read many books, as Aubrey declares, but it is
evident from his writings that he read much, that he
had a taste for literature, and that he developed an
exceptionally clear and forceful English prose. He
knew how to use his mother-tongue with effect and
beauty. The books he read which influenced him most
are difficult to discover. He writes like one familiar
with the field he is exploring, but keeps hidden from
the reader the sources of that familiarity. It is clear,
however, from his life, that he learned from books and
men, from his own experience as he went about, and
not from what we call research and experiment. He
was naturally fertile in ideas and his experiences quick-
ened their activity. He had an ingenious mind which
played freely and freshly with a subject, and suggested
a competence which he did not really have unless that
subject happened to be, like the political situation in
the England of his day, something which forced facts
upon his attention and stimulated his keen perception
of men and affairs. Clearly he knew more about human
nature than about nature at large, more about human
history than the history of the stars, more about the
motions of men than the motions of bodies. Much of
this knowledge he must have gained directly from observation and experience, for it rings true to such a
source, and implies an insight original and keen. Yet

that story of the boy turning the Medea of Euripides
out of Greek into Latin iambics may point to a source
of ideas from which his imagination was early stored.
His first published work, in 1628, was a translation of
eight books of Thucydides' *History of the Pelopon-
nesian War*. Later he translated the *Iliad* and *Odyssey*
of Homer. In his Latin autobiography he speaks of
his early years in the service of the Duke of Devonshire, "who was not only his Lord but truly his friend,"
as that part of his life by far the sweetest, and often
recurring in his dreams, years when he read the histories of Greeks and Romans and their poetry—Flac-
cus, Virgil, Homer, Euripides, Sophocles, Plautus,
Aristophanes, and more. Of the many historians
Thucydides pleased him most because he showed him
how inept democracy is. Here was a whole library on
human nature. Here were men portrayed in legend, in
story, on the stage, in action, in adventure, in war, in
all their heroisms, egotisms, intrigues, enmities, friend-
ships, triumphs, plottings, violences. Hobbes, twin
brother to fear, brought up in an almost illiterate house-
hold and in a little village, going to college at fourteen
to read histories and look at maps, then, in his early
manhood, storing his mind from that library on human
nature, did not look out upon troubled England with
eyes unprepared.

He had, indeed, for a political writer, as good a
preparation as the time afforded. We must, of course,
grant him some genius and also what may be called a
personal bias, for it is evident enough that the reading
of Greek and Latin literature is not itself the promise
of a great achievement to come as a consequence. Many
read and do no more. Their attitude towards life may
be little affected by Homer or Thucydides. With
Hobbes, however, the circumstances of his life and his

habit of mind—what Aubrey calls his "contemplative melancholinesse"—point in a quite different direction. He was timid in action, but courageous in reflection. The melancholy was contemplative, not gloomy. He saw the human struggle for security and peace as a *human* struggle, and so seeing it, could see in Greece and Rome and England illustrations of something universal about man as distinct from those historical circumstances which make him a Greek or a Roman or an Englishman. His bias was for a strong government which would secure peace and order, and it appears from things said about him that he was willing to accept either a Cromwell or a Stuart if that desired security would thereby be attained. He was thus a political philosopher rather than a politician. He lifted experience into the realm of ideas to get as clear a vision as he could of what experience is like. And in his case the realm of ideas had been colored by that reflective melancholy which fed first on the doings of men as portrayed in Greek and Latin literature.

His education and early reading make it difficult to believe that his doctrines of human nature and the state were originally conceived as part of a complete system of philosophy. Certainly the system which he did develop finds little echo in his education. That system owns a close kinship with mathematics and its application to the problems of bodies in motion. But it was only in middle life that Hobbes's interest in mathematics was aroused, and it is not until his second visit to the continent in 1629 that we find clear indications of an interest in problems of motion. And his third visit in 1634 finds him eagerly seeking the acquaintance of such men as Galileo and Mersenne, reading the new science, discussing with learned men and corresponding with them. In Paris he joined a circle about Mersenne, who was living in a monastery near the Place Royale, and whose cell became the resort of local scholars and distinguished foreigners. In 1641 he published in Paris a number of objections to Descartes' *Meditations*, in which the beginnings of his later doctrine of bodies and motion are readily recognized. There is a story told, but difficult to date, that at a gathering of "learned men" the question was asked, What is sense? Hobbes was surprised that no one seemed able to answer. Reflecting on the matter he was led to the conviction that the causes of all things must be sought in the differences in the movements of bodies. This is the cardinal principle of his systematic philosophy. From such facts as these, the conclusion seems fairly certain that the philosophy of Hobbes, as distinct from his political theory, was the consequence of impressions received in middle life. These impressions may have been strong enough to make him resolve to compose a system which would have the state as its culmination. We may take his word for it that he was diverted from this resolve by finding his country "boiling hot with questions of the rights of dominion," so that what was last in order came forth first in time. The *De Cive* of 1647 gives clear evidence, however, that its doctrine of mutual fear did not depend on any antecedent metaphysics.

There would thus seem to be two basic motivations of Hobbes's thinking, different in their origin and independent in their character. The one was derived from his vision of that effort of human beings to adjust their mutual fears, compose their antagonisms, control their egotisms, and secure their lives and property, which effort is both the source and the justification of government. This vision was a consequence of his reading of history, his observation, and his experience. The other motivation was derived from his acquaintance with such men as Galileo and their work. Here his vision was not, first of all, of the human struggle, but of bodies in motion, that vision of the world which Newton later was to round out with such astonishing completeness. In this matter Hobbes's experience may have been a little unusual. The new physics not only revealed to him an unsuspected world, but revealed it to a mind with little or no antecedent prejudice about the constitution of things. The Aristotelian physics which was taught at Oxford, and in contrast to which the new physics was both new and a protest, had apparently not impressed him. It had not filled his mind with a stock of ideas of which he had first to rid himself. He found in the new physics a fresh and unhampered interest. He let his imagination play with it freely. As one reads his "explanations" of the tides, of heat, cold, sound, color, and other physical phenomena, one gets the impression of a mind ingeniously sporting with solutions of problems which had sorely vexed the more competent. Dauntlessly he squares the circle and doubles the cube. He flays the Oxford mathematicians. And because in his own group of the emancipated, Aristotelian physics was obnoxious, he joins in the condemnation of it. His politics was one thing, his physics another. It may be said he could have had the former without the latter, but having the latter, he made it contribute a framework in which the former could be set.

The passage from physics to politics was bridged by Hobbes with the aid of a distinction of which much was made in the physics itself, the distinction between the motion of bodies "when left to themselves" and their motion when influenced by that of other bodies. The former were their natural, and the latter their compounded motions. The problem set by this distinction was to discover how the compounded motions result from the natural. Its implication was, obviously, that there are natural motions which can be ascertained and defined. It seemed fully evident, for example, that a body in motion will "naturally" continue to move in the direction of its own motion unless it is interfered with by some other body; and, given this interference, the resulting change of motion should be calculable. In analogy with the principle of this distinction between natural and compounded motions, Hobbes asks, What will men do "when left to themselves"? What are their "natural" motions? What is the "natural" condition of mankind? Out of the natural motions he discovers, he compounds the movements of men in society. He makes of the body politic a body quite literally. It is a great body, made up of many lesser bodies, and its motion is compounded out of theirs. The frontispiece to the *Leviathan* represents a giant with a crown upon his head, a sword in his right hand and a crosier in his left, rising from behind the hills which overlook a city. Above, there is this legend from Chapter XLI of the Book of Job wherein the leviathan is described: *Non est potestas super terram qui comparetur ei.* The body of the giant in the picture is composed of little men. Sometimes Hobbes speaks of the state—that great leviathan—as an "artificial" body, something which men make, but he construes their making of it as a consequence of their natural motions in conflict. It is the supreme culmination of the simple motions that bodies naturally have as they move from place to place and give place to one another in the space that contains them.

True to this passage from physics to politics, Hobbes divides his system into its three major parts, *de corpore, de homine, de cive*—body, man, state. Strictly speaking, each deals with a body, lifeless body, living body, civil body. The second is made to mediate between the first and the third. Hobbes seems to have been little disturbed by possible difficulties here, or to have suppressed them if he was. He seems to have been content to take the world as he found it, to believe that God had created it and, having created it, left it to follow and compose the motions natural to its parts. The situation, however, imposed upon him a doctrine of human movements or actions. He needed what we call a psychology or science of human behaviour. This he supplied. Looked at from the point of view of to-day, it is remarkable for its anticipations of many a later writer who has followed his course of reasoning without knowing it. The psychology needs, and really receives, little support from the physics. Hobbes links them together more by terminology than by evidence, stressing *motions* of the mind as if the word, when so used by him, was in no sense metaphorical. But the politics depends heavily on the psychology. Hobbes might have admitted, possibly, if pressed, that human beings are naturally gregarious, sociable as well as egotistical, with feelings disposing them to friendship as well as enmity, but he sees them primarily in a position of peril, and, consequently, with a desire for power after power which ceases only in death. It is this insatiate desire which impels them and drives them against their will to submit themselves to a power of their own making which will protect them from themselves. So he has a passionate psychology. Emotions are the driving forces of human nature. They awaken reason in their own interest, and for their own guidance, and it is only with difficulty and labor that reason carries men eventually into that civilized condition in which science and philosophy can flourish. These things are among the blessings of government. So governments must first exist as the organized control of human emotion. The politics is thus, in a sense, the psychology enlarged and socialized.

Hobbes' physics is the weakest part of his system. It contains little in the way of a contribution to the sciences of his own day or since. It is interesting chiefly because of its attempt to align the psychology and the politics with that temper of mind which has produced our natural sciences. And it is interesting as a part of Hobbes's system. He would keep a unity in nature from the movements of bodies in space to the movements of thought in a sovereign's mind. There is often novelty in his explanations of physical occurrences, but there is little novelty in his general conception of what the physical world is like In this he shared the views of those with whom he associated. He shared their views in general, but with the method by which they supported them—mathematical theory and experimentation—he had so little sympathy, and of it so little knowledge, that he wasted many years and many words in attacking those—like Boyle, for example —whom his professions should have led him to support, and in whom he might have found friends instead of enemies. In the matter of the new physics, he was less an aid than a hindrance.

Science and philosophy are, according to Hobbes, generated out of sense, experience, and memory, by means of reasoning and language. He consequently begins the exposition of his system with a consideration of "Computation or Logic." Although in this section of his work, he shows clearly the influence of the logic he had read, and owes more to Aristotle than he would admit, he has a highly individual manner of working out his convictions. He is direct and forceful. He makes his peace with opposite schools of thought by keeping close to a distinction between knowledge of fact and knowledge of the consequences which flow from propositions. Error is abundant in the former and quite real, but error in the latter is only another name for absurdity or senseless speech. He finds small excuse for the poor reasoner. His sense of language is acute. He demolishes many an apparent profundity by reducing it to clear expression. And he used language, both his own and the Latin, with logical power and with beauty of expression. He wrote a rhetoric. He had the sense of style which marks the literary man. The selections from his writings in this volume are so arranged that the reader can follow through Hobbes's system from the logic to the politics after the manner he himself conceived it, and with the aid of extracts in the notes which bring to bear upon the text parallel passages from the other writings.

The impression which Hobbes seems to have made upon his own time was that of a man who ought not to be doing what he did. There was a small circle of friends who genuinely admired him both for his personality and for the acuteness of his mind. At the close of his life, his general reputation seems to have been that of an irresponsible thinker, who might be important mainly because his influence might be bad. He was for giving sovereigns too much power, and he looked to many like an atheist. He had opponents rather than supporters. There was a popular impression that to be a "Hobbist" was to be something quite disgraceful. The term, like our own "materialist," was sufficient to damn a man. He was denounced, among others, by the University of Oxford in 1683. As a philosophical thinker he was speedily eclipsed by John Locke (1632-1704) who, rather than Hobbes, was to become the force which energized British philosophy. Although Hobbes was highly and continuously esteemed on the continent as a political writer, he was well-nigh forgotten in England until the late eighteenth and the nineteenth centuries, when revived interest in social and political questions, and the growing attention to psychology, brought him into consideration. He was then recognized as a man who had something important to say on human nature and society, in spite of the weakness of a system of philosophy which rested on a foundation so naïvely conceived and so inadequately developed.

Although Hobbes may be, as he frequently is, classified as a materialist—if one means thereby a man who conceives that all ultimate explanations of nature and human nature should be in terms of material bodies and motion—the classification obscures and does not clarify those portions of his philosophy which, once read, hold the attention of the reader and stimulate his reflection. The *Leviathan* really needs neither an antecedent physics nor metaphysics to support it. For any genuine appreciation of its value and power, the reader will do well to forget the larger setting in which Hobbes would place it. The worth of the book lies in the picture of man in his social and political relations which its author draws. It is a book about man, the "political animal." As such, it should be read. And as one reads, it is not some system of philosophy which should be used to defend or attack the positions there set forth. It is, rather, history, ancient and modern, the record of man in his social relations, as that record is exposed in books and to daily observation. It is far more profitable, for a critical insight, to look at Russia, Italy, and the United States, than to that system of the physical world with which such names as Galileo and Newton are associated.

FREDERICK J. E. WOODBRIDGE

BIBLIOGRAPHY

THE WRITINGS OF THOMAS HOBBES

1628 The History of the Grecian War written by Thucydides. London.

1636 De Mirabilibus Pecci. London.

1641 Objectiones in Cartesii de Prima Philosophia Meditationes. Paris, about 1641.

1644 Tractatus Opticus. Paris.

1647 Elementa Philosophica de Cive. Amsterdam. A few copies were privately printed in Paris, 1642, with the title, Elementorum Philosophiae Sectio Tertia, De Cive. In English; Philosophical Rudiments concerning Government and Society. London, 1651.

1650 Human Nature. London.

De Corpore Politico, or Elements of Law. London.

Answer to Davenant's Preface before Gondibert. Paris.

1651 Leviathan. London.

1654 Of Liberty and Necessity. London.

1655 Elementa Philosophiae Sectio Prima de Corpore. London. Published in English, London, 1656.

1656 Six Lessons to the Professors of the Mathematics. London.

Questions concerning Liberty, Necessity, and Chance. London.

1657 De Homine, sive Elementorum Philosophiae Sectio Secunda. London.

Marks of the Absurd Geometry &c. of John Wallis. London.

1660 Examinatio et Emendatio Mathematicae Hodiernae. London.

1661 Dialogus Physicus, sive de Natura Aeris. London.

De Duplicatione Cubi. London.

1662 Problemata Physica. London.

Considerations on the Reputation &c. of Thomas Hobbes. London.

1666 De Principiis et Ratiocinatione Geometrarum. London.

1668 Appendix ad Leviathan. Amsterdam.

1669 Quadratum Circuli, Cubatio Sphaerae, Duplicatio Cubi. London.

Letter to the Right Honourable Edward Howard.

1671 Rosetum Geometricum. London.

Three Papers Presented to the Royal Society. London.

1672 Principia et Problemata aliquot Geometrica. London.

Lux Mathematica. London.

1673 The Travels of Ulysses. London.

1674 Epistola ad Anthony à Wood. London.

1675 The Iliads and Odyssies of Homer. London.

1676 Letter to the Duke of Newcastle, on the Controversy about Liberty and Necessity. London.

1678 Decameron Physiologicum. London.

1679 T. Hobbes Malmesburiensis Vita Carmine Expressa. London.

PUBLISHED POSTHUMOUSLY

1680 An Historical Narration concerning Heresy.

Behemoth: the History of the causes of the

Civil Wars of England. London. An edition from a defective manuscript was published without the authority of Hobbes in 1679, shortly before his death.

1681 T. Hobbes Malmesburiensis Vita. London.

The Whole Art of Rhetoric. London.

The Art of Rhetoric. London.

The Art of Sophistry. London.

A Dialogue between a Philosopher and a Student of the Common Laws of England. London.

1682 Answer to Bishop Bramhall's Book called "The Catching of Leviathan." London.

Seven Philosophical Problems. London.

1688 Historia Ecclesiastica. London.

A few letters have been published by Molesworth in Vol. V of the Latin Works, and Vol. VII of the English Works.—*Thomae Hobbes Opera Philosophicae*, ed. Sir William Molesworth, 5 vols., London, 1839. *The English Works of Thomas Hobbes*, ed. Molesworth, 11 vols., London, 1839.

HOBBES
Selections

The practise of Thomas Hobbes and the sense of my indebtedness suggest that I might appropriately begin this volume with an "epistle dedicatory." If I did, it would be addressed to Mr. H. W. Wilson, of the H. W. Wilson Co., formerly of Minneapolis. To his generosity I owe the publication, in 1903, of a volume on the philosopher, and the use of that volume in the preparation of this.

The following selections are taken from the Molesworth edition of Hobbes, London, 1841, and references are to that edition by volume and page.

F. J. E. W.

SELECTIONS FROM

ELEMENTS OF PHILOSOPHY

Part I

COMPUTATION OR LOGIC

CHAPTER I

OF PHILOSOPHY

1. The Introduction.—2. The Definition of Philosophy explained.—3. Ratiocination of the Mind.—4. Properties, what
they are.—5. How Properties are known by Generation, and
contrarily.—6. The Scope of Philosophy.—7. The Utility of
it.—8. The Subject.—9. The Parts of it.—10. The Epilogue.

PHILOSOPHY seems to me to be amongst men now, in
the same manner as corn and wine are said to have been
in the world in ancient time. For from the beginning
there were vines and ears of corn growing here and
there in the fields; but no care was taken for the planting and sowing of them. Men lived therefore upon
acorns; or if any were so bold as to venture upon the
eating of those unknown and doubtful fruits, they did
it with danger of their health. In like manner, every
man brought Philosophy, that is, Natural Reason, into
the world with him; for all men can reason to some
degree, and concerning some things: but where there is
need of a long series of reasons, there most men wander
out of the way, and fall into error for want of method,
as it were for want of sowing and planting, that is, of

1

improving their reason. And from hence it comes to pass, that they who content themselves with daily experience, which may be likened to feeding upon acorns, and either reject, or not much regard philosophy, are commonly esteemed, and are, indeed, men of sounder judgment than those who, from opinions, though not vulgar, yet full of uncertainty, and carelessly received, do nothing but dispute and wrangle, like men that are not well in their wits. I confess, indeed, that that part of philosophy by which magnitudes and figures are computed, is highly improved. But because I have not observed the like advancement in the other parts of it, my purpose is, as far forth as I am able, to lay open the few and first Elements of Philosophy in general, as so many seeds from which pure and true Philosophy may hereafter spring up by little and little.

I am not ignorant how hard a thing it is to weed out of men's minds such inveterate opinions as have taken root there, and been confirmed in them by the authority of most eloquent writers; especially seeing true (that is, accurate) Philosophy professedly rejects not only the paint and false colours of language, but even the very ornaments and graces of the same; and the first grounds of all science are not only not beautiful, but poor, arid, and, in appearance, deformed. Nevertheless, there being certainly some men, though but few, who are delighted with truth and strength of reason in all things, I thought I might do well to take this pains for the sake even of those few. I proceed therefore to the matter, and take my beginning from the very definition of philosophy, which is this.

2. PHILOSOPHY *is such knowledge of effects or appearances, as we acquire by true ratiocination from the knowledge we have first of their causes or generation:*

And again, of such causes or generations as may be from knowing first their effects.[1]

For the better understanding of which definition, we must consider, first, that although Sense and Memory of things, which are common to man and all living creatures, be knowledge, yet because they are given us immediately by nature, and not gotten by ratiocination, they are not philosophy.

Secondly, seeing Experience is nothing but memory; and Prudence, or prospect into the future time, nothing but expectation of such things as we have already had experience of, Prudence also is not to be esteemed philosophy.[2]

By RATIOCINATION, I mean *computation.* Now to compute, is either to collect the sum of many things that are added together, or to know what remains when one thing is taken out of another. *Ratiocination,* therefore, is the same with *addition* and *substraction;* and if any man add *multiplication* and *division,* I will not be against it, seeing multiplication is nothing but addition

---

[1] Compare below Ch. VI, Sec. 1, Ch. XXV, Sec. 1, and the *Leviathan,* Ch. IX.

[2] Compare the following from the *Leviathan,* (M. III, 664). "By which definition [of philosophy] it is evident, that we are not to account as any part thereof, that original knowledge called experience, in which consisteth prudence: because it is not attained by reasoning, but found as well in brute beasts, as in man; and is but a memory of successions of events in times past, wherein the omission of every little circumstance altering the effect, frustrateth the expectation of the most prudent: whereas nothing is produced by reasoning aright, but general, eternal, and immutable truth. Nor are we therefore to give that name to any false conclusions: for he that reasoneth aright in words he understandeth, can never conclude an error: Nor to that which any man knows by supernatural revelation; because it is not acquired by reasoning: Nor that which is gotten by reasoning from the authority of books; because it is not by reasoning from the cause to the effect, nor from the effect to the cause; and is not knowledge but faith."

of equals one to another, and division nothing but a
substraction of equals one from another, as often as is
possible. So that all ratiocination is comprehended in
these two operations of the mind, addition and
substraction.

3. But how by the *ratiocination* of our mind, we add
and subtract in our silent thoughts, without the use of
words, it will be necessary for me to make intelligible
by an example or two. If therefore a man see something afar off and obscurely, although no appellation
had yet been given to anything, he will, notwithstanding, have the same idea of that thing for which now, by
imposing a name on it, we call it *body*. Again, when,
by coming nearer, he sees the same thing thus and thus,
now in one place and now in another, he will have a
new idea thereof, namely, that for which we now call
such a thing *animated*. Thirdly, when standing nearer,
he perceives the figure, hears the voice, and sees other
things which are signs of a rational mind, he has a
third idea, though it have yet no appellation, namely,
that for which we now call anything *rational*. Lastly,
when, by looking fully and distinctly upon it, he conceives all that he has seen as one thing, the idea he has
now is compounded of his former ideas, which are put
together in the mind in the same order in which these
three single names, *body, animated, rational,* are in
speech compounded into this one name, *body-animated-
rational,* or *man*. In like manner, of the several conceptions of *four sides, equality of sides, and right
angles,* is compounded the conception of a *square*. For
the mind may conceive a figure of four sides without
any conception of their equality, and of that equality
without conceiving a right angle; and may join together
all these single conceptions into one conception or one
idea of a square. And thus we see how the conceptions

of the mind are compounded. Again, whosoever sees a man standing near him, conceives the whole idea of that man; and if, as he goes away, he follow him with his eyes only, he will lose the idea of those things which were signs of his being rational, whilst, nevertheless, the idea of a body-animated remains still before his eyes, so that the idea of rational is substracted from the whole idea of man, that is to say, of body-animated-rational, and there remains that of body-animated; and a while after, at a greater distance, the idea of animated will be lost, and that of body only will remain; so that at last, when nothing at all can be seen, the whole idea will vanish out of sight. By which examples, I think, it is manifest enough what is the internal ratiocination of the mind without words.

We must not therefore think that computation, that is, ratiocination, has place only in numbers, as if man were distinguished from other living creatures (which is said to have been the opinion of *Pythagoras*) by nothing but the faculty of numbering; for *magnitude, body, motion, time, degrees of quality, action, conception, proportion, speech and names* (in which all the kinds of philosophy consist) are capable of addition and substraction. Now such things as we add or substract, that is, which we put into an account, we are said to consider, in Greek λογιζεσθαι, in which language also συλλογίζεσθαι signifies to *compute, reason,* or *reckon.*[3]

4. But *effects* and the *appearances* of things to sense, are faculties or powers of bodies, which make us distinguish them from one another; that is to say, conceive one body to be equal or unequal, like or unlike to another body; as in the example above, when by coming near enough to any body, we perceive the motion and

[3] Compare below Ch. IV, and the *Leviathan,* Ch. V and VII, and notes on the latter.

going of the same, we distinguish it thereby from a tree, a column, and other fixed bodies; and so that motion or going is the *property* thereof, as being proper to living creatures, and a faculty by which they make us distinguish them from other bodies.

5. How the knowledge of any effect may be gotten from the knowledge of the generation thereof, may easily be understood by the example of a circle: for if there be set before us a plain figure, having, as near as may be, the figure of a circle, we cannot possibly perceive by sense whether it be a true circle or no; than which, nevertheless, nothing is more easy to be known to him that knows first the generation of the propounded figure. For let it be known that the figure was made by the circumduction of a body whereof one end remained unmoved, and we may reason thus; a body carried about, retaining always the same length, applies itself first to one *radius*, then to another, to a third, a fourth, and successively to all; and, therefore, the same length, from the same point, toucheth the circumference in every part thereof, which is as much as to say, as all the *radii* are equal. We know, therefore, that from such generation proceeds a figure, from whose one middle point all the extreme points are reached unto by equal *radii*. And in like manner, by knowing first what figure is set before us, we may come by ratiocination to some generation of the same, though perhaps not that by which it was made, yet that by which it might have been made; for he that knows that a circle has the property above declared, will easily know whether a body carried about, as is said, will generate a circle or no.

6. The *end* or *scope* of philosophy is, that we may make use to our benefit of effects formerly seen; or that, by application of bodies to one another, we may

produce the like effects of those we conceive in our
mind, as far forth as matter, strength, and industry,
will permit, for the commodity of human life. For the
inward glory and triumph of mind that a man may have
for the mastering of some difficult and doubtful matter,
or for the discovery of some hidden truth, is not worth
so much pains as the study of Philosophy requires; nor
need any man care much to teach another what he
knows himself, if he think that will be the only benefit
of his labour. The end of knowledge is power; and
the use of theorems (which, among geometricians, serve
for the finding out of properties) is for the construction
of problems; and, lastly, the scope of all speculation is
the performing of some action, or thing to be done.

7. But what the *utility* of philosophy is, especially
of natural philosophy and geometry, will be best understood by reckoning up the chief commodities of which
mankind is capable, and by comparing the manner of
life of such as enjoy them, with that of others which
want the same. Now, the greatest commodities of mankind are the arts; namely, of measuring matter and
motion; of moving ponderous bodies; of architecture;
of navigation; of making instruments for all uses; of
calculating the celestial motions, the aspects of the
stars, and the parts of time; of geography, &c. By
which sciences, how great benefits men receive is more
easily understood than expressed. These benefits are
enjoyed by almost all the people of Europe, by most of
those of Asia, and by some of Africa: but the Americans,
and they that live near the Poles, do totally want them.
But why? Have they sharper wits than these? Have
not all men one kind of soul, and the same faculties of
mind? What, then, makes this difference, except philosophy? Philosophy, therefore, is the cause of all these
benefits. But the utility of moral and civil philosophy

is to be estimated, not so much by the commodities we have by knowing these sciences, as by the calamities we receive from not knowing them. Now, all such calamities as may be avoided by human industry, arise from war, but chiefly from civil war; for from this proceed slaughter, solitude, and the want of all things. But the cause of war is not that men are willing to have it; for the will has nothing for object but good, at least that which seemeth good. Nor is it from this, that men know not that the effects of war are evil; for who is there that thinks not poverty and loss of life to be great evils? The cause, therefore, of civil war is, that men know not the causes neither of war nor peace, there being but few in the world that have learned those duties which unite and keep men in peace, that is to say, that have learned the rules of civil life sufficiently. Now, the knowledge of these rules is moral philosophy. But why have they not learned them, unless for this reason, that none hitherto have taught them in a clear and exact method? For what shall we say? Could the ancient masters of Greece, Egypt, Rome, and others, persuade the unskilful multitude to their innumerable opinions concerning the nature of their gods, which they themselves knew not whether they were true or false, and which were indeed manifestly false and absurd; and could they not persuade the same multitude to civil duty, if they themselves had understood it? Or shall those few writings of geometricians which are extant, be thought sufficient for the taking away of all controversy in the matters they treat of, and shall those innumerable and huge volumes of *ethics* be thought unsufficient, if what they teach had been certain and well demonstrated? What, then, can be imagined to be the cause that the writings of those men have increased science, and the writings of these have increased nothing but words, saving that the former were written by men that knew, and the latter by such as knew not, the doctrine they taught only for ostentation of their wit and eloquence?   Nevertheless, I deny not but the reading of some such books is very delightful; for they are most eloquently written, and contain many clear, wholesome and choice sentences, which yet are not universally true, though by them universally pronounced.   From whence it comes to pass, that the circumstances of times, places, and persons being changed, they are no less frequently made use of to confirm wicked men in their purposes, than to make them understand the precepts of civil duties.   Now that which is chiefly wanting in them, is a true and certain rule of our actions, by which we might know whether that we undertake be just or unjust.   For it is to no purpose to be bidden in every thing to do right, before there be a certain rule and measure of right established, which no man hitherto hath established.   Seeing, therefore, from the not knowing of civil duties, that is, from the want of moral science, proceed civil wars, and the greatest calamities of mankind, we may very well attribute to such science the production of the contrary commodities.   And thus much is sufficient, to say nothing of the praises and other contentment proceeding from philosophy, to let you see the utility of the same in every kind thereof.

8. The *subject* of Philosophy, or the matter it treats of, is every body of which we can conceive any generation, and which we may, by any consideration thereof, compare with other bodies, or which is capable of composition and resolution; that is to say, every body of whose generation or properties we can have any knowledge.   And this may be deduced from the definition of philosophy, whose profession it is to search out

the properties of bodies from their generation, or their generation from their properties; and, therefore, where there is no generation or property, there is no philosophy. Therefore it excludes *Theology*, I mean the doctrine of God, eternal, ingenerable, incomprehensible, and in whom there is nothing neither to divide nor compound, nor any generation to be conceived.

It excludes the doctrine of *angels*, and all such things as are thought to be neither bodies nor properties of bodies; there being in them no place neither for composition nor division, nor any capacity of more and less, that is to say, no place for ratiocination.

It excludes *history*, as well *natural* as *political*, though most useful (nay necessary) to philosophy; because such knowledge is but experience, or authority, and not ratiocination.

It excludes all such knowledge as is acquired by Divine inspiration, or revelation, as not derived to us by reason, but by Divine grace in an instant, and, as it were, by some sense supernatural.

It excludes not only all doctrines which are false, but such also as are not well-grounded; for whatsoever we know by right ratiocination, can neither be false nor doubtful; and, therefore, *astrology*, as it is now held forth, and all such divinations rather than sciences, are excluded.

Lastly, the doctrine of *God's worship* is excluded from philosophy, as being not to be known by natural reason, but by the authority of the Church; and as being the object of faith, and not of knowledge.

9. The principal parts of philosophy are two. For two chief kinds of bodies, and very different from one another, offer themselves to such as search after their generation and properties; one whereof being the work of nature, is called a *natural body*, the other is called a

commonwealth, and is made by the wills and agreement of men. And from these spring the two parts of philosophy, called *natural* and *civil*. But seeing that, for the knowledge of the properties of a commonwealth, it is necessary first to know the dispositions, affections, and manners of men, civil philosophy is again commonly divided into two parts, whereof one, which treats of men's dispositions and manners, is called *ethics*; and the other, which takes cognizance of their civil duties, is called *politics*, or simply *civil philosophy*. In the first place, therefore (after I have set down such premises as appertain to the nature of philosophy in general), I will discourse of *bodies natural*; in the second, of the *dispositions and manners of men*; and in the third, of the *civil duties of subjects*.[4]

[4] Compare the *Leviathan*, Ch. IX, and the following from the *Philosophical Rudiments*, "Preface to the Reader," (M. II, xix-xx). "I was studying philosophy for my mind sake, and I had gathered together its first elements in all kinds; and having digested them into three sections by degrees, I thought to have written them, so as in the first I would have treated of *body* and its general properties; in the second of *man* and his special faculties and affections; in the third, of *civil government* and the duties of subjects. Wherefore the first section would have contained the *first philosophy*, and certain elements of physic; in it we would have considered the reasons of *time, place, cause, power, relation, proportion, quantity, figure*, and *motion*. In the second, we would have been conversant about *imagination, memory, intellect, ratiocination, appetite, will, good* and *evil, honest* and *dishonest*, and the like. What this last section handles, I have now already showed you. Whilst I contrive, order, pensively and slowly compose these matters; (for I only do reason, I dispute not); it so happened in the interim, that my country, some few years before the civil wars did rage, was boiling hot with questions concerning the rights of dominion and the obedience due from subjects, the true forerunners of an approaching war; and was the cause which, all those other matters deferred, ripened and plucked from me this third part. Therefore it happens, that what was last in order, is yet come forth first in time." Compare also below Ch. VI, Sec. 6-7. Note

10. To conclude; seeing there may be many who will not like this my definition of philosophy, and will say, that, from the liberty which a man may take of so defining as seems best to himself, he may conclude any thing from any thing (though I think it no hard matter to demonstrate that this definition of mine agrees with the sense of all men); yet, lest in this point there should be any cause of dispute betwixt me and them, I here undertake no more than to deliver the elements of that science by which the effects of anything may be found out from the known generation of the same, or contrarily, the generation from the effects; to the end that they who search after other philosophy, may be admonished to seek it from other principles.

CHAPTER II

OF NAMES

1. The necessity of sensible Moniments or Marks for the help of Memory: a Mark defined.—2. The necessity of Marks for the signification of the conceptions of the Mind.—3. Names supply both those necessities.—4. The Definition of a Name. —5. Names are Signs not of Things, but of our Cogitations. —6. What it is we give Names to.—[7. Names Positive and Negative.—8. Contradictory Names.—9. A Common Name.— 10. Names of the First and Second Intention.—11. Universal, Particular, Individual, and Indefinite Names.—12. Names Univocal and Equivocal.—13. Absolute and Relative Names.—14. Simple and Compounded Names.—15. A Predicament described.—16. Some things to be noted concerning Predicaments.]

1. How unconstant and fading men's thoughts are, and how much the recovery of them depends upon chance, there is none but knows by infallible experience

---

that the Latin titles of Hobbes' chief philosophical writings are *De Corpore*, *De Homine*, and *De Cive*.

in himself. For no man is able to remember quantities
without sensible and present measures, nor colors without sensible and present patterns, nor number without
the names of numbers disposed in order and learned by
heart. So that whatsoever a man has put together in
his mind by ratiocination without such helps, will presently slip from him, and not be revocable but by beginning his ratiocination anew. From which it follows,
that, for the acquiring of philosophy, some sensible
moniments are necessary, by which our past thoughts
may be not only reduced, but also registered every one
in its own order. These moniments I call MARKS,
namely, sensible things taken at pleasure, that, by the
sense of them, such thoughts may be recalled to our
mind as are like those thoughts for which we took them.

2. Again, though some one man, of how excellent a
wit soever, should spend all his time partly in reasoning,
and partly in inventing marks for the help of his memory, and advancing himself in learning; who sees not
that the benefit he reaps to himself will not be much,
and to others none at all? For unless he communicate
his notes with others, his science will perish with him.
But if the same notes be made common to many, and so
one man's inventions be taught to others, sciences will
thereby be increased to the general good of mankind.
It is therefore necessary, for the acquiring of philosophy, that there be certain signs, by which what one
man finds out may be manifested and made known to
others. Now, those things we call SIGNS are the *antecedents of their consequents, and the consequents of
their antecedents, as often as we observe them to go
before or follow after in the same manner.* For example, a thick cloud is a sign of rain to follow, and rain
a sign that a cloud has gone before, for this reason only,
that we seldom see clouds without the consequence of

rain, nor rain at any time but when a cloud has gone before. And of signs, some are *natural*, whereof I have already given an example, others are *arbitrary*, namely, those we make choice of at our own pleasure, as a bush hung up, signifies that wine is to be sold there; a stone set in the ground signifies the bound of a field; and words so and so connected, signify the cogitations and motions of our mind.[1] The difference, therefore, betwixt marks and signs is this, that we make those for our own use, but these for the use of others.

3. Words so connected as that they become signs of

---

[1] Compare the following from *Philosophical Rudiments*. (M. II, 219-220). "There are two kinds of signs; the one *natural*; the other done upon *agreement*, or by express or tacit composition. Now because in every language, the use of *words* and *names* come by appointment, it may also by appointment be altered; for that which depends on and derives its force from the will of men, can by the will of the same men agreeing be changed again or abolished. Such *names* therefore as are *attributed* to God by the appointment of men, can by the same appointment be taken away. Now what can be done by the appointment of men, th·t the city may do. The city therefore by right, that is to say, they who have the power of the whole city, shall judge what *names* or *appellations* are more, what less *honorable* for God; that is to say, what doctrines are to be held and professed concerning the nature of God and his operations. Now actions do signify not by men's appointment, but naturally; even as the effects are signs of their causes. Whereof some are always signs of scorn to them before whom they are committed; as those whereby the body's uncleanness is discovered, and whatsoever men are ashamed to do before those whom they respect. Others are always signs of honor, as to draw near and discourse decently and humbly, to give way or to yield in any matter of private benefit. In these actions the city can alter nothing. But there are infinite others, which, as much as belongs to honour or reproach, are indifferent. Now these, by the institution of the city, may both be made signs of honour, and being made so, do in very deed become so. From whence we may understand, that we must obey the city in whatsoever it shall command to be used for a sign of honouring God, that is to say, for *worship*; provided it can be instituted for a sign of honour; because that is a sign of honour, which by the city's command is used for such."

our thoughts, are called SPEECH, of which every part is a *name*. But seeing (as is said) both marks and signs are necessary for the acquiring of philosophy, (marks by which we may remember our own thoughts, and signs by which we may make our thoughts known to others), names do both these offices; but they serve for marks before they be used as signs. For though a man were alone in the world, they would be useful to him in helping him to remember; but to teach others, (unless there were some others to be taught) of no use at all. Again, names, though standing singly by themselves, are marks, because they serve to recall our own thoughts to mind; but they cannot be signs, otherwise than by being disposed and ordered in speech as parts of the same. For example, a man may begin with a word, whereby the hearer may frame an idea of something in his mind, which, nevertheless, he cannot conceive to be the idea which was in the mind of him that spake, but that he would say something which began with that word, though perhaps not as by itself, but as part of another word. So that the nature of a name consists principally in this, that it is a mark taken for memory's sake; but it serves also by accident to signify and make known to others what we remember ourselves, and, therefore, I will define it thus:

4. *A* NAME *is a word taken at pleasure to serve for a mark, which may raise in our mind a thought like to some thought we had before, and which being pronounced to others, may be to them a sign of what thought the speaker had, or had not before in his mind.* And it is for brevity's sake that I suppose the original of names to be arbitrary, judging it a thing that may be assumed as unquestionable. For considering that new names are daily made, and old ones laid aside; that diverse nations use different names, and how impossible

it is either to observe similitude, or make any comparison betwixt a name and a thing, how can any man imagine that the names of things were imposed from their natures? For though some names of living creatures and other things, which our first parents used, were taught by God himself; yet they were by him arbitrarily imposed, and afterwards, both at the Tower of Babel, and since, in process of time, growing everywhere out of use, are quite forgotten, and in their room have succeeded others, invented and received by men at pleasure. Moreover, whatsoever the common use of words be, yet philosophers, who were to teach their knowledge to others, had always the liberty, and sometimes they both had and will have a necessity, of taking to themselves such names as they please for the signifying of their meaning, if they would have it understood. Nor had mathematicians need to ask leave of any but themselves to name the figures they invented, *parabolas, hyperboles, cissoeides, quadratices,* &c. or to call one magnitude A, another B.

5. But seeing names ordered in speech (as is defined) are signs of our conceptions, it is manifest they are not signs of the things themselves; for that the sound of this word *stone* should be the sign of a stone, cannot be understood in any sense but this, that he that hears it collects that he that pronounces it thinks of a stone. And, therefore, that disputation, whether names signify the matter or form, or something compounded of both, and other like subtleties of the *metaphysics,* is kept up by erring men, and such as understand not the words they dispute about.

6. Nor, indeed, is it at all necessary that every name should be the name of something. For as these, a *man,* a *tree,* a *stone,* are the names of the things themselves, so the images of a man, of a tree, and of a stone, which are represented to men sleeping, have their names also,

though they be not things, but only fictions and phantasms of things. For we can remember these; and, therefore, it is no less necessary that they have names to mark and signify them, than the things themselves. Also this word *future* is a name, but no future thing has yet any being, nor do we know whether that which we call future, shall ever have a being or no. Nevertheless, seeing we use in our mind to knit together things past with those that are present, the name *future* serves to signify such knitting together. Moreover, that which neither is, nor has been, nor ever shall, or ever can be, has a name, namely, *that which neither is nor has been,* &c.; or more briefly this, *impossible.* To conclude; this word *nothing* is a name, which yet cannot be the name of any thing: for when, for example, we substract 2 and 3 from 5, and so nothing remaining, we would call that substraction to mind, this speech *nothing remains,* and in it the word *nothing* is not unuseful. And for the same reason we say truly, *less than nothing* remains, when we substract more from less; for the mind feigns such remains as these for doctrine's sake, and desires, as often as is necessary, to call the same to memory. But seeing every name has some relation to that which is named, though that which we name be not always a thing that has a being in nature, yet it is lawful for doctrine's sake to apply the word *thing* to whatsoever we name; as if it were all one whether that thing be truly existent, or be only feigned.[2]

* * * * * * * *

[2] Compare the following from the *Leviathan* (M. III, 673). "The use of words, is to register to ourselves, and make manifest to others the thoughts and conceptions of our minds. Of which words, some are the names of the things conceived; as the names of all sorts of bodies, that work upon the senses, and leave an impression in the imagination. Others are the names of the imaginations themselves; that is to say, of those ideas, or mental images we have of all things we see, or remember. And others again are names of names; or of

SUPPLEMENT FROM

HUMAN NATURE, CHAPTER V

1. SEEING the *succession* of conceptions in the *mind* are caused, as hath been said before, by the succession they *had* one to another when they were produced by the *senses*, and that there is no conception that hath not been produced immediately before or after innumerable others, by the innumerable acts of sense; it must needs follow, that one *conception* followeth *not* another, according to our election, and the need we have of them, *but* as it *chanceth* us to hear or see such things as shall bring them to our mind. The experience we have hereof, is in such brute beasts, which, having the providence to hide the remains and superfluity of their meat, do nevertheless want the remembrance of the place where they hid it, and thereby make no benefit thereof in their hunger: but man, who in this point beginneth to rank himself somewhat above the nature of beasts, hath observed and remembered the cause of this defect, and to amend the same, hath imagined or devised to set up a visible or other sensible mark, the which, when he seeth it again, may bring to his mind the thought he had when he set it up. A *mark* therefore is a *sensible object* which a man erecteth voluntarily to himself, to the end to *remember* thereby somewhat past, when the

---

different sorts of speech: as *universal, plural, singular,* are the names of names; and *definition, affirmation, negation, true, false, syllogism, interrogation, promise, covenant,* are the names of certain forms of speech. Others serve to show the consequence, or repugnance of one name to another; as when one saith, *a man is a body,* he intendeth that the name of *body* is necessarily consequent to the name of *man*; as being but several names of the same thing, *man*; which consequence is signified by coupling them together with the word *is.*"

same is objected to his sense again: as men that have passed by a rock at sea, set up some mark, thereby to remember their former danger, and avoid it.

2. In the number of these *marks*, are those *human voices*, which we call the *names* or appellations of things sensible by the ear, by which we recall into our mind some conceptions of the things to which we gave those names or appellations; as the appellation *white* bringeth to remembrance the quality of such objects as produce that color or conception in us. A *name* or appellation therefore is the *voice* of a man *arbitrary*, imposed for a *mark* to bring into his mind some conception concerning the thing on which it is imposed.

3. Things named, are either the *objects* themselves, as a man; or the *conception* itself that we have of man, as shape and motion: or some privation, which is when we conceive that there is something which we conceive, not in him; as when we conceive he is not just, not finite, we give him the name of unjust, of infinite, which signify privation or defect; and to the privations themselves we give the names of injustice and infiniteness: so that here be *two sorts* of names; one of *things*, in which we conceive something; or of the conceptions themselves, which are called *positive*: the other of things wherein we conceive *privation* or defect, and those names are called *privative*.

4. By the advantage of *names* it is that we are capable of *science*, which beasts, for want of them are not; nor man, without the use of them: for as a beast misseth not one or two out of many her young ones, for want of those names of order, one, two, and three, and which we call *number*; so neither would a man, without repeating orally or mentally the words of number, know how many pieces of money or other things lie before him.

5. Seeing there be *many* conceptions of *one* and the

same thing, and for *every* conception we give it a *several* name; it followeth that for one and the same thing, we have many names or attributes; as to the same man we give the appellations of *just, valiant, &c.* for divers *virtues*; of *strong, comely, &c.* for divers *qualities* of the *body.* And again, because from divers things we receive like conceptions, many things must needs have the same appellation: as to all things we *see,* we give the same name of *visible*; and to all things we *see moveable,* we give the appellation of *moveable*: and those names we give to *many,* are called *universal* to them all; as the name of man to every particular of mankind: such appellation as we give to *one* only thing, we call *individual,* or singular; as Socrates, and other proper names: or, by circumlocution, he that writ the *Iliads,* for Homer.

6. The universality of *one name* to many things, hath been the cause that men think the *things* are themselves universal; and so seriously contend, that besides Peter and John, and all the rest of the men that are, have been, or shall be in the world, there is yet something else that we call *man,* viz. *man in general,* deceiving themselves, by taking the universal, or general appellation, for the thing it signifieth: for if one should desire the painter to make him the picture of a man, which is as much as to say, of a man in general; he meaneth no more, but that the painter should choose what man he pleaseth to draw, which must needs be some of them that are, or have been, or may be, none of which are *universal.* But when he would have him to draw the picture of the king, or any particular person, he limiteth the painter to that one person he chooseth. It is plain therefore, that there is *nothing universal* but *names*; which are therefore called *indefinite*; because we limit them not ourselves, but leave them to be applied by the

hearer: whereas a singular name is limited and restrained to one of the many things it signifieth; as when
we say, this man, pointing to him, or giving him his
proper name, or by some such other way.[3]

7. The appellations that be *universal*, and common
to many things, are *not* always given to all the *particulars*, (as they ought to be) for like conceptions, and
like considerations in them all; which is the cause that
many of them are *not* of *constant* signification, but bring
into our mind other thoughts than those for which they
were ordained, and these are called equivocal. As for
example, the word faith signifieth the same with belief;
sometimes it signifieth particularly that belief which
maketh a Christian; and sometime it signifieth the
keeping of a promise. Also all *metaphors* are by profession *equivocal*: and there is scarce any word that is
not made *equivocal* by divers contextures of speech, or
by diversity of pronunciation and gesture.

8. This *equivocation* of names maketh it *difficult* to
recover those conceptions for which the name was
ordained: and that not only in the language of other

[3] Compare the following from the *Elements of Philosophy*,
(M. I, 19-20). "A common name, being the name of many
things severally taken, but not collectively of all together (as
man is not the name of all mankind, but of every one, as of
Peter, John, and the rest severally) is therefore called an
universal name; and therefore this word *universal* is never
the name of anything existent in nature, nor of any idea or
phantasm formed in the mind, but always the name of some
word or name; so that when *a living creature, a stone, a spirit*,
or any other thing, is said to be *universal*, it is not to be understood, that any man, stone, &c. ever was or can be universal, but only that these words, *living creatures, stone, &c.*
are *universal names*, that is, names common to many things;
and the conceptions answering them in our mind, are the
images and phantasms of several living creatures, or other
things. And therefore, for the understanding of the extent
of an universal name, we need no other faculty but that of
our imagination, by which we remember that such names bring
sometimes one thing, sometimes another, into our mind."

men, wherein we are to consider the *drift*, and *occasion*, and *contexture* of the speech, as well as the *words* themselves; but also in our discourse, which being derived from the custom and common use of speech, representeth unto us not our own conceptions. It is therefore a great ability in a man, out of the words, contexture, and other circumstances of language, to deliver himself from *equivocation*, and to find out the true meaning of what is said: and this is it we call *understanding*.

9. Of two *appellations*, by the help of this little verb *is*, or something equivalent, we make an *affirmation* or *negation*, either of which in the Schools we call also a *proposition*, and consisteth of two appellations joined together by the said verb *is*: as for example, man is a living creature; or thus, man is not righteous: whereof the former is called an *affirmation*, because the appellation, living creature, is *positive*; the latter a *negative*, because not righteous is *privative*.

10. In *every proposition*, be it affirmative or negative, the latter appellation either comprehendeth the former, as in this proposition, charity is a virtue, the name of virtue comprehendeth the name of charity, and many other virtues beside; and then is the proposition said to be *true* or *truth*: for, *truth*, and a *true proposition*, is all one. Or *else* the *latter* appellation comprehendeth *not* the former; as in this proposition, every man is just; the name of just comprehendeth not every man; for unjust is the name of the far greater part of men: and the proposition is said to be *false*, or falsity: *falsity* and a *false proposition* being also the same thing.

11. In what manner of two propositions, whether *both* affirmative, or *one* affirmative, the *other* negative, is made a *syllogism*, I forbear to write. All this that hath been said of names or propositions, though *necessary*, is but *dry* discourse: and this place is not for the whole

art of logic, which if I enter further into, I ought to pursue: besides, it is not needful; for there be few men which have not so much natural logic, as thereby to discern well enough, whether any conclusion I shall make in this discourse hereafter, be well or ill collected: only thus much I say in this place, that *making of syllogisms* is that we call *ratiocination* or *reasoning*.

12. Now when a man *reasoneth* from *principles* that are *found* indubitable by experience, all deceptions of sense and equivocation of words avoided, the conclusion he maketh is said to be *according to right reason*: but when from his conclusion a man may, by good ratiocination, derive that which is *contradictory* to any evident truth whatsoever, then he is said to have concluded *against reason*: and such a conclusion is called *absurdity*.

13. As the *invention* of *names* hath been *necessary* for the drawing men *out of* ignorance, by calling to their remembrance the necessary *coherence* of one conception to another; so also hath it on the other side precipitated men into *error*: insomuch, that whereas by the benefit of *words* and ratiocination they exceed *brute beasts* in knowledge, and the commodities that accompany the same; so they exceed them also in *error*: for *true* and *false* are things not incident to beasts, because they adhere not to propositions and language; nor have they ratiocination, whereby to multiply one untruth by another, as men have.

14. It is the *nature* almost of every *corporal* thing, being *often moved* in one and the same manner, to receive continually a *greater* and *greater easiness* and aptitude to the *same* motion, insomuch as in time the same becometh so *habitual*, that, to *beget* it, there needs no more than to *begin* it. The *passions* of man, as they are the beginning of *voluntary* motions; so are they the beginning of *speech*, which is the motion of the tongue.

And men desiring to shew others the knowledge, opinions, conceptions, and passions which are in themselves, and to that end having invented *language*, have by that means transferred all that *discursion* of their *mind* mentioned in the former chapter, by the *motion* of their *tongues*, into *discourse* of *words*: and *ratio* now is but *oratio*, for the most part, wherein custom hath so great a power, that the mind suggesteth only the first word; the rest follow *habitually*, and are not followed by the mind; as it is with beggars, when they say their *paternoster*, putting together such words, and in such manner, as in their education they have learned from their nurses, from their companies, or from their teachers, having *no images* or *conceptions* in their mind, answering to the words they speak: and as they have learned themselves, so they teach posterity. Now, if we consider the power of those *deceptions* of the sense, mentioned chapter II, section 10, and also how *unconstantly* names have been settled, and how subject they are to *equivocation*, and how *diversified* by *passion*, (scarce two men agreeing what is to be called good, and what evil; what liberality, what prodigality; what valour, what temerity) and how subject men are to paralogism or fallacy in reasoning, I may in a manner conclude, that it is impossible to *rectify* so many errors of any one man, as must needs proceed from those causes, without beginning *anew* from the very first grounds of all our knowledge and sense; and instead of books, reading over orderly one's own conceptions: in which meaning, I take *nosce teipsum* for a precept worthy the reputation it hath gotten.[4]

[4] Compare on the whole discussion the *Leviathan*, Ch. IV. Hobbes' discussion of *abstract names* is important. Compare on this topic the *Elements of Philosophy*, Ch. III, Sec. 3-4, also the following from the same work, (M. I. 103). "If concerning the name of a body, that is, concerning a concrete

CHAPTER III

OF PROPOSITION

1. Divers kinds of speech.—2. Proposition defined.—3. Subject, predicate, and copula, what they are; and abstract and concrete what.—4. The use and abuse of names abstract.—[5. Proposition, universal and particular.—6. Affirmative and negative.]—7. True and false.—8. True and false belongs to speech, and not to things.—[9. Proposition, primary, not primary, definition, axiom, petition.—10. Proposition, necessary and contingent.—11. Categorical and hypothetical.—12. The same proposition diversely pronounced.—13. Propositions that may be reduced to the same categorical proposition, are equipollent.—14. Universal propositions converted by contradictory names, are equipollent.—15. Negative propositions are the same, whether negation be before or after the copula.—16. Particular propositions simply converted, are equipollent.—17. What are subaltern, contrary, subcontrary, and contradictory propositions.]—18. Consequence, what it is.—19. Falsity cannot follow from truth.—20. How one proposition is the cause of another.

1. From the connexion or contexture of names arise divers kinds of speech, whereof some signify the desires and affections of men; such are, first, *interrogations,* which denote the desire of knowing: as, *Who is a good man?* In which speech there is one name expressed, and another desired and expected from him of whom we ask the same. Then *prayers,* which signify the desire of

name, it be asked, *what is it?* the answer must be made by definition; for the question is concerning the signification of the name. But if it be asked concerning an abstract name, *what is it?* the cause is demanded why a thing appears so or so. As if it be asked, *what is hard?* The answer will be, hard is that, whereof no part gives place, but when the whole gives place. But if it be demanded, *what is hardness?* a cause must be shown why a part does not give place, except the whole give place." Also *An Answer to Bishop Bramhall,* (M. IV, 309). "Essence and all other abstract names, are words artificial belonging to the art of logic, and signify only the manner how we consider the substance itself."

having something; *promises, threats, wishes, commands, complaints,* and other significations of other affections. Speech may also be absurd and insignificant; as when there is a succession of words, to which there can be no succession of thoughts in mind to answer them; and this happens often to such, as, understanding nothing in some subtle matter, do, nevertheless, to make others believe they understand, speak of the same incoherently; for the connexion of incoherent words, though it want the end of speech (which is signification) yet it is speech; and is used by writers of *metaphysics* almost as frequently as speech significative. In philosophy, there is but one kind of speech useful, which some call in Latin *dictum,* others *enuntiatum et pronunciatum*; but most men call it *proposition,* and is the speech of those that affirm or deny, and expresseth truth or falsity.

2. *A* PROPOSITION *is a speech consisting of two names copulated, by which he that speaketh signifies he conceives the latter name to be the name of the same thing whereof the former is the name; or* (which is all one) *that the former name is comprehended by the latter.* For example, this speech, *man is a living creature,* in which two names are copulated by the verb *is,* is a *proposition,* for this reason, that he that speaks it conceives both *living creature* and *man* to be names of the same thing, or that the former name, *man,* is comprehended by the latter name, *living creature.* Now the former name is commonly called the *subject,* or *antecedent,* or the *contained name,* and the latter the *predicate, consequent,* or *containing name.* The sign of connexion amongst most nations is either some word, as the word *is* in the proposition *man is a living creature,* or some case or termination of a word, as in this proposition, *man walketh* (which is equivalent to this, *man is walking*); the termination by which it is said he

walketh, rather than he *is walking*, signifieth that those two are understood to be copulated, or to be names of the same thing.

But there are, or certainly may be, some nations that have no word which answers to our verb *is*, who nevertheless form propositions by the position only of one name after another, as if instead of *man is a living creature*, it should be said *man a living creature*; for the very order of the names may sufficiently show their connection; and they are as apt and useful in philosophy, as if they were copulated by the verb *is*.[1]

3. Wherefore, in every proposition three things are to be considered, *viz.* the two names, which are the *subject*, and the *predicate*, and their *copulation*; both which names raise in our mind the thought of one and the same thing; but the copulation makes us think of the cause for which those names were imposed on that thing. As, for example, when we say *a body is moveable*, though we conceive the same thing to be designed by both those names, yet our mind rests not there, but searches farther what it is *to be a body*, or *to be moveable*, that is, wherein consists the difference betwixt these and other things, for which these are so called, others are not so called. They, therefore, that seek what it is *to be* any thing, as *to be moveable, to be hot, &c.* seek in things the causes of their names.

And from hence arises that distinction of names

---

[1] Compare above, Supplement to Ch. II, Sec. 9. Also the following from the *Leviathan*, (M. III, 674). "When we say, *a man is a living body*, we mean not that the *man* is one thing, the *living body* another, and the *is*, or *being* a third; but that the *man*, and the *living body*, is the same thing; because the consequence, *if he be a man, he is a living body*, is a true consequence, signified by that word *is*. Therefore, *to be a body, to walk, to be speaking, to live, to see*, and the like infinitives; also *corporeity, walking, speaking, life, sight*, and the like, that signify just the same, are the names of *nothing*."

(touched in the last chapter) into *concrete* and *abstract*. For *concrete* is the name of any thing which we suppose to have a being, and is therefore called the *subject*, in Latin *suppositum*, and in Greek ὑποκείμενον; as *body, moveable, moved, figurate, a cubic high, hot, cold, like, equal, Appius, Lentulus,* and the like; and, *abstract* is that which in any subject denotes the cause of the concrete name, as *to be a body, to be moveable, to be moved, to be figurate, to be of such quantity, to be hot, to be cold, to be like, to be equal, to be Appius, to be Lentulus, &c.* Or names equivalent to these, which are most commonly called *abstract* names, as *corporiety, mobility, motion, figure, quantity, heat, cold, likeness, equality,* and (as Cicero has it) *Appiety* and *Lentulity.* Of the same kind also are infinitives; for *to live* and *to move* are the same with *life* and *motion*, or *to be living* and *to be moved.* But *abstract names* denote only the causes of *concrete names*, and not the things themselves. For example, when we see anything, or conceive in our mind any visible thing, that thing appears to us, or is conceived by us, not in one point, but as having parts distant from one another, that is, as being extended and filling some space. Seeing therefore we call the thing so conceived *body*, the cause of that name is, that that thing is *extended*, or the *extension* or *corporiety* of it. So when we see a thing appear sometimes here, sometimes there, and call it *moved* or *removed*, the cause of that name is that it *is moved* or the *motion* of the same.

And these causes of names are the same with the causes of our conceptions, namely, some power of action, or affection of the thing conceived, which some call the manner by which any thing works upon our senses, but by most men they are called *accidents*; I say accidents, not in that sense in which accident is opposed to necessary; but so, as being neither the things themselves, nor parts thereof, do nevertheless accompany the things in such manner, that (saving extension) they may all perish, and be destroyed, but can never be abstracted.

4. There is also this difference betwixt *concrete* and *abstract* names, that those were invented before propositions, but these after; for these could have no being till there were propositions, from whose *copula* they proceed. Now in all matters that concern this life, but chiefly in philosophy, there is both great use and great abuse of *abstract names*; and the use consists in this, that without them we cannot, for the most part, either reason, or compute the properties of bodies; for when we would multiply, divide, add, or subtract heat, light, or motion, if we should double or add them together by concrete names, saying (for example) hot is double to hot, light double to light, or moved double to moved, we should not double the properties, but the bodies themselves that are hot, light, moved, &c. which we would not do. But the abuse proceeds from this, that some men seeing they can consider, that is (as I said before) bring into account the increasings and decreasings of quantity, heat and other accidents, without considering their bodies or subjects (which they call *abstracting*, or making to exist apart by themselves) they speak of accidents, as if they might be separated from all bodies. And from hence proceed the gross errors of writers of metaphysics; for, because they can consider thought without the consideration of body, they infer there is no need of a thinking-body; and because quantity may be considered without considering body, they think also that quantity may be without body, and body without quantity; and that a body has quantity by the addition of quantity to it. From the same fountain spring those insignificant words, *abstract substance, separated essence*, and the like; as also that confusion of words

derived from the Latin verb *est*, as *essence, essentiality, entity, entitative*; besides *reality, aliquiddity, quiddity, &c.* which could never have been heard of among such nations as do not copulate their names by the verb *is*, but by adjective verbs, as runneth, readeth, &c. or by the mere placing of one name after another; and yet seeing such nations compute and reason, it is evident that philosophy has no need of those words *essence, entity,* and other the like barbarous terms.

*   *   *   *   *   *   *   *   *

7. The third distinction is, that one is *true*, another *false*. A *true* proposition is that, whose predicate contains, or comprehends its subject, or whose predicate is the name of every thing, of which the subject is the name; as *man is a living creature* is therefore a true proposition, because whatsoever is called *man*, the same is also called *living creature*; and *some man is sick*, is true, because *sick* is the name of *some man*. That which is not true, or that whose predicate does not contain its subject, is called a *false* proposition, as *man is a stone*.[2]

Now these words *true, truth,* and *true proposition,* are equivalent to one another; for truth consists in speech, and not in the things spoken of; and though *true* be sometimes opposed to *apparent* or *feigned,* yet it is always to be referred to the truth of proposition; for the image of a man in a glass, or a ghost, is therefore denied to be a very man, because this proposition, *a ghost is a man,* is not true; for it cannot be denied but that a ghost is a very ghost. And therefore truth or verity is not any affection of the thing, but of the proposition concerning it. As for that which the writers of metaphysics say, that *a thing, one thing,* and *a very thing,* are equivalent to one another, it is but trifling and

---

[2] Compare above, Supplement to Ch. II, Sec. 10.

childish; for who does not know, that *a man, one man,*
and *a very man,* signify the same.[3]

8. And from hence it is evident, that truth and
falsity have no place but amongst such living creatures
as use speech. For though some brute creatures, looking upon the image of a man in a glass, may be affected
with it, as if it were the man himself, and for this reason
fear it or fawn upon it in vain; yet they do not apprehend it as true or false, but only as like; and in this
they are not deceived. Wherefore, as men owe all their
true ratiocination to the right understanding of speech;
so also they owe their errors to the misunderstanding of
the same; and as all the ornaments of philosophy proceed only from man, so from man also is derived the
ugly absurdity of false opinions. For speech has something in it like to a spider's web, (as it was said of old
of *Solon's* laws) for by contexture of words tender and
delicate wits are ensnared and stopped; but strong wits
break easily through them.[4]

From hence also this may be deduced, that the first
truths were arbitrarily made by those that first of all
imposed names upon things, or received them from the
imposition of others. For it is true (for example) that
man is a living creature, but it is for this reason, that it
pleased men to impose both those names on the same
thing.[5]

*   *   *   *   *   *   *   *   *

[3] Compare below Ch. V, also the *Leviathan,* Ch. IV.

[4] Compare above, Supplement to Ch. II, Sec. 13.

[5] Compare the following from *Philosophical Rudiments,* (M.
II, 302-304). "We grant propositions sometimes, which notwithstanding we receive not into our minds; and this either for
a time, to wit, so long, till by consideration of the consequences we have well examined the truth of them, which we
call *supposing;* or also simply, as through fear of the laws,
which is to *profess,* or *confess* by outward tokens; or for a
voluntary compliance sake, which men use out of civility to
those whom they respect, and for love of peace to others,

18. A proposition is said to *follow* from two other
propositions, when these being granted to be true, it cannot be denied but the other is true also. For example,
let these two propositions, *every man is a living crea-*

---

which is *absolute yielding*. Now the propositions which we
receive for truth, we always grant for some reasons of our
own; and these are derived either from the *proposition itself*,
or from the *person propounding*. They are derived from the
proposition itself, by calling to mind what things those words,
which make up the proposition, do by common consent usually
signify. If so, then the assent which we give, is called
knowledge or *science*. But if we cannot remember what is
certainly understood by those words, but sometimes one thing,
sometimes another seem to be apprehended by us, then we are
said to think. For example, if it be propounded that *two and
three make five*; and by calling to mind, that the order of
numeral words is so appointed by the common consent of
them who are of the same language with us, (as it were, by
a certain contract necessary for human society), that *five*
shall be the name of so many unities as are contained in two
and three taken together, a man assent that this is therefore
true, because two and three together are the same with five:
this assent shall be called knowledge. And to know this
truth is nothing else, but to acknowledge that it is made by
ourselves. For by whose will and rules of speaking the
number | | is called two, | | | is called three, and | | | | | is
called five; by their will also it comes to pass that this
proposition is true, *two and three taken together make five*.
In like manner if we remember what it is that is called *theft*,
and what *injury*; we shall understand by the words themselves, whether it be true that *theft is an injury*, or not.
Truth is the same with a *true proposition*; but *the proposition is true* in which *the word consequent*, which by logicians
is called *the predicate*, embraceth *the word antecedent* in its
amplitude, which they call *the subject*. And to *know truth*,
is the same thing as to *remember* that it was made by ourselves by the very usurpation of the words." Compare also
the following from the *Elements of Philosophy*, (M. I, 130-
131). "All propositions concerning future things, contingent
or not contingent, as this, *it will rain tomorrow*, or this, *to-
morrow the sun will rise*, are either necessarily true, or necessarily false; but we call them contingent, because we do not
yet know whether they be true or false; whereas their verity
depends not upon our knowledge, but upon the foregoing of
their causes. But there are some, who though they confess
this whole proposition, *tomorrow it will either rain, or not*

ture, and, *every living creature is a body,* be supposed true, that is, that *body,* is the name of every living *creature,* and *living creature* the name of *every man.* Seeing therefore, if these be understood to be true, it cannot be understood that *body* is not the name of *every man,* that is, that *every man is a body* is false, this proposition will be said to *follow* from those two, or to be necessarily *inferred* from them.

19. That a true proposition may follow from false propositions, may happen sometimes; but false from true, never. For if these, *every man is a stone,* and *every stone is a living creature,* (which are both false) be granted to be true, it is granted also that *living creature* is the name of *every stone,* and *stone* of *every man,* that is, that *living creature* is the name of *every man*; that is to say, this proposition *every man is a living creature,* is true, as it is indeed true. Wherefore a true proposition may sometimes follow from false. But if any two propositions be true, a false one can never follow from them. For if true follow from false, for this reason only, that the false are granted to be true, then truth from two truths granted will follow in the same manner.

20. Now, seeing none but a true proposition will follow from true, and that the understanding of two propositions to be true, is the cause of understanding that also to be true which is deduced from them; the two antecedent propositions are commonly called the causes

---

rain, to be true, yet they will not acknowledge the parts of it, as, *tomorrow it will rain,* or *tomorrow it will not rain,* to be either of them true by itself; because they say neither this nor that is true *determinately.* But what is this *determinately true,* but true upon our knowledge, or evidently true? And therefore they say no more but that it is not yet known whether it be true or no; but they say it more obscurely, and darken the evidence of the truth with the same words, with which they endeavor to hide their own ignorance."

of the inferred proposition, or conclusion. And from hence it is that logicians say, the *premises* are causes of the *conclusion*; which may pass, though it be not properly spoken; for though understanding be the cause of understanding, yet speech is not the cause of speech. But when they say, the cause of the properties of any thing, is the thing itself, they speak absurdly. For example, if a figure be propounded which is triangular; seeing every triangle has all its angles together equal to two right angles, from whence it follows that all the angles of that figure are equal to two right angles, they say, for this reason, that that figure is the cause of that equality. But seeing the figure does not itself make its angles, and therefore cannot be said to be the *efficient-cause*, they call it the *formal-cause*; whereas indeed it is no cause at all; nor does the property of any figure follow the figure, but has its being at the same time with it; only the knowledge of the figure goes before the knowledge of the properties; and one knowledge is truly the cause of another knowledge, namely the *efficient-cause*.

And thus much concerning *proposition*; which in the progress of philosophy is the first step, like the moving towards of one foot. By the due addition of another step I shall proceed to *syllogism*, and make a complete pace. Of which in the next chapter.

CHAPTER IV

OF SYLLOGISM

1. The definition of syllogism.—2. In a syllogism there are but three terms.—3. Major, minor, and middle term; also major and minor proposition, what they are.—[4. The middle term in every syllogism ought to be determined in both the propositions to one and the same thing.—5. From two particular

propositions nothing can be concluded.—6. A syllogism is
the collection of two propositions into one sum.—7. The figure of a syllogism, what it is.]—8. What is in the mind
answering to a syllogism.—[9. The first indirect figure,
how it is made.—10. The second indirect figure, how made.
—11. How the third indirect figure is made.—12. There are
many moods in every figure, but most of them useless in
philosophy.—13. An hypothetical syllogism when equipollent
to a categorical.]

1. A SPEECH, consisting of three propositions, from two
of which the third follows, is called a SYLLOGISM; and
that which follows is called the *conclusion*; the other
two *premises*. For example, this speech, *every man is
a living creature, every living creature is a body,* therefore, *every man is a body,* is a *syllogism*, because the
third proposition follows from the two first; that is, if
those be granted to be true, this must also be granted
to be true.

2. From two propositions which have not one term
common, no conclusion can follow; and therefore no
syllogism can be made of them. For let any two premises, *a man is a living creature, a tree is a plant,* be both
of them true, yet because it cannot be collected from
them that *plant* is the name of a *man*, or *man* the name
of a *plant*, it is not necessary that this conclusion, *a man
is a plant,* should be true. Corollary: therefore, in the
premises of a *syllogism* there can be but three *terms*.

Besides, there can be no term in the *conclusion*, which
was not in the *premises*. For let any two premises be,
a man is a living creature, a living creature is a body,
yet if any other term be put in the conclusion, as *man
is two-footed*; though it be true, it cannot follow from
the premises, because from them it cannot be collected,
that the name *two-footed* belongs to a *man*; and therefore, again, in every *syllogism* there can be but three
terms.

3. Of these terms, that which is the *predicate* in the conclusion, is commonly called the *major*; that which is the *subject* in the conclusion, the *minor*, and the other is the *middle term*; as in this syllogism, *a man is a living creature, a living creature is a body*, therefore, *a man is a body*, *body* is the *major*, *man* the *minor*, and *living creature* the *middle term*. Also of the premises, that in which the *major term* is found, is called the *major proposition*, and that which has the *minor term*, the *minor proposition*.

*   *   *   *   *   *   *   *   *

8. The thoughts in the mind answering to a direct syllogism, proceed in this manner; first, there is conceived a phantasm of the thing named, with that accident or quality thereof, for which it is in the minor proposition called by that name which is the subject; next, the mind has a phantasm of the same thing with that accident, or quality, for which it hath the name, that in the same proposition is the predicate; thirdly, the thought returns of the same thing as having that accident in it, for which it is called by the name, that is the predicate of the major proposition; and lastly, remembering that all those are the accidents of one and the same thing, it concludes that those three names are also names of one and the same thing; that is to say, the conclusion is true. For example, when this syllogism is made, *man is a living creature, a living creature is a body*, therefore, *man is a body*, the mind conceives first an image of a man speaking or discoursing, and remembers that that, which so appears, is called *man*; then it has the image of the same man moving, and remembers that that, which appears so, is called *living creature*; thirdly, it conceives an image of the same man, as filling some place or space, and remembers that what ap-

pears so is called *body*; and lastly, when it remembers
that that thing, which was extended, and moved and
spake, was one and the same thing, it concludes that
the three names, *man, living creature,* and *body,* are
names of the same thing, and that therefore *man is a
living creature* is a true proposition.   From whence it is
manifest, that living creatures that have not the use of
speech, have no conception or thought in the mind, answering to a syllogism made of universal propositions;
seeing it is necessary to think not only of the thing, but
also by turns to remember the divers names, which for
divers considerations thereof are applied to the same.

*　　*　　*　　*　　*　　*　　*　　*　　*

CHAPTER V

OF ERRING, FALSITY, AND CAPTIONS

1. Erring and falsity how they differ. Error of the mind by
itself without the use of words, how it happens.—2. A
seven-fold incoherency of names, every one of which makes
always a false proposition.—[3. Examples of the first manner of incoherency.—4. Of the second.—5. Of the third.—
6. Of the fourth.—7. Of the fifth.—8. Of the sixth.—9. Of
the seventh.]—10. Falsity of propositions detected by resolving the terms with definitions continued till they come
to simple names, or names that are the most general of
their kind.—[11. Of the fault of a syllogism consisting in
the implication of the terms with the copula.—12. Of the
fault which consists in equivocation.—13. Sophistical captions are oftener faulty in the matter than in the form of
syllogisms.]

1. MEN are subject to *err* not only in affirming and
denying, but also in perception, and in silent cogitation.[1] In affirming and denying, when they call any
thing by a name, which is not the name thereof; as if
from seeing the sun first by reflection in water, and
afterwards again directly in the firmament, we should

[1] Compare below the *Leviathan,* Ch. IV.

to both those appearances give the name of sun, and say there are two suns; which none but men can do, for no other living creatures have the use of names. This kind of error only deserves the name of *falsity*, as arising, not from sense, nor from the things themselves, but from pronouncing rashly; for names have their constitution, not from the species of things, but from the will and consent of men. And hence it comes to pass, that men pronounce *falsely*, by their own negligence, in departing from such appellations of things as are agreed upon, and are not deceived neither by the things, nor by the sense; for they do not perceive that the thing they see is called sun, but they gave it that name from their own will and agreement. Tacit errors, or the errors of sense and cogitation, are made, by passing from one imagination to the imagination of another different thing; or by feigning that to be past, or future, which never was, nor ever shall be; as when, by seeing the image of the sun in water, we imagine the sun itself to be there; or by seeing swords, that there has been or shall be fighting, because it uses to be so for the most part; or when from promises we feign the mind of the promiser to be such and such; or lastly, when from any sign we vainly imagine something to be signified, which is not. And errors of this sort are common to all things that have sense; and yet the deception proceeds neither from our senses, nor from the things we perceive; but from ourselves while we feign such things as are but mere images to be something more than images. But neither things, nor imaginations of things, can be said to be false, seeing they are truly what they are; nor do they, as signs, promise any thing which they do not perform; for they indeed do not promise at all, but we from them; nor do the clouds, but we, from seeing the clouds, say it shall rain. The best way, therefore,

to free ourselves from such errors as arise from natural
signs, is first of all, before we begin to reason concerning such conjectural things, to suppose ourselves
ignorant, and then to make use of our ratiocination; for
these errors proceed from the want of ratiocination;
whereas, errors which consist in affirmation and negation, (that is, the falsity of propositions) proceed only
from reasoning amiss. Of these, therefore, as repugnant
to philosophy, I will speak principally.[2]

2. Errors which happen in reasoning, that is, in
syllogizing, consist either in the falsity of the premises,
or of the inference. In the first of these cases, a syllogism is said to be faulty in the *matter* of it; and in the
second case, in the *form*. I will first consider the matter, namely, how many ways a proposition may be false;
and next the form, and how it comes to pass, that when
the premises are true, the inference is, notwithstanding, false.

Seeing, therefore, that proposition only is true, (chap.
III, art. 7) in which are copulated two names of one
and the same thing; and that always false, in which
names of different things are copulated, look how many
ways names of different things may be copulated, and so
many ways a false proposition may be made.

Now, all things to which we give names, may be
reduced to these four kinds, namely, *bodies, accidents,
phantasms,* and *names* themselves; and therefore, in
every true proposition, it is necessary that the names
copulated, be both of them names of *bodies,* or both
names of *accidents,* or both names of *phantasms,* or both
names of *names.* For names otherwise copulated are
incoherent, and constitute a false proposition. It may
happen, also, that the name of a *body,* of an *accident,*
or of a *phantasm,* may be copulated with the name of a

[2] Compare below the *Leviathan,* Ch. V.

speech. So that copulated names may be incoherent seven manner of ways.

*   *   *   *   *   *   *   *   *

The falsities of propositions in all these several manners, is to be discovered by the definitions of the copulated names.

10. But when names of bodies are copulated with names of bodies, names of accidents with names of accidents, names of names with names of names, and names of phantasms with names of phantasms, if we, nevertheless, remain still doubtful whether such propositions are true, we ought then in the first place to find out the definition of both those names, and again the definitions of such names as are in the former definition, and so proceed by a continual resolution till we come to a simple name, that is, to the most general or most universal name of that kind; and if after all this, the truth or falsity thereof be not evident, we must search it out by philosophy, and ratiocination, beginning from definitions. For every proposition, universally true, is either a definition, or part of a definition, or the evidence of it depends upon definitions.

11. That fault of a syllogism which lies hid in the form thereof, will always be found either in the implication of the copula with one of the terms, or in the equivocation of some word; and in either of these ways there will be four terms, which (as I have shewn) cannot stand in a true syllogism. Now the implication of the copula with either term, is easily detected by reducing the propositions to plain and clear predication; as (for example) if any man should argue thus,

> *The hand toucheth the pen,*
> *The pen toucheth the paper,*
> Therefore, *The hand toucheth the paper;*

the fallacy will easily appear by reducing it, thus:

> *The hand, is, touching the pen,*
> *The pen, is, touching the paper,*
> Therefore, *The hand, is, touching the paper;*

where there are manifestly these four terms, *the hand, touching the pen, the pen,* and *touching the paper.* But the danger of being deceived by sophisms of this kind, does not seem to be so great, as that I need insist longer upon them.

12. And though there may be fallacy in equivocal terms, yet in those that be manifestly such, there is none at all; nor in metaphors, for they profess the transferring of names from one thing to another. Nevertheless, sometimes equivocals (and those not very obscure) may deceive; as in this argumentation:—*It belongs to metaphysics to treat of principles; but the first principle of all, is, that the same thing cannot both exist and not exist at the same time; and therefore it belongs to metaphysics to treat whether the same thing may both exist and not exist at the same time*; where the fallacy lies in the equivocation of the word principle; for whereas Aristotle in the beginning of his *Metaphysics*, says, that *the treating of principles belongs to primary science,* he understands by principles, causes of things, and certain existences which he calls primary; but where he says *a primary proposition is a principle,* by principle, there, he means the beginning and cause of knowledge, that is, the understanding of words, which, if any man want, he is incapable of learning.

13. But the *captions* of sophists and sceptics, by which they were wont, of old, to deride and oppose truth, were faulty for the most part, not in the form, but in the matter of syllogism; and they deceived not others oftener than they were themselves deceived. For the

force of that famous argument of Zeno against motion, consisted in this proposition, *whatsoever may be divided into parts, infinite in number, the same is infinite;* which he, without doubt, thought to be true, yet nevertheless is false. For to be divided into infinite parts, is nothing else but to be divided into as many parts as any man will. But it is not necessary that a line should have parts infinite in number, or be infinite, because I can divide and subdivide it as often as I please; for how many parts soever I make, yet their number is finite; but because he that says parts, simply, without adding how many, does not limit any number, but leaves it to the determination of the hearer, therefore we say commonly, a line may be divided infinitely; which cannot be true in any other sense.

And thus much may suffice concerning syllogism, which is, as it were, the first pace towards philosophy; in which I have said as much as is necessary to teach any man from whence all true argumentation has its force. And to enlarge this treatise with all that may be heaped together, would be as superfluous, as if one should (as I said before) give a young child precepts for the teaching of him to go; for the art of reasoning is not so well learned by precepts as by practice, and by the reading of those books in which the conclusions are all made by severe demonstration. And so I pass on to the way of philosophy, that is, to the method of study.

CHAPTER VI

OF METHOD

1. Method and science defined.—2. It is more easily known concerning singular, than universal things, that they are; and contrarily, it is more easily known concerning universal,

than singular things, why they are, or what are their causes.—3. What it is philosophers seek to know.—4. The first part, by which principles are found out, is purely analytical.—5. The highest causes, and most universal in every kind, are known by themselves.—6. Method from principles found out, tending to science simply, what it is. —7. That method of civil and natural science, which proceeds from sense to principles, is analytical; and again, that, which begins at principles, is synthetical.—8. The method of searching out, whether any thing propounded be matter or accident.—9. The method of seeking whether any accident be in this, or in that subject.—10. The method of searching after the cause of any effect propounded.—11. Words serve to invention, as marks; to demonstration, as signs.—12. The method of demonstration is synthetical.— 13. Definitions only are primary and universal propositions. —14. The nature and definition of a definition.—15. The properties of a definition.—16. The nature of a demonstration.—17. The properties of a demonstration, and order of things to be demonstrated.—18. The faults of a demonstration.—19. Why the analytical method of geometricians cannot be treated of in this place.

1. For the understanding of *method*, it will be necessary for me to repeat the definition of philosophy, delivered above (chap. I, art. 2,) in this manner, *Philosophy is the knowledge we acquire, by true ratiocination, of appearances, or apparent effects, from the knowledge we have of some possible production or generation of the same; and of such production, as has been or may be, from the knowledge we have of the effects.* Method, therefore, in the study of philosophy, *is the shortest way of finding out effects by their known causes, or of causes by their known effects.* But we are then said to know any effect, when we know *that there be causes of the same*, and *in what subject those causes are*, and *in what subject they produce that effect*, and *in what manner they work the same.* And this is the science of causes, or, as they call it, of the διότι. All other science, which is called the ὅτι, is either per-

ception by sense, or the imagination, or memory remaining after such perception.[1]

The first beginnings, therefore, of knowledge, are the phantasms of sense and imagination; and that there be such phantasms we know well enough by nature; but to know why they be, or from what causes they proceed, is the work of ratiocination; which consists (as is said above, in the 1st chapter, art. 2) in *composition,* and *division* or *resolution.* There is therefore no method, by which we find out the causes of things, but is either *compositive* or *resolutive,* or *partly compositive,* and *partly resolutive.* And the resolutive is commonly called *analytical* method, as the compositive is called *synthetical.*

2. It is common to all sorts of method, to proceed from known things to unknown; and this is manifest from the cited definition of philosophy. But in knowledge by sense, the whole object is more known, than any part thereof; as when we see a man, the conception or whole idea of that man is first or more known, than the particular ideas of his being *figurate, animate,* and *rational*; that is, we first see the whole man, and take notice of his being, before we observe in him those other particulars. And therefore in any knowledge of the ὅτι, or that any thing *is,* the beginning of our search is from the whole idea; and contrarily, in our knowledge of the διότι, or of the causes of any thing, that is, in the

[1] Compare above Ch. I, Note 1, also the following from *Human Nature,* (M. IV, 27). "There be *two kinds* of knowledge, whereof the *one* is nothing else but *sense,* or knowledge *original,* and *remembrance* of the same; the *other* is called *science* or knowledge of the *truth of propositions,* and how things are called, and is derived from *understanding.* Both of these sorts are but *experience*; the former being the experience of the effects of things that work upon us from *without,* and the latter experience men have from the proper use of *names* in language: and all experience being, as I have said, but remembrance, all knowledge is remembrance."

sciences, we have more knowledge of the causes of the parts than of the whole. For the cause of the whole is compounded of the causes of the parts; but it is necessary that we know the things that are to be compounded, before we can know the whole compound. Now, by parts, I do not here mean parts of the thing itself, but parts of its nature; as, by the parts of man, I do not understand his head, his shoulders, his arms, &c. but his figure, quantity, motion, sense, reason, and the like; which accidents being compounded or put together, constitute the whole nature of man, but not the man himself. And this is the meaning of that common saying, namely, that some things are more known to us, others more known to nature; for I do not think that they, which so distinguish, mean that something is known to nature, which is known to no man; and therefore, by those things, that are more known to us, we are to understand things we take notice of by our senses, and, by more known to nature, those we acquire the knowledge of by reason; for in this sense it is, that the *whole*, that is, those things that have universal names, (which, for brevity's sake, I call *universal*) are more known to us than the *parts*, that is, such things as have names less universal, (which I therefore call *singular*); and the causes of the parts are more known to nature than the cause of the whole; that is, universals than singulars.

3. In the study of philosophy, men search after science either simply or indefinitely; that is, to know as much as they can, without propounding to themselves any limited question; or they enquire into the cause of some determined appearance, or endeavour to find out the certainty of something in question, as what is the cause of *light*, of *heat*, of *gravity*, of a *figure* propounded, and the like; or in what *subject* any propounded *accident* is inherent; or what may conduce most

to the *generation* of some propounded *effect* from many *accidents*; or in what manner particular causes ought to be compounded for the production of some certain effect. Now, according to this variety of things in question, sometimes the *analytical method* is to be used, and sometimes the *synthetical*.

4. But to those that search after science indefinitely, which consists in the knowledge of the causes of all things, as far forth as it may be attained, (and the causes of singular things are compounded of the causes of universal or simple things) it is necessary that they know the causes of universal things, or of such accidents as are common to all bodies, that is, to all matter, before they can know the causes of singular things, that is, of those accidents by which one thing is distinguished from another. And, again, they must know what those universal things are, before they can know their causes. Moreover, seeing universal things are contained in the nature of singular things, the knowledge of them is to be acquired by reason, that is, by resolution. For example, if there be propounded a conception or *idea* of some singular thing, as of a *square*, this square is to be resolved into a *plain, terminated with a certain number of equal and straight lines and right angles*. For by this resolution we have these things universal or agreeable to all matter, namely, *line, plain,* (which contains *superficies*) *terminated, angle, straightness, rectitude,* and *equality*; and if we can find out the causes of these, we may compound them altogether into the cause of a square. Again, if any man propound to himself the conception of *gold,* he may, by resolving, come to the ideas of *solid, visible, heavy,* (that is, tending to the centre of the earth, or downwards) and many other more universal than gold itself; and these he may resolve again, till he come to such things as are most uni-

versal. And in this manner, by resolving continually, we may come to know what those things are, whose causes being first known severally, and afterwards compounded, bring us to the knowledge of singular things. I conclude, therefore, that the method of attaining to the universal knowledge of things, is purely *analytical*.

5. But the causes of universal things (of those, at least, that have any cause) are manifest of themselves, or (as they say commonly) known to nature; so that they need no method at all; for they have all but one universal cause, which is motion. For the variety of all figures arises out of the variety of those motions by which they are made; and motion cannot be understood to have any other cause besides motion; nor has the variety of those things we perceive by sense, as of *colours, sounds, savours,* &c. any other cause than motion, residing partly in the objects that work upon our senses, and partly in ourselves, in such manner, as that it is manifestly some kind of motion, though we cannot, without ratiocination, come to know what kind. For though many cannot understand till it be in some sort demonstrated to them, that all mutation consists in motion; yet this happens not from any obscurity in the thing itself, (for it is not intelligible that anything can depart either from rest, or from the motion it has, except by motion), but either by having their natural discourse corrupted with former opinions received from their masters, or else for this, that they do not at all bend their mind to the enquiring out of truth.

6. By the knowledge therefore of universals, and of their causes (which are the first principles by which we know the διότι of things) we have in the first place their definitions, (which are nothing but the explication of our simple conceptions.) For example, he that has a true conception of *place*, cannot be ignorant of this definition,

place is that space which is possessed or filled adequately by some body; and so, he that conceives *motion* aright, cannot but know that *motion is the privation of one place, and the acquisition of another.* In the next place, we have their generations or descriptions; as (for example) that *a line is made by the motion of a point, superficies by the motion of a line,* and *one motion by another motion, &c.* It remains, that we enquire what motion begets such and such effects; as, what motion makes a straight line, and what a circular; what motion thrusts, what draws, and by what way; what makes a thing which is seen or heard, to be seen or heard sometimes in one manner, sometimes in another. Now the method of this kind of enquiry, is *compositive.* For first we are to observe what effect a body moved produceth, when we consider nothing in it besides its motion; and we see presently that this makes a line, or length; next, what the motion of a long body produces, which we find to be superficies; and so forwards, till we see what the effects of simple motion are; and then, in like manner, we are to observe what proceeds from the addition, multiplication, substraction, and division, of these motions, and what effects, what figures, and what properties, they produce; from which kind of contemplation sprung that part of philosophy which is called *geometry.*

From this consideration of what is produced by simple motion, we are to pass to the consideration of what effects one body moved worketh upon another; and because there may be motion in all the several parts of a body, yet so as that the whole body remain still in the same place, we must enquire first, what motion causeth such and such motion in the whole, that is, when one body invades another body which is either at rest or in motion, what way, and with what swiftness, the invaded body shall move; and, again, what motion this second

body will generate in a third, and so forwards. From
which contemplation shall be drawn that part of philosophy which treats of motion.

In the third place we must proceed to the enquiry of
such effects as are made by the motion of the parts of
any body, as, how it comes to pass, that things when
they are the same, yet seem not to be the same, but
changed. And here the things we search after are sensible qualities, such as *light, colour, transparency, opa-
city, sound, odour, savour, heat, cold,* and the like; which
because they cannot be known till we know the causes
of sense itself, therefore the consideration of the causes
of *seeing, hearing, smelling, tasting,* and *touching,* belongs to this third place; and all those qualities and
changes, above mentioned, are to be referred to the
fourth place; which two considerations comprehend that
part of philosophy which is called *physics.* And in these
four parts is contained whatsoever in natural philosophy may be explicated by demonstration, properly so
called. For if a cause were to be rendered of natural
appearances in special, as, what are the motions and
influences of the heavenly bodies, and of their parts, the
reason hereof must either be drawn from the parts of
the sciences above mentioned, or no reason at all will be
given, but all left to uncertain conjecture.

After *physics* we must come to *moral philosophy*; in
which we are to consider the motions of the mind,
namely, *appetite, aversion, love, benevolence, hope, fear,
anger, emulation, envy, &c.;* what causes they have, and
of what they be causes. And the reason why these are
to be considered after *physics* is, that they have their
causes in sense and imagination, which are the subject of
physical contemplation. Also the reason, why all these
things are to be searched after in the order above-said,
is, that physics cannot be understood, except we know

first what motions are in the smallest parts of bodies;
nor such motion of parts, till we know what it is that
makes another body move; nor this, till we know what
simple motion will effect. And because all appearance
of things to sense is determined, and made to be of such
and such quality and quantity by compounded motions,
every one of which has a certain degree of velocity, and
a certain and determined way; therefore, in the first
place, we are to search out the ways of motion simply
(in which geometry consists); next the ways of such
generated motions as are manifest; and, lastly, the ways
of internal and invisible motions (which is the enquiry
of natural philosophers). And, therefore, they that
study natural philosophy, study in vain, except they
begin at geometry; and such writers or disputers thereof, as are ignorant of geometry, do but make their
readers and hearers lose their time.

7. *Civil* and *moral philosophy* do not so adhere to
one another, but that they may be severed. For the
causes of the motions of the mind are known, not only
by ratiocination, but also by the experience of every man
that takes the pains to observe those motions within himself. And, therefore, not only they that have attained
the knowledge of the passions and perturbations of the
mind, by the *synthetical method*, and from the very first
principles of philosophy, may by proceeding in the same
way, come to the causes and necessity of constituting
commonwealths, and to get the knowledge of what is
natural right, and what are civil duties; and, in every
kind of government, what are the rights of the commonwealth, and all other knowledge appertaining to civil
philosophy; for this reason, that the principles of the
politics consist in the knowledge of the motions of
the mind, and the knowledge of these motions from the
knowledge of sense and imagination; but even they also

that have not learned the first part of philosophy, namely, *geometry* and *physics*, may, notwithstanding, attain the principles of civil philosophy, by the *analytical method*. For if a question be propounded, as, *whether such an action be just or unjust;* if that *unjust* be resolved into *fact against law*, and that notion *law* into the *command* of him or them that have *coercive power*; and that *power* be derived from the *wills* of men that constitute such power, to the end they may live in peace, they may at last come to this, that the appetites of men and the passions of their minds are such, that, unless they be restrained by some power, they will always be making war upon one another; which may be known to be so by any man's experience, that will but examine his own mind. And, therefore, from hence he may proceed, by compounding, to the determination of the justice or injustice of any propounded action. So that it is manifest, by what has been said, that the method of philosophy, to such as seek science simply, without propounding to themselves the solution of any particular question, is partly analytical, and partly synthetical; namely, that which proceeds from sense to the invention of principles, analytical; and the rest synthetical.

8. To those that seek the cause of some certain and propounded appearance or effect, it happens, sometimes, that they know not whether the thing, whose cause is sought after, be matter or body, or some accident of a body. For though in geometry, when the cause is sought of magnitude, or proportion, or figure, it be certainly known that these things, namely magnitude, proportion, and figure, are accidents; yet in natural philosophy, where all questions are concerning the causes of the phantasms of sensible things, it is not so easy to discern between the things themselves, from which those phan-

tasms proceed, and the appearances of those things to the sense; which have deceived many, especially when the phantasms have been made by light. For example, a man that looks upon the sun, has a certain shining idea of the magnitude of about a foot over, and this he calls the sun, though he know the sun to be truly a great deal bigger; and, in like manner, the phantasm of the same thing appears sometimes round, by being seen afar off, and sometimes square, by being nearer. Whereupon it may well be doubted, whether that phantasm be matter, or some body natural, or only some accident of a body; in the examination of which doubt we may use this method. The properties of matter and accidents already found out by us, by the synthetical method, from their definitions, are to be compared with the idea we have before us; and if it agree with the properties of matter or body, then it is a body; otherwise it is an accident. Seeing, therefore, matter cannot by any endeavor of ours be either made or destroyed, or increased, or diminished, or moved out of its place, whereas that idea appears, vanishes, is increased and diminished, and moved hither and thither at pleasure; we may certainly conclude that it is not a body, but an accident only. And this method is *synthetical*.

9. But if there be a doubt made concerning the subject of any known accident (for this may be doubted sometimes, as in the precedent example, doubt may be made in what subject that splendour and apparent magnitude of the sun is), then our enquiry must proceed in this manner. First, matter in general must be divided into parts, as, into object, medium, and the sentient itself, or such other parts as seem most conformable to the thing propounded. Next, these parts are severally to be examined how they agree with the definition of the subject; and such of them as are not

capable of that accident are to be rejected. For example, if by any true ratiocination the sun be found to be greater than its apparent magnitude, then that magnitude is not in the sun; if the sun be in one determined straight line, and one determined distance, and the magnitude and splendour be seen in more lines and distances than one, as it is in reflection or refraction, then neither that splendour nor apparent magnitude are in the sun itself, and, therefore, the body of the sun cannot be the subject of that splendour and magnitude. And for the same reasons the air and other parts will be rejected, till at last nothing remain which can be the subject of that splendour and magnitude but the sentient itself. And this method, in regard the subject is divided into parts, is analytical; and in regard the properties, both of the subject and accident, are compared with the accident concerning whose subject the enquiry is made, it is synthetical.

10. But when we seek after the cause of any propounded effect, we must in the first place get into our mind an exact notion or idea of that which we call cause, namely, that *a cause is the sum or aggregate of all such accidents, both in the agents and the patient, as concur to the producing of the effect propounded; all which existing together, it cannot be understood but that the effect existeth with them; or that it can possibly exist if any one of them be absent.* This being known, in the next place we must examine singly every accident that accompanies or precedes the effect, as far forth as it seems to conduce in any manner to the production of the same, and see whether the propounded effect may be conceived to exist, without the existence of any of those accidents; and by this means separate such accidents, as do not concur, from such as concur to produce the said effect; which being done, we are to put together

the concurring accidents, and consider whether we can
possibly conceive, that when these are all present, the
effect propounded will not follow; and if it be evident
that the effect will follow, then that aggregate of accidents is the entire cause, otherwise not; but we must still
search out and put together other accidents. For example, if the cause of light be propounded to be sought
out; first, we examine things without us, and find
that whensoever light appears, there is some principal
object, as it were the fountain of light, without which
we cannot have any perception of light; and, therefore,
the concurrence of that object is necessary to the generation of light. Next we consider the medium, and find,
that unless it be disposed in a certain manner, namely,
that it be transparent, though the object remain the
same, yet the effect will not follow; and, therefore,
the concurrence of transparency is also necessary to the
generation of light. Thirdly, we observe our own body,
and find that by the indisposition of the eyes, the brain,
the nerves, and the heart, that is, by obstructions,
stupidity, and debility, we are deprived of light, so that
a fitting disposition of the organs to receive impressions
from without is likewise a necessary part of the cause
of light. Again, of all the accidents inherent in the
object, there is none that can conduce to the effecting of
light, but only action (or a certain motion), which cannot be conceived to be wanting, whensoever the effect is
present; for, that anything may shine, it is not requisite
that it be of such or such magnitude or figure, or that
the whole body of it be moved out of the place it is in
(unless it may perhaps be said, that in the sun, or other
body, that which causes light is the light it hath in
itself; which yet is but a trifling exception, seeing nothing is meant thereby but the cause of light; as if any
man should say that the cause of light is that in the

sun which produceth it); it remains, therefore, that the action, by which light is generated, is motion only in the parts of the object. Which being understood, we may easily conceive what it is the medium contributes, namely, the continuation of that motion to the eye; and, lastly, what the eye and the rest of the organs of the sentient contribute, namely, the continuation of the same motion to the last organ of sense, the heart. And in this manner the cause of light may be made up of motion continued from the original of the same motion, to the original of vital motion, light being nothing but the alteration of vital motion, made by the impression upon it of motion continued from the object. But I give this only for an example, for I shall speak more at large of light, and the generation of it, in its proper place. In the mean time it is manifest, that in the searching out of causes, there is need partly of the analytical, and partly of the synthetical method; of the analytical, to conceive how circumstances conduce severally to the production of effects; and of the synthetical, for the adding together and compounding of what they can effect singly by themselves. And thus much may serve for the method of invention. It remains that I speak of the method of teaching, that is, of demonstration, and of the means by which we demonstrate.

11. In the method of invention, the use of words consists in this, that they may serve for marks, by which whatsoever we have found out may be recalled to memory; for without this all our inventions perish, nor will it be possible for us to go on from principles beyond a syllogism or two, by reason of the weakness of memory. For example, if any man, by considering a triangle set before him should find that all its angles together taken are equal to two right angles, and that by thinking of the same tacitly, without any use of words either under-

stood or expressed; and it should happen afterwards that another triangle, unlike the former, or the same in different situation, should be offered to his consideration, he would not know readily whether the same property were in this last or no, but would be forced, as often as a different triangle were brought before him (and the difference of triangles is infinite) to begin his contemplation anew; which he would have no need to do if he had the use of names, for every universal name denotes the conceptions we have of infinite singular things. Nevertheless, as I said above, they serve as *marks* for the help of our memory, whereby we register to ourselves our own inventions; but not as *signs* by which we declare the same to others; so that a man may be a philosopher alone by himself, without any master; Adam had this capacity. But to teach, that is, to demonstrate, supposes two at the least, and syllogistical speech.

12. And seeing teaching is nothing but leading the mind of him we teach, to the knowledge of our inventions, in that track by which we attained the same with our own mind; therefore, the same method that served for our invention, will serve also for demonstration to others, saving that we omit the first part of method which proceeded from the sense of things to universal principles, which, because they are principles, cannot be demonstrated; and seeing they are known by nature, (as we said above in the 5th article) they need no demonstration, though they need explication. The whole method, therefore, of demonstration, is *synthetical*, consisting of that order of speech which begins from primary or most universal propositions, which are manifest of themselves, and proceeds by a perpetual composition of propositions into syllogisms, till at last the learner understand the truth of the conclusion sought after.

13. Now, such principles are nothing but definitions,[2] whereof there are two sorts; one of names, that signify such things as have some conceivable cause, and another of such names as signify things of which we can conceive no cause at all. Names of the former kind are, *body*, or *matter, quantity*, or *extension, motion*, and whatsoever is common to all matter. Of the second kind, are *such a body, such and so great motion, so great magnitude, such figure*, and whatsoever we can distinguish one body from another by. And names of the former kind are well enough defined, when, by speech as short as may be, we raise in the mind of the hearer perfect and clear ideas or conceptions of the things named, as when we define motion to be *the leaving of one place, and the acquiring of another continually;* for though no thing moved, nor any cause of motion be in that definition, yet, at the hearing of that speech, there will come into the mind of the hearer an *idea* of motion clear enough. But definitions of things, which may be understood to have some cause, must consist of such names as express the cause or manner of their generation, as when we define a circle to be a figure made by the circumduction of a straight line in a plane, &c. Besides definitions, there is no other proposition that ought to be called primary, or (according to severe truth) be received into the number of principles.[3] For

---

[2] Compare the following from *Philosophical Rudiments*, (M. II, 305). "The explication of words, whereby the matter enquired after is propounded, is conducible to knowledge; nay, the only way *to know*, is by *definition*."

[3] Compare the following from *Elements of Philosophy*, (M. I, 36). "*Primary* [proposition] is that wherein the subject is explicated by a predicate of many names, as *man is a body, animated, rational*; for that which is comprehended in the name *man*, is more largely expressed in the names *body, animated*, and *rational*, joined together; and it is called *primary*, because it is first in ratiocination; for nothing can be proved, without understanding first the name of the thing in ques-

those *axioms of Euclid*, seeing they may be demonstrated, are no principles of demonstration, though they have by the consent of all men gotten the authority of principles, because they need not be demonstrated. Also, those *petitions*, or *postulata*, (as they call them) though they be principles, yet they are not principles of demonstration, but of construction only; that is, not of science, but of power; or (which is all one) not of *theorems*, which are speculations, but of *problems*, which belong to practice, or the doing of something. But as for those common received opinions, *Nature abhors vacuity, Nature doth nothing in vain*, and the like, which are neither evident in themselves, nor at all to be demonstrated, and which are oftener false than true, they are much less to be acknowledged for principles.

To return, therefore, to definitions; the reason why I say that the cause and generation of such things, as have any cause or generation, ought to enter into their definitions, is this. The end of science is the demonstration of the causes and generations of things; which if they be not in the definitions, they cannot be found in the conclusion of the first syllogism, that is made from those definitions; and if they be not in the first conclusion, they will not be found in any further conclusion deduced from that; and, therefore, by proceeding in this manner, we shall never come to science; which is against the scope and intention of demonstration.[4]

---

tion. Now *primary* propositions are nothing but definitions, or parts of definitions, and these only are the principles of demonstration, being truths constituted arbitrarily by the inventors of speech, and therefore not to be demonstrated."

[4] Compare the following from *Six Lessons, etc.* (M. VII, 212). "Of true and evident definitions, the best are those which declare the cause or generation of that subject, whereof the proper passions are to be demonstrated. For science is

14. Now, seeing definitions (as I have said) are principles, or primary propositions, they are therefore speeches; and seeing they are used for the raising of an *idea* of some thing in the mind of the learner, whensoever that thing has a name, the definition of it can be nothing but the explication of that name by speech; and if that name be given it for some compounded conception, the definition is nothing but a resolution of that name into its most universal parts. As when we define man, saying *man is a body animated, sentient, rational,* those names, *body animated, &c.* are parts of that whole name *man;* so that definitions of this kind always consist of *genus* and *difference;* the former names being all, till the last, *general;* and the last of all, *difference.* But if any name be the most universal in its kind, then the definition of it cannot consist of *genus* and *difference,* but is to be made by such circumlocution, as best explicateth the force of that name. Again, it is possible, and happens often, that the *genus* and *difference* are put together, and yet make no definition; as these words, *a straight line,* contain both the *genus* and *difference;* but are not a definition, unless we should think a straight line may be thus defined, *a straight line is a straight line:* and yet if there were added another name, consisting of different words, but signifying the same thing which these signify, then these might be the definition of that name. From what has been said, it may be understood how a definition ought to be defined, namely, *that it is a proposition, whose predicate resolves the subject, when it may; and when it may not, it exemplifies the same.*[5]

---

that knowledge which is derived from the comprehension of the cause."

[5] Compare the following from *Questions concerning Liberty, etc.* (M. V, 370-371.) "A right definition is that which determineth the signification of the word defined, to the end

15. The properties of a definition are:

First, that it takes away equivocation, as also all
that multitude of distinctions, which are used by such
as think they may learn philosophy by disputation.
For the nature of a definition is to define, that is, to
determine the signification of the defined name, and to
pare from it all other signification besides what is contained in the definition itself; and therefore one definition does as much, as all the distinctions (how many
soever) that can be used about the name defined.

Secondly, that it gives an universal notion of the
thing defined, representing a certain universal picture
thereof, not to the eye, but to the mind. For as when
one paints a man, he paints the image of some man;
so he, that defines the name man, makes a representation of some man to the mind.

Thirdly, that it is not necessary to dispute whether
definitions are to be admitted or no. For when a master
is instructing his scholar, if the scholar understand all
the parts of the thing defined, which are resolved in
the definition, and yet will not admit of the definition,
there needs no further controversy betwixt them, it
being all one as if he refused to be taught. But if he

---

that in the discourse where it is used, the meaning of it may
be constant and without equivocation. This is the measure
of a definition, and intelligible to an English reader. But the
Bishop, that measures it by the genus and the difference,
thinks, it seems, though he write English, he writes not to an
English reader unless he also be a Schoolman. I confess the
rule is good, that we ought to define, when it can be done,
by using first some more general term, and then by restrain-
ing the signification of that general term, till it be the same
with that of the word defined. And this general term the
School calls *genus*, and the restraint *difference*. This, I say,
is a good rule where it can be done; for some words are so
general, that they cannot admit a more general in their
definition."

understand nothing, then certainly the definition is faulty; for the nature of a definition consists in this, that it exhibit a clear idea of the thing defined; and principles are either known by themselves, or else they are not principles.

Fourthly, that, in philosophy, definitions are before defined names. For in teaching philosophy, the first beginning is from definitions; and all progression in the same, till we come to the knowledge of the thing compounded, is compositive. Seeing, therefore, definition is the explication of a compounded name by resolution, and the progression is from the parts to the compound, definitions must be understood before compounded names; nay, when the names of the parts of any speech be explicated, it is not necessary that the definition should be a name compounded of them. For example, when these names, *equilateral, quadrilateral, right-angled*, are sufficiently understood, it is not necessary in geometry that there should be at all such a name as *square*; for defined names are received in philosophy for brevity's sake only.

Fifthly, that compounded names, which are defined one way in some one part of philosophy, may in another part of the same be otherwise defined; as a *parabola* and an *hyperbole* have one definition in geometry, and another in rhetoric; for definitions are instituted and serve for the understanding of the doctrine which is treated of. And, therefore, as in one part of philosophy, a definition may have in it some one fit name for the more brief explanation of some proposition in geometry; so it may have the same liberty in other parts of philosophy; for the use of names is particular (even where many agree to the set of them) and arbitrary.

Sixthly, that no name can be defined by any one

word; because no one word is sufficient for the resolving
of one or more words.

Seventhly, that a defined name ought not to be re-
peated in the definition. For a defined name is the
whole compound, and a definition is the resolution of
that compound into parts; but no total can be part of
itself.

16. Any two definitions, that may be compounded
into a syllogism, produce a conclusion; which, because
it is derived from principles, that is, from definitions, is
said to be demonstrated; and the derivation or composition itself is called a demonstration. In like manner, if a syllogism be made of two propositions, whereof
one is a definition, the other a demonstrated conclusion,
or neither of them is a definition, but both formerly
demonstrated, that syllogism is also called a demonstration, and so successively. The definition therefore of a
demonstration is this, *a demonstration is a syllogism, or
series of syllogisms, derived and continued, from the
definitions of names, to the last conclusion.* And from
hence it may be understood, that all true ratiocination,
which taketh its beginning from true principles, produceth science, and is true demonstration. For as for
the original of the name, although that, which the
Greeks called ἀπόδειξις, and the Latins *demonstratio,*
was understood by them for that sort only of ratiocination, in which, by the describing of certain lines and
figures, they placed the thing they were to prove, as it
were before men's eyes, which is properly ἀποδεικνύειν,
or to *shew* by the figure; yet they seem to have done
it for this reason, that unless it were in geometry, (in
which only there is place for such figures) there was
no ratiocination certain, and ending in science, their
doctrines concerning all other things being nothing but
controversy and clamour; which, nevertheless, hap-

pened, not because the truth to which they pretended could not be made evident without figures, but because they wanted true principles, from which they might derive their ratiocination; and, therefore, there is no reason but that if true definitions were premised in all sorts of doctrines, the demonstrations also would be true.[6]

17. It is proper to methodical demonstration,

First, that there be a true succession of one reason to another, according to the rules of syllogizing delivered above.

Secondly, that the premises of all syllogisms be demonstrated from the first definitions.[7]

[6] Compare the following from *Six Lessons, etc.* (M. VII, 183-184.) "Of arts, some are demonstrable, others indemonstrable; and demonstrable are those the construction of the subject whereof is in the power of the artist himself, who, in his demonstration, does no more but deduce the consequences of his own operation. The reason whereof is this, that the science of every subject is derived from a precognition of the causes, generatioñ, and construction of the same; and consequently where the causes are known, there is place for demonstration, but not where the causes are to seek for. Geometry therefore is demonstrable, for the lines and figures from which we reason are drawn and described by ourselves; and civil philosophy is demonstrable, because we make the commonwealth ourselves. But because of natural bodies we know not the construction, but seek it from the effects, there lies no demonstration of what the causes be we seek for, but only of that what they may be."

[7] Compare the following from *Six Lessons, etc.* (M. VII, 211-212.) "There be but two causes from which can spring an error in the demonstration of any conclusion in any science whatsoever; and those are ignorance or want of understanding, and negligence. For as in the adding together of many and great numbers, he cannot fail that knoweth the rules of addition, and is also all the way so careful, as not to mistake one number or one place for another; so in any other science, he that is perfect in the rules of logic, and is so watchful over his pen, as not to put one word for another, can never

Thirdly, that after definitions, he that teaches or
demonstrates any thing, proceed in the same method by
which he found it out; namely, that in the first place
those things be demonstrated, which immediately succeed to universal definitions (in which is contained that
part of philosophy which is called *philosophia prima*).[8]
Next, those things which may be demonstrated by
simple motion (in which geometry consists). After
geometry, such things as may be taught or shewed by
manifest action, that is, by thrusting from, or pulling

---

fail of making a true, though not perhaps the shortest and
easiest demonstration. The rules of demonstration are but of
two kinds: one, that the principles be true and evident definitions; the other, that the inferences be necessary."

[8] Compare the following from the *Leviathan*. (M. III,
671.) "There is a certain *philosophia prima*, on which all
other philosophy ought to depend; and consisteth principally,
in right limiting of the significations of such appellations, or
names, as are of all others the most universal; which limita-
tions serve to avoid ambiguity and equivocation in reasoning;
and are commonly called definitions; such as are the definitions of body, time, place, matter, form, essence, subject,
substance, accident, power, act, finite, infinite, quantity,
quality, motion, action, passion, and divers others, necessary
to the explaining of a man's conceptions concerning the nature and generation of bodies." Also the following from *Six
Questions, etc.* (M. VII, 226.) "Words understood are but
the seed, and no part of the harvest of philosophy. And this
seed was it, which Aristotle went about to sow in his twelve
books of *metaphysics*, and in his eight books concerning the
hearing of *natural philosophy*. And in these books he defineth
time, place, substance or essence, quantity, relation, &c., that
from thence might be taken the definitions of the most general words for principles in the several parts of science. So
that all definitions proceed from common understanding; of
which, if any man rightly write, he may properly call his
writing *philosophia prima*, that is, the seeds, or the grounds
of philosophy. And this is the method I have used, defining
place, magnitude, and the other the most general appellations
in that part which I entitle *philosophia prima*." That is, in
the part entitled *Elements of Philosophy* or *De Corpore*.

towards. And after these, the motion or mutation of the invisible parts of things, and the doctrine of sense and imaginations, and of the internal passions, especially those of men, in which are comprehended the grounds of civil duties, or civil philosophy; which takes up the last place. And that this method ought to be kept in all sorts of philosophy, is evident from hence, that such things as I have said are to be taught last, cannot be demonstrated, till such as are propounded to be first treated of, be fully understood. Of which method no other example can be given, but that treatise of the elements of philosophy, which I shall begin in the next chapter, and continue to the end of the work.

18. Besides those *paralogisms*, whose fault lies either in the falsity of the premises, or the want of true composition, of which I have spoken in the precedent chapter, there are two more, which are frequent in demonstration; one whereof is commonly called *petitio principii*; the other is the supposing of a *false cause*; and these do not only deceive unskilful learners, but sometimes masters themselves, by making them take that for well demonstrated, which is not demonstrated at all. *Petitio principii* is, when the conclusion to be proved is disguised in other words, and put for the definition or principle from whence it is to be demonstrated; and thus, by putting for the cause of the thing sought, either the thing itself or some effect of it, they make a circle in their demonstration. As for example, he that would demonstrate that the earth stands still in the center of the world, and should suppose the earth's gravity to be the cause thereof, and define gravity to be a quality by which every heavy body tends towards the center of the world, would lose his labour; for the question is, what is the cause of

that quality in the earth? and, therefore, he that supposes gravity to be the cause, puts the thing itself for its own cause.

Of a *false cause* I find this example in a certain treatise where the thing to be demonstrated is the motion of the earth. He begins, therefore, with this, that seeing the earth and the sun are not always in the same situation, it must needs be that one of them be locally moved, which is true; next, he affirms that the vapours, which the sun raises from the earth and sea, are, by reason of this motion, necessarily moved, which also is true; from whence he infers the winds are made, and this may pass for granted; and by these winds he says, the waters of the sea are moved, and by their motion the bottom of the sea, as if it were beaten forwards, moves round; and let this also be granted; wherefore, he concludes, the earth is moved; which is, nevertheless, a paralogism. For, if that wind were the cause why the earth was, from the beginning, moved round, and the motion either of the sun or the earth were the cause of that wind, then the motion of the sun or the earth was before the wind itself; and if the earth were moved, before the wind was made, then the wind could not be the cause of the earth's revolution; but, if the sun were moved, and the earth stand still, then it is manifest the earth might remain unmoved, notwithstanding that wind; and therefore that motion was not made by the cause which he allegeth. But paralogisms of this kind are very frequent among the writers of *physics*, though none can be more elaborate than this in the example given.

19. It may to some men seem pertinent to treat in this place of that art of the geometricians, which they call *logistica*, that is, the art, by which, from supposing

the thing in question to be true, they proceed by ratiocination, till either they come to something known, by which they may demonstrate the truth of the thing sought for; or to something which is impossible, from whence they collect that to be false, which they supposed true. But this art cannot be explicated here, for this reason, that the method of it can neither be practised, nor understood, unless by such as are well versed in geometry; and among geometricians themselves, they, that have most theorems in readiness, are the most ready in the use of this *logistica*; so that, indeed, it is not a distinct thing from geometry itself; for there are, in the method of it, three parts; the first whereof consists in the finding out of equality betwixt known and unknown things, which they call equation; and this equation cannot be found out, but by such as know perfectly the nature, properties, and transpositions of proportion, as also the addition, subtraction, multiplication, and division of lines and superficies, and the extraction of roots; which are the parts of no mean geometrician. The second is, when an equation is found, to be able to judge whether the truth or falsity of the question may be deduced from it, or no; which yet requires greater knowledge. And the third is, when such an equation is found, as is fit for the solution of the question, to know how to resolve the same in such manner, that the truth or falsity may thereby manifestly appear; which, in hard questions, cannot be done without the knowledge of the nature of crooked-lined figures; but he that understands readily the nature and properties of these, is a complete geometrician. It happens besides, that for the finding out of equations, there is no certain method, but he is best able to do it, that has the best natural wit.

Part II

THE FIRST GROUNDS OF PHILOSOPHY

CHAPTER VII

OF PLACE AND TIME

1. Things that have no existence, may nevertheless be understood and computed.—2. What is Space.—3. Time.—4. Part.—5. Division.—6. One.—7. Number.—8. Composition.—9. The whole.—10. Spaces and times contiguous, and continual.—11. Beginning, end, way, finite, infinite.—12. What is infinite in power. Nothing infinite can be truly said to be either whole, or one; nor infinite spaces or times, many.—13. Division proceeds not to the least.

1. In the teaching of natural philosophy, I cannot begin better (as I have already shewn) than from *privation*; that is, from feigning the world to be annihilated. But, if such annihilation of all things be supposed, it may perhaps be asked, what would remain for any man (whom only I except from this universal annihilation of things) to consider as the subject of philosophy, or at all to reason upon; or what to give names unto for ratiocination's sake.

I say, therefore, there would remain to that man ideas of the world, and of all such bodies as he had, before their annihilation, seen with his eyes, or perceived by any other sense; that is to say, the memory and imagination of magnitudes, motions, sounds, colours, &c. as also of their order and parts. All which things, though they be nothing but ideas and phantasms, happening internally to him that imagineth; yet they will appear as if they were external, and not at all depending upon any power of the mind. And these are the things to which he would give names, and subtract them from, and compound them with one another. For seeing, that after the destruction of all other things, I suppose man still remaining, and namely that he thinks, imagines, and remembers, there can be nothing for him to think of but what is past; nay, if we do but observe diligently what it is we do when we consider and reason, we shall find, that though all things be still remaining in the world, yet we compute nothing but our own phantasms. For when we calculate the magnitude and motions of heaven or earth, we do not ascend into heaven that we may divide it into parts, or measure the motions thereof, but we do it sitting still in our closets or in the dark. Now things may be considered, that is, be brought into account, either as internal accidents of our mind, in which manner we consider them when the question is about some faculty of the mind; or as species of external things, not as really existing, but appearing only to exist, or to have a being without us. And in this manner we are now to consider them.

2. If therefore we remember, or have a phantasm of any thing that was in the world before the supposed annihilation of the same; and consider, not that the thing was such or such, but only that it had a being without the mind, we have presently a conception of that we call *space*: an imaginary space indeed, because a mere phantasm, yet that very thing which all men call so. For no man calls it space for being already filled, but because it may be filled; nor does any man think bodies carry their places away with them, but that the same space contains sometimes one, sometimes another body; which could not be if space should always accompany the body which is once in it. And this is of itself so manifest, that I should not think it needed any explaining at all, but that I find space to be

falsely defined by certain philosophers who infer from
thence, one, that the world is infinite (for taking *space*
to be the extension of bodies and thinking extension
may encrease continually, he infers that bodies may be
infinitely extended); and, another, from the same definition, concludes rashly, that it is impossible even to God
himself to create more worlds than one; for, if another
world were to be created, he says, that seeing there is
nothing without this world, and therefore (according to
his definition) no space, that new world must be placed
in nothing; but in nothing nothing can be placed; which
he affirms only, without showing any reason for the
same; whereas the contrary is the truth: for more cannot
be put into a space already filled, so much is empty
space fitter than that, which is full, for the receiving
of new bodies. Having therefore spoken thus much for
these men's sakes, and for theirs that assent to them, I
return to my purpose, and define *space* thus: SPACE *is
the phantasm of a thing existing without the mind
simply*; that is to say, that phantasm, in which we
consider no other accident, but only that it appears
without us.

3. As a body leaves a phantasm of its magnitude in
the mind, so also a moved body leaves a phantasm of
its motion, namely, an idea of that body passing out
of one space into another by continual succession. And
this idea, or phantasm, is that, which (without receding
much from the common opinion, or from *Aristotle's*
definition) I call *Time*. For seeing all men confess a
year to be time, and yet do not think a year to be the
accident or affection of any body, they must needs
confess it to be, not in the things without us, but only
in the thought of the mind. So when they speak of the
times of their predecessors, they do not think after
their predecessors are gone, that their times can be

any where else than in the memory of those that remember them. And as for those that say, days, years,
and months are the motions of the sun and moon, seeing
it is all one to say, motion *past* and motion *destroyed,*
and that *future* motion is the same with motion which
is not yet begun, they say that, which they do not mean,
that there neither is, nor has been, nor shall be any
time: for of whatsoever it may be said, *it has been* or
it shall be, of the same also it might have been said
heretofore, or may be said hereafter *it is.* What then
can days, months, and years, be, but the names of such
computations made in our mind? *Time* therefore is a
phantasm, but a phantasm of motion, for if we would
know by what moments time passes away, we make use
of some motion or other, as of the sun, of a clock, of
the sand in an hourglass, or we mark some line upon
which we imagine something to be moved, there being
no other means by which we can take notice of any
time at all. And yet, when I say *time* is a phantasm of
motion, I do not say this is sufficient to define it by;
for this word *time* comprehends the notion of *former*
and *latter,* or of succession in the motion of a body, in
as much as it is first *here* then *there.* Wherefore a complete definition of *time* is such as this, TIME *is the phantasm of before and after in motion*; which agrees with
this definition of *Aristotle, time is the number of motion
according to former and latter*; for that numbering is an
act of the mind; and therefore it is all one to say, *time
is the number of motion according to former and latter*;
and *time is a phantasm of motion numbered.* But that
other definition, *time is the measure of motion,* is not
so exact, for we measure time by motion and not motion
by time.

4. One space is called *part* of another space, and one
time *part* of another time, when this contains that and

something besides. From whence it may be collected,
that nothing can rightly be called a PART, but that which
is compared with something that contains it.

5. And therefore to *make parts,* or to *part* or DIVIDE
space or *time,* is nothing else but to consider one and
another within the same; so that if any man *divide*
space or time, the diverse conceptions he has are more,
by one, than the parts he makes; for his first conception
is of that which is to be divided, then of some part of it,
and again of some other part of it, and so forwards as
long as he goes on in dividing.

But it is to be noted, that here, by *division,* I do not
mean the severing or pulling asunder of one space or
time from another (for does any man think that one
hemisphere may be separated from the other hemisphere, or the first hour from the second?) but diversity
of consideration; so that division is not made by the
operation of the hands of the mind.

6. When space or time is considered among other
spaces or times, it is said to be ONE, namely *one of them;*
for except one space might be added to another, and
subtracted from another space, and so of time, it would
be sufficient to say space or time simply, and superfluous
to say one space or one time, if it could not be conceived that there were another. The common definition
of *one,* namely, that *one is that which is undivided,* is
obnoxious to an absurd consequence; for it may thence
be inferred, that whatsoever is divided is many things,
that is, that every divided thing, is divided things, which
is insignificant.

7. NUMBER is *one* and *one,* or *one one* and *one,* and
so forwards; namely, *one* and *one* make the number
two, and *one one* and *one* the number *three;* so are all
other numbers made; which is all one as if we should
say, *number is unities.*

8. To COMPOUND space of spaces, or time of times, is first to consider them one after another, and then altogether as one; as if one should reckon first the head, the feet, the arms, and the body, severally, and then for the account of them all together put *man*. And that which is so put for all the severals of which it consists, is called the WHOLE; and those severals, when by the division of the whole they come again to be considered singly, are parts thereof; and therefore the *whole* and *all the parts taken together* are the same thing. And as I noted above, that in *division* it is not necessary to pull the parts asunder; so in *composition*, it is to be understood, that for the making up of a whole there is no need of putting the parts together, so as to make them touch one another, but only of collecting them into one sum in the mind. For thus all men, being considered together, make up the whole of mankind, though never so much dispersed by time and place; and twelve hours, though the hours of several days, may be compounded into one number of twelve.

9. This being well understood, it is manifest, that nothing can rightly be called a whole, that is not conceived to be compounded of parts, and that it may be divided into parts; so that if we deny that a thing has parts, we deny the same to be a whole. For example, if we say the soul can have no parts, we affirm that no soul can be a whole soul. Also it is manifest, that nothing has parts till it be divided; and when a thing is divided, the parts are only so many as the division makes them. Again, that a part of a part is a part of the whole; and thus any part of the number *four*, as *two*, is a part of the number *eight*; for *four* is made of *two* and *two*; but eight is compounded of *two, two,* and *four,* and therefore *two,* which is a part of the part *four,* is also a part of the whole *eight.*

10. Two spaces are said to be CONTIGUOUS, when there is no other space betwixt them. But two times, betwixt which there is no other time, are called immediate, as A B, B C. And any two spaces, as well as times, are said to be CONTINUAL, when they have one common part, as A C, B D, where the

A B C

A B C D

part B C is common; and more spaces and times are continual, when every two which are next one another are continual.

11. That part which is between two other parts, is called a MEAN; and that which is not between two other parts, an EXTREME. And of extremes, that which is first reckoned is the BEGINNING, and that which last, the END; and all the means together taken are the WAY. Also, *extreme parts* and *limits* are the same thing. And from hence it is manifest, that *beginning* and *end* depend upon the order in which we number them; and that to *terminate* or *limit* space and time, is the same thing with *imagining their beginning and end*; as also that every thing is FINITE or INFINITE, according as we imagine or not imagine it *limited* or *terminated* every way; and that the *limits* of any number are *unities*, and of these, that which is the first in our numbering is the *beginning*, and that which we number last, is the *end*. When we say number is *infinite*, we mean only that no number is expressed; for when we speak of the numbers *two, three, a thousand,* &c. they are always *finite*. But when no more is said but this, *number is infinite*, it is to be understood as if it were said, this name *number* is an *indefinite name*.

12. Space or time is said to be *finite in power*, or *terminable*, when there may be assigned a number of finite spaces or times, as of paces or hours, than which there can be no greater number of the same measure

in that space or time; and *infinite in power* is that space or time, in which a greater number of the said paces or hours may be assigned, than any number that can be given. But we must note, that, although in that space or time which is infinite in power, there may be numbered more paces or hours than any number that can be assigned, yet their number will always be finite; for every number is finite. And therefore his ratiocination was not good, that undertaking to prove the world to be finite, reasoned thus; *If the world be infinite, then there may be taken in it some part which is distant from us an infinite number of paces: but no such part can be taken; wherefore the world is not infinite*; because that consequence of the major proposition is false; for in an infinite space, whatsoever we take or design in our mind, the distance of the same from us is a finite space; for in the very designing of the place thereof, we put an end to that space, of which we ourselves are the beginning; and whatsoever any man with his mind cuts off both ways from infinite, he determines the same, that is, he makes it finite.

Of infinite space or time, it cannot be said that it is a *whole* or *one*: not a *whole*, because not compounded of parts: for seeing parts, how many soever they be, are severally finite, they will also, when they are all put together, make a whole finite: nor *one*, because nothing can be said to be one, except there be another to compare it with; but it cannot be conceived that there are two spaces, or two times, infinite. Lastly, when we make question whether the world be finite or infinite, we have nothing in our mind answering to the name *world*; for whatsoever we imagine, is therefore finite, though our computation reach the fixed stars, or the ninth or tenth, nay, the thousandth sphere. The meaning of the question is this only, whether God has actually made so great an addition of body to body, as we are able to make of space to space.

13. And, therefore, that which is commonly said, that space and time may be divided infinitely, is not to be so understood, as if there might be any infinite or external division; but rather to be taken in this sense, *whatsoever is divided, is divided into such parts as may again be divided*; or thus, *the least divisible thing is not to be given*; or, as geometricians have it, *no quantity is so small, but a less may be taken*; which may easily be demonstrated in this manner. Let any space or time, that which was thought to be the least divisible, be divided into two equal parts, A and B. I say either of them, as A, may be divided again. For suppose the part A to be contiguous to the part B of one side, and of the other side to some other space equal to B. This whole space, therefore, being greater than the space given, is divisible. Wherefore, if it be divided into two equal parts, the part in the middle, which is A, will be also divided into two equal parts; and therefore A was divisible.

CHAPTER VIII

OF BODY AND ACCIDENT

1. Body defined.—2. Accident defined.—3. How an accident may be understood to be in its subject.—4. Magnitude, what it is.—5. Place, what it is, and that it is immovable.—6. What is full and empty.—7. Here, there, somewhere, what they signify.—8. Many bodies cannot be in one place, nor one body in many places.—9. Contiguous and continual, what they are.—10. The definition of motion. No motion intelligible but with time.—11. What it is to be at rest, to have been moved, and to be moved. No motion to be conceived, without the conception of past and future.—12. A point, a line, superficies and solid, what they are.—13. Equal, greater, and less in bodies and magnitudes, what

they are.—14. One and the same body has always one and
the same magnitude.—15. Velocity, what it is.—16. Equal,
greater, and less in times, what they are.—17. Equal,
greater, and less, in velocity, what.—18. Equal, greater,
and less, in motion, what.—19. That which is at rest, will
always be at rest, except it be moved by some external
thing; and that which is moved, will always be moved, unless it be hindered by some external thing.—20. Accidents
are generated and destroyed, but bodies not so.—21. An
accident cannot depart from its subject.—22. Nor be moved.
—23. Essence, form and matter, what they are.—24. First
matter, what.—25. That the whole is greater than any part
thereof, why demonstrated.

1. HAVING understood what imaginary space is, in
which we supposed nothing remaining without us, but
all those things to be destroyed, that, by existing heretofore, left images of themselves in our minds; let us
now suppose some one of those things to be placed
again in the world, or created anew. It is necessary,
therefore, that this new-created or replaced thing do not
only fill some part of the space above mentioned, or be
coincident and coextended with it, but also that it have
no dependence upon our thought. And this is that
which, for the extension of it, we commonly call *body*;
and because it depends not upon our thought, we say is
a thing subsisting of itself; as also *existing*, because
without us; and, lastly, it is called the *subject*, because
it is so placed in and *subjected* to imaginary space, that
it may be understood by reason, as well as perceived by
sense. The definition, therefore of *body* may be this,
*a body is that, which having no dependence upon our
thought, is coincident or coextended with some part of
space*.

2. But what an *accident* is cannot so easily be explained by any definition, as by examples. Let us
imagine, therefore, that a body fills any space, or is
coextended with it; that coextension is not the coex-

tended body, and, in like manner, let us imagine that
the same body is removed out of its place; that removing
is not the removed body: or let us think the same not
removed; that not removing or rest is not the resting
body. What, then, are these things? They are *accidents* of that body. But the thing in question is, *what
is an accident?* which is an enquiry after that which we
know already, and not that which we should enquire
after. For who does not always and in the same manner understand him that says any thing is extended, or
moved or not moved? But most men will have it be
said that *an accident is something,* namely, some part
of a natural thing, when, indeed, it is no part of the
same. To satisfy these men, as well as may be, they
answer best that define an *accident* to be *the manner
by which any body is conceived*; which is all one as if
they should say, *an accident is that faculty of any body,
by which it works in us a conception of itself.* Which
definition, though it be not an answer to the question
propounded, yet it is an answer to that question which
should have been propounded, namely, *whence does it
happen that one part of any body appears here, another
there?* For this is well answered thus: *it happens from
the extension of that body,* Or, *how comes it to pass
that the whole body, by succession, is seen now here,
now there?* and the answer will be, *by reason of its
motion.* Or, lastly, *whence is it that any body possesseth the same space for sometime?* and the answer will
be, *because it is not moved.* For if concerning the name
of a body, that is, concerning a concrete name, it be
asked, *what is it?* the answer must be made by definition; for the question is concerning the signification of
the name. But if it be asked concerning an abstract
name, *what is it?* the cause is demanded why a thing
appears so or so. As if it be asked, *what is hard?* The

answer will be, hard is that, whereof no part gives place, but when the whole gives place. But if it be demanded, *what is hardness?* a cause must be shewn why a part does not give place, except the whole give place. Wherefore, I define *an accident* to be *the manner of our conception of body.*

3. When an *accident* is said *to be in a body,* it is not so to be understood, as if any thing were contained in that body; as if, for example, redness were in blood, in the same manner, as blood is in a bloody cloth, that is, as a part in the whole; for so, an accident would be a body also. But, as magnitude, or rest, or motion, is in that which is great, or which resteth, or which is moved, (which, how it is to be understood, every man understands) so also, it is to be understood, that every other accident *is in* its subject. And this, also, is explicated by *Aristotle* no otherwise than negatively, namely, that *an accident is in its subject, not as any part thereof, but so as that it may be away, the subject still remaining*; which is right, saving that there are certain accidents which can never perish except the body perish also; for no body can be conceived to be without extension, or without figure. All other accidents, which are not common to all bodies, but peculiar to some only, as *to be at rest, to be moved, colour, hardness,* and the like, do perish continually, and are succeeded by others, yet so, as that the body never perisheth. And as for the opinion that some may have, that all other accidents are not in their bodies in the same manner that extension, motion, rest, or figure, are in the same; for example, that colour, heat, odour, virtue, vice, and the like, are otherwise in them, and, as they say, *inherent*; I desire they would suspend their judgment for the present, and expect a little, till it be found out by ratiocination, whether these very accidents are not also

certain motions either of the mind of the perceiver, or
of the bodies themselves which are perceived; for in
the search of this, a great part of natural philosophy
consists.

4. The *extension* of a body, is the same thing with
the *magnitude* of it, or that which some call *real space*.
But this *magnitude* does not depend upon our cogitation, as imaginary space doth; for this is an effect of
our imagination, but *magnitude* is the cause of it; this
is an accident of the mind, that of a body existing out
of the mind.

5. That space, by which word I here understand
imaginary space, which is coincident with the magnitude of any body, is called the *place* of that body; and
the body itself is that which we call the *thing placed*.
Now *place*, and the *magnitude* of the *thing placed*,
differ. First in this, that a body keeps always the same
magnitude, both when it is at rest, and when it is moved;
but when it is moved, it does not keep the same *place*.
Secondly in this, that *place* is a phantasm of any body
of such and such quantity and figure; but *magnitude* is
the peculiar accident of every body; for one body may
at several times have several places, but has always
one and the same magnitude. Thirdly in this, that *place*
is nothing out of the mind, nor magnitude any thing
within it. And lastly, *place* is feigned extension, but
magnitude true extension; and a placed body is not
extension, but a thing extended. Besides, *place is immovable*; for, seeing that which is moved, is understood
to be carried from place to place, if place were moved,
it would also be carried from place to place, so that
one place must have another place, and that place another place, and so on infinitely, which is ridiculous.
And as for those, that, by making *place* to be of the
same nature with *real space*, would from thence main-

tain it to be immovable, they also make place, though they do not perceive they make it so, to be a mere phantasm. For whilst one affirms that place is therefore said to be immovable, because space in general is considered there; if he had remembered that nothing is general or universal besides names or signs, he would easily have seen that that space, which he says is considered in general, is nothing but a phantasm, in the mind or the memory, of a body of such magnitude and such figure. And whilst another says: real space is made immovable by the understanding; as when, under the superficies of running water, we imagine other and other water to come by continual succession, that superficies fixed there by the understanding, is the *immovable place* of the river: what else does he make it to be but a phantasm, though he do it obscurely and in perplexed words? Lastly, the nature of place does not consist in the *superficies of the ambient*, but in *solid space*; for the whole placed body is coextended with its whole place, and every part of it with every answering part of the same place; but seeing every placed body is a solid thing, it cannot be understood to be coextended with superficies. Besides, how can any whole body be moved, unless all its parts be moved together with it? Or how can the internal parts of it be moved, but by leaving their place? But the internal parts of a body cannot leave the superficies of an external part contiguous to it; and, therefore, it follows, that if place be the superficies of the ambient, then the parts of a body moved, that is, bodies moved, are not moved.

6. Space, or place, that is possessed by a body, is called *full*, and that which is not so possessed, is called *empty*.

7. *Here, there, in the country, in the city*, and other the like names, by which answer is made to the question

where is it? are not properly names of place, nor do they of themselves bring into the mind the place that is sought; for *here* and *there* signify nothing, unless the thing be shewn at the same time with the finger or something else; but when the eye of him that seeks, is, by pointing or some other sign, directed to the thing sought, the place of it is not hereby defined by him that answers, but found out by him that asks the question. Now such shewings as are made by words only, as when we say, *in the country*, or *in the city*, are some of greater latitude than others, as when we say, *in the country, in the city, in such a street, in a house, in the chamber, in bed, &c.* For these do, by little and little, direct the seeker nearer to the proper place; and yet they do not determine the same, but only restrain it to a lesser space, and signify no more, than that the place of the thing is within a certain space designed by those words, as a part is in the whole. And all such names, by which answer is made to the question *where?* have, for the their *genus*, the name *somewhere*. From whence it may be understood, that whatsoever is somewhere, is in some place properly so called, which place is part of that greater space that is signified by some of these names, *in the country, in the city*, or the like.

8. A body, and the magnitude, and the place thereof, are divided by one and the same act of the mind; for, to divide an extended body, and the extension thereof, and the idea of that extension, which is place, is the same with dividing any one of them; because they are coincident, and it cannot be done but by the mind, that is by the division of space. From whence it is manifest, that neither two bodies can be together in the same place, nor one body be in two places at the same time. Not two bodies in the same place; because when a body that fills its whole place is divided into two, the place

itself is divided into two also, so that there will be two places. Not one body in two places; for the place that a body fills being divided into two, the placed body will be also divided into two; for, as I said, a place and the body that fills that place, are divided both together; and so there will be two bodies.

9. Two bodies are said to be *contiguous* to one another, and *continual,* in the same manner as spaces are; namely, *those are contiguous, between which there is no space.* Now, by space I understand, here as formerly, an idea or phantasm of a body. Wherefore, though between two bodies there be put no other body, and consequently no magnitude, or, as they call it, real space, yet if another body may be put between them, that is, if there intercede any imagined space which may receive another body, then those bodies are not contiguous. And this is so easy to be understood that I should wonder at some men, who being otherwise skilful enough in philosophy, are of a different opinion, but that I find that most of those that affect metaphysical subtleties wander from truth, as if they were led out of their way by an *ignis fatuus.* For can any man that has his natural senses, think that two bodies must therefore necessarily touch one another, because no other body is between them? Or that there can be no *vacuum,* because *vacuum* is nothing, or as they call it, *non ens?* Which is as childish, as if one should reason thus; no man can fast, because to fast is to eat nothing; but nothing cannot be eaten. *Continual, are any two bodies that have a common part; and more than two are continual, when every two, that are next to one another, are continual.*

10. Motion *is a continual relinquishing of one place, and acquiring of another*; and that place which is relinquished is commonly called the *terminus a quo,* as that

which is acquired is called the *terminus ad quem*; I say a continual relinquishing, because no body, how little soever, can totally and at once go out of its former place into another, so, but that some part of it will be in a part of a place which is common to both, namely, to the relinquished and the acquired places. For example, let any body be in the place A C B D; the same body cannot come into the place B D E F, but it must first be in G H I K, whose part A G B I E
G H B D is common to both the
places A C B D, and G H I K,
and whose part B D I K, is common to both the places G H I K, C H D K F
and B D E F. Now it cannot be conceived that any thing can be moved without time; for time is, by the definition of it, a phantasm, that is, a conception of motion; and, therefore, to conceive that any thing may be moved without time, were to conceive motion without motion, which is impossible.

11. *That is said to be at rest, which, during any time, is in one place; and that to be moved, or to have been moved, which, whether it be now at rest or moved, was formerly in another place than that which it is now in.* From which definitions it may be inferred, first, that *whatsoever is moved, has been moved*; for if it be still in the same place in which it was formerly, it is at *rest*; but if it be in another place, it has been *moved*, by the definition of *moved*. Secondly, that *what is moved, will yet be moved*; for that which is moved, leaveth the place where it is, and therefore will be in another place, and consequently will be moved still. Thirdly, that *whatsoever is moved, is not in one place during any time, how little soever that time be*; for by the definition of rest, that which is in one place during any time, is at rest.

There is a certain sophism against motion, which seems to spring from the not understanding of this last proposition. For they say, that, *if any body be moved, it is moved either in the place where it is, or in the place where it is not; both which are false; and therefore nothing is moved.* But the falsity lies in the major proposition; for that which is moved, is neither moved in the place where it is, nor in the place where it is not; but from the place where it is, to the place where it is not. Indeed it cannot be denied but that whatsoever is moved, is moved somewhere, that is, within some space; but then the place of that body is not that whole space, but a part of it, as is said above in the seventh article. From what is above demonstrated, namely, that whatsoever is moved, has also been moved, and will be moved, this also may be collected, that there can be no conception of motion, without conceiving past and future time.

12. Though there be no body which has not some magnitude, yet if, when any body is moved, the magnitude of it be not at all considered, the way it makes is called a *line*, or one single dimension; and the space, through which it passeth, is called *length*; and the body itself, a *point*; in which sense the earth is called a *point*, and the way of its yearly revolution, the *ecliptic line*. But if a body, which is moved, be considered as *long*, and be supposed to be so moved, as that all the several parts of it be understood to make several lines, then the way of every part of that body is called *breadth*, and the space which is made is called *superficies*, consisting of two dimensions, one whereof to every several part of the other is applied whole. Again, if a body be considered as having *superficies*, and be understood to be so moved, that all the several parts of it describe

several lines, then the way of every part of that body is called *thickness* or *depth*, and the space which is made is called *solid*, consisting of three dimensions, any two whereof are applied whole to every several part of the third.

But if a body be considered as *solid*, then it is not possible that all the several parts of it should describe several lines; for what way soever it be moved, the way of the following part will fall into the way of the part before it, so that the same solid will still be made which the foremost superficies would have made by itself. And therefore there can be no other dimension in any body, as it is a body, than the three which I have now described; though, as it shall be shewed hereafter, *velocity*, which is motion according to *length*, may, by being applied to all the parts of a *solid*, make a magnitude of motion, consisting of four dimensions; as the goodness of gold, computed in all the parts of it, makes the price and value thereof.

13. *Bodies*, how many soever they be, that can fill every one the place of every one, are said to be *equal* every one to every other. Now, one body may fill the same place which another body filleth, though it be not of the same figure with that other body, if so be that it may be understood to be reducible to the same figure, either by flexion or transposition of the parts. And *one body is greater than another body, when a part of that is equal to all this; and less, when all that is equal to a part of this.* Also, *magnitudes* are *equal*, or *greater*, or *lesser*, than one another, for the same consideration, namely, when the bodies, of which they are the magnitudes, are either *equal*, or *greater*, or *less*, &c.

14. One and the same body is always of one and the same magnitude. For seeing a body and the magnitude

and place thereof cannot be comprehended in the mind
otherwise than as they are coincident, if any body be
understood to be at rest, that is, to remain in the same
place during some time, and the magnitude thereof be
in one part of that time greater, and in another part
less, that body's place, which is one and the same, will
be coincident sometimes with greater, sometimes with
less magnitude, that is, the same place will be greater
and less than itself, which is impossible. But there
would be no need at all of demonstrating a thing that
is in itself so manifest, if there were not some, whose
opinion concerning bodies and their magnitudes is, that
a body may exist separated from its magnitude, and
have greater or less magnitude bestowed upon it, making
use of this principle for the explication of the nature of
rarum and *densum.*

15. Motion, in as much as a certain length may in a
certain time be transmitted by it, is called VELOCITY or
swiftness: &c. For though *swift* be very often understood with relation to *slower* or *less swift,* as great is
in respect of less, yet nevertheless, as magnitude is by
philosophers taken absolutely for extension, so also
velocity or *swiftness* may be put absolutely for motion
according to length.

16. Many motions are said to be made in equal
times, when every one of them begins and ends together
with some other motion, or if it had begun together,
would also have ended together with the same. For
time, which is a phantasm of motion, cannot be reckoned
but by some exposed motion; as in dials by the motion
of the sun or of the hand; and if two or more motions
begin and end with this motion, they are said to be
made in equal times; from whence also it is easy to
understand what it is to be moved in greater or longer

time, and in less time or not so long; namely, that that is longer moved, which beginning with another, ends later; or ending together, began sooner.

17. Motions are said to be equally swift, when equal lengths are transmitted in equal times; and greater swiftness is that, wherein greater length is passed in equal time, or equal length in less time. Also that swiftness by which equal lengths are passed in equal parts of time, is called *uniform* swiftness or motion; and of motions *not uniform*, such as become swifter or slower by equal increasings or decreasings in equal parts of time, are said to be *accelerated* or *retarded uniformly*.

18. But motion is said to be greater, less, and equal, not only in regard of the length which is transmitted in a certain time, that is, in regard of swiftness only, but of swiftness applied to every smallest particle of magnitude; for when any body is moved, every part of it is also moved; and supposing the parts to be halves, the motions of those halves have their swiftness equal to one another, and severally equal to that of the whole; but the motion of the whole is equal to those two motions, either of which is of equal swiftness with it; and therefore it is one thing for two motions to be equal to one another, and another thing for them to be equally swift. And this is manifest in two horses that draw abreast, where the motion of both the horses together is of equal swiftness with the motion of either of them singly; but the motion of both is greater than the motion of one of them, namely, double. Wherefore *motions are said to be simply equal to one another, when the swiftness of one, computed in every part of its magnitude, is equal to the swiftness of the other computed also in every part of its magnitude: and greater than one another, when the swiftness of one computed as*

above, is greater than the swiftness of the other so com-
puted; and less, when less. Besides, the magnitude of
motion computed in this manner is that which is commonly called FORCE.

19. *Whatsoever is at rest, will always be at rest,*
unless there be some other body besides it, which, by
endeavouring to get into its place by motion, suffers it
no longer to remain at rest. For suppose that some
finite body exist and be at rest, and that all space besides
be empty; if now this body begin to be moved, it will
certainly be moved some way; seeing therefore there
was nothing in that body which did not dispose it to
rest, the reason why it is moved this way is in something
out of it; and in like manner, if it had been moved any
other way, the reason of motion that way had also been
in something out of it; but seeing it was supposed that
nothing is out of it, the reason of its motion one way
would be the same with the reason of its motion every
other way, wherefore it would be moved alike all ways
at once; which is impossible.

In like *manner, whatsoever is moved, will always be*
moved, except there be some other body besides it, which
causeth it to rest. For if we suppose nothing to be
without it, there will be no reason why it should rest
now, rather than at another time; wherefore its motion
would cease in every particle of time alike; which is not
intelligible.

20. When we say a living creature, a tree, or any
other specified body is *generated* or *destroyed*, it is not
to be so understood as if there were made a body of
that which is not-body, or not a body of a body, but
of a living creature not a living creature, of a tree not
a tree, &c. that is, that those accidents for which we
call one thing a living creature, another thing a tree,

and another by some other name, are generated and destroyed; and that therefore the same names are not to
be given to them now, which were given them before.
But that magnitude for which we give to any thing the
name of body is neither generated nor destroyed. For
though we may feign in our mind that a point may
swell to a huge bulk, and that this may again contract
itself to a point; that is, though we may imagine something to arise where before was nothing, and nothing
to be there where before was something, yet we cannot
comprehend in our mind how this may possibly be done
in nature. And therefore philosophers, who tie themselves to natural reason, suppose that a body can neither
be generated nor destroyed, but only that it may appear
otherwise than it did to us, that is, under different
species, and consequently be called by other and other
names; so that that which is now called man, may at
another time have the name of not-man; but that which
is once called body, can never be called not-body. But
it is manifest that all other accidents besides magnitude
or extension may be generated and destroyed; as when
a white thing is made black, the whiteness that was in
it perisheth, and the blackness that was not in it is now
generated; and therefore, bodies and the accidents under
which they appear diversely have this difference, that
bodies are things, and not generated; accidents are
generated, and not things.

21. And therefore, when any thing appears otherwise
than it did by reason of other and other accidents, it is
not to be thought that an accident goes out of one
subject into another, (for they are not, as I said above,
in their subjects as a part in the whole, or as a contained thing in that which contains it, or as a master of
a family in his house), but that one accident perisheth,
and another is generated. For example, when the hand,

being moved, moves the pen, motion does not go out of the hand into the pen; for so the writing might be continued though the hand stood still; but a new motion is generated in the pen, and is the pen's motion.

22. And therefore also it is improper to say, an accident is moved; as when, instead of saying, *figure is an accident of a body carried away*, we say, *a body carries away its figure*.

23. Now that accident for which we give a certain name to any body, or the accident which denominates its subject, is commonly called the ESSENCE thereof; as rationality is the essence of a man; whiteness, of any white thing, and extension the essence of a body. And the same essence, in as much as it is generated, is called the FORM. Again, a body, in respect of any accident, is called the SUBJECT, and in respect of the form it is called the MATTER.

Also, the production or perishing of any accident makes its subject be said *to be changed*; only the production or perishing of form makes it be said it is *generated* or *destroyed*; but in all generation and mutation, the name of *matter* still remains. For a table made of wood is not only wooden, but wood; and a statue of brass is brass as well as brazen; though Aristotle, in his *Metaphysics*, says, that whatsoever is made of any thing ought not to be called ἐκεινὸ, but ἐκέινινον; as that which is made of wood, not ξύλον, but ξύλινον, that is, not wood, but wooden.

24. And as for that matter which is common to all things, and which philosophers, following Aristotle, usually call *materia prima*, that is, *first matter*, it is not any body distinct from all other bodies, nor is it one of them. What then is it? A mere name; yet a name which is not of vain use; for it signifies a conception of body without the consideration of any form or other

accident except only magnitude or extension, and aptness to receive form and other accident. So that whensoever we have use of the name *body in general,* if we
use that of *materia prima,* we do well. For as when a
man not knowing which was first, water or ice, would
find out which of the two were the matter of both, he
would be fain to suppose some third matter which were
neither of these two; so he that would find out what is
the matter of all things, ought to suppose such as is not
the matter of anything that exists. Wherefore *materia
prima* is nothing; and therefore they do not attribute
to it either form or any other accident besides quantity; whereas all singular things have their forms and
accidents certain.

Materia prima, therefore, is body in general, that is,
body considered universally, not as having neither form
nor any accident, but in which no form nor any other
accident but quantity are at all considered, that is, they
are not drawn into argumentation.

25. From what has been said, those axioms may be
demonstrated, which are assumed by Euclid in the beginning of his first element, about the equality and
inequality of magnitudes; of which, omitting the rest,
I will here demonstrate only this one, *the whole is
greater than any part thereof;* to the end that the
reader may know that those axioms are not indemonstrable, and therefore not principles of demonstration;
and from hence learn to be wary how he admits any
thing for a principle, which is not at least as evident as
these are. *Greater* is defined to be that, whose part is
equal to the whole of another. Now if we suppose any
whole to be A, and a part of it to be B; seeing the
whole B is equal to itself, and the same B is a part of
A; therefore a part of A will be equal to the whole B.

Wherefore, by the definition above, A is greater than B; which was to be proved.

CHAPTER IX

OF CAUSE AND EFFECT

1. Action and passion, what they are.—2. Action and passion mediate and immediate.—3. Cause simply taken. Cause without which no effect follows, or cause necessary by supposition.—4. Cause efficient and material.—5. An entire cause is always sufficient to produce its effect. At the same instant that the cause is entire, the effect is produced. Every effect has a necessary cause.—6. The generation of effects is continual. What is the beginning in causation.—7. No cause of motion but in a body contiguous and moved.—8. The same agents and patients, if alike disposed, produce like effects though at different times.—9. All mutation is motion.—10. Contingent accidents, what they are.

1. A BODY is said to work upon or *act*, that is to say, *do* something to another body, when it either generates or destroys some accident in it: and the body in which an accident is generated or destroyed is said to *suffer*, that is, to have something *done* to it by another body; as when one body by putting forwards another body generates motion in it, it is called the AGENT; and the body in which motion is so generated, is called the PATIENT; so fire that warms the hand is the *agent*, and the hand, which is warmed, is the *patient*. That accident, which is generated in the patient, is called the EFFECT.

2. When an agent and patient are contiguous to one another, their action and passion are then said to be *immediate*, otherwise, *mediate*; and when another body, lying betwixt the agent and patient, is contiguous to them both, it is then itself both an agent and a patient; an agent in respect of the body next after it, upon which it works, and a patient in respect of the body next

before it, from which it suffers. Also, if many bodies
be so ordered that every two which are next to one another be contiguous, then all those that are betwixt the
first and the last are both agents and patients, and the
first is an agent only, and the last a patient only.

3. An agent is understood to *produce* its determined
or certain effect in the patient, according to some certain
accident or accidents, with which both it and the patient
are affected; that is to say, the agent hath its effect
precisely such, not because it is a body, but because such
a body, or so moved. For otherwise all agents, seeing
they are all bodies alike, would produce like effects in
all patients. And therefore the fire, for example, does
not warm, because it is a body, but because it is hot;
nor does one body put forward another body because
it is a body, but because it is moved into the place of
that other body. The cause, therefore, of all effects
consists in certain accidents both in the agents and in
the patients; which when they are all present, the effect
is produced; but if any one of them be wanting, it is
not produced; and that accident either of the agent or
patient, without which the effect cannot be produced, is
called *causa sine qua non*, or *cause necessary by supposition*, as also the *cause requisite for the production
of the effect*. But a CAUSE simply, or *an entire cause,
is the aggregate of all the accidents both of the agents
how many soever they be, and of the patient, put together; which when they are all supposed to be present,
it cannot be understood but that the effect is produced
at the same instant; and if any one of them be wanting,
it cannot be understood but that the effect is not
produced.*

4. The aggregate of accidents in the agent or agents,
requisite for the production of the effect, the effect being
produced, is called the *efficient cause* thereof; and the

aggregate of accidents in the patient, the effect being produced, is usually called the *material cause*; I say the effect being produced; for where there is no effect, there can be no cause; for nothing can be called a cause, where there is nothing that can be called an effect. But the efficient and material causes are both but partial causes, or parts of that cause, which in the next precedent article I called an entire cause. And from hence it is manifest, that the effect we expect, though the agents be not defective on their part, may nevertheless be frustrated by a defect in the patient; and when the patient is sufficient, by a defect in the agents.

5. An entire cause is always sufficient for the production of its effect, if the effect be at all possible. For let any effect whatsoever be propounded to be produced; if the same be produced, it is manifest that the cause which produced it was a sufficient cause; but if it be not produced, and yet be possible, it is evident that something was wanting either in some agent, or in the patient, without which it could not be produced; that is, that some accident was wanting which was requisite for its production; and therefore, that cause was not *entire*, which is contrary to what was supposed.

It follows also from hence, that in whatsoever instant the cause is entire, in the same instant the effect is produced. For if it be not produced, something is still wanting, which is requisite for the production of it; and therefore the cause was not entire, as was supposed.

And seeing a necessary cause is defined to be that, which being supposed, the effect cannot but follow; this also may be collected, that whatsoever effect is produced at any time, the same is produced by a necessary cause. For whatsoever is produced, in as much as it is produced, had an entire cause, that is, had all those things, which

being supposed, it cannot be understood but that the
effect follows; that is, it had a necessary cause. And
in the same manner it may be shewn, that whatsoever
effects are hereafter to be produced, shall have a necessary cause; so that all the effects that have been, or
shall be produced, have their necessity in things
antecedent.

6. And from this, that whensoever the cause is entire,
the effect is produced in the same instant, it is manifest
that causation and the production of effects consist in
a certain continual progress; so that as there is a continual mutation in the agent or agents, by the working
of other agents upon them, so also the patient, upon
which they work, is continually altered and changed.
For example: as the heat of the fire increases more and
more, so also the effects thereof, namely, the heat of
such bodies as are next to it, and again, of such other
bodies as are next to them, increase more and more
accordingly; which is already no little argument that all
mutation consists in motion only; the truth whereof
shall be further demonstrated in the ninth article. But
in this progress of causation, that is of action and passion, if any man comprehend in his imagination a part
thereof, and divide the same into parts, the first part or
beginning of it cannot be considered otherwise than as
action or cause; for, if it should be considered as effect
or passion, then it would be necessary to consider something before it, for its cause or action; which cannot be,
for nothing can be before the beginning. And in like
manner, the last part is considered only as effect; for it
cannot be called cause, if nothing follow it; but after
the last, nothing follows. And from hence it is, that in
all action the beginning and cause are taken for the same
thing. But every one of the intermediate parts are both

action and passion, and cause and effect, according as they are compared with the antecedent or subsequent part.

7. There can be no cause of motion, except in a body contiguous and moved. For let there be any two bodies which are not contiguous, and betwixt which the intermediate space is empty, or, if filled, filled with another body which is at rest; and let one of the propounded bodies be supposed to be at rest; I say it shall always be at rest. For if it shall be moved, and the cause of that motion, by the 8th chapter, article 19, will be some external body; and, therefore, if between it and that external body there be nothing but empty space, then whatsoever the disposition be of that external body or the patient itself, yet if it be supposed to be now at rest, we may conceive it will continue so till it be touched by some other body. But seeing cause, by the definition, is the aggregate of all such accidents, which being supposed to be present, it cannot be conceived but that the effect will follow, those accidents, which are either in external bodies, or in the patient itself, cannot be the cause of future motion. And in like manner, seeing we may conceive that whatsoever is at rest will still be at rest, though it be touched by some other body, except that other body is moved; therefore in a contiguous body, which is at rest, there can be no cause of motion. Wherefore there is no cause of motion in any body, except it be contiguous and moved.

The same reason may serve to prove that whatsoever is moved, will always be moved on in the same way and with the same velocity, except it be hindered by some other contiguous and moved body; and consequently that no bodies, either when they are at rest, or when there is an interposition of vacuum, can generate or extinguish or lessen motion in other bodies. There is one that has written that things moved are more resisted by things at rest, than by things contrarily moved; for this reason, that he conceived motion not to be so contrary to motion as rest. That which deceived him was, that the words *rest* and *motion* are but contradictory names; whereas motion, indeed, is not resisted by rest, but by contrary motion.

8. But if a body work upon another body at one time, and afterwards the same body work upon the same body at another time, so that both the agent and patient, and all their parts, be in all things as they were; and there be no difference, except only in time, that is, that one action be former, the other later in time; it is manifest itself, that the effects will be equal and like, as not differing in anything besides time. And as effects themselves proceed from their causes, so the diversity of them depends upon the diversity of their causes also.

9. This being true, it is necessary that mutation can be nothing else but motion of the parts of that body which is changed. For first, we do not say anything is changed, but that which appears to our senses otherwise than it appeared formerly. Secondly, both those appearances are effects produced in the sentient; and, therefore, if they be different, it is necessary, by the preceding article, that either some part of the agent, which was formerly at rest, is now moved, and so the mutation consists in this motion; or some part, which was formerly moved, is now otherwise moved, and so also the mutation consists in this new motion; or which, being formerly moved, is now at rest, which, as I have shewn above, cannot come to pass without motion; and so again, mutation is motion; or lastly, it happens in

some of these manners to the patient, or some of its parts; so the mutation, howsoever it be made, will consist in the motion of the parts, either of the body which is perceived, or of the sentient body, or of both. Mutation therefore is motion, namely, of the parts either of the agent or of the patient; which was to be demonstrated. And to this it is consequent, that rest cannot be the cause of anything, nor can any action proceed from it; seeing neither motion nor mutation can be caused by it.

10. Accidents, in respect of other accidents which precede them, or are before them in time, and upon which they do not depend as upon their causes, are called *contingent* accidents; I say, in respect of those accidents by which they are not generated; for, in respect of their causes, all things come to pass with equal necessity; for otherwise they would have no causes at all; which, of things generated, is not intelligible.

CHAPTER X

OF POWER AND ACT

1. Power and cause are the same thing.—2. An act is produced at the same instant in which the power is plenary.—3. Active and passive power are parts only of plenary power. —4. An act, when said to be possible.—5. An act necessary and contingent, what.—6. Active power consists in motion. —7. Cause, formal and final, what they are.

1. CORRESPONDENT to *cause* and *effect*, are POWER and ACT; nay, those and these are the same things; though, for divers considerations, they have divers names. For whensoever any agent has all those accidents which are necessarily requisite for the production of some effect in the patient, then we say that agent has *power* to

produce that effect, if it be applied to a patient. But, as I have shewn in the precedent chapter, those accidents constitute the efficient cause; and therefore the same accidents, which constitute the efficient cause, constitute also the *power* of the agent. Wherefore the *power of the agent* and the *efficient cause* are the same thing. But they are considered with this difference, that *cause* is so called in respect of the effect already produced, and power in respect of the same effect to be produced hereafter; so that *cause* respects the past, *power* the future time. Also, the *power of the agent* is that which is commonly called *active power*.

In like manner, whensoever any patient has all those accidents which it is requisite it should have, for the production of some effect in it, we say it is in the *power* of that patient to produce that effect, if it be applied to a fitting agent. But those accidents, as is defined in the precedent chapter, constitute the material cause; and therefore the *power of the patient*, commonly called *passive power*, and *material cause*, are the same thing; but with this different consideration, that in cause the past time, and in power the future, is respected. Wherefore the power of the agent and patient together, which may be called entire or *plenary power*, is the same thing with *entire cause*; for they both consist in the sum or aggregate of all the accidents, as well in the agent as in the patient, which are requisite for the production of the effect. Lastly, as the accident produced is, in respect of the cause, called an effect, so in respect of the power, it is called an *act*.

2. As therefore the effect is produced in the same instant in which the cause is entire, so also every act that may be produced, is produced in the same instant in which the power is plenary. And as there can be no

effect but from a sufficient and necessary cause, so also no act can be produced but by sufficient power, or that power by which it could not but be produced.

3. And as it is manifest, as I have shewn, that the efficient and material causes are severally and by themselves parts only of an entire cause, and cannot produce any effect but by being joined together, so also power, active and passive, are parts only of plenary and entire power; nor, except they be joined, can any act proceed from them; and therefore these powers, as I said in the first article, are but conditional, namely, *the agent has power, if it be applied to a patient; and the patient has power, if it be applied to an agent*; otherwise neither of them have power, nor can the accidents, which are in them severally, be properly called powers; nor any action be said to be possible for the power of the agent alone or of the patient alone.

4. For that is an impossible act, for the production of which there is no power plenary. For seeing plenary power is that in which all things concur, which are requisite for the production of an act, if the power shall never be plenary, there will always be wanting some of those things, without which the act cannot be produced; wherefore that act shall never be produced; that is, that act is IMPOSSIBLE: and every act, which is not impossible, is POSSIBLE. Every act, therefore, which is possible, shall at some time be produced; for if it shall never be produced, then those things shall never concur which are requisite for the production of it; wherefore that act is *impossible*, by the definition; which is contrary to what was supposed.

5. A *necessary act* is that, the production whereof it is impossible to hinder; and therefore every act, that shall be produced, shall necessarily be produced; for,

that it shall not be produced, is impossible; because, as is already demonstrated, every possible act shall at some time be produced; nay, this proposition, *what shall be, shall be,* is as necessary a proposition as this, *a man is a man.*

But here, perhaps, some man may ask whether those future things, which are commonly called *contingents,* are necessary. I say, therefore, that generally all contingents have their necessary causes, as is shewn in the preceding chapter; but are called contingents in respect of other events, upon which they do not depend; as the rain, which shall be tomorrow, shall be necessary, that is, from necessary causes; but we think and say it happens by chance, because we do not yet perceive the causes thereof, though they exist now; for men commonly call that *casual or contingent,* whereof they do not perceive the necessary cause; and in the same manner they used to speak of things past, when not knowing whether a thing be done or no, they say it is possible it never was done.

Wherefore, all propositions concerning future things, contingent or not contingent, as this, *it will rain tomorrow,* or this, *tomorrow the sun will rise,* are either necessarily true, or necessarily false; but we call them contingent, because we do not yet know whether they be true or false; whereas their verity depends not upon our knowledge, but upon the foregoing of their causes. But there are some, who though they confess this whole proposition, *tomorrow it will either rain, or not rain,* to be true, yet they will not acknowledge the parts of it, as *tomorrow it will rain,* or *tomorrow it will not rain,* to be either of them true by itself; because they say neither this nor that is true *determinately.* But what is this *determinately true,* but true upon our knowledge, or evidently true? And therefore they say no more but that it is not yet known whether it be true or no; but they say it more obscurely, and darken the evidence of the truth with the same words, with which they endeavour to hide their own ignorance.

6. In the 9th article of the preceding chapter, I have shewn that the efficient cause of all motion and mutation consists in the motion of the agent or agents; and in the first article of this chapter, that the power of the agent is the same thing with the efficient cause. From whence it may be understood, that all active power consists in motion also; and that power is not a certain accident, which differs from all acts, but is, indeed, an act, namely, motion, which is therefore called power, because another act shall be produced by it afterwards. For example, if of three bodies the first put forward the second, and this the third, the motion of the second, in respect of the first which produceth it, is the act of the second body; but, in respect of the third, it is the active power of the same second body.

7. The writers of metaphysics reckon up two other causes besides the *efficient* and *material*, namely, the ESSENCE, which some call the *formal cause*, and the END, or *final cause*; both which are nevertheless efficient causes. For when it is said the essence of a thing is the cause thereof, *as to be rational is the cause of man*, it is not intelligible; for it is all one, as if it were said, *to be a man is the cause of man*; which is not well said. And yet the knowledge of the *essence* of anything, is the cause of the knowledge of the thing itself; for, if I first know that a thing is *rational*, I know from thence, that the same is *man*; but this is no other than an efficient cause. A *final cause* has no place but in such things as have sense and will; and this also I shall prove hereafter to be an efficient cause.

Part IV

PHYSICS
OR THE PHENOMENA OF NATURE

CHAPTER XXV

OF SENSE AND ANIMAL MOTION

1. The connexion of what hath been said with that which
followeth.—2. The investigation of the nature of sense, and
the definition of sense.—3. The subject and object of sense.
—4. The organs of sense.—5. All bodies are not indued
with sense.—6. But one phantasm at one and the same time.
—7. Imagination the remains of past sense, which also is
memory. Of sleep.—8. How phantasms suceed one another.
—9. Dreams, whence they proceed.—10. Of the senses, their
kinds, their organs, and phantasms proper and common.—
11. The magnitude of images, how and by what it is determined.—12. Pleasure, pain, appetite, and aversion, what
they are.—13. Deliberation and will, what.

1. I HAVE, in the first chapter, defined philosophy to
be *knowledge of effects acquired by true ratiocination,*
from knowledge first had of their causes and generation;
and of such causes or generations as may be, from
former knowledge of their effects or appearances.
There are, therefore, two methods of philosophy; one,
from the generation of things to their possible effects;
and the other, from their effects or appearances to some
possible generation of the same. In the former of these
the truth of the first principles of our ratiocination,
namely definitions, is made and constituted by ourselves, whilst we consent and agree about the appellations of things. And this part I have finished in the
foregoing chapters; in which, if I am not deceived, I
have affirmed nothing, saving the definitions themselves,

which hath not good coherence with the definitions I have given; that is to say, which is not sufficiently demonstrated to all those, that agree with me in the use of words and appellations; for whose sake only I have written the same. I now enter upon the other part; which is the finding out by the appearances or effects of nature, which we know by sense, some ways and means by which they may be, I do not say they are, generated. The principles, therefore, upon which the following discourse depends, are not such as we ourselves make and pronounce in general terms, as definitions; but such, as being placed in the things themselves by the Author of Nature, are by us observed in them; and we make use of them in single and particular, not universal propositions. Nor do they impose upon us any necessity of constituting theorems; their use being only, though not without such general propositions as have been already demonstrated, to show us the possibility of some production or generation. Seeing therefore, the science, which is here taught, hath its principles in the appearances of nature, and endeth in the attaining of some knowledge of natural causes, I have given to this part the title of PHYSICS, or the *Phenomena of Nature*. Now such things as appear, or are shown to us by nature, we call phenomena or appearances.

Of all the phenomena or appearances which are near us, the most admirable is apparition itself, τὸ φαίνεσθαι; namely, that some natural bodies have in themselves the patterns almost of all things, and others of none at all. So that if the appearances be the principles by which we know all other things, we must needs acknowledge sense to be the principle by which we know those principles, and that all the knowledge we have is derived from it. And as for the causes of sense, we cannot begin our search of them from any other phenomenon than that of sense itself. But you will say, by what sense shall we take notice of sense? I answer, by sense itself, namely, by the memory which for some time remains in us of things sensible, though they themselves pass away. For he that perceives that he hath perceived, remembers.

In the first place, therefore, the causes of our perception, that is, the causes of those ideas and phantasms which are perpetually generated within us whilst we make use of our senses, are to be enquired into; and in what manner their generation proceeds. To help which inquisition, we may observe first of all, that our phantasms or ideas are not always the same; but that new ones appear to us, and old ones vanish, according as we apply our organs of sense, now to one object, now to another. Wherefore they are generated, and perish. And from hence it is manifest, that they are some change or mutation in the sentient.

2. Now that all mutation or alteration is motion or endeavour (and endeavour also is motion) in the internal parts of the thing that is altered, hath been proved (in art. 9, chap. VIII) from this, that whilst even the least parts of any body remain in the same situation in respect of one another, it cannot be said that any alteration, unless perhaps that the whole body together hath been moved, hath happened to it; but that it both appeareth and is the same it appeared and was before. Sense, therefore, in the sentient, can be nothing else but motion in some of the internal parts of the sentient; and the parts so moved are parts of the organs of sense. For the parts of our body, by which we perceive any thing, are those we commonly call the organs of sense. And so we find what is the subject of our sense, namely, that in which are the phantasms;

and partly also we have discovered the nature of sense, namely, that it is some internal motion in the sentient.

I have shown besides (in chap. IX, art. 7) that no motion is generated but by a body contiguous and moved: from whence it is manifest, that the immediate cause of sense or perception consists in this, that the first organ of sense is touched and pressed. For when the uttermost part of the organ is pressed, it no sooner yields, but the part next within it is pressed also; and, in this manner, the pressure or motion is propagated through all the parts of the organ to the innermost. And thus also the pressure of the uttermost part proceeds from the pressure of some more remote body, and so continually, till we come to that from which, as from its fountain, we derive the phantasm or idea that is made in us by our sense. And this, whatsoever it be, is that we commonly call *the object*. Sense, therefore, is some internal motion in the sentient, generated by some internal motion of the parts of the object, and propagated through all the media to the innermost part of the organ. By which words I have almost defined what sense is.

Moreover, I have shown (art. 2, chap. XV) that all resistance is endeavour opposite to another endeavour, that is to say, reaction. Seeing, therefore, there is in the whole organ, by reason of its own internal natural motion, some resistance or reaction against the motion which is propagated from the object to the innermost part of the organ, there is also in the same organ an endeavour opposite to the endeavour which proceeds from the object; so that when that endeavour inwards is the last action in the act of sense, then from the reaction, how little soever the duration of it be, a phantasm or idea hath its being; which, by reason that the endeavour is now outwards, doth always appear as something situate without the organ. So that now I shall give you the whole definition of sense, as it is drawn from the explication of the causes thereof and the order of its generation, thus: SENSE *is a phantasm, made by the reaction and endeavour outwards in the organ of sense, caused by an endeavour inwards from the object, remaining for some time more or less.*

3. The *subject* of sense is the *sentient* itself, namely, some living creature; and we speak more correctly, when we say a living creature seeth, than when we say the eye seeth. The object is the thing received; and it is more accurately said, that we see the sun, than that we see the light. For light and colour, and heat and sound, and other qualities which are commonly called sensible, are not objects, but phantasms in the sentients. For a phantasm is the act of sense, and differs no otherwise from sense than *fieri*, that is, being a doing, differs from *factum esse*, that is, being done; which difference, in things that are done in an instant, is none at all; and a phantasm is made in an instant. For in all motion which proceeds by perpetual propagation, the first part being moved moves the second, the second the third, and so on to the last, and that to any distance, how great soever. And in what point of time the first or foremost part proceeded to the place of the second, which is thrust on, in the same point of time the last save one proceeded into the place of the last yielding part; which by reaction, in the same instant, if the reaction be strong enough, makes a phantasm; and a phantasm being made, perception is made together with it.

4. The *organs* of sense, which are in the sentient, are such parts thereof, that if they be hurt, the very generation of phantasms is thereby destroyed, though all the rest of the parts remain entire. Now these parts in

the most of living creatures are found to be certain
spirits and membranes, which, proceeding from the
pia mater, involve the brain and all the nerves; also the
brain itself, and the arteries which are in the brain;
and such other parts, as being stirred, the heart also,
which is the fountain of all sense, is stirred together
with them. For whensoever the action of the object
reacheth the body of the sentient, that action is by
some nerve propagated to the brain; and if the nerve
leading thither be so hurt or obstructed, that the motion
can be propagated no further, no sense follows. Also
if the motion be intercepted between the brain and the
heart by the defect of the organ by which the action
is propagated, there will be no perception of the object.

5. But though all sense, as I have said, be made by
reaction, nevertheless it is not necessary that every
thing that reacteth should have sense. I know there
have been philosophers, and those learned men, who
have maintained that all bodies are endued with sense.
Nor do I see how they can be refuted, if the nature
of sense be placed in reaction only. And, though by
the reaction of bodies inanimate a phantasm might be
made, it would nevertheless cease, as soon as ever the
object were removed. For unless those bodies had organs, as living creatures have, fit for the retaining of
such motion as is made in them, their sense would be
such, as that they should never remember the same.
And therefore this hath nothing to do with that sense
which is the subject of my discourse. For by sense, we
commonly understand the judgment we make of objects
by their phantasms; namely, by comparing and distinguishing those phantasms; which we could never do, if
that motion in the organ, by which the phantasm is
made, did not remain there for some time, and make the
same phantasm return. Wherefore sense, as I here

understand it, and which is commonly so called, hath necessarily some memory adhering to it, by which former and later phantasms may be compared together, and distinguished from one another.

Sense, therefore, properly so called, must necessarily have in it a perpetual variety of phantasms, that they may be discerned one from another. For if we should suppose a man to be made with clear eyes, and all the rest of his organs of sight well disposed, but endued with no other sense; and that he should look only upon one thing, which is always of the same colour and figure, without the least appearance of variety, he would seem to me, whatsoever others may say, to see, no more than I seem to myself to feel the bones of my own limbs by my organs of feeling; and yet those bones are always and on all sides touched by a most sensible membrane. I might perhaps say he were astonished, and looked upon it; but I should not say he saw it; it being almost all one for a man to be always sensible of one and the same thing, and not to be sensible at all of any thing.

6. And yet such is the nature of sense, that it does not permit a man to discern many things at once. For seeing the nature of sense consists in motion; as long as the organs are employed about one object, they cannot be so moved by another at the same time, as to make by both their motions one sincere phantasm of each of them at once. And therefore two several phantasms will not be made by two objects working together, but only one phantasm compounded from the action of both.

Besides, as when we divide a body, we divide its place; and when we reckon many bodies, we must necessarily reckon as many places; and contrarily, as I have shown in the seventh chapter; so what number soever we say there be of times, we must understand the same number of motions also; and as oft as we count many motions, so oft we reckon many times. For though the object we look upon be of divers colours, yet with those divers colours it is but one varied object, and not variety of objects.

Moreover, whilst those organs which are common to all the senses, such as are those parts of every organ which proceed in men from the root of the nerves to the heart, are vehemently stirred by a strong action from some one object, they are, by reason of the contumacy which the motion, they have already, gives them against the reception of all other motion, made the less fit to receive any other impression from whatsoever other objects, to what sense soever those objects belong. And hence it is, that an earnest studying of one object, takes away the sense of all other objects for the present. For *study* is nothing else but a possession of the mind, that is to say, a vehement motion made by some one object in the organs of sense, which are stupid to all other motions as long as this lasteth; according to what was said by Terence, *"Populus studio stupidus in funambulo animum occuparat."* For what is *stupor* but that which the Greeks call ἀναισθησία, that is, a cessation from the sense of other things? Wherefore at one and the same time, we cannot by sense perceive more than one single object; as in reading, we see the letters successively one by one, and not all together, though the whole page be presented to our eye; and though every several letter be distinctly written there, yet when we look upon the whole page at once, we read nothing.

From hence it is manifest, that every endeavour of the organ outwards, is not to be called sense, but that only, which at several times is by vehemence made stronger and more predominant than the rest; which deprives us of the sense of other phantasms, no otherwise than the sun deprives the rest of the stars of light, not by hindering their action, but by obscuring and hiding them with his excess of brightness.

7. But the motion of the organ, by which a phantasm is made, is not commonly called sense, except the object be present. And the phantasm remaining after the object is removed or past by, is called *fancy*, and in Latin *imaginatio*; which word, because all phantasms are not images, doth not fully answer the signification of the word *fancy* in its general acceptation. Nevertheless I may use it safely enough, by understanding it for the Greek φαντασία.

IMAGINATION therefore is nothing else but *sense decaying*, or *weakened*, by the absence of the object. But what may be the cause of this decay or weakening? Is the motion the weaker, because the object is taken away? If it were, then phantasms would always and necessarily be less clear in the imagination, than they are in sense; which is not true. For in dreams, which are the imaginations of those that sleep, they are no less clear than in sense itself. But the reason why in men waking the phantasms of things past are more obscure than those of things present, is this, that their organs being at the same time moved by other present objects, those phantasms are the less predominant. Whereas in sleep, the passages being shut up, external action doth not at all disturb or hinder internal motion.

If this be true, the next thing to be considered, will be, whether any cause may be found out, from the supposition whereof it will follow, that the passage is shut up from the external objects of sense to the internal organ. I suppose, therefore, that by the continual action of objects, to which a reaction of the organ, and more especially of the spirits, is necessarily consequent, the organ is wearied, that is, its parts are no longer

moved by the spirits without some pain; and consequently the nerves being abandoned and grown slack,
they retire to their fountain, which is the cavity either
of the brain or of the heart; by which means the action
which proceeded by the nerves is necessarily intercepted.
For action upon a patient, that retires from it, makes
but little impression at the first; and at last, when the
nerves are by little and little slackened, none at all.
And therefore there is no more reaction, that is, no
more sense, till the organ being refreshed by rest, and
by a supply of new spirits recovering strength and
motion, the sentient awaketh. And thus it seems to be
always, unless some other preternatural cause inter-
vene; as heat in the internal parts from lassitude, or
from some disease stirring the spirits and other parts
or the organ in some extraordinary manner.

8. Now it is not without cause, nor so casual a thing
as many perhaps think it, that phantasms in this their
great variety proceed from one another; and that the
same phantasms sometimes bring into the mind other
phantasms like themselves, and at other times extremely
unlike. For in the motion of any continued body, one
part follows another by cohesion; and therefore, whilst
we turn our eyes and other organs successively to many
objects, the motion which was made by every one of
them remaining, the phantasms are renewed as often as
any one of those motions comes to be predominant above
the rest; and they become predominant in the same order
in which at any time formerly they were generated by
sense. So that when by length of time very many
phantasms have been generated within us by sense, then
almost any thought may arise from any other thought;
insomuch that it may seem to be a thing indifferent and
casual, which thought shall follow which. But for the
most part this is not so uncertain a thing to waking as

to sleeping men. For the thought or phantasm of the
desired end brings in all the phantasms, that are means
conducing to that end, and that in order backwards from
the last to the first, and again forwards from the beginning to the end. But this supposes both appetite, and
judgment to discern what means conduce to the end,
which is gotten by experience; and experience is store
of phantasms, arising from the sense of very many
things. For φαντάζεσθαι and *meminisse, fancy* and
memory, differ only in this, that memory supposeth the
time past, which fancy doth not. In memory, the
phantasms we consider are as if they were worn out
with time; but in our fancy we consider them as they
are; which distinction is not of the things themselves,
but of the considerations of the sentient. For there is
in memory something like that which happens in looking
upon things at a great distance; in which as the small
parts of the object are not discerned, by reason of their
remoteness; so in memory, many accidents and places
and parts of things, which were formerly perceived by
sense, are by length of time decayed and lost.

The perpetual arising of phantasms, both in sense
and imagination, is that which we commonly call discourse of the mind, and is common to men with other
living creatures. For he that thinketh, compareth the
phantasms that pass, that is, taketh notice of their
likeness or unlikeness to one another. And as he that
observes readily the likenesses of things of different
natures, or that are very remote from one another, is
said to have a good fancy; so he is said to have a good
judgment, that finds out the unlikenesses or differences
of things that are like one another. Now this observation of differences is not perception made by a common
organ of sense, distinct from sense or perception properly so called, but is memory of the differences of par-

ticular phantasms remaining for some time; as the distinction between hot and lucid, is nothing else but the memory both of a heating, and of an enlightening object.

9. The phantasms of men that sleep, are *dreams*. Concerning which we are taught by experience these five things. First, that for the most part there is neither order nor coherence in them. Secondly, that we dream of nothing but what is compounded and made up of the phantasms of sense past. Thirdly, that sometimes they proceed, as in those that are drowsy, from the interruption of their phantasms by little and little, broken and altered through sleepiness; and sometimes also they begin in the midst of sleep. Fourthly, that they are clearer than the imaginations of waking men, except such as are made by sense itself, to which they are equal in clearness. Fifthly, that when we dream, we admire neither the places nor the looks of the things that appear to us. Now from what hath been said, it is not hard to show what may be the causes of these phenomena. For as for the first, seeing all order and coherence proceeds from frequent looking back to the end, that is, from consultation; it must needs be, that seeing in sleep we lose all thought of the end, our phantasms succeed one another, not in that order which tends to any end, but as it happeneth, and in such manner, as objects present themselves to our eyes when we look indifferently upon all things before us, and see them, not because we would see them, but because we do not shut our eyes; for then they appear to us without any order at all. The second proceeds from this, that in the silence of sense there is no new motion from the objects, and therefore no new phantasm, unless we call that new, which is compounded of old ones, as a chimera, a golden mountain, and the like. As for the third, why a

dream is sometimes as it were the continuation of sense, made up of broken phantasms, as in men distempered with sickness, the reason is manifestly this, that in some of the organs sense remains, and in others it faileth. But how some phantasms may be revived, when all the exterior organs are benumbed with sleep, is not so easily shown. Nevertheless that, which hath already been said, contains the reason of this also. For whatsoever strikes the *pia mater*, reviveth some of those phantasms that are still in motion in the brain; and when any internal motion of the heart reacheth that membrane, then the predominant motion in the brain makes the phantasm. Now the motions of the heart are appetites and aversions, of which I shall presently speak further. And as appetites and aversions are generated by phantasms, so reciprocally phantasms are generated by appetites and aversions. For example, heat in the heart proceeds from anger and fighting; and again, from heat in the heart, whatsoever be the cause of it, is generated anger and the image of an enemy, in sleep. And as love and beauty stir up heat in certain organs; so heat in the same organs, from whatsoever it proceeds, often causeth desire and the image of an unresisting beauty. Lastly, cold doth in the same manner generate fear in those that sleep, and causeth them to dream of ghosts, and to have phantasms of horror and danger; as fear also causeth cold in those that wake. So reciprocal are the motions of the heart and brain. The fourth, namely, that the things we seem to see and feel in sleep, are as clear as in sense itself, proceeds from two causes; one, that having then no sense of things without us, that internal motion which makes the phantasm, in the absence of all other impressions, is predominant; and the other, that the parts of our phantasms which are decayed and worn out by time, are made up with other fictitious parts. To conclude, when we dream, we do not wonder at strange places and the appearances of things unknown to us, because admiration requires that the things appearing be new and unusual, which can happen to none but those that remember former appearances; whereas in sleep, all things appear as present.

But it is here to be observed, that certain dreams, especially such as some men have when they are between sleeping and waking, and such as happen to those that have no knowledge of the nature of dreams and are withal superstitious, were not heretofore nor are now accounted dreams. For the apparitions men thought they saw, and the voices they thought they heard in sleep, were not believed to be phantasms, but things subsisting of themselves, and objects without those that dreamed. For to some men, as well sleeping as waking, but especially to guilty men, and in the night, and in hallowed places, fear alone, helped a little with the stories of such apparitions, hath raised in their minds terrible phantasms, which have been and are still deceitfully received for things really true, under the names of *ghosts* and *incorporeal substances*.

10. In most living creatures there are observed five kinds of senses, which are distinguished by their organs, and by their different kinds of phantasms; namely, *sight, hearing, smell, taste,* and *touch*; and these have their organs peculiar to each of them severally, and partly common to them all. The organ of sight is partly animate, and partly inanimate. The inanimate parts are the three humours; namely, the watery humour, which by the interposition of the membrane called uvea, the perforation whereof is called the apple of the eye, is contained on one side by the first concave superficies of the eye, and on the other side by the ciliary processes,

and the coat of the crystalline humour; the crystalline, which, hanging in the midst between the ciliary processes, and being almost of spherical figure, and of a thick consistence, is enclosed on all sides with its own transparent coat; and the vitreous or glassy humour, which filleth all the rest of the cavity of the eye, and is somewhat thicker than the watery humour, but thinner than the crystalline. The animate part of the organ is, first, the membrane *choroeides*, which is a part of the *pia mater*, saving that it is covered with a coat derived from the marrow of the optic nerve, which is called the *retina*; and this *choroeides*, seeing it is part of the *pia mater*, is continued to the beginning of the *medulla spinalis* within the scull, in which all the nerves which are within the head have their roots. Wherefore all the animal spirits that the nerves receive, enter into them there; for it is not imaginable that they can enter into them anywhere else. Seeing therefore sense is nothing else but the action of objects propagated to the furthest part of the organ; and seeing also that animal spirits are nothing but vital spirits purified by the heart, and carried from it by the arteries; it follows necessarily, that the action is derived from the heart by some of the arteries to the roots of the nerves which are in the head, whether those arteries be the *plexus retiformis*, or whether they be other arteries which are inserted into the substance of the brain. And, therefore, those arteries are the complement or the remaining part of the whole organ of sight. And this last part is a common organ to all the senses; whereas, that which reacheth from the eye to the roots of the nerves is proper only to sight. The proper organ of hearing is the tympanum of the ear and its own nerve; from which to the heart the organ is common. So the proper organs of smell and taste are nervous membranes, in the palate and tongue for the taste, and in the nostrils for the smell; and from the roots of those nerves to the heart all is common. Lastly, the proper organ of touch are nerves and membranes dispersed through the whole body; which membranes are derived from the root of the nerves. And all things else belonging alike to all the senses seem to be administered by the arteries, and not by the nerves.

The proper phantasm of sight is light; and under this name of light, colour also, which is nothing but perturbed light, is comprehended. Wherefore the phantasm of a lucid body is light; and of a coloured body, colour. But the object of sight, properly so called, is neither light nor colour, but the body itself which is lucid, or enlightened, or coloured. For light and colour, being phantasms of the sentient, cannot be accidents of the object. Which is manifest enough from this, that visible things appear oftentimes in places in which we know assuredly they are not, and that in different places they are of different colours, and may at one and the same time appear in divers places. Motion, rest, magnitude, and figure, are common both to the sight and touch; and the whole appearance together of figure, and light or colour, is by the Greeks commonly called εἶδος, and εἴδωλον, and ἰδέα; and by the Latins, *species* and *imago*; all which names signify no more but appearance.

The phantasm, which is made by hearing, is sound; by smell, odour; by taste, savour; and by touch, hardness and softness, heat and cold, wetness, oiliness, and many more, which are easier to be distinguished by sense than words. Smoothness, roughness, rarity, and density, refer to figure, and are therefore common both to touch and sight. And as for the objects of hearing, smell, taste, and touch, they are not sound, odour, savour, hardness, &c., but the bodies themselves from which sound, odour, savour, hardness, &c. proceed; of the causes of which, and of the manner how they are produced, I shall speak hereafter.

But these phantasms, though they be effects in the sentient, as subject, produced by objects working upon the organs; yet there are also other effects besides these, produced by the same objects in the same organs; namely certain motions proceeding from sense, which are called *animal motions*. For seeing in all sense of external things there is mutual action and reaction, that is, two endeavours opposing one another, it is manifest that the motion of both of them together will be continued every way, especially to the confines of both the bodies. And when this happens in the internal organ, the endeavour outwards will proceed in a solid angle, which will be greater, and consequently the idea greater, than it would have been if the impression had been weaker.

11. From hence the natural cause is manifest, first, why those things seem to be greater, which, *cæteris paribus*, are seen in a greater angle; secondly, why in a serene cold night, when the moon doth not shine, more of the fixed stars appear than at another time. For their action is less hindered by the serenity of the air, and not obscured by the greater light of the moon, which is then absent; and the cold, making the air more pressing, helpeth or strengtheneth the action of the stars upon our eyes; in so much as stars may then be seen which are seen at no other time. And this may suffice to be said in general concerning sense made by the reaction of the organ. For, as for the place of the image, the deceptions of sight, and other things of which we have experience in ourselves by sense, seeing they depend for the most part upon the fabric itself

of the eye of man, I shall speak of them then when I come to speak of man.

12. But there is another kind of sense, of which I will say something in this place, namely, the sense of pleasure and pain, proceeding not from the reaction of the heart outwards, but from continual action from the outermost part of the organ towards the heart. For the original of life being in the heart, that motion in the sentient, which is propagated to the heart, must necessarily make some alteration or diversion of vital motion, namely, by quickening or slackening, helping or hindering the same. Now when it helpeth, it is pleasure; and when it hindereth, it is pain, trouble, grief, &c. And as phantasms seem to be without, by reason of the endeavour outwards, so pleasure and pain, by reason of the endeavour of the organ inwards, seem to be within; namely, there where the first cause of the pleasure or pain is; as when the pain proceeds from a wound, we think the pain and the wound are both in the same place.

Now vital motion is the motion of the blood, perpetually circulating (as hath been shown from many infallible signs and marks by Doctor Harvey, the first observer of it) in the veins and arteries. Which motion, when it is hindered by some other motion made by the action of sensible objects, may be restored again either by bending or setting strait the parts of the body; which is done when the spirits are carried now into these, now into other nerves, till the pain, as far as is possible, be quite taken away. But if vital motion be helped by motion made by sense, then the parts of the organ will be disposed to guide the spirits in such manner as conduceth most to the preservation and augmentation of that motion, by the help of the nerves. And in animal motion this is the very first endeavour, and found even in the embryo; which while it is in the womb, moveth its limbs with voluntary motion, for the avoiding of whatsoever troubleth it, or for the pursuing of what pleaseth it. And this first endeavour, when it tends towards such things as are known by experience to be pleasant, is called *appetite*, that is, an approaching; and when it shuns what is troublesome, *aversion*, or flying from it. And little infants, at the beginning and as soon as they are born, have appetite to very few things, as also they avoid very few, by reason of their want of experience and memory; and therefore they have not so great a variety of animal motion as we see in those that are more grown. For it is not possible, without such knowledge as is derived from sense, that is, without experience and memory, to know what will prove pleasant or hurtful; only there is some place for conjecture from the looks or aspects of things. And hence it is, that though they do not know what may do them good or harm, yet sometimes they approach and sometimes retire from the same thing, as their doubt prompts them. But afterwards, by accustoming themselves by little and little, they come to know readily what is to be pursued and what to be avoided; and also to have a ready use of their nerves and other organs, in the pursuing and avoiding of good and bad. Wherefore appetite and aversion are the first endeavours of animal motion.

Consequent to this first endeavour, is the impulsion into the nerves and retraction again of animal spirits, of which it is necessary there be some receptacle or place near the original of the nerves; and this motion or endeavour is followed by a swelling and relaxation of the muscles; and lastly, these are followed by contraction and extension of the limbs, which is animal motion.

13. The considerations of appetites and aversions are divers. For seeing living creatures have sometimes appetite and sometimes aversion to the same thing, as they think it will either be for their good or their hurt; while that vicissitude of appetites and aversions remains in them, they have that series of thoughts which is called *deliberation*; which lasteth as long as they have it in their power to obtain that which pleaseth, or to avoid that which displeaseth them. Appetite, therefore, and aversion are simply so called as long as they follow not deliberation. But if deliberation have gone before, then the last act of it, if it be appetite, is called *will*; if aversion, *unwillingness*. So that the same thing is called both will and appetite; but the consideration of them, namely, before and after deliberation, is divers. Nor is that which is done within a man whilst he willeth any thing, different from that which is done in other living creatures, whilst, deliberation having preceded, they have appetite.

Neither is the freedom of willing or not willing, greater in man, than in other living creatures. For where there is appetite, the entire cause of appetite hath preceded; and, consequently, the act of appetite could not choose but follow, that is, hath of necessity followed (as is shown in chap. IX, art. 5). And therefore such a liberty as is free from necessity, is not to be found in the will either of men or beasts. But if by liberty we understand the faculty or power, not of willing, but of doing what they will, then certainly that liberty is to be allowed to both, and both may equally have it, whensoever it is to be had.

Again, when appetite and aversion do with celerity succeed one another, the whole series made by them hath its name sometimes from one, sometimes from the other. For the same deliberation, whilst it inclines sometimes to one, sometimes to the other, is from appetite called *hope*, and from aversion, *fear*. For where there is no hope, it is not to be called fear, but *hate*; and where no fear, not hope, but *desire*. To conclude, all the passions, called passions of the mind, consist of appetite and aversion, except pure pleasure and pain, which are a certain fruition of good or evil; as anger is aversion from some imminent evil, but such as is joined with appetite of avoiding that evil by force. But because the passions and perturbations of the mind are innumerable, and many of them not to be discerned in any creatures besides men; I will speak of them more at large in that section which is concerning *man*. As for those objects, if there be any such, which do not at all stir the mind, we are said to contemn them.

And thus much of sense in general. In the next place I shall speak of sensible objects.

CHAPTER XXVI

OF THE WORLD AND OF THE STARS

1. The magnitude and duration of the world, inscrutable.—[2. No place in the world empty.—3. The arguments of Lucretius for vacuum, invalid.—4. Other arguments for the establishing of vacuum, invalid.]—5. Six suppositions for the salving of the phenomena of nature.—6. Possible causes of the motions annual and diurnal; [and of the apparent direction, station, and retrogradation of the planets.—7. The supposition of simple motion, why likely.—8. The cause of the eccentricity of the annual motion of the earth.—9. The cause why the moon hath always one and the same face turned towards the earth.—10. The cause of the tides of the ocean.—11. The cause of the precession of the equinoxes.]

1. CONSEQUENT to the contemplation of sense is the contemplation of bodies, which are the efficient causes

or objects of sense. Now every object is either a part
of the whole world, or an aggregate of parts. The
greatest of all bodies, or sensible objects, is the world
itself; which we behold when we look round about us
from this point of the same which we call the earth.
Concerning the world, as it is one aggregate of many
parts, the things that fall under inquiry are but few;
and those we can determine, none. Of the whole world
we may inquire what is its magnitude, what its duration, and how many there be, but nothing else. For
as for place and time, that is to say, magnitude and
duration, they are only our own fancy of a body simply
so called, that is to say, of a body indefinitely taken,
as I have shown before in chapter VII. All other
phantasms are of bodies or objects, as they are distinguished from one another; as colour, the phantasm
of coloured bodies; sound of bodies that move the sense
of hearing, &c. The questions concerning the magnitude of the world are whether it be finite or infinite,
full or not full; concerning its duration, whether it had
a beginning, or be eternal; and concerning the number,
whether there be one or many; though as concerning
the number, if it were of infinite magnitude, there could
be no controversy at all. Also if it had a beginning,
then by what cause and of what matter it was made;
and again, from whence that cause and that matter
had their being, will be new questions; till at last we
come to one or many eternal cause or causes. And the
determination of all these things belongeth to him that
professeth the universal doctrine of philosophy, in case
as much could be known as can be sought. But the
knowledge of what is infinite can never be attained by
a finite inquirer. Whatsoever we know that are men,
we learn it from our phantasms; and of infinite, whether
magnitude or time, there is no phantasm at all; so that

it is impossible either for a man or any other creature
to have any conception of infinite. And though a man
may from some effect proceed to the immediate cause
thereof, and from that to a more remote cause, and
so ascend continually by right ratiocination from cause
to cause; yet he will not be able to proceed eternally,
but wearied will at last give over, without knowing
whether it were possible for him to proceed to an end
or not. But whether we suppose the world to be finite
or infinite, no absurdity will follow. For the same
things which now appear, might appear, whether the
Creator had pleased it should be finite or infinite. Besides, though from this, that nothing can move itself, it
may rightly be inferred that there was some first eternal
movent; yet it can never be inferred, though some
used to make such inference, that that movent was
eternally immoveable, but rather eternally moved. For
as it is true, that nothing is moved by itself; so it is
true also that nothing is moved but by that which is
already moved. The questions therefore about the
magnitude and beginning of the world, are not to be
determined by philosophers, but by those that are lawfully authorized to order the worship of God. For as
Almighty God, when he had brought his people into
Judaea, allowed the priests the first fruits reserved to
himself; so when he had delivered up the world to the
disputations of men, it was his pleasure that all opinions
concerning the nature of infinite and eternal, known
only to himself, should, as the first fruits of wisdom,
be judged by those whose ministry he meant to use
in the ordering of religion. I cannot therefore commend those that boast they have demonstrated, by
reasons drawn from natural things, that the world had
a beginning. They are contemned by idiots, because
they understand them not; and by the learned, because

they understand them; by both deservedly. For who can commend him that demonstrates thus? "If the world be eternal, then an infinite number of days, or other measures of time, preceded the birth of Abraham. But the birth of Abraham preceded the birth of Isaac; and therefore one infinite is greater than another infinite, or one eternal than another eternal; which" he says, "is absurd." This demonstration is like his, who from this, that the number of even numbers is infinite, would conclude that there are as many even numbers as there are numbers simply, that is to say, the even numbers are as many as all the even and odd together. They, which in this manner take away eternity from the world, do they not by the same means take away eternity from the Creator of the world? From this absurdity therefore they run into another, being forced to call eternity *nunc stans*, a standing still of the present time, or an abiding now; and, which is much more absurd, to give to the infinite number of numbers the name of unity. But why should eternity be called an abiding now, rather than an abiding then? Wherefore there must either be many eternities, or *now* and *then* must signify the same. With such demonstrators as these, that speak in another language, it is impossible to enter into disputation. And the men, that reason thus absurdly, are not idiots, but, which makes the absurdity unpardonable, geometricians, and such as take upon them to be judges, impertinent, but severe judges of other men's demonstrations. The reason is this, that as soon as they are entangled in the words *infinite* and *eternal*, of which we have in our mind no idea, but that of our own insufficiency to comprehend them, they are forced either to speak something absurd, or, which they love worse, to hold their peace. For geometry hath in it somewhat like wine, which, when new, is windy; but afterwards though less pleasant, yet more wholesome. Whatsoever therefore is true, young geometricians think demonstrable; but elder not. Wherefore I purposely pass over the questions of infinite and eternal, contenting myself with that doctrine concerning the beginning and magnitude of the world, which I have been persuaded to by the holy Scriptures and fame of the miracles which confirm them; and by the custom of my country, and reverence due to the laws. And so I pass on to such things as it is not unlawful to dispute of.

*   *   *   *   *   *   *   *   *

5. First, therefore, I suppose that the immense space, which we call the world, is the aggregate of all bodies which are either consistent and visible, as the earth and the stars; or invisible, as the small atoms which are disseminated through the whole space between the earth and the stars; and lastly, that most fluid ether, which so fills all the rest of the universe, as that it leaves in it no empty place at all.

Secondly, I suppose with Copernicus, that the greater bodies of the world, which are both consistent and permanent, have such order amongst themselves, as that the sun hath the first place, Mercury the second, Venus the third, the Earth with the moon going about it the fourth, Mars the fifth, Jupiter with his attendants the sixth, Saturn the seventh; and after these, the fixed stars have their several distances from the sun.

Thirdly, I suppose that in the sun and the rest of the planets there is and always has been a simple circular motion.

Fourthly, I suppose that in the body of the air there are certain other bodies intermingled, which are not fluid; but withal that they are so small, that they are not perceptible by sense; and that these also have their proper simple motion, and are some of them more, some less hard or consistent.

Fifthly, I suppose with Kepler that as the distance between the sun and the earth is to the distance between the moon and the earth, so the distance between the moon and the earth is to the semidiameter of the earth.

As for the magnitude of the circles, and the times in which they are described by the bodies which are in them, I will suppose them to be such as shall seem most agreeable to the phenomena in question.

6. The causes of the different seasons of the year, and of the several variations of days and nights in all the parts of the superficies of the earth, have been demonstrated, first by Copernicus, and since by Kepler, Galileus, and others, from the supposition of the earth's diurnal revolution about its own axis, together with its annual motion about the sun in the ecliptic according to the order of the signs; and thirdly, by the annual revolution of the same earth about its own centre, contrary to the order of the signs. I suppose with Copernicus, that the diurnal revolution is from the motion of the earth, by which the equinoctial circle is described about it. And as for the other two annual motions, they are the efficient cause of the earth's being carried about in the ecliptic in such manner, as that its axis is always kept parallel to itself. Which parallelism was for this reason introduced, lest by the earth's annual revolution its poles should seem to be necessarily carried about the sun, contrary to experience. I have, in art. 10, chap. XXI, demonstrated, from the supposition of simple circular motion in the sun, that the earth is so carried about the sun, as that its axis is thereby kept always parallel to itself. Wherefore, from these two supposed motions in the sun, the one simple circular

motion, the other circular motion about its own centre, it may be demonstrated that the year hath both the same variations of days and nights, as have been demonstrated by Copernicus.

*   *   *   *   *   *   *   *   *

[There follow in the text four chapters in which Hobbes attempts to set forth the causes of light, heat, colours, cold, wind, hard, ice, restitution of bodies bent, diaphanous, lightning and thunder, heads of rivers, sound, odor, savor, touch, and gravity or weight. The principles of the explanation are, for a general understanding of Hobbes' doctrine of natural bodies, more important than the details. These principles he finds to be consistency or degrees of tenacity, magnitude, motion, and figure; and in terms of these he frames hypotheses regarding the causes of the phenomena enumerated above. The following paragraphs contain his general statement.]

Besides the stars, of which I have spoken in the last chapter, whatsoever other bodies there be in the world, they may be all comprehended under the name of intersidereal bodies. And these I have already supposed to be either the most fluid aether, or such bodies whose parts have some degree of cohesion. Now, these differ from one another in their several *consistencies, magnitudes, motions,* and *figures.* In consistency, I suppose some bodies to be harder, others softer through all the several degrees of *tenacity.* In magnitude, some to be greater, others less, and many unspeakably little. For we must remember that, by the understanding, quantity is divisible into divisibles perpetually. And, therefore, if a man could do as much with his hands as he can with his understanding, he would be able to take from

any given magnitude a part which should be less than
any other magnitude given. But the Omnipotent
Creator of the world can actually form a part of any
thing take another part, as far as we by our understanding can conceive the same to be divisible. Wherefore there is no impossible smallness of bodies. And
what hinders but that we may think this likely? For
we know there are some living creatures so small that
we can scarce see their whole bodies. Yet even these
have their young ones; their little veins and other
vessels, and their eyes so small as that no microscope
can make them visible. So that we cannot suppose any
magnitude so little, but that our very supposition is
actually exceeded by nature. Besides, there are now
such microscopes commonly made, that the things we see
with them appear a hundred thousand times bigger than
they would do if we looked upon them with our bare
eyes. Nor is there any doubt but that by augmenting
the power of these microscopes (for it may be augmented as long as neither matter nor the hands of work-
men are wanting) every one of those hundred thousandth parts might yet appear a hundred thousand times
greater than they did before. Neither is the smallness
of some bodies to be more admired than the vast greatness of others. For it belongs to the same Infinite
Power, as well to augment infinitely as infinitely to
diminish. To make the great orb, namely, that whose
radius reacheth from the earth to the sun, but as a point
in respect of the distance between the sun and fixed
stars; and, on the contrary, to make a body so little, as
to be in the same proportion less than any other visible
body, proceeds equally from one and the same Author
of Nature. But this of the immense distance of the fixed
stars, which for a long time was accounted an incredible
thing, is now believed by almost all the learned. Why

then should not that other, of the smallness of some bodies, become credible at some time or other? For the Majesty of God appears no less in small things than in great; and as it exceedeth human sense in the immense greatness of the universe, so also it doth in the smallness of the parts thereof. Nor are the first elements of compositions, nor the first beginnings of actions, nor the first moments of times more credible, than that which is now believed of the vast distance of the fixed stars.

Some things are acknowledged by mortal men to be very great, though finite, as seeing them to be such. They acknowledge also that some things, which they do not see, may be of infinite magnitude. But they are not presently nor without great study persuaded, that there is any mean between infinite and the greatest of those things which either they see or imagine. Nevertheless, when after meditation and contemplation many things which we wondered at before are now grown more familiar to us, we then believe them, and transfer our admiration from the creatures to the Creator. But how little soever some bodies may be, yet I will not suppose their quantity to be less than is requisite for the salving of the phenomena. And in like manner I shall suppose their motion, namely, their velocity and slowness, and the variety of their figures, to be only such as the explication of their natural causes requires. And lastly, I suppose, that the parts of the pure aether, as if it were the first matter, have no motion at all but what they receive from bodies which float in them, and are not themselves fluid.

*   *   *   *   *   *   *   *   *

And thus much concerning the nature of body in general; with which I conclude this my first section of the Elements of Philosophy. In the first, second, and

third parts, where the principles of ratiocination consist in our own understanding, that is to say, in the
legitimate use of such words as we ourselves constitute,
all the theorems, if I be not deceived, are rightly demonstrated.   The fourth part depends upon hypotheses;
which unless we know them to be true, it is impossible
for us to demonstrate that those causes, which I have
there explicated, are the true causes of the things whose
productions I have derived from them.

Nevertheless, seeing I have assumed no hypothesis,
which is not both possible and easy to be comprehended;
and seeing also that I have reasoned aright from those
assumptions, I have withal sufficiently demonstrated
that they may be the true causes; which is the end of
physical contemplation.   If any other man from other
hypotheses shall demonstrate the same or greater things,
there will be greater praise and thanks due to him than
I demand for myself, provided his hypotheses be such
as are conceivable.   For as for those that say anything
may be moved or produced by *itself*, by *species*, by *its
own power*, by *substantial forms*, by *incorporeal substances*, by *instinct*, by *antiperistasis*, by *antipathy*,
sympathy, *occult quality*, and other empty words of
schoolmen, their saying so is to no purpose.

LEVIATHAN

OR

THE MATTER, FORM, AND POWER

OF A

COMMONWEALTH

ECCLESIASTICAL AND CIVIL

The Epistle Dedicatory

TO MY MOST HONOR'D FRIEND

MR. FRANCIS GODOLPHIN,

OF GODOLPHIN

HONOR'D SIR,

YOUR most worthy brother, MR. SIDNEY GODOLPHIN, when he lived, was pleased to think my studies something, and otherwise to oblige me, as you know, with real testimonies of his good opinion, great in themselves, and the greater for the worthiness of his person. For there is not any virtue that disposeth a man, either to the service of God, or to the service of his country, to civil society, or private friendship, that did not manifestly appear in his conversation, not as acquired by necessity, or affected upon occasion, but inherent, and

shining in a generous constitution of his nature. Therefore, in honour and gratitude to him, and with devotion to yourself, I humbly dedicate unto you this my
discourse of Commonwealth. I know not how the
world will receive it, nor how it may reflect on those
that shall seem to favour it. For in a way beset with
those that contend, on one side for too great liberty,
and on the other side for too much authority, 'tis hard
to pass between the points of both unwounded. But
yet, methinks, the endeavour to advance the civil power,
should not be by the civil power condemned; nor private
men, by reprehending it, declare they think that power
too great. Besides, I speak not of the men, but, in the
abstract, of the seat of power, (like to those simple and
unpartial creatures in the Roman Capitol, that with their
noise defended those within it, not because they were
they, but there), offending none, I think, but those without, or such within, if there be any such, as favour them.
That which perhaps may most offend, are certain texts
of Holy Scripture, alleged by me to other purpose than
ordinarily they use to be by others. But I have done it
with due submission, and also, in order to my subject,
necessarily; for they are the outworks of the enemy,
from whence they impugn the civil power. If notwithstanding this, you find my labour generally decried, you
may be pleased to excuse yourself, and say, I am a man
that love my own opinions, and think all true I say,
that I honoured your brother, and honour you, and have
presumed on that, to assume the title, without your
knowledge, of being, as I am,

SIR,

Your most humble,

and most obedient Servant,

THOMAS HOBBES.

Paris, April $^{15}/_{25}$, 1651.

THE INTRODUCTION

Nature, the art whereby God hath made and governs the world, is by the *art* of man, as in many other things, so in this also imitated, that it can make an artificial animal. For seeing life is but a motion of limbs, the beginning whereof is in some principal part within; why may we not say, that all *automata* (engines that move themselves by springs and wheels as doth a watch) have an artificial life? For what is the *heart*, but a *spring*; and the *nerves*, but so many *strings*; and the *joints*, but so many *wheels*, giving motion to the whole body, such as was intended by the artificer? *Art* goes yet further, imitating that rational and most excellent work of nature, *man*. For by art is created that great Leviathan called a Commonwealth, or State, in Latin Civitas, which is but an artificial man; though of greater stature and strength than the natural, for whose protection and defense it was intended; and in which the *sovereignty* is an artificial *soul*, as giving life and motion to the whole body; the *magistrates*, and other *officers* of judicature and execution, artificial *joints*; *reward* and *punishment*, by which fastened to the seat of the sovereignty every joint and member is moved to perform his duty, are the *nerves*, that do the same in the body natural; the *wealth* and *riches* of all the particular members, are the *strength*; *salus populi*, the *people's safety*, its *business*; *counsellors*, by whom all things needful for it to know are suggested unto it, are the *memory*; *equity*, and *laws*, an artificial *reason* and *will*; *concord, health; sedition, sickness; and civil war, death*. Lastly, the *pacts* and *covenants*, by which the parts of this body politic were at first made, set together, and united, resemble that *fiat*, or the *let us make man*, pronounced by God in the creation.

To describe the nature of this artificial man, I will consider

First, the *matter* thereof, and the *artificer*; both which is *man*.

Secondly, *how*, and by what *covenants* it is made; what are the *rights* and just *power* or *authority* of a *sovereign*; and what it is that *preserveth* or *dissolveth* it.

Thirdly, what is a *Christian commonwealth*.

Lastly, what is the *kingdom of darkness*.

Concerning the first, there is a saying much usurped of late, that *wisdom* is acquired, not by reading of *books*, but of *men*. Consequently whereunto, those persons, that for the most part can give no other proof of being wise, take great delight to show what they think they have read in men, by uncharitable censures of one another behind their backs. But there is another saying not of late understood, by which they might learn truly to read one another, if they would take the pains; that is, *nosce teipsum, read thyself*: which was not meant, as it is now used, to countenance, either the barbarous state of men in power, towards their inferiors; or to encourage men of low degree, to a saucy behaviour towards their betters; but to teach us, that from the similitude of the thoughts and passions of one man, to the thoughts and passions of another, whosoever looketh into himself, and considereth what he doth, when he does *think, opine, reason, hope, fear,* &c. and upon what grounds; he shall thereby read and know, what are the thoughts and passions of all other men upon the like occasions. I say the similitude of *passions*, which are the same in all men, *desire, fear, hope,* &c; not the similitude of the *objects* of the passions, which are the things *desired, feared, hoped,* &c: for these the con-

stitution individual, and particular education, do so vary,
and they are so easy to be kept from our knowledge,
that the characters of man's heart, blotted and con-
founded as they are with dissembling, lying, counter-
feiting, and erroneous doctrines, are legible only to him
that searcheth hearts. And though by men's actions we
do discover their design sometimes; yet to do it without comparing them with our own, and distinguishing
all circumstances, by which the case may come to be
altered, is to decypher without a key, and be for the
most part deceived, by too much trust, or by too much
diffidence; as he that reads, is himself a good or evil
man.

But let one man read another by his actions never so
perfectly, it serves him only with his acquaintance, which
are but few. He that is to govern a whole nation,
must read in himself, not this or that particular man;
but mankind: which though it be hard to do, harder than
to learn any language or science; yet when I shall have
set down my own reading orderly, and perspicuously,
the pains left another, will be only to consider, if he
also find not the same in himself. For this kind of
doctrine admitteth no other demonstration.

Part I

OF MAN

CHAPTER I

OF SENSE

CONCERNING the thoughts of man, I will consider them
first singly, and afterwards in train, or dependence upon
one another. Singly, they are every one a *representa-*

tion or *appearance,* of some quality, or other accident of a body without us, which is commonly called an *object*. Which object worketh on the eyes, ears, and other parts of a man's body; and by diversity of working produceth diversity of appearances.

The original of them all, is that which we call SENSE, for there is no conception in a man's mind, which hath not at first, totally or by parts, been begotten upon the organs of sense. The rest are derived from that original.

To know the natural cause of sense, is not very necessary to the business now in hand; and I have elsewhere written of the same at large. Nevertheless, to fill each part of my present method, I will briefly deliver the same in this place.

The cause of sense, is the external body, or object, which presseth the organ proper to each sense, either immediately, as in the taste and touch; or mediately, as in seeing, hearing, and smelling; which pressure, by the mediation of the nerves, and other strings and membranes of the body, continued inwards to the brain and heart, causeth there a resistance, or counter-pressure, or endeavour of the heart to deliver itself, which endeavour, because *outward,* seemeth to be some matter without. And this *seeming,* or *fancy,* is that which men call *sense*; and consisteth, as to the eye, in a *light,* or *colour figured*; to the ear, in a *sound*; to the nostril, in an *odour*; to the tongue and palate, in a *savour*; and to the rest of the body, in *heat, cold, hardness, softness,* and such other qualities as we discern by *feeling*. All which qualities, called *sensible,* are in the object, that causeth them, but so many several motions of the matter, by which it presseth our organs diversely. Neither in us that are pressed, are they any thing else, but divers motions; for motion produceth nothing but motion. But their appearance to us is fancy, the same waking, that dreaming. And as pressing, rubbing, or striking the eye, makes us fancy a light; and pressing the ear, produceth a din; so do the bodies also we see, or hear, produce the same by their strong, though unobserved action. For if those colours and sounds were in the bodies, or objects that cause them, they could not be severed from them, as by glasses, and in echoes by reflection, we see they are; where we know the thing we see is in one place, the appearance in another. And though at some certain distance, the real and very object seem invested with the fancy it begets in us; yet still the object is one thing, the image or fancy is another. So that sense, in all cases, is nothing else but original fancy, caused, as I have said, by the pressure, that is, by the motion, of external things upon our eyes, ears, and other organs thereunto ordained.

But the philosophy-schools, through all the universities of Christendom, grounded upon certain texts of Aristotle, teach another doctrine, and say, for the cause of *vision*, that the thing seen, sendeth forth on every side a *visible species*, in English, *a visible show, apparition,* or *aspect*, or *a being seen*; the receiving whereof into the eye is *seeing*. And for the cause of *hearing*, that the thing heard, sendeth forth an *audible species*, that is an *audible aspect*, or *audible being seen*; which entering at the ear maketh *hearing*. Nay, for the cause of *understanding* also, they say the thing understood, sendeth forth an *intelligible species*, that is, an *intelligible being seen*; which, coming into the understanding, makes us understand. I say not this, as disproving the use of universities; but because I am to speak hereafter of their office in a commonwealth, I must let you see on all occasions by the way, what things would be amended in them; amongst which the frequency of insignificant speech is one.

SUPPLEMENT FROM

HUMAN NATURE

CHAPTER II

ORIGINALLY all *conceptions* proceed from the *action* of the thing itself, whereof it is the conception: now when the action is *present*, the conception it produceth is also called *sense*; and the thing by whose action the same is produced, is called the *object of the sense*.

By our several *organs* we have several *conceptions* of several qualities in the objects; for by *sight* we have a conception or image composed of *colour* and *figure*, which is all the notice and knowledge the object imparteth to us of its nature by the eye. By *hearing* we have a conception called *sound*, which is all the knowledge we have of the quality of the object from the ear. And so the rest of the senses are also conceptions of several qualities, or natures of their objects.

Because the *image* in vision consisting of *colour* and *shape* is the knowledge we have of the qualities of the object of that sense; it is no hard matter for a man to fall into this opinion, that the same *colour* and *shape* are the *very qualities themselves*; and for the same cause, that *sound* and *noise* are the *qualities of the bell*, or of the air. And this opinion hath been so long received, that the *contrary* must needs appear a great paradox; and yet the introduction of *species visible* and *intelligible* (which is necessary for the maintenance of that opinion) passing to and fro from the *object*, is *worse* than any paradox, as being a plain *impossibility*. I shall therefore endeavour to make plain these points:

That the subject wherein colour and image are inherent, is *not* the *object* or thing seen.

That there is nothing *without us* (really) which we call an *image* or colour.

That the said image or colour is but an *apparition* unto us of the *motion*, agitation, or alteration, which the *object* worketh in the *brain*, or spirits, or some internal substance of the head.

That as in *vision*, so also in conceptions that arise from the *other senses*, the subject of their *inherence* is not the *object*, but the *sentient*.

Every man hath so much experience as to have seen the *sun* and the other visible objects by reflection in the *water* and *glasses*; and this alone is sufficient for this conclusion, that *colour* and *image* may be there where the *thing seen* is *not*. But because it may be said that notwithstanding the *image* in the water be not in the object, but a thing merely *phantastical*, yet there may be *colour* really in the thing itself: I will urge further this experience, that divers times men see directly the *same* object *double*, as *two candles* for *one*, which may happen from distemper, or otherwise without distemper if a man will, the organs being either in their right temper, or equally distempered; the *colours* and *figures* in two such images of the same thing *cannot be inherent* therein, because the thing seen cannot be in *two places*.

One of these images therefore is *not inherent* in the object: but seeing the organs of the sight are then in equal temper or distemper, the *one* of them is no more inherent than the *other*; and consequently *neither* of them both are in the object; which is the first proposition, mentioned in the precedent number.

Secondly, that the image of any thing by *reflection* in

a *glass* or *water* or the like, is *not* any thing *in* or *behind* the glass, or *in* or *under* the water, every man may grant to himself; which is the second proposition.

For the third, we are to consider, first that upon every *great agitation* or *concussion* of the *brain* (as it happeneth from a stroke, especially if the stroke be upon the eye) whereby the optic nerve suffereth any great violence, there *appeareth* before the *eyes* a certain light, which light is *nothing without,* but an apparition only, all that is real being the concussion or motion of the parts of that nerve; from which experience we may conclude, that *apparition of light is really nothing but motion* within. If therefore from *lucid bodies* there can be derived *motion,* so as to affect the optic nerve in such manner as is proper thereunto, there will follow an *image* of light somewhere in that line by which the motion was last derived to the eye; that is to say, in the object, if we look directly on it, and in the glass or water, when we look upon it in the line of reflection, which in effect is the third proposition; namely, that image and colour is but an apparition to us of that motion, agitation, or alteration which the object worketh in the brain or spirits, or some *internal* substance in the head.

But that *from all lucid,* shining and illuminate bodies, there is a *motion produced* to the eye, and, through the eye, to the *optic* nerve, and so into the *brain,* by which that apparition of *light* or *colour* is affected, is not hard to prove. And first, it is evident that the *fire,* the only lucid body here upon earth, worketh by *motion* equally every way; insomuch as the motion thereof *stopped* or inclosed, it is presently *extinguished,* and no more fire. And further, that that motion, whereby the fire worketh, is *dilation,* and *contraction* of itself *alternately,* commonly called *scintillation* or glowing, is manifest also by experience. From such *motion* in the fire must needs arise a *rejection* or casting from itself of that part of the *medium* which is *contiguous* to it, whereby that part also rejecteth the *next*, and so successively one part beateth back another to the very *eye*; and in the same manner the *exterior* part of the eye presseth the *interior*, (the laws of refraction still observed). Now the interior coat of the eye is nothing else but a piece of the *optic* nerve; and therefore the motion is still continued thereby into the *brain*, and by *resistance* or reaction of the brain, is also a *rebound* into the optic nerve again; which we *not conceiving* as motion or rebound from *within*, do think it is *without*, and call it *light*; as hath been already shewed by the experience of a stroke. We have no reason to doubt, that the fountain of light, the *sun*, worketh by any other ways than the *fire*, at least in this matter. And thus all *vision* hath its original from such *motion* as is here described: for where there is no light, there is no sight; and therefore *colour* also must be the same thing with *light*, as being the effect of the lucid bodies: their *difference* being only this, that when the light cometh *directly* from the fountain to the eye, or *indirectly* by reflection from *clean* and *polite* bodies, and such as have *not* any particular motion internal to alter it, we call it *light*; but when it cometh to the eye by reflection from *uneven, rough,* and coarse bodies, or such as are affected with internal motion of their own that may alter it, then we call it *colour*; colour and light differing only in this, that the one is *pure*, and the other *perturbed* light. By that which hath been said, not only the truth of the third proposition, but also the whole manner of producing light and colour, is apparent.

As colour is not inherent in the object, but an effect thereof upon us, caused by such motion in the object, as hath been described: so neither is *sound* in the thing we hear, but in ourselves. One manifest sign thereof is, that as a man may *see*, so also he may *hear double* or *treble*, by multiplication of *echoes*, which echoes are sounds as well as the original; and *not* being in one and the *same place*, cannot be *inherent* in the body that maketh them. Nothing can make anything which is not in itself: the *clapper* hath no *sound* in it, but *motion*, and maketh motion in the internal parts of the bell; so the *bell* hath motion, and not sound, that imparteth *motion* to the *air*; and the *air* hath motion, but not sound; the *air* imparteth motion by the *ear* and *nerve* unto the *brain*; and the brain hath motion but not sound; from the *brain*, it reboundeth back into the nerves *outward*, and thence it becometh an *apparition without*, which we call *sound*. And to proceed to the *rest* of the *senses*, it is apparent enough, that the *smell* and *taste* of the *same thing*, are *not* the *same* to *every man*; and therefore are not in the thing *smelt* or *tasted*, but in the men. So likewise the *heat* we feel from the fire is manifestly in *us*, and is quite *different* from the heat which is in the *fire*: for *our* heat is *pleasure* or *pain*, according as it is *great* or *moderate*; but in the *coal* there is no such thing. By this the fourth and last proposition is proved, *viz.* that as in vision, so also the conceptions that arise from *other* senses, the subject of their inherence is not in the object, but in the sentient.

And from hence also it followeth, that *whatsoever accidents* or qualities our senses make us think there be in the *world*, they be *not* there, but are *seeming* and *apparitions* only: the things that really *are* in the world without us, are those *motions* by which these seemings are caused. And this is the *great deception of sense*, which also is to be by sense *corrected*: for as sense telleth me, when I see *directly*, that the colour seemeth to *be* in the object; so also sense telleth me, when I see by *reflection*, that colour is not in the object.[1]

CHAPTER II

OF IMAGINATION

THAT when a thing lies still, unless somewhat else stir it, it will lie still for ever, is a truth that no man doubts of. But that when a thing is in motion, it will eternally be in motion, unless somewhat else stay it, though the reason be the same, namely, that nothing can change itself, is not so easily assented to. For men measure, not only other men, but all other things, by themselves; and because they find themselves subject after motion, to pain, and lassitude, think everything else grows weary of motion, and seeks repose of its own accord; little considering, whether it be not some other motion, wherein that desire of rest they find in themselves, consisteth. From hence it is, that the schools say, heavy bodies fall downwards, out of an appetite to rest, and to conserve their nature in that place which is most proper for them; ascribing appetite, and knowledge of what is good for their conservation, which is more than man has, to things inanimate, absurdly.

When a body is once in motion, it moveth, unless something else hinder it, eternally; and whatsoever hindereth it cannot in an instant, but in time, and by degrees, quite extinguish it; and as we see in the water, though the wind cease, the waves give not over rolling for a long time after: so also it happeneth in that motion, which is made in the internal parts of a man,

[1] Compare also above *Elements of Philosophy*, Ch. XXV.

then, when he sees, dreams, &c. For after the object is removed, or the eye shut, we still retain an image of the thing seen, though more obscure than when we see it. And this is it, the Latins call *imagination,* from the image made in seeing; and apply the same, though improperly, to all the other senses. But the Greeks call it *fancy*; which signifies *appearance,* and is as proper to one sense, as to another. IMAGINATION therefore is nothing but *decaying sense*; and is found in men, and many other living creatures, as well sleeping, as waking.

The decay of sense in men waking, is not the decay of the motion made in sense; but an obscuring of it, in such manner as the light of the sun obscureth the light of the stars; which stars do no less exercise their virtue, by which they are visible, in the day than in the night. But because amongst many strokes, which our eyes, ears, and other organs receive from external bodies, the predominant only is sensible; therefore, the light of the sun being predominant, we are not affected with the action of the stars. And any object being removed from our eyes, though the impression it made in us remain, yet other objects more present succeeding, and working on us, the imagination of the past is obscured, and made weak, as the voice of a man is in the noise of the day. From whence it followeth, that the longer the time is, after the sight or sense of any object, the weaker is the imagination. For the continual change of man's body destroys in time the parts which in sense were moved: so that distance of time, and of place, hath one and the same effect in us. For as at a great distance of place, that which we look at appears dim, and without distinction of the smaller parts; and as voices grow weak, and inarticulate; so also, after great distance of time, our imagination of the past is weak; and we lose, for example, of cities we have seen, many particular

streets, and of actions, many particular circumstances.[1]
This *decaying sense,* when we would express the thing
itself, I mean *fancy* itself, we call *imagination,* as I
said before: but when we would express the decay, and
signify that the sense is fading, old, and past, it is called

[1] Compare *Elements of Philosophy,* (M. I, 396). "But the
motion of the organ, by which a phantasm is made, is not
commonly called sense, except the object be present. And
the phantasm remaining after the object is removed or past
by, is called *fancy,* and in Latin *imaginatio;* which word, because all phantasms are not images, doth not fully answer the
signification of the word *fancy* in its general acceptation.
Nevertheless I may use it safely enough by understanding it
for the Greek Φαντασία. IMAGINATION therefore is nothing
else but *sense decaying,* or *weakened,* by the absence of the
object. But what may be the cause of this decay or weakening? Is the motion the weaker, because the object is taken
away? If it were, then phantasms would always and necessarily be less clear in the imagination, than they are in sense;
which is not true. For in dreams, which are the imaginations
of those that sleep, they are no less clear than in sense itself.
But the reason why in men waking the phantasms of things
past are more obscure than those of things present, is this, that
their organs being at the same time moved by other present
objects, those phantasms are the less predominant. Whereas
in sleep, the passages being shut up, external action doth not
at all disturb or hinder internal motion." Compare also
Questions Concerning Liberty (M. V. 358-359). "If the
Bishop had observed what he does himself, when he deliberates, reasons, understands, or imagines, he would have
known what to make of all I have said in this Number. He
would have known that consideration, understanding, reason,
and all the passions of the mind, are imaginations. That to
consider a thing, is to imagine it; that to understand a thing,
is to imagine it; that to hope and fear, are to imagine the
things hoped for and feared. The difference between them
is, that when we imagine the consequence of anything, we are
said to consider that thing; and when we have imagined anything from a sign, and especially from those signs we call
names, we are said to understand his meaning that maketh the
sign; and when we reason, we imagine the consequence of
affirmations and negations joined together; and when we hope
or fear, we imagine things good or hurtful to ourselves: insomuch as all these are but imaginations diversely named from
different circumstances: as any man may perceive as easily as
he can look into his own thoughts."

memory. So that imagination and memory are but one thing, which for divers considerations hath divers names.[2]

Much memory, or memory of many things, is called

[2] Compare *Elements of Philosophy*, (M. I, 398). "For Φαντάζεσθαι and *meminisse, fancy* and *memory,* differ only in this, that memory supposeth the time past, which fancy doth not. In memory, the phantasms we consider are as if they were worn out with time; but in our fancy we consider them as they are; which distinction is not of the things themselves, but of the considerations of the sentient. For there is in memory something like that which happens in looking upon things at a great distance; in which as the small parts of the object are not discerned, by reason of their remoteness; so in memory, many accidents and places and parts of things, which were formerly perceived by sense, are by length of time decayed and lost." Also *Human Nature* (M. IV, 12). "For the *manner* by which we take notice of a conception *past,* we are to remember, that in the *definition* of *imagination,* it is said to be a conception by *little* and *little decaying,* or growing more *obscure.* An *obscure* conception is that which representeth the *whole object* together, but *none* of the *smaller parts* by themselves; and as *more* or *fewer* parts be represented, so is the conception or representation said to be *more* or *less clear.* Seeing then the *conception,* which when it was *first* produced by sense, was *clear,* and represented the *parts* of the object *distinctly*; and when it cometh *again* is *obscure,* we find *missing* somewhat that we expected; by which we judge it *past* and *decayed.* For example, a man that is present in a foreign *city,* seeth not only *whole* streets, but can also distinguish particular *houses,* and *parts* of houses; but departed thence, he cannot distinguish them so particularly in his mind as he did, some *house* or turning escaping him; yet is this to *remember*: when *afterwards* there escape him *more* particulars, this is also to *remember,* but *not* so well. In process of time, the *image* of the city *returneth* but as a *mass* of building *only,* which is *almost* to have *forgotten* it. Seeing then remembrance is *more* or *less,* as we find more or less obscurity, why may not we well think *remembrance* to be nothing else but the *missing of parts,* which every man expecteth should succeed after they have a conception of the whole? To see at a great distance of place, and to remember at a great distance of time, is to have like conceptions of the thing: for there wanteth distinction of parts in both; the one conception being weak by operation at distance, the other by decay."

experience.[3]   Again, imagination being only of those
things which have been formerly perceived by sense,
either all at once, or by parts at several times; the
former, which is the imagining the whole object as it
was presented to the sense, is *simple* imagination, as
when one imagineth a man, or horse, which he hath seen
before.   The other is *compounded*; as when, from the
sight of a man at one time, and of a horse at another,
we conceive in our mind a Centaur.   So when a man
compoundeth the image of his own person with the
image of the actions of another man, as when a man
imagines himself a Hercules or an Alexander, which
happeneth often to them that are much taken with reading of romances, it is a compound imagination, and
properly but a fiction of the mind.   There be also other
imaginations that rise in men, though waking, from the
great impression made in sense: as from gazing upon
the sun, the impression leaves an image of the sun before
our eyes a long time after; and from being long and
vehemently attent upon geometrical figures, a man shall
in the dark, though awake, have the images of lines
and angles before his eyes; which kind of fancy hath
no particular name, as being a thing that doth not commonly fall into men's discourse.

The imaginations of them that sleep are those we call
dreams.   And these also, as all other imaginations, have
been before, either totally or by parcels, in the sense.

---

[3] Compare *Human Nature*, (M. IV, 16).   "The *remembrance*
of succession of one thing to another, that is, of what was
antecedent, and what *consequent*, and what *concomitant*, is
called an *experiment*; whether the same be made by us *voluntarily*, as when a man putteth any thing into the fire, to see
what effect the fire will produce upon it: or *not* made by us,
as when we remember a fair morning after a red evening.
To have had many *experiments*, is what we call *experience*,
which is nothing else but *remembrance* of what antecedents
have been followed by what consequents."

And because in sense, the brain and nerves, which are
the necessary organs of sense, are so benumbed in sleep,
as not easily to be moved by the action of external
objects, there can happen in sleep no imagination, and
therefore no dream, but what proceeds from the agitation of the inward parts of man's body; which inward
parts, for the connexion they have with the brain, and
other organs, when they be distempered, do keep the
same in motion; whereby the imaginations there
formerly made, appear as if a man were waking; saving
that the organs of sense being now benumbed, so as there
is no new object, which can master and obscure them
with a more vigorous impression, a dream must needs
be more clear, in this silence of sense, than our waking
thoughts. And hence it cometh to pass, that it is a hard
matter, and by many thought impossible, to distinguish
exactly between sense and dreaming. For my part,
when I consider that in dreams I do not often nor constantly think of the same persons, places, objects, and
actions, that I do waking; nor remember so long a
train of coherent thoughts, dreaming, as at other times;
and because waking I often observe the absurdity of
dreams, but never dream of the absurdities of my waking thoughts; I am well satisfied, that being awake, I
know I dream not, though when I dream I think myself awake.

And seeing dreams are caused by the distemper of
some of the inward parts of the body, divers distempers
must needs cause different dreams. And hence it is
that lying cold breedeth dreams of fear, and raiseth
the thought and image of some fearful object, the motion
from the brain to the inner parts and from the inner
parts to the brain being reciprocal; and that as anger
causeth heat in some parts of the body when we are
awake, so when we sleep the overheating of the same

parts causeth anger, and raiseth up in the brain the imagination of an enemy. In the same manner, as natural kindness, when we are awake, causeth desire, and desire maketh heat in certain other parts of the body; so also too much heat in those parts, while we sleep, raiseth in the brain the imagination of some kindness shown. In sum, our dreams are the reverse of our waking imaginations; the motion when we are awake beginning at one end, and when we dream at another.[4]

[4] Compare *Elements of Philosophy*, (M. I, 339). "The phantasms of men that sleep, are *dreams*. Concerning which we are taught by experience these five things. First, that for the most part there is neither order nor coherence in them. Secondly, that we dream of nothing but what is compounded and made up of the phantasms of sense past. Thirdly, that sometimes they proceed, as in those that are drowsy, from the interruption of their phantasms by little and little, broken and altered through sleepiness; and sometimes also they begin in the midst of sleep. Fourthly, that they are clearer than the imaginations of waking men, except such as are made by sense itself, to which they are equal in clearness. Fifthly, that when we dream, we admire neither the places nor the looks of the things that appear to us. Now from what hath been said, it is not hard to show what may be the causes of these phenomena. For as for the first, seeing all order and coherence proceeds from frequent looking back to the end, that is, from consultation; it must needs be, that seeing in sleep we lose all thought of the end, our phantasms succeed one another, not in that order which tends to any end, but as it happeneth, and in such manner, as objects present themselves to our eyes when we look indifferently upon all things before us, and see them, not because we would see them, but because we do not shut our eyes; for then they appear to us without any order at all. The second proceeds from this, that in the silence of sense there is no new motion from the objects, and therefore no new phantasm, unless we call that new, which is compounded of old ones, as a chimera, a golden mountain, and the like. As for the third, why a dream is sometimes as it were the continuation of sense, made up of broken phantasms, as in men distempered with sickness, the reason is manifestly this, that in some of the organs sense remains, and in others it faileth. But how some phantasms may be revived, when all the exterior organs are benumbed with sleep, is not so easily shown. Nevertheless that, which

The most difficult discerning of a man's dream, from his waking thoughts, is then, when by some accident we observe not that we have slept: which is easy to happen to a man full of fearful thoughts, and whose conscience

---

hath already been said, contains the reason of this also. For whatsoever strikes the *pia mater*, reviveth some of those phantasms that are still in motion in the brain; and when any internal motion of the heart reacheth that membrane, then the predominant motion in the brain makes the phantasm. Now the motions of the heart are appetites and aversions, of which I shall presently speak further. And as appetites and aversions are generated by phantasms, so reciprocally phantasms are generated by appetites and aversions. * * * * The fourth, namely, that the things we seem to see and feel in sleep, are as clear as in sense itself, proceeds from two causes; one, that having then no sense of things without us, that internal motion which makes the phantasm, in the absence of all other impressions, is predominant; and the other, that the parts of our phantasms which are decayed and worn out by time, are made up with other fictitious parts. To conclude, when we dream, we do not wonder at strange places and the appearances of things unknown to us, because admiration requires that the things appearing be new and unusual, which can happen to none but those that remember former appearances; whereas in sleep, all things appear as present. But it is here to be observed, that certain dreams, especially such as some men have when they are between sleeping and waking, and such as happen to those that have no knowledge of the nature of dreams and are withal superstitious, were not heretofore nor are now accounted dreams. For the apparitions men thought they saw, and the voices they thought they heard in sleep, were not believed to be phantasms, but things subsisting of themselves, and objects without those that dreamed. For to some men, as well sleeping as waking, but especially to guilty men, and in the night, and in hallowed places, fear alone, helped a little with the stories of such apparitions, hath raised in their minds terrible phantasms, which have been and are still deceitfully received for things really true, under the names of *ghosts* and *incorporeal substances*." Also *Human Nature*, (M. IV. 10, 13-14). "The *causes* of dreams, if they be natural, are the *actions* or violence of the *inward* parts of a man upon his *brain*, by which the *passages* of sense by sleep *benumbed*, are *restored* to their motion. The signs by which this appeareth to be so, are the *differences* of dreams (old men commonly dream oftener, and have their dreams more

is much troubled; and that sleepeth, without the circumstances of going to bed or putting off his clothes, as one that noddeth in a chair. For he that taketh pains, and industriously lays himself to sleep, in case any uncouth

---

painful than young) proceeding from the *different* accidents of man's body, as dreams of *lust*, as dreams of *anger*, according as the heart, or other parts within, work more or less upon the brain, by more or less *heat*; so also the descents of different *sorts of phlegm* maketh us a dream of different tastes of meats and drinks; and I believe there is a *reciprocation* of motion from the brain to the vital parts, and back from the vital parts to the brain; whereby not only *imagination* begetteth *motion* in those parts; but also motion in those parts begetteth imagination like to that by which it was begotten. If this be true, and that *sad* imaginations nourish the *spleen*, then we see also a cause, why a strong *spleen* reciprocally causeth *fearful dreams*, and why the effects of *lasciviousness* may in a dream produce the image of some person that had *caused* them. Another sign that dreams are caused by the action of the inward parts, is the *disorder* and casual consequence of one conception or image to another: for when we are *waking*, the *antecedent* thought or conception introduceth, and is the cause of the *consequent*, as the water followeth a man's finger upon a dry and level table; but in *dreams* there is commonly *no coherence*, and when there is, it is by chance, which must needs proceed from this, that the *brain* in dreams is *not restored* to its motion in every part alike: whereby it cometh to pass, that our thoughts appear like the stars between flying clouds, not in the order which a man would choose to observe them, but as the uncertain flight of broken clouds permits. * * * And from this that hath been said, there followeth, that a man can *never know* he *dreameth*; he *may* dream he *doubteth*, whether it be a dream or no: but the clearness of the imagination representeth every thing with as many parts as doth sense itself, and consequently, he can take notice of nothing but as present; whereas to think he dreameth, is to think those his conceptions, that is to say dreams, obscurer than they were in the sense: so that he must think them both as clear, and not as clear as sense; which is impossible. From the same ground it proceedeth, that men *wonder not* in their dreams at place and persons, as they would do waking: for waking, a man would think it strange to be in a place where he never was before, and remember nothing how he came there; but in a dream, there cometh little of that kind into consideration. The *clearness* of conception in a dream, taketh away *distrust*, un-

and exhorbitant fancy come unto him, cannot easily think it other than a dream. We read of Marcus Brutus, (one that had his life given him by Julius Cæsar, and was also his favourite, and notwithstanding murdered him), how at Philippi, the night before he gave battle to Augustus Cæsar, he saw a fearful apparition, which is commonly related by historians as a vision; but considering the circumstances, one may easily judge to have been but a short dream. For sitting in his tent, pensive and troubled with the horror of his rash act, it was not hard for him, slumbering in the cold, to dream of that which most affrighted him; which fear, as by degrees it made him wake, so also it must needs make the apparition by degrees to vanish; and having no assurance that he slept, he could have no cause to think it a dream, or anything but a vision. And this is no very rare accident; for even they that be perfectly awake, if they be timorous and superstitious, possessed with fearful tales, and alone in the dark, are subject to the like fancies, and believe they see spirits and dead men's ghosts walking in churchyards; whereas it is either their fancy only, or else the knavery of such persons as make use of such superstitious fear, to pass disguised in the night, to places they would not be known to haunt.

From this ignorance of how to distinguish dreams, and other strong fancies, from vision and sense, did arise the greatest part of the religion of the Gentiles in time

---

less the *strangeness* be *excessive*, as to think himself fallen from on high without hurt, and then most commonly he *waketh*. Nor is it *impossible* for a man to be so far deceived, as when his dream is *past*, to think it real: for if he dream of such things as are ordinarily in his mind, and in such order as he useth to do waking, and withal that he laid him down to sleep in the place where he findeth himself when he awaketh; all which may happen: I know no κριτήριον or mark by which he can discern whether it were a dream or not, and therefore do the less wonder to hear a man sometimes to tell his dream for a truth, or to take it for a vision."

past, that worshipped satyrs, fawns, nymphs, and the like; and now-a-days the opinion that rude people have of fairies, ghosts, and goblins, and of the power of witches. For as for witches, I think not that their witchcraft is any real power; but yet that they are justly punished, for the false belief they have that they can do such mischief, joined with their purpose to do it if they can; their trade being nearer to a new religion than to a craft or science. And for fairies, and walking ghosts, the opinion of them has, I think, been on purpose either taught or not confuted, to keep in credit the use of exorcism, of crosses, of holy water, and other such inventions of ghostly men. Nevertheless, there is no doubt, but God can make unnatural apparitions; but that he does it so often, as men need to fear such things, more than they fear the stay or change of the course of nature, which he also can stay, and change, is no point of Christian faith. But evil men under pretext that God can do anything, are so bold as to say anything when it serves their turn, though they think it untrue; it is the part of a wise man, to believe them no farther, than right reason makes that which they say, appear credible. If this superstitious fear of spirits were taken away, and with it, prognostics from dreams, false prophecies, and many other things depending thereon, by which crafty ambitious persons abuse the simple people, men would be much more fitted than they are for civil obedience.

And this ought to be the work of the schools: but they rather nourish such doctrine. For, not knowing what imagination or the senses are, what they receive, they teach: some saying, that imaginations rise of themselves, and have no cause; others, that they rise most commonly from the will; and that good thoughts are blown (inspired) into a man by God, and evil thoughts by the

Devil; or that good thoughts are poured (infused) into a man by God, and evil ones by the Devil. Some say the senses receive the species of things, and deliver them to the common sense; and the common sense delivers them over to the fancy, and the fancy to the memory, and the memory to the judgment, like handling of things from one to another with many words making nothing understood.

The imagination that is raised in man, or any other creature indued with the faculty of imagining, by words, or other voluntary signs, is that we generally call *understanding*; and is common to man and beast. For a dog by custom will understand the call, or the rating of his master; and so will many other beasts. That understanding which is peculiar to man, is the understanding not only his will, but his conceptions and thoughts, by the sequel and contexture of the names of things into affirmations, negations, and other forms of speech; and of this kind of understanding I shall speak hereafter.[5]

CHAPTER III

OF THE CONSEQUENCE OR TRAIN OF IMAGINATIONS

By *Consequence*, or TRAIN of thoughts, I understand that succession of one thought to another, which is

[5] Compare below p. 173. Also *Human Nature*, (M. IV, 23). "This *equivocation* of names maketh it *difficult* to recover those conceptions for which the name was ordained; and that not only in the language of other men, wherein we are to consider the *drift*, and *occasion*, and *contexture* of the speech, as well as the *words* themselves; but also in our discourse, which being derived from the custom and common use of speech, representeth unto us not our own conceptions. It is therefore a great ability in a man, out of the words, contexture, and other circumstances of language, to deliver himself from *equivocation*, and to find out the true meaning of what is said: and this is it we call *understanding*."

called, to distinguish it from discourse in words, *mental discourse*.

When a man thinketh on any thing whatsoever, his next thought after, is not altogether so casual as it seems to be. Not every thought to every thought succeeds indifferently. But as we have no imagination, whereof we have not formerly had sense, in whole, or in parts; so we have no transition from one imagination to another, whereof we never had the like before in our senses. The reason whereof is this. All fancies are motions within us, relics of those made in the sense: and those motions that immediately succeeded one another in the sense, continue also together after sense: insomuch as the former coming again to take place, and be predominant, the latter followeth, by coherence of the matter moved, in such manner, as water upon a plane table is drawn which way any one part of it is guided by the finger. But because in sense, to one and the same thing perceived, sometimes one thing, sometimes another succeedeth, it comes to pass in time, that in the imagining of any thing, there is no certainty what we shall imagine next; only this is certain, it shall be something that succeeded the same before, at one time or another.[1]

[1] Compare *Human Nature*, (M. IV, 15). "The *cause* of the *coherence* or consequence of one conception to another, is their first *coherence* of consequence at that *time* when they are produced by sense: as for example, from St. Andrew the mind runneth to St. Peter, because their names are read together; from St. Peter, to a *stone*, for the same cause; from *stone* to *foundation*, because we see them together; and for the same cause, from foundation to *church*, and from church to *people*, and from people to *tumult*: and according to this example, the mind may run almost from anything to anything. But as in the *sense* the conception of cause and effect may succeed one another; so may they after sense in the *imagination*: and for the most part they do so; the *cause* whereof is the *appetite* of them, who, having a conception of the *end*, have next unto it a conception of the next *means* to

This train of thoughts, or mental discourse, is of two sorts. The first is *unguided, without design,* and inconstant; wherein there is no passionate thought, to govern and direct those that follow, to itself, as the end and scope of some desire, or other passion: in which case the thoughts are said to wander, and seem impertinent one to another, as in a dream. Such are commonly the thoughts of men, that are not only without company, but also without care of anything; though even then their thoughts are as busy as at other times, but without harmony; as the sound which a lute out of tune would yield to any man; or in tune, to one that could not play. And yet in this wild ranging of the mind, a man may oft-times perceive the way of it, and the dependence of one thought upon another. For in a discourse of our present civil war, what could seem more impertinent, than to ask, as one did, what was the value of a Roman penny? Yet the coherence to me was manifest enough. For the thought of the war, introduced the thought of the delivering up the king to his enemies; the thought of that, brought in the thought of the delivering up of Christ; and that again the thought of the thirty pence, which was the price of that treason; and thence easily followed that malicious question, and all this in a moment of time; for thought is quick.

The second is more constant; as being *regulated* by some desire, and design. For the impression made by such things as we desire, or fear, is strong, and permanent, or, if it cease for a time, of quick return: so strong it is sometimes, as to hinder and break our sleep. From desire, ariseth the thought of some means we have seen

that end: as, when a man, from a thought of *honour* to which he hath an appetite, cometh to the thought of *wisdom,* which is the next means thereunto; and from thence to the thought of *study,* which is the next means to wisdom."

produce the like of that which we aim at; and from the
thought of that, the thought of means to that mean; and
so continually, till we come to some beginning within
our own power. And because the end, by the greatness
of the impression, comes often to mind, in case our
thoughts begin to wander, they are quickly again reduced into the way: which observed by one of the seven
wise men, made him give men this precept, which is now
worn out, *Respice finem;* that is to say, in all your
actions, look often upon what you would have, as the
thing that directs all your thoughts in the way to attain it.

The train of regulated thoughts is of two kinds; one,
when of an effect imagined we seek the causes, or means
that produce it: and this is common to man and beast.
The other is, when imagining anything whatsoever, we
seek all the possible effects, that can by it be produced;
that is to say, we imagine what we can do with it, when
we have it. Of which I have not at any time seen any
sign, but in man only; for this is a curiosity hardly incident to the nature of any living creature that has no
other passion but sensual, such as are hunger, thirst,
lust, and anger. In sum, the discourse of the mind,
when it is governed by design, is nothing but *seeking,*
or the faculty of invention, which the Latins called
sagacitas, and *solertia*; a hunting out of the causes, of
some effect, present or past; or of the effects, of some
present or past cause. Sometimes a man seeks what he
hath lost; and from that place, and time, wherein he
misses it, his mind runs back, from place to place, and
time to time, to find where, and when he had it; that
is to say, to find some certain, and limited time and
place, in which to begin a method of seeking. Again,
from thence, his thoughts run over the same places and
times, to find what action, or other occasion might make

him lose it. This we call *remembrance,* or calling to mind: the Latins call it *reminiscentia,* as it were a *re-conning* of our former actions.

Sometimes a man knows a place determinate, within the compass whereof he is to seek; and then his thoughts run over all the parts thereof, in the same manner as one would sweep a room, to find a jewel; or as a spaniel ranges the field, till he find a scent; or as a man should run over the alphabet, to start a rhyme.

Sometimes a man desires to know the event of an action; and then he thinketh of some like action past, and the events thereof one after another; supposing like events will follow like actions. As he that foresees what will become of a criminal, re-cons what he has seen follow on the like crime before; having this order of thoughts, the crime, the officer, the prison, the judge, and the gallows. Which kind of thoughts, is called *foresight,* and *prudence,* or *providence*; and sometimes *wisdom*; though such conjecture, through the difficulty of observing all circumstances, be very fallacious. But this is certain; by how much one man has more experience of things past, than another, by so much also he is more prudent, and his expectations the seldomer fail him. The *present* only has a being in nature; things *past* have a being in the memory only, but things *to come* have no being at all; the *future* being but a fiction of the mind, applying the sequels of actions passed, to the actions that are present; which with most certainty is done by him that has most experience, but not with certainty enough. And though it be called prudence, when the event answereth our expectation; yet in its own nature, it is but presumption. For the foresight of things to come, which is providence, belongs only to him by whose will they are to come. From him only, and supernaturally, proceeds prophecy. The best prophet naturally is the best guesser; and the best guesser, he that is most versed and studied in the matters he guesses at: for he hath most *signs* to guess by.

A *sign* is the evident antecedent of the consequent; and contrarily, the consequent of the antecedent, when the like consequences have been observed, before: and the oftener they have been observed, the less uncertain is the sign. And therefore he that has most experience in any kind of business, has most signs, whereby to guess at the future time; and consequently is the most prudent: and so much more prudent than he that is new in that kind of business, as not to be equalled by any advantage of natural and extemporary wit: though perhaps many young men think the contrary.

Nevertheless it is not prudence that distinguisheth man from beast. There be beasts, that at a year old observe more, and pursue that which is for their good, more prudently, than a child can do at ten.

As prudence is a *presumption* of the *future*, contracted from the *experience* of time *past*: so there is a presumption of things past taken from other things, not future, but past also. For he that hath seen by what courses and degrees a flourishing state hath first come into civil war, and then to ruin; upon the sight of the ruins of any other state, will guess, the like war, and the like courses have been there also. But this conjecture, has the same uncertainty almost with the conjecture of the future; both being grounded only upon experience.[2]

[2] The chapter corresponding to this in *Human Nature* (M. IV, 18), closes with the following caveats of concluding from experience. "As in conjecture concerning things past and future, it is prudence to conclude from experience, what is like to come to pass, or to have passed already; so it is an error to conclude from it, that *it is* so or so *called*; that is to say, we cannot from experience conclude, that anything is to be called *just* or *unjust, true* or *false*, or any proposition

There is no other act of man's mind, that I can remember, naturally planted in him, so as to need no other
thing, to the exercise of it, but to be born a man, and
live with the use of his five senses. Those other faculties, of which I shall speak by and by, and which seem
proper to man only, are acquired and increased by study
and industry; and of most men learned by instruction,
and discipline; and proceed all from the invention of
words, and speech. For besides sense, and thoughts,
and the train of thoughts, the mind of man has no other
motion; though by the help of speech, and method,
the same faculties may be improved to such a height,
as to distinguish men from all other living creatures.

Whatsoever we imagine is *finite*. Therefore there
is no idea, or conception of any thing we call *infinite*.
No man can have in his mind an image of infinite magnitude; nor conceive infinite swiftness, infinite time, or
infinite force, or infinite power. When we say anything
is infinite, we signify only, that we are not able to
conceive the ends, the bounds of the things named; having no conception of the thing, but of our own inability.
And therefore the name of God is used, not to make
us conceive him, for he is incomprehensible; and his
greatness, and power are unconceivable; but that we
may honour him. Also because, whatsoever, as I said
before, we conceive, has been perceived first by sense,

---

universal whatsoever, except it be from remembrance of the
use of names imposed arbitrarily by men: for example, to
have heard a sentence given in the like case, the like sentence
a thousand times is not enough to conclude that the sentence
is just; though most men have no other means to conclude
by: but it is *necessary*, for the drawing of such a conclusion,
to *trace* and *find out*, by many experiences, what men do
mean by calling things just and unjust. Further, there is
another *caveat* to be taken in concluding by experience,
* * * that is, that we conclude such things to be without,
that are within us."

either all at once, or by parts; a man can have no thought, representing anything, not subject to sense. No man therefore can conceive anything, but he must conceive it in some place; and indued with some determinate magnitude; and which may be divided into parts; nor that anything is all in this place, and all in another place at the same time; nor that two, or more things can be in one, and the same place at once: for none of these things ever have, nor can be incident to sense; but are absurd speeches, taken upon credit, without any signification at all, from deceived philosophers, and deceived, or deceiving schoolmen.

CHAPTER IV

OF SPEECH [1]

THE invention of *printing*, though ingenious, compared with the invention of *letters*, is no great matter. But who was the first that found the use of letters, is not known. He that first brought them into Greece, men say was Cadmus, the son of Agenor, king of Phœnicia. A profitable invention for continuing the memory of time passed, and the conjunction of mankind, dispersed into so many, and distant regions of the earth; and withal difficult, as proceeding from a watchful observation of the divers motions of the tongue, palate, lips, and other organs of speech; whereby to make as many differences of characters, to remember them. But the most noble and profitable invention of all other, was that of SPEECH, consisting of *names* or *appellations*, and their connexion; whereby men register their thoughts; recall them when they are past; and also declare them one to another for mutual utility and conversation; without

[1] Compare above *Elements of Philosophy*, Ch. II.

which, there had been amongst men, neither commonwealth, nor society, nor contract, nor peace, no more
than amongst lions, bears, and wolves. The first author
of *speech* was God himself, that instructed Adam how
to name such creatures as he presented to his sight;
for the Scripture goeth no further in this matter. But
this was sufficient to direct him to add more names, as
the experience and use of the creatures should give him
occasion; and to join them in such manner by degrees,
as to make himself understood; and so by succession of
time, so much language might be gotten, as he had
found use for; though not so copious, as an orator or
philosopher has need of: for I do not find anything in
the Scripture, out of which, directly or by consequence,
can be gathered, that Adam was taught the names of all
figures, numbers, measures, colours, sounds, fancies,
relations; much less the names of words and speech, as
*general, special, affirmative, negative, interrogative,
optative, infinitive,* all which are useful; and least of all,
of *entity, intentionality, quiddity,* and other insignificant
words of the school.

But all this language gotten, and augmented by Adam
and his posterity, was again lost at the Tower of Babel,
when, by the hand of God, every man was stricken, for
his rebellion, with an oblivion of his former language.
And being hereby forced to disperse themselves into
several parts of the world, it must needs be, that the
diversity of tongues that now is, proceeded by degrees
from them, in such manner, as need, the mother of all
inventions, taught them; and in tract of time grew
everywhere more copious.

The general use of speech, is to transfer our mental
discourse, into verbal; or the train of our thoughts, into
a train of words; and that for two commodities, whereof one is the registering of the consequences of our

thoughts; which being apt to slip out of our memory, and put us to a new labour, may again be recalled, by such words as they were marked by. So that the first use of names is to serve for *marks*, or *notes* of remembrance. Another is, when many use the same words, to signify, by their connexion and order, one to another, what they conceive, or think of each matter; and also what they desire, fear, or have any other passion for. And for this use they are called *signs*. Special uses of speech are these: first, to register, what by cogitation, we find to be the cause of anything, present or past; and what we find things present or past may produce, or effect; which in sum, is acquiring of arts. Secondly, to show to others that knowledge which we have attained, which is, to counsel and teach one another. Thirdly, to make known to others our wills and purposes, that we may have the mutual help of one another. Fourthly, to please and delight ourselves and others, by playing with our words, for pleasure or ornament, innocently.

To these uses, there are also four correspondent abuses. First, when men register their thoughts wrong, by the inconstancy of the signification of their words; by which they register for their conception, that which they never conceived, and so deceive themselves. Secondly, when they use words metaphorically; that is, in other sense than that they are ordained for; and thereby deceive others. Thirdly, by words, when they declare that to be their will, which is not. Fourthly, when they use them to grieve one another; for seeing nature hath armed living creatures, some with teeth, some with horns, and some with hands, to grieve an enemy, it is but an abuse of speech, to grieve him with the tongue, unless it be one whom we are obliged to govern; and then it is not to grieve, but to correct and amend.

The manner how speech serveth to the remembrance of the consequence of causes and effects, consisteth in the imposing of *names*, and the *connexion* of them.

Of names, some are *proper*, and singular to one only thing, as *Peter, John, this man, this tree*; and some are *common* to many things, *man, horse, tree*; every of which, though but one name, is nevertheless the name of divers particular things; in respect of all which together, it is called an *universal*; there being nothing in the world universal but names; for the things named are every one of them individual and singular.

One universal name is imposed on many things, for their similitude in some quality, or other accident; and whereas a proper name bringeth to mind one thing only, universals recall any one of those many.

And of names universal, some are of more, and some of less extent; the larger comprehending the less large; and some again of equal extent, comprehending each other reciprocally. As for example: the name *body* is of larger signification than the word *man*, and comprehendeth it; and the names *man* and *rational*, are of equal extent, comprehending mutually one another. But here we must take notice, that by a name is not always understood, as in grammar, one only word; but sometimes, by circumlocution, many words together. For all these words, *he that in his actions observeth the laws of his country*, make but one name, equivalent to this one word, *just*.

By this imposition of names, some of larger, some of stricter signification, we turn the reckoning of the consequences of things imagined in the mind, into a reckoning of the consequences of appellations. For example: a man that hath no use of speech at all, such as

is born and remains perfectly deaf and dumb, if he set
before his eyes a triangle, and by it two right angles,
such as are the corners of a square figure, he may, by
meditation, compare and find, that the three angles of
that triangle, are equal to those two right angles that
stand by it. But if another triangle be shown him,
different in shape from the former, he cannot know,
without a new labour, whether the three angles of that
also be equal to the same. But he that hath the use of
words, when he observes, that such quality was consequent, not to the length of the sides, nor to any other
particular thing in his triangle; but only to this, that
the sides were straight, and the angles three; and that
that was all, for which he named it a triangle; will
boldly conclude universally, that such equality of angles
is in all triangles whatsoever; and register his invention
in these general terms, *every triangle hath its three
angles equal to two right angles*. And thus the consequence found in one particular, comes to be registered
and remembered, as a universal rule, and discharges
our mental reckoning, of time and place, and delivers
us from all labour of the mind, saving the first, and
makes that which was found true *here*, and *now*, to be
true in *all times* and *places*.

But the use of words in registering our thoughts is
in nothing so evident as in numbering. A natural fool
that could never learn by heart the order of numeral
words, as *one, two,* and *three,* may observe every stroke
of the clock, and nod to it, or say *one, one, one,* but can
never know what hour it strikes. And it seems, there
was a time when those names of number were not in
use; and men were fain to apply their fingers of one
or both hands, to those things they desired to keep account of; and that thence it proceeded, that now our
numeral words are but ten, in any nation, and in some

but five; and then they begin again. And he that can
tell ten, if he recite them out of order, will lose himself,
and not know when he has done. Much less will he be
able to add, and subtract, and perform all other operations of arithmetic. So that without words there is no
possibility of reckoning of numbers; much less of magnitudes, of swiftness, of force, and other things, the
reckonings whereof are necessary to the being, or well-
being of mankind.

When two names are joined together into a consequence, or affirmation, as thus, *a man is a living creature;* or thus, *if he be a man, he is a living creature;*
if the latter name, *living creature,* signify all that the
former name *man* signifieth, then the affirmation, or consequence, is *true;* otherwise *false.* For *true* and *false*
are attributes of speech, not of things. And where
speech is not, there is neither *truth* nor *falsehood; error*
there may be, as when we expect that which shall not
be, or suspect what has not been; but in neither case can
a man be charged with untruth.

Seeing then that truth consisteth in the right ordering of names in our affirmations, a man that seeketh
precise truth had need to remember what every name he
uses stands for, and to place it accordingly, or else he
will find himself entangled in words, as a bird in lime
twigs, the more he struggles the more belimed. And
therefore in geometry, which is the only science that it
hath pleased God hitherto to bestow on mankind, men
begin at settling the significations of their words; which
settling of significations they call *definitions,* and place
them in the beginning of their reckoning.

By this it appears how necessary it is for any man
that aspires to true knowledge, to examine the definitions of former authors; and either to correct them,
where they are negligently set down, or to make them

himself. For the errors of definitions multiply themselves according as the reckoning proceeds, and lead men into absurdities, which at last they see, but cannot avoid, without reckoning anew from the beginning, in which lies the foundation of their errors. From whence it happens, that they which trust to books do as they that cast up many little sums into a greater, without considering whether those little sums were rightly cast up or not; and at last finding the error visible, and not mistrusting their first grounds, know not which way to clear themselves, but spend time in fluttering over their books; as birds that entering by the chimney, and finding themselves enclosed in a chamber, flutter at the false light of a glass window, for want of wit to consider which way they came in. So that in the right definition of names lies the first use of speech; which is the acquisition of science: and in wrong, or no definitions, lies the first abuse; from which proceed all false and senseless tenets; which make those men that take their instruction from the authority of books, and not from their own meditation, to be as much below the condition of ignorant men, as men endued with true science are above it. For between true science and erroneous doctrines, ignorance is in the middle. Natural sense and imagination are not subject to absurdity. Nature itself cannot err; and as men abound in copiousness of language, so they become more wise, or more mad than ordinary. Nor is it possible without letters for any man to become either excellently wise, or, unless his memory be hurt by disease or ill constitution of organs, excellently foolish. For words are wise men's counters, they do but reckon by them; but they are the money of fools, that value them by the authority of an Aristotle, a Cicero, or a Thomas, or any other doctor whatsoever, if but a man.

Subject to names, is whatsoever can enter into or be considered in an account, and be added one to another to make a sum, or subtracted one from another and leave a remainder. The Latins called accounts of money *rationes*, and accounting *ratiocinatio*; and that which we in bills or books of account call *items*, they call *nomina*, that is *names*; and thence it seems to proceed, that they extended the word *ratio* to the faculty of reckoning in all other things. The Greeks have but one word, λόγος for both *speech* and *reason*; not that they thought there was no speech without reason, but no reasoning without speech: and the act of reasoning they called *syllogism*, which signifieth summing up of the consequences of one saying to another. And because the same thing may enter into account for divers accidents, their names are, to show that diversity, diversly wrested and diversified. This diversity of names may be reduced to four general heads.

First, a thing may enter into account for *matter* or *body*; as *living, sensible, rational, hot, cold, moved, quiet;* with all which names the word *matter*, or *body*, is understood; all such being names of matter.

Secondly, it may enter into account, or be considered, for some accident or quality which we conceive to be in it; as for *being moved*, for *being so long*, for *being hot*, &c.; and then, of the name of the thing itself, by a little change or wresting, we make a name for that accident, which we consider; and for *living* put into the account *life*; for *moved, motion*; for *hot, heat*; for *long, length*; and the like: and all such names are the names of the accidents and properties by which one matter and body is distinguished from another. These are called *names abstract*, because severed, not from matter, but from the account of matter.

Thirdly, we bring into account the properties of our

own bodies, whereby we make such distinction; as when anything is seen by us, we reckon not the thing itself, but the sight, the colour, the idea of it in the fancy: and when anything is heard, we reckon it not, but the hearing or sound only, which is our fancy or conception of it by the ear; and such are names of fancies.

Fourthly, we bring into account, consider, and give names, to *names* themselves, and to *speech*: for *general, universal, special, equivocal,* are names of names. And *affirmation, interrogation, commandment, narration, syllogism, sermon, oration,* and many other such, are names of speeches. And this is all the variety of names *positive*; which are put to mark somewhat which is in nature, or may be feigned by the mind of man, as bodies that are, or may be conceived to be; or of bodies, the properties that are, or may be feigned to be; or words and speech.

There be also other names, called *negative,* which are notes to signify that a word is not the name of the thing in question; as these words, *nothing, no man, infinite, indocible, three want four,* and the like; which are nevertheless of use in reckoning, or in correcting of reckoning, and call to mind our past cogitations, though they be not names of anything, because they make us refuse to admit of names not rightly used.

All other names are but insignificant sounds; and those of two sorts. One when they are new, and yet their meaning not explained by definition; whereof there have been abundance coined by schoolmen, and puzzled philosophers.

Another, when men make a name of two names, whose significations are contradictory and inconsistent; as this name, an *incorporeal body*, or, which is all one, an *incorporeal substance*, and a great number more. For whensoever any affirmation is false, the two names of which it is composed, put together and made one, signify nothing at all. For example, if it be a false affirmation to say *a quadrangle is round,* the word *round quadrangle* signifies nothing, but is a mere sound. So likewise, if it be false to say that virtue can be poured, or blown up and down, the words *inpoured virtue, inblown virtue,* are as absurd and insignificant as a *round quadrangle.* And therefore you shall hardly meet with a senseless and insignificant word, that is not made up of some Latin or Greek names. A Frenchman seldom hears our Saviour called by the name of *parole,* but by the name of *verbe* often; yet *verbe* and *parole* differ no more, but that one is Latin and the other French.

When a man, upon the hearing of any speech, hath those thoughts which the words of that speech and their connexion were ordained and constituted to signify, then he is said to understand it; *understanding* being nothing else but conception caused by speech. And therefore if speech be peculiar to man, as for ought I know it is, then is understanding peculiar to him also. And therefore of absurd and false affirmations, in case they be universal, there can be no understanding; though many think they understand then, when they do but repeat the words softly, or con them in their mind.

What kinds of speeches signify the appetites, aversions, and passions of man's mind; and of their use and abuse, I shall speak when I have spoken of the passions.

The names of such things as affect us, that is, which please and displease us, because all men be not alike affected with the same thing, nor the same man at all times, are in the common discourses of men of *inconstant* signification. For seeing all names are imposed to signify our conceptions, and all our affections are but conceptions, when we conceive the same things differently, we can hardly avoid different naming of them.

For though the nature of that we conceive, be the same; yet the diversity of our reception of it, in respect of different constitutions of body, and prejudices of opinion, gives every thing a tincture of our different passions. And therefore in reasoning a man must take heed of words; which besides the signification of what we imagine of their nature, have a signification also of the nature, disposition, and interest of the speaker; such as are the names of virtues and vices; for one man calleth *wisdom*, what another calleth *fear*; and one *cruelty*, what another *justice*; one *prodigality*, what another *magnanimity*; and one *gravity*, what another *stupidity*, &c. And therefore such names can never be true grounds of any ratiocination. No more can metaphors, and tropes of speech; but these are less dangerous, because they profess their inconstancy; which the other do not.

CHAPTER V

OF REASON AND SCIENCE

When a man *reasoneth*, he does nothing else but conceive a sum total, from *addition* of parcels; or conceive a remainder, from *subtraction* of one sum from another; which, if it be done by words, is conceiving of the consequence of the names of all the parts, to the name of the whole; or from the names of the whole and one part, to the name of the other part. And though in some things, as in numbers, besides adding and subtracting, men name other operations, as *multiplying* and *dividing*, yet they are the same; for multiplication, is but adding together of things equal; and division, but subtracting of one thing, as often as we can. These operations are not incident to numbers only, but to all manner of

things that can be added together, and taken on
of another. For as arithmeticians teach to add
subtract in *numbers*; so the geometricians teach
same in *lines, figures*, solid and superficial, *angles, pro-
portions, times*, degrees of *swiftness, force, power*, and
the like; the logicians teach the same in *consequences of
words*; adding together two *names* to make an *affirmation*, and two *affirmations* to make a *syllogism*; and
many syllogisms to make a *demonstration*; and from the
sum, or *conclusion* of a *syllogism*, they subtract one
proposition to find the other. Writers of politics add
together *pactions* to find men's *duties*; and lawyers, *laws*
and *facts*, to find what is *right* and *wrong* in the actions
of private men. In sum, in what matter soever there
is place for *addition* and *subtraction*, there also is place
for *reason*; and where these have no place, there *reason*
has nothing at all to do.

Out of all which we may define, that is to say determine, what that is, which is meant by this word *reason*, when we reckon it amongst the faculties of the
mind. For REASON, in this sense, is nothing but *reckoning*, that is adding and subtracting, of the consequences
of general names agreed upon for the *marking* and
signifying of our thoughts; I say *marking* them when
we reckon by ourselves, and *signifying*, when we demonstrate or approve our reckonings to other men.[1]

And, as in arithmetic, unpractised men must, and
professors themselves may often, err, and cast up false;
so also in any other subject of reasoning, the ablest,
most attentive, and most practised men may deceive
themselves, and infer false conclusions; not but that
reason itself is always right reason, as well as arithmetic is a certain and infallible art: but no one man's
reason, nor the reason of any one number of men, makes

[1] Compare above *Elements of Philosophy*, chap. I, art. 3.

the certainty; no more than an account is therefore
well cast up, because a great many men have unani-
mously approved it. And therefore, as when there is a
controversy in an account, the parties must by their
own accord, set up, for right reason, the reason of some
arbitrator, or judge, to whose sentence they will both
stand, or their controversy must either come to blows,
or be undecided, for want of a right reason constituted
by nature; so it is also in all debates of what kind
soever. And when men that think themselves wiser than
all others, clamour and demand right reason for judge,
yet seek no more, but that things should be determined,
by no other men's reason but their own, it is as intoler-
able in the society of men, as it is in play after trump
is turned, to use for trump on every occasion, that suite
whereof they have most in their hand. For they do
nothing else, that will have every of their passions, as
it comes to bear sway in them, to be taken for right
reason, and that in their own controversies: bewraying
their want of right reason, by the claim they lay to it.[2]

[2] Compare below p. 284, n. Also *Philosophical Rudiments*,
(M. II, 268). "Furthermore, all these things, to build castles,
houses, temples; to move, carry, take away mighty weights; to
send securely over seas; to contrive engines, serving for all
manner of uses; to be well acquainted with the face of the
whole world, the courses of the stars, the seasons of the year,
the accounts of the times, and the nature of all things; to
understand perfectly all natural and civil rights; and all
manner of sciences, which, comprehended under the title of
philosophy, are necessary partly to live, partly to live well;
I say, the understanding of these (because Christ hath not
delivered it) is to be learnt from reasoning; that is to say, by
making necessary consequences, having first taken the beginning from experience. But men's reasonings are sometimes
right, sometimes wrong; and consequently, that which is concluded and held for a truth, is sometimes truth, sometimes
error. Now errors, even about these philosophical points, do
sometimes public hurt, and give occasions of great seditions
and injuries. It is needful therefore, as oft as any controversy ariseth in these matters contrary to public good and

The use and end of reason, is not the finding of the
sum and truth of one, or a few consequences, remote
from the first definitions, and settled significations of
names, but to begin at these, and proceed from one consequence to another. For there can be no certainty of

---

common peace, that there be somebody to judge of the reasoning, that is to say, whether that which is inferred, be
rightly inferred or not; that so the controversy may be ended.
But there are no rules given by Christ to this purpose,
neither came he into the world to teach *logic*. It remains
therefore that the judges of such controversies, be the same
with those whom God by nature had instituted before, namely,
those who in each city are constituted by the sovereign.
Moreover, if a controversy be raised of the accurate and
proper signification, that is, the definition of those names or
appellations which are commonly used; insomuch as it is
needful for the peace of the city, or the distribution of right,
to be determined; the determination will belong to the city.
For men, by reasoning, do search out such kind of definitions
in their observation of diverse conceptions, for the signification whereof those appellations were used at diverse times and
for diverse causes. But the decision of the question, whether
a man do reason rightly, belongs to the city. For example,
if a woman bring forth a child of an unwonted shape, and
the law forbid to kill a man; the question is, whether the
child be a man. It is demanded therefore, what a man is.
No man doubts but the city shall judge it, and that without
taking an account of Aristotle's definition, that man is a
rational creature." Also *De Corpore Politico*, (M. IV, 225).
"In the state of nature, where every man is his own judge,
and differeth from other concerning the names and appellations of things, and from those differences arise quarrels and
breach of peace, it was necessary there should be a common
measure of all things, that might fall in controversy. As for
example; of what is to be called right, what good, what virtue,
what much, what little, what *meum* and *tuum*, what a pound,
what a quart, &c. For in these things private judgments
may differ, and beget controversy. This common measure,
some say, is *right reason*: with whom I should consent, if
there were any such thing to be found or known in *rerum
natura*. But commonly they that call for *right reason* to
decide any controversy, do mean their own. But this is certain, seeing *right reason* is not existent, the reason of some
man or men must supply the place thereof; and that man or
men, is he or they, that have the sovereign power, as hath

the last conclusion, without a certainty of all those affirmations and negations, on which it was grounded and
inferred. As when a master of a family, in taking an
account, casteth up the sums of all the bills of expense
into one sum, and not regarding how each bill is
summed up, by those that give them in account; nor
what it is he pays for; he advantages himself no more,
than if he allowed the account in gross, trusting to
every of the accountants' skill and honesty: so also in
reasoning of all other things, he that takes up conclusions on the trust of authors, and doth not fetch them
from the first items in every reckoning, which are the
significations of names settled by definitions, loses his
labour; and does not know anything, but only believeth.

When a man reckons without the use of words, which
may be done in particular things, as when upon the
sight of any one thing, we conjecture what was likely
to have preceded, or is likely to follow upon it; if that
which he thought likely to follow, follows not, or that
which he thought likely to have preceded it, hath not
preceded it, this is called *error*; to which even the most
prudent men are subject. But when we reason in words
of general signification, and fall upon a general infer-

---

been already proved; and consequently the civil laws are to
all subjects the measures of their actions, whereby to determine, whether they be right or wrong, profitable or unprofitable, virtuous or vicious; and by them the use and definition
of all names not agreed upon, and tending to controversy,
shall be established." Compare also above *Elements of
Philosophy*, Ch. I, Sec. 2, with notes, p. 2f; and *Human Nature*
(M. IV, 24). "Now when a man *reasoneth* from *principles*
that are *found* indubitable by experience, all deceptions of
sense and equivocation of words avoided, the conclusion he
maketh is said to be *according to right reason*: but when
from his conclusion a man may, by good ratiocination, derive
that which is *contradictory* to any evident truth whatsoever,
then he is said to have concluded *against reason*: and such a
conclusion is called *absurdity*."

ence which is false, though it be commonly called *error,* it is indeed an *absurdity,* or senseless speech. For error is but a deception, in presuming that somewhat is passed, or to come; of which, though it were not past, or not to come, yet there was no impossibility discoverable. But when we make a general assertion, unless it be a true one, the possibility of it is inconceivable. And words whereby we conceive nothing but the sound, are those we call *absurd, insignificant,* and *nonsense.* And therefore if a man should talk to me of a *round quadrangle;* or, *accidents of bread in cheese;* or *immaterial substances;* or of *a free subject; a free will;* or any *free,* but free from being hindered by opposition, I should not say he were in an error, but that his words were without meaning, that is to say, absurd.

I have said before, in the second chapter, that a man did excel all other animals in this faculty, that when he conceived any thing whatsoever, he was apt to enquire the consequences of it, and what effects he could do with it. And now I add this other degree of the same excellence, that he can by words reduce the consequences he finds to general rules, called *theorems,* or *aphorisms;* that is, he can reason, or reckon, not only in number, but in all other things, whereof one may be added unto, or subtracted from another.

But this privilege is allayed by another; and that is, by the privilege of absurdity; to which no living creature is subject, but man only. And of men, those are of all most subject to it, that profess philosophy. For it is most true that Cicero saith of them somewhere; that there can be nothing so absurd, but may be found in the books of philosophers. And the reason is manifest. For there is not one of them that begins his ratiocination from the definitions, or explications of the names they are to use; which is a method that hath been used only in geometry; whose conclusions have thereby been made indisputable.

I. The first cause of absurd conclusions I ascribe to the want of method; in that they begin not their ratiocination from definitions; that is, from settled significations of their words: as if they could cast account, without knowing the value of the numeral words, *one, two,* and *three*.

And whereas all bodies enter into account upon divers considerations, which I have mentioned in the precedent chapter; these considerations being diversely named, divers absurdities proceed from the confusion, and unfit connexion of their names into assertions. And therefore,

II. The second cause of absurd assertions, I ascribe to the giving of names of *bodies* to *accidents*; or of *accidents* to *bodies*; as they do, that say, *faith is infused,* or *inspired*; when nothing can be *poured*, or *breathed* into anything, but body; and that, *extension* is *body*; that *phantasms* are *spirits*, &c.

III. The third I ascribe to the giving of the names of the *accidents* of *bodies without us,* to the *accidents* of our *own bodies*; as they do that say, the *colour is in the body; the sound is in the air,* &c.

IV. The fourth, to the giving of the names of *bodies* to *names,* or *speeches*; as they do that say, that *there be things universal*; that *a living creature is genus,* or *a general thing*, &c.

V. The fifth, to the giving of the names of *accidents* to *names* and *speeches*; as they do that say, *the nature of a thing is its definition; a man's command is his will*; and the like.

VI. The sixth, to the use of metaphors, tropes, and other rhetorical figures, instead of words proper. For though it be lawful to say, for example, in common speech, *the way goeth, or leadeth hither, or thither; the proverb says this or that,* whereas ways cannot go, nor proverbs speak; yet in reckoning, and seeking of truth, such speeches are not to be admitted.

VII. The seventh, to names that signify nothing; but are taken up, and learned by rote from the schools, as *hypostatical, transubstantiate, consubstantiate, eternal-now,* and the like canting of schoolmen.[3]

To him that can avoid these things it is not easy to fall into any absurdity, unless it be by the length of an account; wherein he may perhaps forget what went before. For all men by nature reason alike, and well, when they have good principles. For who is so stupid, as both to mistake in geometry, and also to persist in it, when another detects his error to him?

By this it appears that reason is not, as sense and memory, born with us; nor gotten by experience only, as prudence is; but attained by industry; first in apt imposing of names; and secondly by getting a good and orderly method in proceeding from the elements, which are names, to assertions made by connexion of one of them to another; and so to syllogisms, which are the connexions of one assertion to another, till we come to a knowledge of all the consequences of names appertaining to the subject in hand; and that is it, men call SCIENCE. And whereas sense and memory are but knowledge of fact, which is a thing past and irrevocable. *Science* is the knowledge of consequences, and dependence of one fact upon another:[4] by which, out of that we can presently do, we know how to do something else when we will, or the like another time; because when we see how anything comes about, upon what causes, and by what manner; when the like causes come

---

[3] Compare above, *Elements of Philosophy,* Ch. v.
[4] Compare *Leviathan* (M. III, 368). "Reason serves only to convince the truth, not of fact, but, of consequence."

into our power, we see how to make it produce the like effects.

Children therefore are not endued with reason at all, till they have attained the use of speech; but are called reasonable creatures, for the possibility apparent of having the use of reason in time to come. And the most part of men, though they have the use of reasoning a little way, as in numbering to some degree; yet it serves them to little use in common life; in which they govern themselves, some better, some worse, according to their differences of experience, quickness of memory, and inclinations to several ends; but specially according to good or evil fortune, and the errors of one another. For as for *science*, or certain rules of their actions, they are so far from it, they know not what it is. Geometry they have thought conjuring; but for other sciences, they who have not been taught the beginnings and some progress in them, that they may see how they be acquired and generated, are in this point like children, that having no thought of generation, are made believe by the women that their brothers and sisters are not born, but found in the garden.

But yet they that have no *science*, are in better, and nobler condition, with their natural prudence; than men, that by mis-reasoning, or by trusting them that reason wrong, fall upon false and absurd general rules. For ignorance of causes, and of rules, does not set men so far out of their way, as relying on false rules, and taking for causes of what they aspire to, those that are not so, but rather causes of the contrary.

To conclude, the light of human minds is perspicuous words, but by exact definitions first snuffed, and purged from ambiguity; *reason* is the *pace*; increase of *science*, the *way*; and the benefit of mankind, the *end*. And, on the contrary, metaphors, and senseless and ambiguous words, are like *ignes fatui*; and reasoning upon them is wandering amongst innumerable absurdities; and their end, contention and sedition, or contempt.

As much experience is *prudence*; so, is much science *sapience*. For though we usually have one name of wisdom for them both, yet the Latins did always distinguish between *prudentia* and *sapientia*; ascribing the former to experience, the latter to science. But to make their difference appear more clearly, let us suppose one man endued with an excellent natural use and dexterity in handling his arms; and another to have added to that dexterity, an acquired science, of where he can offend, or be offended by his adversary, in every possible posture or guard: the ability of the former, would be to the ability of the latter, as prudence to sapience; both useful; but the latter infallible. But they that trusting only to the authority of books, follow the blind blindly, are like him that, trusting to the false rules of a master of fence, ventures presumptuously upon an adversary, that either kills or disgraces him.[5]

[5] Compare above, p. 44, n. 1, and below *Leviathan*, Chapters VII and IX. Also *Human Nature*, (M. IV, 28, 50). "Knowledge thereof, which we call *science*, I define to be *evidence of truth*, from some beginning or principle of *sense*: for the truth of a proposition is never evident, until we conceive the meaning of the words or terms whereof it consisteth, which are always conceptions of the mind: nor can we remember those conceptions, without the thing that produced the same by our senses. The *first* principle of knowledge is, that we have such and such *conceptions*; the *second*, that we have thus and thus *named* the things whereof they are conceptions; the *third* is, that we have *joined* those *names* in such manner as to make true propositions; the *fourth* and last is, that we have *joined* those *propositions* in such manner as they be concluding, and the truth of the conclusion said to be known. And of these two kinds of knowledge, whereof the former is *experience of fact*, and the latter *evidence of truth*; as the *former*, if it be great, is called *prudence*; so the *latter*, if it be much, hath usually been called, both by ancient and modern writers, *sapience* or wisdom: and of this *latter, man* only is

The signs of science are some, certain and infallible; some, uncertain. Certain, when he that pretendeth the science of anything, can teach the same: that is to say, demonstrate the truth thereof perspicuously to another;

---

capable; of the *former, brute beasts* also participate. * * * * Forasmuch as all *knowledge* beginneth from *experience*, therefore also *new experience* is the beginning of *new knowledge*, and the increase of experience the beginning of the increase of knowledge. Whatsoever therefore happeneth new to a man, giveth him matter of *hope* of *knowing* somewhat that he knew *not before*. And this hope and expectation of future knowledge from anything that happeneth new and strange, is that passion which we commonly call *admiration*; and the same considered as appetite, is called *curiosity*, which is appetite of knowledge. As in the discerning of faculties, *man leaveth* all community with *beasts* at the faculty of *imposing names*; so also doth he surmount their nature at this *passion of curiosity*. For when a beast seeth anything new and strange to him, he considereth it so far only as to discern whether it be likely to serve his turn, or hurt him, and accordingly approacheth nearer to it, or fleeth from it: whereas man, who in most events remembereth in what manner they were caused and begun, looketh for the cause and beginning of everything that ariseth new unto him. And from this passion of admiration and curiosity, have arisen not only the invention of names, but also supposition of such causes of all things as they thought might produce them. And from this beginning is derived all *philosophy*; as *astronomy* from the admiration of the course of heaven; *natural philosophy* from the strange effects of the elements and other bodies. And from the degrees of curiosity, proceed also the degrees of knowledge amongst men: for, to a man in the chase of riches or authority, (which in respect of knowledge are but sensuality) it is a diversity of little pleasure, whether it be the motion of the sun or the earth that maketh the day, or to enter into other contemplations of any strange accident, otherwise than whether it conduce or not to the end he pursueth. Because *curiosity* is *delight*, therefore also *novelty* is so, but especially that novelty from which a man conceiveth an *opinion* true or false of *bettering* his own estate; for, in such case, they stand affected with the hope that all gamesters have while the cards are shuffling." Note the limitation of knowledge expressed in *Philosophical Rudiments*, (M. II, 217). "It is supposed *that all things in the natural kingdom of God are enquired into by reason only*, that is to say, out of the principles of natural science. But we are so uncertain, when only some particular events answer to his pretence, and upon many occasions prove so as he says they must. Signs of prudence are all uncertain; because to observe by experience, and remember all circumstances that may alter the success, is impossible. But in any business, whereof a man has not infallible science to proceed by; to forsake his own natural judgment, and be guided by general sentences read in authors, and subject to many exceptions, is a sign of folly, and generally scorned by the name of pedantry. And even of those men themselves, that in councils of the commonwealth love to show their reading of politics and history, very few do it in their domestic affairs, where their particular interest is concerned; having prudence enough for their private affairs: but in public they study more the reputation of their own wit, than the success of another's business.

CHAPTER VI

OF THE INTERIOR BEGINNINGS OF VOLUNTARY MOTIONS; COMMONLY CALLED THE PASSIONS; AND THE SPEECHES BY WHICH THEY ARE EXPRESSED

THERE be in animals, two sorts of *motions* peculiar to them: one called *vital*; begun in generation, and continued without interruption through their whole life; such as are the *course* of the *blood*, the *pulse*, the *breath-*

---

far off by these to attain to the knowledge of the nature of God, that we cannot so much as reach to the full understanding of all the qualities of our own bodies, or of any other creatures. Wherefore there comes nothing from these disputes, but a rash imposition of names to the divine Majesty according to the small measure of our conceptions." Also below, p. 391.

ing, the *concoction, nutrition, excretion,* &c., to which motions there needs no help of imagination: the other is *animal motion,* otherwise called *voluntary motion;* as to *go,* to *speak,* to *move* any of our limbs, in such manner as is first fancied in our minds.[1] That sense is motion in the organs and interior parts of man's body, caused by the action of the things we see, hear, &c.; and that fancy is but the relics of the same motion, remaining after sense, has been already said in the first and second chapters. And because *going, speaking,* and the like voluntary motions, depend always upon a precedent thought of *whither, which way,* and *what;* it is evident, that the imagination is the first internal beginning of all voluntary motion. And although unstudied men do not conceive any motion at all to be there, where the thing moved is invisible; or the space it is moved in is, for the shortness of it, insensible; yet that doth not hinder, but that such motions are. For let a space be never so little, that which is moved over a greater space, whereof that little one is part, must first be moved over that. These small beginnings of motion, within the body of man, before they appear in walking, speaking, striking, and other visible actions, are commonly called ENDEAVOUR.[2]

[1] Compare *Elements of Philosophy,* above, pp. 121-2.
[2] Compare *Elements of Philosophy.* (M. I, 206.) "I define ENDEAVOUR *to be motion made in less space and time than can be given;* that is, *less than can be determined or assigned by exposition or number;* that is, *motion made through the length of a point, and in an instant or point of time.* For the explaining of which definition it must be remembered, that by a point is not to be understood that which has no quantity, or which cannot by any means be divided; for there is no such thing in nature; but that, whose quantity is not at all considered, that is, whereof neither quantity nor any part is computed in demonstration; so that a point is not to be taken for an indivisible, but for an undivided thing; as also an instant is to be taken for an undivided, and not for an

This endeavour, when it is toward something which causes it, is called APPETITE, or DESIRE; the latter, being the general name; and the other oftentimes restrained to signify the desire of food, namely *hunger* and *thirst*. And when the endeavour is fromward something, it is generally called AVERSION. These words, *appetite* and *aversion,* we have from the Latins; and they both of them signify the motions, one of approaching, the other of retiring. So also do the Greek words for the same, which are ὁρμή and ἀφορμή. For nature itself does often press upon men those truths, which afterwards, when they look for somewhat beyond nature, they stumble at. For the Schools find in mere appetite to go, or move, no actual motion at all: but because some motion they must acknowledge, they call it metaphorical motion; which is but an absurd speech: for though words may be called metaphorical; bodies and motions can not.

That which men desire, they are also said to LOVE: and to HATE those things for which they have aversion. So that desire and love are the same thing; save that by desire, we always signify the absence of the object; by love, most commonly the presence of the same. So also by aversion, we signify the absence; and by hate, the presence of the object.

---

indivisible time. In like manner, endeavour is to be conceived as motion; but so as that neither the quantity of the time in which, nor of the line in which it is made, may in demonstration be at all brought into comparison with the quantity of that time, or of that line of which it is a part. And yet, as a point may be compared with a point, so one endeavour may be compared with another endeavour, and one may be found to be greater or less than another." Also *Decameron Physiologicum,* (M. VII, 87). "In all motion, as in all quantity, you must take the beginning of your reckoning from the least supposed motion. And this I call the first endeavour of the movement; which endeavour, how weak soever, is also motion."

Of appetites and aversions, some are born with men; as appetite of food, appetite of excretion, and exoneration, which may also and more properly be called aversions, from somewhat they feel in their bodies; and some other appetites, not many. The rest, which are appetites of particular things, proceed from experience, and trial of their effects upon themselves or other men. For of things we know not at all, or believe not to be, we can have no further desire, than to taste and try. But aversion we have for things, not only which we know have hurt us, but also that we do not know whether they will hurt us, or not.

Those things which we neither desire, nor hate, we are said to *contemn*; CONTEMPT being nothing else but an immobility, or contumacy of the heart, in resisting the action of certain things; and proceeding from that the heart is already moved otherwise, by other more potent objects; or from want of experience of them.

And because the constitution of a man's body is in continual mutation, it is impossible that all the same things should always cause in him the same appetites, and aversions: much less can all men consent, in the desire of almost any one and the same object.

But whatsoever is the object of any man's appetite or desire, that is it which he for his part calleth *good*: and the object of his hate and aversion, evil; and of his contempt, *vile* and *inconsiderable*. For these words of good, evil, and contemptible, are ever used with relation to the person that useth them: there being nothing simply and absolutely so; nor any common rule of good and evil, to be taken from the nature of the objects themselves; but from the person of the man, where there is no commonwealth; or, in a commonwealth, from the person that representeth it; or from an arbitrator or judge, whom men disagreeing shall by consent set up, and make his sentence the rule thereof.[3]

[3] Compare below p. 327, Sec. 31. Also *Philosophical Rudiments*, (M. II, 77). "Since it no less, nay, it much more conduceth to peace, to prevent brawls from arising than to appease them being risen; and that all controversies are bred from hence, that the opinions of men differ concerning *meum* and *tuum, just* and *unjust, profitable* and *unprofitable, good* and *evil, honest* and *dishonest*, and the like; which every man esteems according to his own judgment: it belongs to the same chief power to make some common rules for all men, and to declare them publicly, by which every man may know what may be called his, what another's, what just, what unjust, what honest, what dishonest, what good, what evil; that is summarily, what is to be done, what to be avoided in our common course of life. But those rules and measures are usually called the civil laws, or the laws of the city, as being the commands of him who hath the supreme power in the city. And the *civil laws*, (that we may define them) are nothing else but *the commands of him who hath the chief authority in the city, for direction of the future actions of his citizens*." (M. II, 150.) "But one and the first which disposeth them to sedition is this, *that the knowledge of good and evil belongs to each single man*. In the state of nature indeed, where every man lives by equal right, and has not by any mutual pacts submitted to the command of others, we have granted this to be true. * * * But in the civil state it is false. For it was shown that the civil laws were the rules of *good* and *evil, just* and *unjust, honest* and *dishonest*; that therefore what the legislator commands, must be held for *good*, and what he forbids for *evil*. And the legislator is ever that person who hath the supreme power in the commonweal, that is to say, the monarch in a monarchy. We have confirmed the same truth in chap. XI, art. 2, out of the words of Solomon. For if private men may pursue that as good and shun that as evil, which appears to them to be so, to what end serve those words of his: *Give therefore unto thy servant an understanding heart, to judge thy people, that I may discern between good and evil?* Since therefore it belongs to kings to discern between *good* and *evil*, wicked are those, though usual, sayings, *that he only is a king who does righteously*, and *that kings must not be obeyed unless they command us just things*; and many other such like. Before there was any government, *just* and *unjust* had no being, their nature only being relative to some command: and every action in its own nature is indifferent; that it becomes *just* or *unjust*, proceeds from the right of the magistrate. Legitimate kings therefore

The Latin tongue has two words, whose significations approach to those of good and evil; but are not precisely the same; and those are *pulchrum* and *turpe*. Whereof the former signifies that, which by some ap-

---

make the things they command just, by commanding them, and those which they forbid, unjust, by forbidding them. But private men, while they assume to themselves the knowledge of *good* and *evil*, desire to be even as kings; which cannot be with the safety of the commonweal. The most ancient of all God's commands is (Gen. ii. 17): *Thou shalt not eat of the tree of knowledge of good and evil*: and the most ancient of all diabolical temptations, (Gen. iii. 5): *Ye shall be as gods, knowing good and evil;* and God's expostulation with man, (verse II): *Who told thee that thou wert naked? Hast thou eaten of the tree, whereof I commanded thee that thou shouldst not eat?* As if he had said, how comest thou to judge that nakedness, wherein it seemed good to me to create thee, to be shameful, except thou have arrogated to thyself the knowledge of *good* and *evil*." (M. II. 196.) "We all measure *good* and *evil* by the pleasure or pain we either feel at present, or expect hereafter." Also below pp. 310-11, and *Leviathan*, (M. III, 680). "Aristotle, and other heathen philosophers, define good and evil, by the appetite of men; and well enough, as long as we consider them governed every one by his own law; for in the condition of men that have no other law by their own appetites, there can be no general rule of good, and evil actions. But in a commonwealth this measure is false: not the appetite of private men, but the law, which is the will and appetite of the state, is the measure. And yet is this doctrine still practiced; and men judge the goodness or wickedness of their own, and of other men's actions, and of the actions of the commonwealth itself, by their own passions; and no man calleth good or evil, but that which is so in his own eyes, without any regard at all to the public laws; except only monks, and friars, that are bound by vow to that simple obedience to their superior, to which every subject ought to think himself bound by the law of nature to the civil sovereign. And this private measure of good, is a doctrine, not only vain, but also pernicious to the public state." Also *Human Nature*, (M. IV. 32). "Every man, for his own part, calleth that which *pleaseth*, and is delightful to himself, *good*; and that *evil* which *displeaseth* him: insomuch that while every man *differeth* from another in *constitution*, they differ also from one another concerning the common distinction of good and evil. Nor is there any such thing as absolute goodness, considered without relation: for even the goodness which we

parent signs promiseth good; and the latter, that which
promiseth evil. But in our tongue we have not so
general names to express them by. But for *pulchrum*
we say in some things, *fair*; in others, *beautiful*, or

apprehend in God Almighty, is *his goodness to us*. And as we
call *good* and *evil* the *things* that please and displease; so call
we *goodness* and *badness*, the *qualities* or *powers* whereby they
do it: and the signs of that goodness are called by the Latins
in one word *pulchritudo*, and the signs of evil, *turpitudo*; to
which we have no words precisely answerable." Also *De
Corpore Politico*, (M. IV, 109-111). "Every man by natural
passion, calleth that good which pleaseth him for the present,
or so far forth as he can foresee; and in like manner, that
which displeaseth him, evil. And therefore he that foreseeth
the whole way to his preservation, which is the end that every
one by nature aimeth at, must also call it good, and the
contrary evil. And this is that good and evil, which not every
man in passion calleth so, but all men by reason. And therefore the fulfilling of all these laws is good in reason, and the
breaking of them evil. And so also the habit, or disposition,
or intention to fulfill them good; and the neglect of them evil.
And from hence cometh that distinction of *malum poenae*,
and *malum culpae*; for *malum poenae* is any pain or molestation of the mind whatsoever; but *malum culpae* is that action
which is contrary to reason and the law of nature: as also the
habit of doing according to these and other laws of nature,
that tend to our preservation, is that we call *virtue*; and the
habit of doing the contrary, *vice*. As for example, justice is
that habit by which we stand to covenants, injustice the contrary vice; equity that habit by which we allow equality of
nature, arrogancy the contrary vice; gratitude the habit whereby we requite the benefit and trust of others, ingratitude the
contrary vice; temperance the habit by which we abstain from
all things that tend to our destruction, intemperance the contrary vice; prudence, the same with virtue in general. As for
the common opinion, that virtue consisteth in mediocrity, and
vice in extremes, I see no ground for it, nor can find any such
mediocrity. Courage may be virtue, when the daring is
extreme, if the cause be good, and extreme fear no vice when
the danger is extreme. To give a man more than his due,
is no injustice, though it be to give him less: and in gifts it
is not the sum that maketh liberality, but the reason. And so
in all other virtues and vices. I know that this doctrine of
mediocrity is Aristotle's, but his opinions concerning virtue
and vice, are no other than those, which were received then,
and are still by the generality of men unstudied, and therefore

handsome, or *gallant,* or *honourable,* or *comely,* or
amiable; and for *turpe, foul, deformed, ugly, base,
nauseous,* and the like, as the subject shall require; all
which words, in their proper places, signify nothing else

not very likely to be accurate. The sum of virtue is to be
sociable with them that will be sociable, and formidable to
them that will not. And the same is the sum of the law of
nature: for in being sociable, the law of nature taketh place
by way of peace and society; and to be formidable, is the law
of nature in war, where to be feared is a protection a man
hath from his own power: and as the former consisteth in
actions of equity and justice, the latter consisteth in actions
of honour. And equity, justice, and honour, contain all virtues
whatsoever." Also *Questions Concerning Liberty,* (M. V,
192). "There hath been in the Schools derived from *Aristotle's
Metaphysics,* an old proverb rather than an axiom: *ens, bonum, et verum convertuntur.* From hence the Bishop hath
taken this notion of a metaphysical goodness, and his doctrine
that whatsoever hath a being is good; and by this interpreteth
the words of Gen. i. 31: *God saw all that he had made, and
it was very good.* But the reason of those words is, that *good*
is relative to those that are pleased with it, and not of absolute
signification to all men. God therefore saith, that all that he
had made was very good, because he was pleased with the
creatures of his own making. But if all things were absolutely
good, we should be all pleased with their *being,* which we are
not, when the actions that depend upon their being are hurtful
to us. And therefore, to speak properly, nothing is good or
evil but in regard of the action that proceedeth from it, and
also of the person to whom it doth good or hurt. Satan is evil
to us, because he seeketh our destruction, but good to God,
because he executeth his commandments. And so his *metaphysical goodness* is but an idle term, and not the member
of a distinction. And as for natural goodness and evilness, that
also is but the goodness and evilness of actions; as some herbs
are good because they nourish, others evil because they poison
us; and one horse is good because he is gentle, strong, and
carrieth a man easily; another bad, because he resisteth, goeth
hard, or otherwise displeaseth us; and that quality of gentleness, if there were no more laws amongst men than there is
amongst beasts, would be as much a moral good in a horse
or other beast as in a man. It is the law from whence proceeds the difference between the moral and the natural goodness: so that it is well enough said by him, that 'moral
goodness is the conformity of an action with right reason';
and better said than meant; for this *right reason,* which is the

but the *mien*, or countenance, that promiseth good and
evil. So that of good there be three kinds; good in the
promise, that is *pulchrum*; good in effect, as the end
desired, which is called *jucundum, delightful*; and good
as the means, which is called *utile, profitable*; and as

---

law, is no otherwise certainly right than by our making it so
by our approbation of it and voluntary subjection to it. For
the lawmakers are men, and may err, and think that law,
which they make, is for the good of the people sometimes when
it is not. And yet the actions of subjects, if they be conformable to the law, are morally good, and yet cease not to be
naturally good; and the praise of them passeth to the Author
of nature, as well as of any other good whatsoever. From
whence it appears that moral praise is not, as he says, from the
good use of liberty, but from obedience to the laws; nor moral
dispraise from the bad use of liberty, but from disobedience
to the laws. And for his consequence, 'if all things be necessary, then moral liberty is quite taken away, and with it all
true praise and dispraise,' there is neither truth in it, nor
argument offered for it; for there is nothing more necessary
than the consequence of *voluntary* actions to the *will*. And
whereas I had said, that to say a thing is good, is to say it
is as I or another would wish, or as the state would have it,
or according to the law of the land, he answers, that 'I mistake infinitely." And his reason is, because 'we often wish
what is profitable or delightful, without regarding as we ought
what is honest.' There is no man living that seeth all the
consequences of an action from the beginning to the end,
whereby to weigh the whole sum of the good with the whole
sum of the evil consequence. We choose no further than we
can weigh. That is good to every man, which is so far good
as he can see. All the real good, which we call honest and
morally virtuous, is that which is not repugnant to the law,
civil or natural; for the law is all the right reason we have,
and, (though he, as often as it disagreeth with his own reason,
deny it), is the infallible rule of moral goodness. The reason
whereof is this, that because neither mine nor the Bishop's
reason is right reason fit to be a rule of our moral actions,
we have therefore set up over ourselves a sovereign governor,
and agreed that his laws shall be unto us, whatsoever they
be, in the place of right reason, to dictate to us what is really
good. In the same manner as men in playing turn up trump,
and as in playing their game their morality consisteth in not
renouncing, so in our civil conversation our morality is all
contained in not disobeying of the laws."

many of evil: for *evil* in promise, is that they call *turpe*; evil in effect, and end, is *molestum, unpleasant, troublesome*; and evil in the means, *inutile, unprofitable, hurtful.*

As, in sense, that which is really within us, is, as I have said before, only motion, caused by the action of external objects, but in apparence; to the sight, light and colour; to the ear, sound; to the nostril, odour, &c.: so, when the action of the same object is continued from the eyes, ears, and other organs to the heart, the real effect there is nothing but motion, or endeavour; which consisteth in appetite, or aversion, to or from the object moving. But the apparence, or sense of that motion, is that we either call *delight,* or *trouble of mind.*

This motion, which is called appetite, and for the apparence of it *delight,* and *pleasure,* seemeth to be a corroboration of vital motion, and a help thereunto; and therefore such things as caused delight, were not improperly called *jucunda, a juvando,* from helping or fortifying; and the contrary, *molesta, offensive,* from hindering, and troubling the motion vital.

Pleasure therefore, or *delight,* is the apparence, or sense of good; and *molestation,* or *displeasure,* the apparence, or sense of evil. And consequently all appetite, desire, and love, is accompanied with some delight more or less; and all hatred and aversion, with more or less displeasure and offence.

Of pleasures or delights, some arise from the sense of an object present; and those may be called *pleasure of sense;* the word *sensual,* as it is used by those only that condemn them, having no place till there be laws. Of this kind are all onerations and exonerations of the body; as also all that is pleasant, in the *sight, hearing, smell, taste,* or *touch.* Others arise from the expectation, that proceeds from foresight of the end, or consequence of things; whether those things in the sense please or displease. And these are *pleasures of the mind* of him that draweth those consequences, and are generally called JOY. In the like manner, displeasures are some in the sense, and called PAIN; others in the expectation of consequences, and are called GRIEF.[4]

These simple passions called *appetite, desire, love, aversion, hate, joy,* and *grief,* have their names for divers considerations diversified. As first, when they one succeed another, they are diversely called from the opinion men have of the likelihood of attaining what they desire. Secondly, from the object loved or hated. Thirdly, from the consideration of many of them together. Fourthly, from the alteration or succession itself.

For *appetite,* with an opinion of attaining, is called HOPE.

The same, without such opinion, DESPAIR.

Aversion, with opinion of HURT from the object, FEAR.

The same, with hope of avoiding that hurt by resistance, COURAGE.

Sudden *courage,* ANGER.

Constant *hope,* CONFIDENCE of ourselves.

Constant *despair,* DIFFIDENCE of ourselves.

[4] Compare *Elements of Philosophy,* above, p. 121. Also *Human Nature,* (M. IV, 31). "*Conceptions* and *apparitions* are nothing *really,* but *motion* in some internal substance of the *head;* which motion *not stopping* there, but proceeding to the *heart,* of necessity must either *help* or *hinder* the motion which is called *vital;* when it *helpeth,* it is called *delight, contentment,* or *pleasure,* which is nothing but motion about the heart, as conception is nothing but motion in the head: and the *objects* that cause it are called *pleasant* or *delightful,* or by some name equivalent; the Latins have *jucundum, a juvando* from helping; and the same delight, with reference to the object, is called *love:* but when such motion *weakeneth* or *hindereth* the vital motion, then it is called *pain;* and in relation to that which causeth it, *hatred,* which the Latins express sometimes by *odium,* and sometimes by *taedium.*"

Anger for great hurt done to another, when we conceive the same to be done by injury, INDIGNATION.

Desire of good to another, BENEVOLENCE, GOOD WILL, CHARITY. If to man generally, GOOD NATURE.

Desire of riches, COVETOUSNESS; a name used always in signification of blame; because men contending for them, are displeased with one another attaining them; though the desire in itself be to be blamed, or allowed, according to the means by which these riches are sought.

Desire of office, or precedence, AMBITION: a name used also in the worse sense, for the reason before mentioned.

Desire of things that conduce but a little to our ends, and fear of things that are of but little hindrance, PUSILLANIMITY.

Contempt of little helps and hindrances, MAGNANIMITY.

Magnanimity, in danger of death or wounds, VALOUR, FORTITUDE.

Magnanimity in the use of riches, LIBERALITY.

Pusillanimity in the same, WRETCHEDNESS, MISERABLENESS, or PARSIMONY; as it is liked or disliked.

Love of persons for society, KINDNESS.

Love of persons for pleasing the sense only, NATURAL LUST.

Love of the same, acquired from rumination, that is, imagination of pleasure past, LUXURY.

Love of one singularly, with desire to be singularly beloved, THE PASSION OF LOVE. The same, with fear that the love is not mutual, JEALOUSY.

Desire, by doing hurt to another, to make him condemn some fact of his own, REVENGEFULNESS.

Desire to know why, and how, CURIOSITY; such as is in no living creature but *man*: so that man is distinguished, not only by his reason, but also by this singular

passion from other *animals*; in whom the appetite of
food, and other pleasures of sense, by predominance,
take away the care of knowing causes; which is a lust
of the mind, that by a perseverance of delight in the
continual and indefatigable generation of knowledge,
exceedeth the short vehemence of any carnal pleasure.

Fear of power invisible, feigned by the mind, or
imagined from tales publicly allowed, RELIGION; not
allowed, SUPERSTITION. And when the power imagined,
is truly such as we imagine, TRUE RELIGION.

Fear, without the apprehension of why, or what,
PANIC TERROR, called so from the fables, that make Pan
the author of them; whereas, in truth, there is always
in him that so feareth first, some apprehension of the
cause, though the rest run away by example, every one
supposing his fellow to know why. And therefore this
passion happens to none but in a throng, or multitude
of people.

Joy, from apprehension of novelty, ADMIRATION;
proper to man, because it excites the appetite of knowing the cause.

Joy, arising from imagination of a man's own power
and ability, is that exultation of the mind which is
called GLORYING: which if grounded upon the experience of his own former actions, is the same with *confidence*: but if grounded on the flattery of others; or
only supposed by himself, for delight in the consequences of it, is called VAIN-GLORY: which name is
properly given; because a well grounded *confidence* begetteth attempt; whereas the supposing of power does
not, and is therefore rightly called *vain*.

Grief, from opinion of want of power, is called
DEJECTION of mind.

The *vain-glory* which consisteth in the feigning or
supposing of abilities in ourselves, which we know are

not, is most incident to young men, and nourished by the histories, or fictions of gallant persons; and is corrected oftentimes by age, and employment.

Sudden glory, is the passion which maketh those *grimaces* called LAUGHTER; and is caused either by some sudden act of their own, that pleaseth them; or by the apprehension of some deformed thing in another, by comparison whereof they suddenly applaud themselves. And it is incident most to them, that are conscious of the fewest abilities in themselves; who are forced to keep themselves in their own favour, by observing the imperfections of other men. And therefore much laughter at the defects of others, is a sign of pusillanimity. For of great minds, one of the proper works is, to help and free others from scorn; and compare themselves only with the most able.

On the contrary, *sudden dejection,* is the passion that causeth WEEPING; and is caused by such accidents, as suddenly take away some vehement hope, or some prop of their power: and they are most subject to it, that rely principally on helps external, such as are women, and children. Therefore some weep for the loss of friends; others for their unkindness; others for the sudden stop made to their thoughts of revenge, by reconciliation. But in all cases, both laughter, and weeping, are sudden motions; custom taking them both away. For no man laughs at old jests; or weeps for an old calamity.

Grief, for the discovery of some defect of ability, is SHAME, or the passion that discovereth itself in BLUSHING; and consisteth in the apprehension of some thing dishonourable; and in young men, is a sign of the love of good reputation, and commendable; in old men it is a sign of the same; but because it comes too late, not commendable.

The *contempt* of good reputation is called IMPUDENCE.

Grief, for the calamity of another, is PITY; and ariseth from the imagination that the like calamity may befall himself; and therefore is called also COMPASSION, and in the phrase of this present time a FELLOW-FEELING: and therefore for calamity arriving from great wickedness, the best men have the least pity; and for the same calamity those hate pity, that think themselves least obnoxious to the same.

Contempt, or little sense of the calamity of others, is that which men call CRUELTY; proceeding from security of their own fortune. For, that any man should take pleasure in other men's great harms; without other end of his own, I do not conceive it possible.

Grief, for the success of a competitor in wealth, honour, or other good, if it be joined with endeavour to enforce our own abilities to equal or exceed him, is called EMULATION: but joined with endeavour to supplant, or hinder a competitor, ENVY.

When in the mind of man, appetites, and aversions, hopes, and fears, concerning one and the same thing, arise alternately; and divers good and evil consequences of the doing, or omitting the thing propounded, come successively into our thoughts; so that sometimes we have an appetite to it; sometimes an aversion from it; sometimes hope to be able to do it; sometimes despair, or fear to attempt it; the whole sum of desires, aversions, hopes and fears continued till the thing be either done, or thought impossible, is that we call DELIBERATION.

Therefore of things past, there is no *deliberation*; because manifestly impossible to be changed: nor of things known to be impossible, or thought so; because men know, or think such deliberation vain. But of things impossible, which we think possible, we may deliberate; not knowing it is in vain. And it is called *deliberation*; because it is a putting an end to the *liberty* we had of doing, or omitting, according to our own appetite, or aversion.

This alternate succession of appetites, aversions, hopes and fears, is no less in other living creatures than in man: and therefore beasts also deliberate.

Every *deliberation* is then said to *end*, when that whereof they deliberate, is either done, or thought impossible; because till then we retain the liberty of doing, or omitting; according to our appetite, or aversion.

In *deliberation*, the last appetite, or aversion, immediately adhering to the action, or to the omission thereof, is that we call the WILL; the act, not the faculty, of *willing*. And beasts that have *deliberation*, must necessarily also have *will*. The definition of the *will*, given commonly by the Schools, that it is a *rational appetite*, is not good. For if it were, then could there be no voluntary act against reason. For a *voluntary act* is that, which proceedeth from the *will*, and no other. But if instead of a rational appetite, we shall say an appetite resulting from a precedent deliberation, then the definition is the same that I have given here. *Will*, therefore, *is the last appetite in deliberating*. And though we say in common discourse, a man had a will once to do a thing, that nevertheless he forbore to do; yet that is properly but an inclination, which makes no action voluntary; because the action depends not of it, but of the last inclination, or appetite. For if the intervenient appetites, make any action voluntary; then by the same reason all intervenient aversions, should make the same action involuntary; and so one and the same action, should be both voluntary and involuntary.

By this it is manifest, that not only actions that have their beginning from covetousness, ambition, lust, or other appetites to the thing propounded; but also those

that have thèir beginning from aversion, or fear of those
consequences that follow the omission, are *voluntary
actions*.[5]

[5] Compare *Elements of Philosophy*, above p. 123, and *Leviathan*, (M. III, 360). "Sense, memory, understanding, reason,
and opinion are not in our power to change; but always, and
necessarily such, as the things we see, hear, and consider
suggest unto us; and therefore are not effects of our will,
but our will of them." Also *Human Nature*, (M. IV, 67).
"It hath been declared already, how *external* objects cause
conceptions, and conceptions, *appetite* and *fear*, which are the
first unperceived beginnings of our actions: for *either* the
actions immediately follow the first appetite, as when we do
anything upon a sudden; *or else* to our first appetite there
succeedeth some conception of evil to happen to us by such
actions, which is fear, and which holdeth us from proceeding.
And to that fear may succeed a new appetite, and to that
appetite another fear alternately, till the action be either
done, or some accident come between, to make it impossible;
and so this alternate appetite and fear ceaseth. This *alternate
succession of appetite and fear* during all the time the action
is in our power to do or not to do, is that we call *deliberation*;
which name hath been given it for that part of the definition
wherein it is said that it lasteth so long as the action, whereof
we deliberate, is in our power: for, so long we have liberty to
do or not to do; and deliberation signifieth a taking away of
our own liberty. *Deliberation* therefore requireth in the action
deliberated *two conditions*; one, that it be *future*; the other,
that there be *hope* of doing it, or possibility of not doing it;
for, *appetite* and *fear* are *expectations* of the future; and
there is no expectation of good, without hope; or of evil,
without possibility: of *necessaries* therefore there is *no deliberation*. In deliberation, the last appetite, as also the last
fear, is called *will*, viz. the last appetite, will to do, or will to
omit. It is all one therefore to say *will* and *last will*: for,
though a man express his present inclination and appetite
concerning the disposing of his goods, by words or writings;
yet shall it not be counted his will, because he hath still liberty
to dispose of them otherways: but when death taketh away
that liberty, then it is his will. *Voluntary* actions and omis-
sions are such as have beginning in the *will*; all other are
involuntary, or *mixed voluntary*; *involuntary*, such as he
doth by necessity of nature, as when he is pushed, or falleth,
and thereby doth good or hurt to another: *mixed*, such as
participate of both; as when a man is carried to prison, going
is voluntary, to the prison, is involùntary: the example of

The forms of speech by which the passions are expressed, are partly the same, and partly different from those, by which we express our thoughts. And first, generally all passions may be expressed *indicatively*;

him that throweth his goods out of a ship into the sea, to save his person, is of an action altogether voluntary: for, there is nothing therein involuntary, but the hardness of the choice, which is not his action, but the action of the winds: what he himself doth, is no more against his will, than to flee from danger is against the will of him that seeth no other means to preserve himself. *Voluntary* also are the actions that proceed from sudden *anger*, or *other* sudden *appetite* in such men as can discern good or evil: for, in them the time precedent *is* to be judged deliberation: for then also he deliberateth in what cases it is good to strike, deride, or do any other action proceeding from anger or other such sudden passion. *Appetite, fear, hope,* and the rest of the passions are *not* called *voluntary*; for they proceed *not from, but are the will*; and the will is not voluntary: for, a man can no more say he will will, than he will will will, and so make an infinite repetition of the word [*will*]; which is absurd, and insignificant. Forasmuch as *will to do is appetite,* and *will to omit, fear*; the *cause* of *appetite* and *fear* is the *cause* also of our *will*: but the propounding of the benefits and harms, that is to say, of reward and punishment, is the cause of our appetite, and of our fears, and therefore also of our wills, so far forth as we believe that such rewards and benefits as are propounded, shall arrive unto us; and consequently, our *wills* follow our *opinions*, as our *actions* follow our *wills*; in which sense they say truly, and properly, that say the world is governed by opinion. When the wills of many concur to one and the same action and effect, this *concourse* of their *wills* is called *consent*; by which we must not understand one will of many men, for every man hath his several will, but many wills to the producing of one effect: but when the *wills* of two divers men *produce* such actions as are reciprocally *resistant* one to the other, this is called *contention*; and, being upon the persons one of another, *battle*: whereas actions proceeding from *consent*, are mutual *aid*. When many wills are involved or included in the will of one or more consenting, (which how it may be, shall be hereafter declared) then is that involving of many wills in one or more, called *union*. In *deliberations* interrupted, as they may be by *diversion* of other business, or by *sleep*, the last *appetite* of such part of the deliberation is called *intention*, or *purpose*." Also *Human Nature* (M. IV, 240). "He is *free* to do a thing, that may do as *I love, I fear, I joy, I deliberate, I will, I command*: but some of them have particular expressions by themselves, which nevertheless are not affirmations, unless it be when they serve to make other inferences, besides that of the passion they proceed from. Deliberation is expressed *subjunctively*; which is a speech proper to signify suppositions, with their consequences; as, *if this be done, then this will follow*; and differs not from the language of reasoning, save that reasoning is in general words; but deliberation for the most part is of particulars. The language of desire, and aversion, is *imperative*; as *do this, forbear that*; which when the party is obliged to do, or forbear, is *command*; otherwise *prayer*; or else *counsel*. The language of vain-glory, of indignation, pity and revengefulness, *optative*: but of the desire to know, there is a peculiar expression called *interrogative*; as, *what is it, when shall it, how is it done*, and *why so?* other language of the passions I find none: for cursing, swearing, reviling, and the like, do not signify as speech; but as the actions of a tongue accustomed.

These forms of speech, I say, are expressions, or voluntary significations of our passions: but certain signs they be not; because they may be used arbitrarily, whether they that use them, have such passions or not. The best signs of passions present, are either in the

---

it if he have the will to do it, and may forbear, if he have the will to forbear. And yet if there be a *necessity* that he shall have the *will* to do it, the action is necessarily to follow: and if there be a *necessity* that he shall have the *will* to forbear, the forbearing also will be necessary. The question therefore is not, whether a man be a *free agent*, that is to say, whether he can write or forbear, speak or be silent, according to his *will*; but, whether the *will* to write, and the *will* to forbear, come upon him according to his *will*, or according to anything else in his own power. I acknowledge this *liberty*, that I *can* do it if I *will*; but to say, I can *will* if I *will*, I take to be an absurd speech." Compare also *Leviathan*, (below, p. 369).

countenance, motions of the body, actions, and ends, or aims, which we otherwise know the man to have.

And because in deliberation, the appetites, and aversions, are raised by foresight of the good and evil consequences, and sequels of the action whereof we deliberate; the good or evil effect thereof dependeth on the foresight of a long chain of consequences, of which very seldom any man is able to see the end. But for so far as a man seeth, if the good in those consequences be greater than the evil, the whole chain is that which writers call *apparent,* or *seeming good.* And contrarily, when the evil exceedeth the good, the whole is *apparent,* or *seeming evil*: so that he who hath by experience, or reason, the greatest and surest prospect of consequences, deliberates best himself; and is able when he will, to give the best counsel unto others.

Continual success in obtaining those things which a man from time to time desireth, that is to say, continual prospering, is that men call FELICITY; I mean the felicity of this life. For there is no such thing as perpetual tranquillity of mind, while we live here; because life itself is but motion, and can never be without desire, nor without fear, no more than without sense. What kind of felicity God hath ordained to them that devoutly honour Him, a man shall no sooner know, than enjoy; being joys, that now are as incomprehensible, as the word of school-men *beatifical vision* is unintelligible.

The form of speech whereby men signify their opinion of the goodness of anything, is PRAISE. That whereby they signify the power and greatness of anything, is MAGNIFYING. And that whereby they signify the opinion they have of a man's felicity, is by the Greeks called μακαρισμός, for which we have no name in our tongue. And thus much is sufficient for the present purpose, to have been said of the PASSIONS.

SUPPLEMENT FROM

LIBERTY AND NECESSITY

MY OPINION ABOUT LIBERTY AND NECESSITY.[6]

FIRST I conceive, that when it cometh into a man's mind to do or not to do some certain action, if he have no time to *deliberate*, the doing it or abstaining *necessarily* follow the *present* thought he hath of the *good* or *evil* consequence thereof to himself. As for example, in sudden *anger*, the *action* shall follow the thought of *revenge*; in sudden *fear*, the thought of *escape*. Also when a man hath time to *deliberate*, but deliberates not, because never anything appeared that could make him doubt of the consequence, the *action* follows his opinion of the *goodness* or *harm* of it. These actions I call VOL-UNTARY, my Lord, if I understand him aright that calls them SPONTANEOUS. I call them *voluntary*, because those *actions* that follow immediately the *last* appetite, are *voluntary*, and here where is one only appetite, that one is the last. Besides, I see it is reasonable to punish a *rash* action, which could not be justly done by man to man, unless the same were *voluntary*. For no *action* of a man can be said to be without *deliberation*, though never so sudden, because it is supposed he had time to *deliberate* all the precedent time of his life, whether he should do that kind of action or not. And hence it is, that he that killeth in a sudden passion of *anger*, shall nevertheless be justly put to *death*, because all the time, wherein he was able to consider whether to kill were

⁶M. IV, 272-278.

good or evil, shall be held for one continual *deliberation*, and consequently the killing shall be judged to proceed from *election*.

Secondly, I conceive when a man *deliberates* whether he shall do a thing or not do it, that he does nothing else but consider whether it be better for himself to do it or not to do it. And to *consider* an action, is to imagine the *consequences* of it, both *good* and *evil*. From whence is to be inferred, that *deliberation* is nothing else but *alternate* imagination of the *good* and *evil* sequels of an *action*, or, which is the same thing, alternate *hope* and *fear*, or alternate *appetite* to do or quit the action of which he *deliberateth*.

Thirdly, I conceive that in all *deliberations*, that is to say, in all alternate *succession* of contrary *appetites*, the last is that which we call the WILL, and is immediately before the doing of the action, or next before the doing of it become impossible. All other *appetites* to do, and to quit, that come upon a man during his deliberations, are called *intentions* and *inclinations*, but not *wills*, there being but one *will*, which also in this case may be called the *last will*, though the *intentions* change often.

Fourthly, I conceive that those *actions*, which a man is said to do upon *deliberation*, are said to be *voluntary*, and done upon *choice* and *election*, so that *voluntary* action, and action proceeding from *election* is the same thing; and that of a *voluntary agent*, it is all one to say, he is *free*, and to say, he hath not made an end of *deliberating*.

Fifthly, I conceive *liberty* to be rightly defined in this manner: *Liberty is the absence of all the impediments to action that are not contained in the nature and intrinsical quality of the agent.* As for example, the water is said to descend *freely*, or to have *liberty* to

descend by the channel of the river, because there is no
impediment that way, but not across, because the banks
are impediments. And though the water cannot ascend,
yet men never say it wants the *liberty* to ascend, but
the *faculty* or *power*, because the impediment is in the
nature of the water, and intrinsical. So also we say,
he that is tied, wants the *liberty* to go, because the
impediment is not in him, but in his bands; whereas
we say not so of him that is sick or lame, because the
impediment is in himself.

Sixthly, I conceive that nothing taketh beginning
from *itself*, but from the *action* of some other immediate *agent* without itself. And that therefore, when
first a man hath an *appetite* or *will* to something, to
which immediately before he had no appetite nor will,
the *cause* of his *will*, is not the *will* itself, but *something*
else not in his own disposing. So that whereas it is out
of controversy, that of *voluntary* actions the *will* is the
necessary cause, and by this which is said, the *will* is
also *caused* by other things whereof it disposeth not, it
followeth, that *voluntary actions* have all of them *necessary* causes, and therefore are *necessitated*.

Seventhly, I hold that to be a *sufficient cause*, to
which nothing is wanting that is needful to the producing of the *effect*. The same also is a *necessary* cause.
For if it be possible that a *sufficient* cause shall not
bring forth the *effect*, then there wanteth somewhat
which was needful to the producing of it, and so the
cause was not *sufficient*; but if it be impossible that a
sufficient cause should not produce the *effect*, then is a
sufficient cause a *necessary* cause, for that is said to
produce an effect *necessarily* that cannot but produce it.
Hence it is manifest, that whatsoever is produced, is
produced *necessarily*; for whatsoever is produced hath
had a *sufficient* cause to produce it, or else it had not

been; and therefore also *voluntary* actions are *necessitated*.

Lastly, that ordinary *definition* of a *free agent*, namely, *that a* free agent *is that, which, when all things are present which are needful to produce the* effect, *can nevertheless not produce it*, implies a contradiction, and is nonsense; being as much as to say, the cause may be *sufficient*, that is to say, *necessary*, and yet the *effect* shall not follow.

MY REASONS

For the first five points, wherein it is explicated I, what *spontaneity* is; II, *what deliberation* is; III, what *will, propension*, and *appetite* are; IV, what a *free agent* is: V, what *liberty* is; there can no other proof be offered but every man's own experience, by reflection on himself, and remembering what he useth in his mind, that is, what he himself meaneth when he saith an action is *spontaneous*, a man *deliberates*, such is his *will*, that *agent* or that *action* is *free*. Now he that reflecteth so on himself, cannot but be satisfied, that *deliberation* is the *consideration of the good and evil sequels of an action to come*; that by *spontaneity* is meant *inconsiderate action*, or else nothing is meant by it; that *will* is the *last act of our deliberation*; that a *free agent* is he *that can do if he will*, and *forbear if he will*; and that *liberty* is *the absence of external impediments*. But to those that out of custom speak not what they conceive, but what they hear, and are not able, or will not take the pains to consider what they think when they hear such words, no argument can be sufficient, because *experience* and *matter of fact* are not verified by other men's arguments, but by every man's own *sense* and *memory*. For example, how can it be proved that

to *love* a thing and to think it *good* is all one, to a man
that doth not mark his own meaning by those words?
Or how can it be proved that *eternity* is not *nunc stans*
to a man that says those words by custom, and never
considers how he can conceive the thing in his mind?

Also the sixth point, that a man cannot imagine anything to begin *without a cause,* can no other way be
made known, but by trying how he can imagine it; but
if he try, he shall find as much reason, if there be no
cause of the thing, to conceive it should begin at one
time as another, that he hath equal reason to think it
should begin at all times, which is impossible, and therefore he must think there was some special cause why
it began then, rather than sooner or later; or else that
it began never, but was *eternal.*

For the seventh point, which is, that all *events* have
necessary causes, it is there proved, in that they have
sufficient causes.   Further let us in this place also suppose any event never so casual, as the throwing, for
example, *ames ace* upon a pair of dice, and see, if it must
not have been *necessary* before it was thrown.   For seeing it was thrown, it had a *beginning,* and consequently
a *sufficient* cause to produce it, consisting partly in the
dice, partly in outward things, as the posture of the
parts of the *hand,* the measure of *force* applied by
the caster, the posture of the parts of the *table,* and the
like.   In sum, there was nothing wanting which was
necessarily requisite to the producing of that particular
cast, and consequently the cast was necessarily thrown;
for if it had not been thrown, there had wanted somewhat requisite to the throwing of it, and so the cause
had not been *sufficient.*   In the like manner it may be
proved that every other accident, how *contingent* soever
it seem, or how *voluntary* soever it be, is produced *necessarily,* which is that that my Lord Bishop disputes

against. The same may be proved also in this manner. Let the case be put, for example, of the weather. *It is necessary that to-morrow it shall rain or not rain.* If therefore it be not *necessary* it shall rain, it is *necessary* it shall not rain, otherwise there is no necessity that the proposition, *it shall rain or not rain,* should be true. I know there be some that say, it may necessarily be true that one of the two shall come to pass, but not, singly that it shall rain, or that it shall not rain, which is as much to say, *one* of them is *necessary,* yet neither of them is *necessary*; and therefore to seem to avoid that absurdity, they make a distinction, that neither of them is true *determinate,* but *indeterminate*; which distinction either signifies no more but this, one of them is true, but we know not which, and so the necessity remains, though we know it not; or if the meaning of the distinction be not that, it hath no meaning, and they might as well have said, one of them is true *Titirice,* but neither of them, *Tu patulice.*

The last thing, in which also consisteth the whole controversy, namely that there is no such thing as an agent, *which when all things requisite to action are present, can nevertheless forbear to produce it*; or, which is all one, that there is no such thing as *freedom from necessity,* is easily inferred from that which hath been before alleged. For if it be an *agent,* it can *work*; and if it *work,* there is nothing wanting of what is requisite to produce the *action,* and consequently the cause of the action is *sufficient*; and if *sufficient,* then also *necessary,* as hath been proved before.

And thus you see how the *inconveniences,* which his Lordship objecteth must follow upon the holding of *necessity,* are avoided, and the *necessity* itself *demonstratively* proved. To which I could add, if I thought it good logic, the *inconvenience* of denying *necessity,* as that it destroyeth both the *decrees* and the *prescience* of God Almighty; for whatsoever God hath *purposed* to bring to pass by *man*, as an instrument, or forseeth shall come to pass; a man, if he have *liberty*, such as his Lordship affirmeth, from *necessitation*, might frustrate, and make not to come to pass, and God should either not *foreknow* it, and not *decree* it, or he should *foreknow* such things shall be, as shall never be, and *decree* that which shall never *come to pass*.

CHAPTER VII

OF THE ENDS, OR RESOLUTIONS OF DISCOURSE

OF ALL *discourse*, governed by desire of knowledge, there is at last an *end*, either by attaining, or by giving over. And in the chain of discourse, wheresoever it be interrupted, there is an end for that time.

If the discourse be merely mental, it consisteth of thoughts that the thing will be, and will not be; or that it has been, and has not been, alternately. So that wheresoever you break off the chain of the man's discourse, you leave him in a presumption of *it will be*, or, *it will not be*; or, *it has been*, or, *has not been*. All which is *opinion*.[1] And that which is alternate appetite, in deliberating concerning good and evil; the same is alternate opinion, in the enquiry of the truth of *past*, and *future*. And as the last appetite in deliberation, is called the *will*; so the last opinion in search of the truth of past, and future, is called the JUDGMENT,[2] or *reso-*

[1] Compare above p. 201, n. 5.
[2] Hobbes does not usually use the term in this sense. For his usual meaning compare above pp. 114-15, below pp. 218-19 and *Human Nature*, (M. IV, 55). "A man delighteth

lute and *final sentence* of him that *discourseth*. And as
the whole chain of appetites alternate, in the question of
good, or bad, is called *deliberation*; so the whole chain
of opinions alternate, in the question of true, or false, is
called DOUBT.

No discourse whatsoever, can end in absolute knowledge of fact, past, or to come. For, as for the knowledge
of fact, it is originally, sense; and ever after, memory.
And for the knowledge of consequence, which I have
said before is called science, it is not absolute, but conditional. No man can know by discourse, that this, or
that, is, has been, or will be; which is to know absolutely: but only, that if this be, that is; if this has been,
that has been; if this shall be, that shall be: which is
to know conditionally; and that not the consequence of
one thing to another; but of one name of a thing, to
another name of the same thing.

And therefore, when the discourse is put into speech,
and begins with the definitions of words, and proceeds
by connexion of the same into general affirmations, and
of these again into syllogisms; the end or last sum is
called the conclusion; and the thought of the mind by
it signified, is that conditional knowledge, or knowledge
of the consequence of words, which is commonly called

---

himself either with finding expected *similitude* of things, otherwise much unlike, in which men place the excellency of
fancy, * * * * * * * or else in discerning suddenly
dissimilitude in things that otherwise appear the same. And
this virtue of the mind is that by which men attain to exact
and perfect *knowledge*; and the pleasure thereof consisteth
in continual instruction, and in distinction of places, persons,
and seasons, and is commonly termed by the name of *judgment*; for, to judge is nothing else, but to distinguish or
discern: and both *fancy* and *judgment* are commonly comprehended under the name of *wit*, which seemeth to be a tenuity
and agility of spirits, contrary to that restiness of the spirits
supposed in those that are dull."

SCIENCE.[3] But if the first ground of such discourse, be not definitions; or if the definitions be not rightly joined together into syllogisms, then the end or conclusion, is again OPINION, namely of the truth of somewhat said, though sometimes in absurd and senseless words, without possibility of being understood. When two, or more, men know of one and the same fact, they are said to be CONSCIOUS of it one to another; which is as much as to know it together. And because such are fittest witnesses of the facts of one another, or of a third; it was, and ever will be reputed a very evil act, for any man to speak against his *conscience*: or to corrupt or force another so to do: insomuch that the plea of conscience, has been always hearkened unto very diligently in all times. Afterwards, men made use of the same word metaphorically, for the knowledge of their own secret facts, and secret thoughts; and therefore it is rhetorically said, that the conscience is a thousand witnesses. And last of all, men, vehemently in love with their own new opinions, though never so absurd, and obstinately bent to maintain them, gave those their opinions also that reverenced name of conscience, as if they would have it seem unlawful, to change or speak against them; and so pretend to know they are true, when they know at most, but that they think so.[4]

[3] For other references to knowledge and science see above Chapter V, below Chapter IX, and index.

[4] Compare *Human Nature*, (M. IV, 29). "It is either *science* or *opinion* which we commonly mean by the word *conscience*: for men say that such and such a thing is true in or upon their conscience; which they *never* do, when they think it *doubtful*; and therefore they *know*, or *think* they know it to be true. But men, when they say things upon their conscience, are not therefore presumed certainly to know the truth of what they say; it remaineth then, that that word is used by them that have an *opinion*, *not* only of the *truth* of the thing, *but* also of their *knowledge* of it, to which the *truth* of the

When a man's discourse beginneth not at definitions,
it beginneth either at some other contemplation of his
own, and then it is still called opinion; or it beginneth
at some saying of another, of whose ability to know

---

proposition is consequent. *Conscience* I therefore define to be
opinion of evidence." (M. IV, 163). "A subject may no
more govern his own actions according to his own discretion
and judgment, or, which is all one, conscience, as the present
occasions from time to time shall dictate to him; but must
be tied to do according to that will only, which once for all
he had long ago laid up, and involved in the wills of the major
part of an assembly, or in the will of some one man. But this
is really no inconvenience. For, as it hath been showed before,
it is the only means, by which we have any possibility of preserving ourselves. For if every man were allowed this liberty
of following his conscience, in such difference of consciences,
they would not live together in peace an hour. But it appeareth a great inconvenience to every man in particular, to be
debarred of this liberty, because every one apart considereth
it as in himself, and not as in the rest; by which means,
liberty appeareth in the likeness of rule and government over
others. For where one man is at liberty, and the rest bound,
there that one hath government; which honour, he that understandeth not so much, demanding by the name simply of
liberty, thinketh it a great grievance and injury to be denied
it." (M. IV, 172). "To take away this scruple of conscience,
concerning obedience to human laws, amongst those that interpret to themselves the word of God in the Holy Scriptures,
I propound to their consideration, first, that no human law
is intended to oblige the conscience of a man, unless it break
out into action, either of the tongue, or other part of the
body. The law made thereupon would be of none effect,
because no man is able to discern, but by word or other action
whether such law be kept or broken." (M. IV, 186). "And
though it be true, whatsoever a man does against his conscience, is sin; yet the obedience in these cases, is neither sin,
nor against the conscience. For the conscience being nothing
else but a man's settled judgment and opinion, when he hath
once transferred his right of judging to another, that which
shall be commanded, is no less his judgment, than the judgment of that other. So that in obedience to laws, a man doth
still according to his own conscience, but not his private conscience. And whatsoever is done contrary to private conscience, is then a sin, when the laws have left him to his own
liberty, and never else. And then whatsoever a man doth,
not only believing it is ill done, but doubting whether it be

the truth, and of whose honesty in not deceiving, he doubteth not; and then the discourse is not so much concerning the thing, as the person; and the resolution is called BELIEF, and FAITH: *faith, in* the man; *belief,* both *of* the man, and *of* the truth of what he says. So' that in belief are two opinions: one of the saying of the man; the other of his virtue. To *have faith in,* or *trust to,* or *believe a man,* signify the same thing; namely, an opinion of the veracity of the man: but to *believe what is said,* signifieth only an opinion of the truth of the saying. But we are to observe that this phrase, *I believe in*; as also the Latin, *credo in*; and the Greek, πιστεύω εἰς, are never used but in the writings of divines. Instead of them, in other writings are put, *I believe him; I trust him; I have faith in him; I rely on him*: and in Latin, *credo illi: fido illi*: and in Greek, πιστεύω αὐτῷ: and that this singularity of the ecclesiastic use of the word hath raised many disputes about the right object of the Christian faith.

But by *believing in,* as it is in the creed, is meant, not trust in the person; but confession and acknowledgment of the doctrine. For not only Christians, but all manner of men do so believe in God, as to hold

---

ill or not, is done ill, in case he may lawfully omit the doing." Also *Leviathan* (M. III, 311). "Another doctrine repugnant to civil society, is, that *whatsoever a man does against his conscience, is sin;* and it dependeth on the presumption of making himself judge of good and evil. For a man's conscience, and his judgment is the same thing, and as the judgment, so also the conscience may be erroneous. Therefore, though he that is subject to no civil law, sinneth in all he does against his conscience, because he has no other rule to follow but his own reason; yet it is not so with him that lives in a commonwealth; because the law is the public conscience, by which he hath already undertaken to be guided. Otherwise in such diversity, as there is of private consciences, which are but private opinions, the commonwealth must needs be distracted, and no man dare to obey the sovereign power, further than it shall seem good in his own eyes."

all for truth they hear him say, whether they understand it, or not; which is all the faith and trust can possibly be had in any person whatsoever: but they do not all believe the doctrine of the creed.

From whence we may infer, that when we believe any saying whatsoever it be, to be true, from arguments taken, not from the thing itself, or from the principles of natural reason, but from the authority, and good opinion we have, of him that hath said it; then is the speaker, or person we believe in, or trust in, and whose word we take, the object of our faith; and the honour done in believing, is done to him only. And consequently, when we believe that the Scriptures are the word of God, having no immediate revelation from God himself, our belief, faith, and trust is in the church; whose word we take, and acquiesce therein. And they that believe that which a prophet relates unto them in the name of God, to take the word of the prophet, do honour to him, and in him trust, and believe, touching the truth of what he relateth, whether he be a true, or a false prophet. And so it is also with all other history. For if I should not believe all that is written by historians, of the glorious acts of *Alexander*, or *Caesar*; I do not think the ghost of *Alexander*, or *Caesar*, had any just cause to be offended; or anybody else, but the historian. If *Livy* say the gods made once a cow speak, and we believe it not; we distrust not God therein, but *Livy*. So that it is evident, that whatsoever we believe, upon no other reason, than what is drawn from authority of men only, and their writings; whether they be sent from God or not, is faith in men only.[5]

[5] Compare *Philosophical Rudiments*, (M. II, 304). "But when our reasons, for which we assent to some proposition, derive not from the *proposition itself*, but from the *person propounding,* whom we esteem so learned that he is not deceived, and we see no reason why he should deceive us; our

CHAPTER VIII

OF THE VIRTUES COMMONLY CALLED INTELLECTUAL; AND THEIR CONTRARY DEFECTS

VIRTUE generally, in all sorts of subjects, is somewhat that is valued for eminence; and consisteth in comparison. For if all things were equal in all men,

---

assent, because it grows not from any confidence of our own, but from another man's knowledge, is called *faith*. And by the confidence of whom we do believe, we are said *to trust them*, or *to trust in them*. By what hath been said, the difference appears, first, between *faith* and *profession*; for that is always joined with inward assent, this not always. That is an inward persuasion of the mind, this an outward obedience. Next, between *faith* and *opinion*: for this depends on our own reason, that on the good esteem we have of another. Lastly, between *faith* and *knowledge*; for this deliberately takes a proposition broken and chewed; that swallows it down whole and entire. The explication of words, whereby the matter enquired after is propounded, is conducible to knowledge; nay, the only way *to know*, is by definition. But this is prejudicial to *faith*; for those things which exceed human capacity, and are propounded to be believed, are never more evident by explication, but, on the contrary, more obscure and harder to be credited. And the same thing befalls a man, who endeavours to demonstrate *the mysteries of faith* by natural reason, which happens to a sick man, who will needs chew before he will swallow his wholesome but bitter pills; whence it comes to pass, that he presently brings them up again; which perhaps would otherwise, if he had taken them well down, have proved his remedy." Also *Human Nature*, (M. IV, 30). "*Belief*, which is the admitting of propositions upon *trust*, in many cases is no less free from *doubt*, than perfect and manifest *knowledge*: for as there is nothing whereof there is not some cause; so, when there is doubt, there must be some cause thereof conceived. Now there be many things which we receive from *report of others*, of which it is impossible to imagine any cause of *doubt*: for what can be opposed against the consent of all men, in things they can

nothing would be prized. And by *virtues intellectual*, are always understood such abilities of the mind, as men praise, value, and desire should be in themselves; and go commonly under the name of a *good wit*; though the same word *wit*, be used also, to distinguish one certain ability from the rest.[1]

These *virtues* are of two sorts; *natural*, and *acquired*. By natural, I mean not, that which a man hath from his birth: for that is nothing else but sense; wherein men differ so little one from another, and from brute beasts, as it is not to be reckoned amongst virtues. But I mean, that *wit*, which is gotten by use only, and experience; without method, culture, or instruction. This NATURAL WIT, consisteth principally in two things; *celerity of imagining*, that is, swift succession of one thought to another; and *steady direction* to some approved end. On the contrary a slow imagination, maketh that defect, or fault of the mind, which is commonly called DULLNESS, *stupidity*, and sometimes by other names that signify slowness of motion, or difficulty to be moved.

And this difference of quickness, is caused by the difference of men's passions; that love and dislike, some one thing, some another: and therefore some men's thoughts run one way, some another; and are held to, and observe differently the things that pass through their imagination. And whereas in this succession of men's thoughts, there is nothing to observe in the things they think on, but either in what they be *like one another*, or in what they be *unlike*, or *what they serve for*, or *how they serve to such a purpose*; those that ob-

---

know, and have no cause to report otherwise than they are, such as is a great part of our *histories*, unless a man would say that all the world had *conspired to deceive him*."

[1] For the distinction of moral virtues see above p. 189, n. 3.

serve their similitudes, in case they be such as are but rarely observed by others, are said to have a *good wit*; by which, in this occasion, is meant a *good fancy*. But they that observe their differences, and dissimilitudes; which is called *distinguishing*, and *discerning*, and *judging* between thing and thing; in case such discerning be not easy, are said to have a *good judgment*; and particularly in matter of conversation and business, wherein, times, places, and persons are to be discerned, this virtue is called DISCRETION. The former, that is, fancy, without the help of judgment, is not commended as a virtue: but the latter which is judgment, and discretion, is commended for itself, without the help of fancy. Besides the discretion of times, places, and persons, necessary to a good fancy, there is required also an often application of his thoughts to their end; that is to say, to some use to be made of them. This done; he that hath this virtue, will be easily fitted with similitudes, that will please, not only by illustrations of his discourse, and adorning it with new and apt metaphors; but also, by the rarity of their invention. But without steadiness, and direction to some end, a great fancy is one kind of madness; such as they have, that entering into any discourse, are snatched from their purpose, by every thing that comes in their thought, into so many, and so long digressions, and parentheses, that they utterly lose themselves: which kind of folly, I know no particular name for: but the cause of it is: sometimes want of experience; whereby that seemeth to a man new and rare, which doth not so to others: sometimes pusillanimity; by which that seems great to him, which other men think a trifle: and whatsoever is new, or great, and therefore thought fit to be told, withdraws a man by degrees from the intended way of his discourse.

In a good poem, whether it be *epic*, or *dramatic*; as

also in *sonnets, epigrams,* and other pieces, both judgment and fancy are required: but the fancy must be
more eminent: because they please for the extravagancy;
but ought not to please by indiscretion.

In a good history, the judgment must be eminent;
because the goodness consisteth, in the method, in the
truth, and in the choice of the actions that are most
profitable to be known. Fancy has no place, but only
in adorning the style.

In orations of praise, and in invectives, the fancy
is predominant; because the design is not truth, but
to honour or dishonour; which is done by noble, or by
vile comparisons. The judgment does but suggest what
circumstances make an action laudable, or culpable.

In hortatives, and pleadings, as truth, or disguise
serveth best to the design in hand; so is the judgment,
or the fancy most required.

In demonstration, in counsel, and all rigorous search
of truth, judgment does all, except sometimes the understanding have need to be opened by some apt similitude;
and then there is so much use of fancy. But for metaphors, they are in this case utterly excluded. For
seeing they openly profess deceit; to admit them into
counsel, or reasoning, were manifest folly.

And in any discourse whatsoever, if the defect of
discretion be apparent, how extravagant soever the
fancy be, the whole discourse will be taken for a sign
of want of wit; and so will it never when the discretion
is manifest, though the fancy be never so ordinary.

The secret thoughts of a man run over all things,
holy, profane, clean, obscene, grave, and light, without
shame, or blame; which verbal discourse cannot do,
farther than the judgment shall approve of the time,
place, and persons. An anatomist, or a physician may
speak, or write his judgment of unclean things: because

it is not to please, but profit: but for another man to write his extravagant, and pleasant fancies of the same, is as if a man, from being tumbled into the dirt, should come and present himself before good company. And it is the want of discretion that makes the difference. Again, in professed remissness of mind, and familiar company, a man may play with the sounds, and equivocal significations of words; and that many times with encounters of extraordinary fancy: but in a sermon, or in public, or before persons unknown, or whom we ought to reverence; there is no gingling of words that will not be accounted folly: and the difference is only in the want of discretion. So that where wit is wanting, it is not fancy that is wanting, but discretion. Judgment therefore without fancy is wit, but fancy without judgment, not.

When the thoughts of a man, that has a design in hand, running over a multitude of things, observe how they conduce to that design; or what design they may conduce unto; if his observations be such as are not easy, or usual, this wit of his is called PRUDENCE; and depends on much experience, and memory of the like things, and their consequences heretofore. In which there is not so much difference of men; as there is in their fancies and judgment; because the experience of men equal in age, is not much unequal, as to the quantity; but lies in different occasions; every one having his private designs. To govern well a family, and a kingdom, are not different degrees of prudence; but different sorts of business; no more than to draw a picture in little, or as great, or greater than the life, are different degrees of art. A plain husbandman is more prudent in affairs of his own house, than a privy-councillor in the affairs of another man.

To prudence, if you add the use of unjust, or dis-

honest means, such as usually are prompted to men by
fear, or want; you have that crooked wisdom, which is
called CRAFT; which is the sign of pusillanimity. For
magnanimity is contempt of unjust, or dishonest helps.
And that which the Latins call *versutia*, translated into
English, *shifting*, and is a putting off of a present
danger or incommodity, by engaging into a greater, as
when a man robs one to pay another, is but a shorter-
sighted craft, called *versutia*, from *versura*, which signifies taking money at usury for the present payment
of interest.

As for *acquired wit*, I mean acquired by method
and instruction, there is none but reason; which is
grounded on the right use of speech, and produceth the
sciences. But of reason and science I have already
spoken, in the fifth and sixth chapters.

The causes of this difference of wits are in the passions; and the difference of passions proceedeth, partly
from the different constitution of the body, and partly
from different education. For if the difference proceeded from the temper of the brain, and the organs of
sense, either exterior or interior, there would be no less
difference of men in their sight, hearing, or other senses,
than in their fancies and discretions. It proceeds therefore from the passions; which are different, not only
from the difference of men's complexions; but also from
their difference of customs, and education.[2]

[2] Compare *Human Nature*, (M. IV, 54). "Having shewed
in the precedent chapters, that sense proceedeth from the
action of external objects upon the *brain*, or some internal
substance of the *head*; and that the *passions* proceed from
the alteration there made, and continued to the *heart*; it is
consequent in the next place, seeing the diversity of degrees
in knowledge in divers men, to be greater than may be
ascribed to the divers *tempers* of their brain, to declare *what
other causes* may produce such *odds*, and excess of *capacity*,
as we daily observe in one man above another. As for that
difference which ariseth from *sickness*, and such accidental

The passions that most of all cause the difference of wit, are principally, the more or less desire of power, of riches, of knowledge, and of honour. All which may be reduced to the first, that is, desire of power. For riches, knowledge, and honour, are but several sorts of power.

And therefore, a man who has no great passion for any of these things; but is, as men term it, indifferent; though he may be so far a good man, as to be free from giving offence; yet he cannot possibly have either a great fancy, or much judgment. For the thoughts are to the desires, as scouts, and spies, to range abroad, and find the way to the things desired: all steadiness of the

---

distempers, I omit the same, as impertinent to this place, and consider it only in such as have their *health*, and *organs* well disposed. If the difference were in the natural temper of the brain, I can imagine no reason why the same should not appear first and most of all in the senses, which being equal both in the wise and less wise, infer an equal temper in the common organ (namely the brain) of all the senses. But we see by experience, that *joy* and *grief* proceed *not* in *all* men from the *same causes*, and that men differ very much in the constitution of the body; whereby, that which helpeth and furthereth *vital constitution* in one, and is therefore delightful, hindereth it and crosseth it in another, and therefore causeth grief. The *difference* therefore of *wits* hath its original *from* the *different passions*, and from the *ends* to which the appetite leadeth them. And first, those men whose ends are *sensual* delight, and generally are addicted to *ease, food, onerations* and *exonerations* of the body, must needs be the *less* thereby delighted with those *imaginations* that *conduce not* to those ends, such as are imaginations of *honour* and *glory*, which, as I have said before, have respect to the future: for sensuality consisteth in the pleasure of the senses, which please only for the present, and take away the inclination to observe such things as conduce to honour, and consequently maketh men less curious, and less ambitious, whereby they less consider the way either to knowledge or other power; in which two consisteth all the excellency of power cognitive. And this is it which men call *dullness*, and proceedeth from the appetite of sensual or bodily delight. And it may well be conjectured that such passion hath its beginning from a *grossness* and *difficulty* of the *motion* of the *spirit* about the *heart*."

mind's motion, and all quickness of the same, proceeding from thence: for as to have no desire, is to be dead: so to have weak passions, is dullness; and to have passions indifferently for everything, GIDDINESS, and *distraction*; and to have stronger and more vehement passions for anything, than is ordinarily seen in others, is that which men call MADNESS.

Whereof there be almost as many kinds, as of the passions themselves. Sometimes the extraordinary and extravagant passion, proceedeth from the evil constitution of the organs of the body, or harm done them; and sometimes the hurt, and indisposition of the organs, is caused by the vehemence, or long continuance of the passion. But in both cases the madness is of one and the same nature.

The passion, whose violence, or continuance, maketh madness, is either great *vain-glory*; which is commonly called *pride*, and *self-conceit*; or great *dejection* of mind.

Pride, subjecteth a man to anger, the excess whereof, is the madness called RAGE and FURY. And thus it comes to pass that excessive desire of revenge, when it becomes habitual, hurteth the organs, and becomes rage: that excessive love, with jealousy, becomes also rage: excessive opinion of a man's own self, for divine inspiration, for wisdom, learning, form and the like, becomes distraction and giddiness: the same, joined with envy, rage: vehement opinion of the truth of anything, contradicted by others, rage.

Dejection subjects a man to causeless fears; which is a madness, commonly called MELANCHOLY; apparent also in divers manners; as in haunting of solitudes and graves; in superstitious behaviour; and in fearing, some one, some another particular thing. In sum, all passions that produce strange and unusual behaviour, are called by the general name of madness. But of the several kinds of madness, he that would take the pains, might enrol a legion. And if the excesses be madness, there is no doubt but the passions themselves, when they tend to evil, are degrees of the same.

For example, though the effect of folly, in them that are possessed of an opinion of being inspired, be not visible always in one man, by any very extravagant action, that proceedeth from such passion; yet, when many of them conspire together, the rage of the whole multitude is visible enough. For what argument of madness can there be greater, than to clamour, strike, and throw stones at our best friends? Yet this is somewhat less than such a multitude will do. For they will clamour, fight against, and destroy those, by whom all their lifetime before, they have been protected, and secured from injury. And if this be madness in the multitude, it is the same in every particular man. For as in the midst of the sea, though a man perceive no sound of that part of the water next him, yet he is well assured, that part contributes as much to the roaring of the sea, as any other part of the same quantity; so also, though we perceive no great unquietness in one or two men, yet we may be well assured, that their singular passions, are parts of the seditious roaring of a troubled nation. And if there were nothing else that betrayed their madness; yet that very arrogating such inspiration to themselves, is argument enough. If some man in Bedlam should entertain you with sober discourse; and you desire in taking leave, to know what he were, that you might another time requite his civility; and he should tell you, he were God the Father; I think you need expect no extravagant action for argument of his madness.

This opinion of inspiration, called commonly, private spirit, begins very often, from some lucky finding of an error generally held by others; and not knowing, or not remembering, by what conduct of reason, they came to so singular a truth, (as they think it, though it be many times an untruth they light on) they presently admire themselves, as being in the special grace of God Almighty, who hath revealed the same to them supernaturally, by his Spirit.

Again, that madness is nothing else, but too much appearing passion, may be gathered out of the effects of wine, which are the same with those of the evil disposition of the organs. For the variety of behaviour in men that have drunk too much, is the same with that of madmen: some of them raging, others loving, others laughing, all extravagantly, but according to their several domineering passions: for the effect of the wine, does but remove dissimulation, and take from them the sight of the deformity of their passions. For, I believe, the most sober men, when they walk alone without care and employment of the mind, would be unwilling the vanity and extravagance of their thoughts at that time should be publicly seen; which is a confession, that passions unguided, are for the most part mere madness.

The opinions of the world, both in ancient and later ages, concerning the cause of madness, have been two; some deriving them from the passions; some, from demons, or spirits, either good or bad, which they thought might enter into a man, possess him, and move his organs in such strange and uncouth manner, as madmen use to do. The former sort therefore, called such men, madmen: but the latter, called them sometimes *demoniacs*, that is, possessed with spirits; sometimes *enurgumeni*, that is, agitated or moved with spirits; and now in Italy they are called, not only *pazzi*, madmen; but also *spiritati*, men possessed.

There was once a great conflux of people in Abdera,

a city of the Greeks, at the acting of the tragedy of *Andromeda,* upon an extreme hot day; whereupon a great many of the spectators falling into fevers, had this accident from the heat, and from the tragedy together, that they did nothing but pronounce iambics, with the names of Perseus and Andromeda; which, together with the fever, was cured by the coming on of winter; and this madness was thought to proceed from the passion imprinted by the tragedy. Likewise there reigned a fit of madness in another Grecian city, which seized only the young maidens; and caused many of them to hang themselves. This was by most then thought an act of the Devil. But one that suspected, that contempt of life in them, might proceed from some passion of the mind, and supposing that they did not contemn also their honour, gave counsel to the magistrates, to strip such as so hanged themselves, and let them hang out naked. This, the story says, cured that madness. But on the other side, the same Grecians, did often ascribe madness to the operation of Eumenides, or Furies; and sometimes of Ceres, Phœbus, and other gods; so much did men attribute to phantasms, as to think them aëreal living bodies; and generally to call them spirits. And as the Romans in this, held the same opinion with the Greeks, so also did the Jews; for they called madmen prophets, or, according as they thought the spirits good or bad, demoniacs; and some of them called both prophets and demoniacs, madmen; and some called the same man both demoniac, and madman. But for the Gentiles it is no wonder, because diseases and health, vices and virtues, and many natural accidents, were with them termed, and worshipped as demons. So that a man was to understand by demon, as well, sometimes an ague, as a devil. But for the Jews to have such

opinion, is somewhat strange. For neither Moses nor
Abraham pretended to prophecy by possession of a
spirit; but from the voice of God; or by a vision or
dream: nor is there anything in his law, moral or cere-
monial, by which they were taught, there was any such
enthusiasm, or any possession. When God is said,
(*Numb.* xi. 25) to take from the spirit that was in
Moses, and give to the seventy elders, the Spirit of
God (taking it for the substance of God) is not divided.
The Scriptures, by the Spirit of God in man, mean a
man's spirit, inclined to godliness. And where it is
said, (*Exod.* xxiii. 8) *"whom I have filled with the
spirit of wisdom to make garments for Aaron,"* is not
meant a spirit put into them, that can make garments,
but the wisdom of their own spirits in that kind of
work. In the like sense, the spirit of man, when it
produceth unclean actions, is ordinarily called an unclean spirit, and so other spirits, though not always,
yet as often as the virtue or vice so styled, is extraordinary, and eminent. Neither did the other prophets
of the old Testament pretend enthusiasm; or, that God
spake in them; but to them, by voice, vision, or dream;
and the *burthen of the Lord* was not possession, but
command. How then could the Jews fall into this
opinion of possession? I can imagine no reason, but
that which is common to all men; namely, the want of
curiosity to search natural causes: and their placing
felicity in the acquisition of the gross pleasures of the
senses, and the things that most immediately conduce
thereto. For they that see any strange, and unusual
ability, or defect, in a man's mind; unless they see
withal, from what cause it may probably proceed, can
hardly think it natural; and if not natural, they must
needs think it supernatural; and then what can it be,

but that either God or the Devil is in him? And hence
it came to pass, when our Saviour (*Mark* iii. 21) was
compassed about with the multitude, those of the house
doubted he was mad, and went out to hold him: but
the Scribes said he had Beelzebub, and that was it, by
which he cast out devils; as if the greater madman had
awed the lesser: and that (*John* x. 20) some said,
he hath a devil, and is mad; whereas others holding
him for a prophet, said, *these are not the words of one
that hath a devil.* So in the old Testament he that came
to anoint Jehu, (2 *Kings* ix. 11) was a prophet; but
some of the company asked Jehu, *what came that madman for?* So that in sum, it is manifest, that whosoever behaved himself in extraordinary manner, was
thought by the Jews to be possessed either with a good,
or evil spirit; except by the Sadducees, who erred so far
on the other hand, as not to believe there were at all
any spirits, which is very near to direct atheism; and
thereby perhaps the more provoked others to term such
men demoniacs, rather than madmen.

But why then does our Saviour proceed in the cur-
ing of them, as if they were possessed; and not as if
they were mad? To which I can give no other kind of
answer, but that which is given to those that urge the
Scripture in like manner against the opinion of the
motion of the earth. The Scripture was written to
shew unto men the kingdom of God, and to prepare
their minds to become his obedient subjects; leaving
the world, and the philosophy thereof, to the disputation of men, for the exercising of their natural reason.
Whether the earth's, or sun's motion make the day, and
night; or whether the exorbitant actions of men, proceed from passion, or from the devil, so we worship
him not, it is all one, as to our obedience, and subjection

to God Almighty; which is the thing for which the Scripture was written. As for that our Saviour speaketh to the disease, as to a person; it is the usual phrase of all that cure by words only, as Christ did, and enchanters pretend to do, whether they speak to a devil or not. For is not Christ also said (*Matt.* viii. 26) to have rebuked the winds? Is not he said also (*Luke* iv. 39) to rebuke a fever? Yet this does not argue that a fever is a devil. And whereas many of the devils are said to confess Christ; it is not necessary to interpret those places otherwise, than that those madmen confessed him. And whereas our Saviour (*Matt.* xii. 43) speaketh of an unclean spirit, that having gone out of a man, wandereth through dry places, seeking rest, and finding none, and returning into the same man, with seven other spirits worse than himself; it is manifestly a parable, alluding to a man, that after a little endeavour to quit his lusts, is vanquished by the strength of them; and becomes seven times worse than he was. So that I see nothing at all in the Scripture, that requireth a belief, that demoniacs were any other thing but madmen.

There is yet another fault in the discourses of some men; which may also be numbered amongst the sorts of madness; namely, that abuse of words, whereof I have spoken before in the fifth chapter, by the name of absurdity. And that is, when men speak such words, as put together, have in them no signification at all; but are fallen upon by some, through misunderstanding of the words they have received, and repeat by rote; by others from intention to deceive by obscurity. And this is incident to none but those, that converse in questions of matters incomprehensible, as the School-men; or in questions of abstruse philosophy. The common

sort of men seldom speak insignificantly, and are therefore, by those other egregious persons counted idiots.
But to be assured their words are without any thing
correspondent to them in the mind, there would need
some examples; which if any man require, let him take
a School-man in his hands and see if he can translate
any one chapter concerning any difficult points, as the
Trinity; the Deity; the nature of Christ; transubstantiation; free-will, &c. into any of the modern
tongues, so as to make the same intelligible; or into
any tolerable Latin, such as they were acquainted withal,
that lived when the Latin tongue was vulgar. What is
the meaning of these words, *The first cause does not
necessarily inflow anything into the second, by force of
the essential subordination of the second causes, by
which it may help it to work?* They are the translation
of the title of the sixth chapter of *Suarez'* first book,
Of the concourse, motion, and help of God. When men
write whole volumes of such stuff, are they not mad,
or intend to make others so? And particularly, in the
question of transubstantiation; where after certain
words spoken; they that say, the white*ness*, round*ness*,
magni*tude*, quali*ty*, corruptibili*ty*, all which are incorporeal, &c. go out of the wafer, into the body of our
blessed Saviour, do they not make those *nesses*, *tudes*,
and *ties*, to be so many spirits possessing his body?
For by spirits, they mean always things, that being incorporeal, are nevertheless moveable from one place to
another. So that this kind of absurdity, may rightly
be numbered amongst the many sorts of madness; and
all the time that guided by clear thoughts of their
worldly lust, they forbear disputing, or writing thus,
but lucid intervals. And thus much of the virtues and
defects intellectual.

TABLE TO
FOLLOW
CHAPTER IX

Consequences from the accidents common to all bodies natural; which are *quantity*, and *motion*.

Consequences from the accidents of bodies natural; which is called NATURAL PHILOSOPHY.

Consequences from the qualities of bodies *transient*, such as some times appear, some times vanish, *Meteorology* . . . .

PHYSICS or consequences from *qualities*.

Consequences from the qualities of the *stars*.

Consequences from the qualities of bodies *permanent*.

Consequences of the qualities from *liquid* bodies, that fill the space between the stars; such as are the *air*, or substances ethereal.

Consequences from the qualities of *bodies terrestrial*.

SCIENCE, that is, knowledge of consequences; which is called also PHILOSOPHY.

Consequences from the accidents of *politic* bodies; which is called POLITICS, and CIVIL PHILOSOPHY.

1. Of consequences from the *institution* of COMMONWEALTHS, to the *rights* and *duties* of the body politic or *sovereign*.

2. Of consequences from the same, to the *duty* and *right* of the *subjects*.

Consequences from quantity, and motion *indeterminate;* which being the principles or first foundation of philosophy is called *Philosophia Prima.* — PHILOSOPHIA PRIMA.

Consequences from quantity and motion determined.
- By Figure — Mathematics. — GEOMETRY.
- By Number. — Mathematics. — ARITHMETIC.

Consequences from motion and quantity determined.

Consequences from the motion and quantity of bodies in special.
- Consequences from the motion and quantity of the greater parts of the world, as the *earth* and *stars.* — *Cosmography.* — ASTRONOMY. GEOGRAPHY.
- Consequences from the motions of special kinds, and figures of body. — *Mechanics.* Doctrine of *weight.* — *Science of* ENGINEERS. ARCHITECTURE. NAVIGATION.

.... — METEOROLOGY.

Consequences from the *light* of the stars. Out of this, and the motion of the sun, is made the science of..... — SCIOGRAPHY.

Consequences from the *influences* of the stars........ — ASTROLOGY.

Consequences from the parts of the earth, that are *without* sense.
- Consequences from the qualities of *minerals,* as *stones, metals,* &c.
- Consequences from the qualities of *vegetables.*

Consequences from the qualities of *animals*

Consequences from the qualities of *animals in general.*
- Consequences from *vision*... — OPTICS.
- Consequences from *sounds*.. — MUSIC.
- Consequences from the rest of the *senses.*

Consequences from the qualities of *men in special.*
- Consequences from the *passions* of men .... — ETHICS.
- Consequences from *speech.*
  - In *magnifying, vilifying,* &c. — POETRY.
  - In *persuading,* — RHETORIC.
  - In *reasoning,* — LOGIC.
  - In *contracting.* — THE *Science* of JUST AND UNJUST.

CHAPTER IX

OF THE SEVERAL SUBJECTS OF KNOWLEDGE

THERE are of KNOWLEDGE two kinds; whereof one is *knowledge of fact*: the other *knowledge of the consequence of one affirmation to another*. The former is nothing else, but sense and memory, and is *absolute knowledge*; as when we see a fact doing, or remember it done: and this is the knowledge required in a witness. The latter is called *science*; and is *conditional*; as when we know, that, *if the figure shown be a circle, then any straight line through the center shall divide it into two equal parts*. And this is the knowledge required in a philosopher; that is to say, of him that pretends to reasoning.

The register of *knowledge of fact* is called *history*. Whereof there be two sorts: one called *natural history*; which is the history of such facts, or effects of nature, as have no dependence on man's *will*; such as are the histories of *metals, plants, animals, regions,* and the like. The other, is *civil history*; which is the history of the voluntary actions of men in commonwealths.

The registers of science, are such *books* as contain the *demonstrations* of consequences of one affirmation, to another; and are commonly called *books of philosophy*; whereof the sorts are many, according to the diversity of the matter; and may be divided in such manner as I have divided them in the foregoing table.[1] [See pp. 232-33]

---

[1] Compare on the general subject of knowledge and science, Chapters V and VII of *Leviathan*. Also *Philosophical Rudiments*, (M. II, iii). "Wisdom, properly so called, is nothing else but this: *the perfect knowledge of the truth in all matters whatsoever*. Which being derived from the registers and records of *things*; and that as it were through the conduit of certain definite appellations; cannot possibly be the work of a

CHAPTER XII

OF RELIGION

SEEING there are no signs, nor fruit of *religion*, but in man only; there is no cause to doubt, but that the seed of *religion*, is also only in man; and consisteth in some peculiar quality, or at least in some eminent degree thereof, not to be found in any other living creatures.

And first, it is peculiar to the nature of man, to be inquisitive into the causes of the events they see, some more, some less; but all men so much, as to be curious in the search of the causes of their own good and evil fortune.

Secondly, upon the sight of anything that hath a beginning, to think also it had a cause, which determined the same to begin, then when it did, rather than sooner or later.

Thirdly, whereas there is no other felicity of beasts, but the enjoying of their quotidian food, ease, and lusts; as having little or no foresight of the time to come, for want of observation, and memory of the order, consequence, and dependence of the things they see; man ob-

---

sudden acuteness, but of a well-balanced reason; which by the compendium of a word, we call *philosophy*. For by this it is that a way is open to us, in which we travel from the contemplation of particular things to the inference or result of universal actions. Now look, how many sorts of things there are, which properly fall within the cognizance of human reason; into so many branches does the tree of philosophy divide itself. And, from the diversity of the matter about which they are conversant, there hath been given to those branches a diversity of names too. For treating of figures, it is called *geometry*; of motion, *physics*; of natural right, *morals*; put altogether, and they make up *philosophy*. Just as the British, the Atlantic, and the Indian seas being diversely christened from the diversity of their shores, do notwithstanding all together make up *the ocean*."

serveth how one event hath been produced by another;
and remembereth in them antecedence and consequence;
and when he cannot assure himself of the true causes
of things, (for the causes of good and evil fortune
for the most part are invisible,) he supposes causes of
them, either such as his own fancy suggesteth; or
trusteth the authority of other men, such as he thinks
to be his friends, and wiser than himself.

The two first, make anxiety. For being assured that
there be causes of all things that have arrived hitherto,
or shall arrive hereafter; it is impossible for a man,
who continually endeavoureth to secure himself against
the evil he fears, and procure the good he desireth, not
to be in a perpetual solicitude of the time to come; so
that every man, especially those that are over provident,
are in a state like to that of Prometheus. For as
Prometheus, which interpreted, is, *the prudent man,*
was bound to the hill Caucasus, a place of large prospect, where, an eagle feeding on his liver, devoured in
the day, as much as was repaired in the night: so that
man, which looks too far before him, in the care of
future time, hath his heart all the day long, gnawed
on by fear of death, poverty, or other calamity; and
has no repose, nor pause of his anxiety, but in sleep.

This perpetual fear, always accompanying mankind
in the ignorance of causes, as it were in the dark, must
needs have for object something. And therefore when
there is nothing to be seen, there is nothing to accuse,
either of their good, or evil fortune, but some *power,*
or agent *invisible*: in which sense perhaps it was, that
some of the old poets said, that the gods were at first
created by human fear: which spoken of the gods, that
is to say, of the many gods of the Gentiles, is very
true. But the acknowledging of one God, eternal, infinite, and omnipotent, may more easily be derived,

from the desire men have to know the causes of natural
bodies, and their several virtues, and operations; than
from the fear of what was to befall them in time to
come. For he that from any effect he seeth come to
pass, should reason to the next and immediate cause
thereof, and from thence to the cause of that cause, and
plunge himself profoundly in the pursuit of causes;
shall at last come to this, that there must be, as even
the heathen philosophers confessed, one first mover;
that is, a first, and an eternal cause of all things; which
is that which men mean by the name of God: and all
this without thought of their fortune; the solicitude
whereof, both inclines to fear, and hinders them from
the search of the causes of other things; and thereby
gives occasion of feigning of as many gods, as there
be men that feign them.

And for the matter, or substance of the invisible
agents, so fancied; they could not by natural cogitation,
fall upon any other conceit, but that it was the same with
that of the soul of man; and that the soul of man, was
of the same substance, with that which appeareth in a
dream, to one that sleepeth; or in a looking-glass, to
one that is awake; which, men not knowing that such
apparitions are nothing else but creatures of the fancy,
think to be real, and external substances; and therefore
call them ghosts; as the Latins called them *imagines*,
and *umbrae*; and thought them spirits, that is, thin
aerial bodies; and those invisible agents, which they
feared, to be like them; save that they appear, and
vanish when they please. But the opinion that such
spirits were incorporeal, or immaterial, could never enter
into the mind of any man by nature; because, though
men may put together words of contradictory signification, as *spirit*, and *incorporeal*; yet they can never have
the imagination of any thing answering to them: and

therefore, men that by their own meditation, arrive to the acknowledgment of one infinite, omnipotent, and eternal God, chose rather to confess he is incomprehensible, and above their understanding, than to define his nature by *spirit incorporeal*, and then confess their definition to be unintelligible: or if they give him such a title, it is not *dogmatically*, with intention to make the divine nature understood; but *piously*, to honour him with attributes, of significations, as remote as they can from the grossness of bodies visible.

Then, for the way by which they think these invisible agents wrought their effects; that is to say, what immediate causes they used, in bringing things to pass, men that know not what it is that we call *causing*, that is, almost all men, have no other rule to guess by, but by observing, and remembering what they have seen to precede the like effect at some other time, or times before, without seeing between the antecedent and subsequent event, any dependence or connexion at all: and therefore from the like things past, they expect the like things to come; and hope for good or evil luck, superstitiously, from things that have no part at all in the causing of it: as the Athenians did for their war at Lepanto, demand another Phormio; the Pompeian faction for their war in Africa, another Scipio; and others have done in divers other occasions since. In like manner they attribute their fortune to a stander-by, to a lucky or unlucky place, to words spoken, especially if the name of God be amongst them; as charming and conjuring, the liturgy of witches; insomuch as to believe, they have power to turn a stone into bread, bread into a man, or any thing into any thing.

Thirdly, for the worship which naturally men exhibit to powers invisible, it can be no other, but such expressions of their reverence, as they would use towards men;

gifts, petitions, thanks, submission of body, considerate addresses, sober behaviour, premeditated words, swearing, that is, assuring one another of their promises, by invoking them. Beyond that reason suggesteth nothing; but leaves them either to rest there; or for further ceremonies, to rely on those they believe to be wiser than themselves.

Lastly, concerning how these invisible powers declare to men the things which shall hereafter come to pass, especially concerning their good or evil fortune in general, or good or ill success in any particular undertaking, men are naturally at a stand; save that using to conjecture of the time to come, by the time past, they are very apt, not only to take casual things, after one or two encounters, for prognostics of the like encounter ever after, but also to believe the like prognostics from other men, of whom they have once conceived a good opinion.

And in these four things, opinion of ghosts, ignorance of second causes, devotion towards what men fear, and taking of things casual for prognostics, consisteth the natural seed of *religion*, which by reason of the different fancies, judgments, and passions of several men, hath grown up into ceremonies so different, that those which are used by one man, are for the most part ridiculous to another.

For these seeds have received culture from two sorts of men. One sort have been they, that have nourished, and ordered them, according to their own invention. The other have done it, by God's commandment, and direction; but both sorts have done it, with a purpose to make those men that relied on them, the more apt to obedience, laws, peace, charity, and civil society. So that the religion of the former sort, is a part of human politics; and teacheth part of the duty which earthly kings require of their subjects. And the religion of the latter sort is divine politics; and containeth precepts to those that have yielded themselves subjects in the kingdom of God. Of the former sort, were all the founders of common-wealths, and the law-givers of the Gentiles: of the latter sort, were Abraham, Moses, and our blessed Saviour; by whom have been derived unto us the laws of the kingdom of God.

And for that part of religion, which consisteth in opinions concerning the nature of powers invisible, there is almost nothing that has a name, that has not been esteemed amongst the Gentiles, in one place or another, a god, or devil; or by their poets feigned to be inanimated, inhabited, or possessed by some spirit or other.

The unformed matter of the world, was a god, by the name of Chaos.

The heaven, the ocean, the planets, the fire, the earth, the winds, were so many gods.

Men, women, a bird, a crocodile, a calf, a dog, a snake, an onion, a leek, were deified. Besides that, they filled almost all places, with spirits called *demons*: the plains, with Pan, and Panises, or Satyrs; the woods, with Fawns, and Nymphs; the sea, with Tritons, and other Nymphs; every river, and fountain, with a ghost of his name, and with Nymphs; every house with its *Lares*, or familiars; every man with his *Genius*; hell with ghosts, and spiritual officers, as Charon, Cerberus, and the Furies; and in the night time, all places with *larvae, lemures,* ghosts of men deceased, and a whole kingdom of fairies and bugbears. They have also ascribed divinity, and built temples to meer accidents, and qualities; such as are time, night, day, peace, concord, love, contention, virtue, honour, health, rust, fever, and the like; which when they prayed for, or against, they prayed to, as if there were ghosts of those names

hanging over their heads, and letting fall, or withhold-
ing that good, or evil, for, or against which they prayed.
They invoked also their own wit, by the name of Muses;
their own ignorance, by the name of Fortune; their own
lusts by the name of Cupid; their own rage, by the name
of Furies; their own privy members, by the name of
Priapus; and attributed their pollutions, to Incubi, and
Succubæ: insomuch as there was nothing, which a poet
could introduce as a person in his poem, which they did
not make either a *god*, or a *devil*.

The same authors of the religion of the Gentiles, observing the second ground for religion, which is men's
ignorance of causes; and thereby their aptness to attribute their fortune to causes, on which there was no dependence at all apparent, took occasion to obtrude on
their ignorance, instead of second causes, a kind of
second and ministerial gods; ascribing the cause of
fecundity, to Venus; the cause of arts, to Apollo; of
subtlety and craft, to Mercury; of tempests and storms,
to Aeolus; and of other effects, to other gods; insomuch
as there was amongst the heathen almost as great variety
of gods, as of business.

And to the worship, which naturally men conceived
fit to be used towards their gods, namely, oblations,
prayers, thanks, and the rest formerly named; the same
legislators of the Gentiles have added their images, both
in picture, and sculpture; that the more ignorant sort,
that is to say, the most part or generality of the people,
thinking the gods for whose representation they were
made, were really included, and as it were housed within
them, might so much the more stand in fear of them:
and endowed them with lands, and houses, and officers,
and revenues, set apart from all other human uses; that
is, consecrated, and made holy to those their idols; as
caverns, groves, woods, mountains, and whole islands;

and have attributed to them, not only the shapes, some
of men, some of beasts, some of monsters; but also the
faculties, and passions of men and beasts: as sense,
speech, sex, lust, generation, and this not only by mixing
one with another, to propagate the kind of gods; but also
by mixing with men, and women, to beget mongrel gods,
and but inmates of heaven, as Bacchus, Hercules, and
others; besides anger, revenge, and other passions of
living creatures, and the actions proceeding from them,
as fraud, theft, adultery, sodomy, and any vice that may
be taken for an effect of power, or a cause of pleasure;
and all such vices, as amongst men are taken to be
against law, rather than against honour.

Lastly, to the prognostics of time to come; which are
naturally, but conjectures upon experience of time past;
and supernaturally, divine revelation; the same authors
of the religion of the Gentiles, partly upon pretended
experience, partly upon pretended revelation, have
added innumerable other superstitious ways of divina-
tion; and made men believe they should find their fortunes, sometimes in the ambiguous or senseless answers
of the priests at Delphi, Delos, Ammon, and other
famous oracles; which answers, were made ambiguous
by design, to own the event both ways; or absurd, by
the intoxicating vapour of the place, which is very frequent in sulphurous caverns: sometimes in the leaves of
the Sybils; of whose prophecies, like those perhaps of
Nostradamus (for the fragments now extant seem to be
the invention of later times), there were some books in
reputation in the time of the Roman republic: sometimes
in the insignificant speeches of madmen, supposed to be
possessed with a divine spirit, which possession they
called enthusiasm; and these kinds of foretelling events,
were accounted theomancy, or prophecy: sometimes in
the aspect of the stars at their nativity; which was

called horoscopy, and esteemed a part of judiciary
astrology: sometimes in their own hopes and fears,
called thumomancy, or presage: sometimes in the pre-
diction of witches, that pretended conference with the
dead; which is called necromancy, conjuring, and witchcraft; and is but juggling and confederate knavery:
sometimes in the casual flight, or feeding of birds;
called augury: sometimes in the entrails of a sacrificed
beast; which was *aruspicina*: sometimes in dreams:
sometimes in croaking of ravens, or chattering of birds:
sometimes in the lineaments of the face; which was
called metoposcopy; or by palmistry in the lines of the
hand; in casual words, called *omina*: sometimes in monsters, or unusual accidents; as eclipses, comets, rare
meteors, earthquakes, inundations, uncouth births, and
the like, which they call *portenta*, and *ostenta*, because
they thought them to portend, or foreshow some great
calamity to come; sometimes, in mere lottery, as cross
and pile; counting holes in a sieve; dipping of verses in
Homer, and Virgil; and innumerable other such vain
conceits. So easy are men to be drawn to believe any
thing, from such men as have gotten credit with them;
and can with gentleness, and dexterity, take hold of
their fear, and ignorance.

And therefore the first founders, and legislators of
commonwealths among the Gentiles, whose ends were
only to keep the people in obedience, and peace, have
in all places taken care; first, to imprint in their minds
a belief, that those precepts which they gave concerning
religion, might not be thought to proceed from their own
device, but from the dictates of some god, or other
spirit; or else that they themselves were of a higher
nature than mere mortals, that their laws might the
more easily be received: so Numa Pompilius pretended
to receive the ceremonies he instituted amongst the

Romans, from the nymph Egeria: and the first king and
founder of the kingdom of Peru, pretended himself and
his wife to be the children of the Sun; and Mahomet,
to set up his new religion, pretended to have confer-
ences with the Holy Ghost, in form of a dove. Secondly,
they have had a care, to make it believed, that the same
things were displeasing to the gods, which were forbidden by the laws. Thirdly, to prescribe ceremonies,
supplications, sacrifices, and festivals, by which they
were to believe, the anger of the gods might be ap-
peased; and that ill success in war, great contagions
of sickness, earthquakes, and each man's private misery,
came from the anger of the gods, and their anger from
the neglect of their worship, or the forgetting, or mis-
taking some point of the ceremonies required. And
though amongst the ancient Romans, men were not forbidden to deny, that which in the poets is written of
the pains, and pleasures after this life: which divers
of great authority, and gravity in that state have in
their harangues openly derided; yet that belief was
always more cherished, than the contrary.

And by these, and such other institutions, they obtained in order to their end, which was the peace of the
commonwealth, that the common people in their misfor-
tunes, laying the fault on neglect, or error in their
ceremonies, or on their own disobedience to the laws,
were the less apt to mutiny against their governors; and
being entertained with the pomp, and pastime of festivals, and public games, made in honour of the gods,
needed nothing else but bread to keep them from dis-
content, murmuring, and commotion against the state.
And therefore the Romans, that had conquered the
greatest part of the then known world, made no scruple
of tolerating any religion whatsoever in the city of
Rome itself; unless it had something in it, that could

not consist with their civil government; nor do we read, that any religion was there forbidden, but that of the Jews; who, being the peculiar kingdom of God, thought it unlawful to acknowledge subjection to any mortal king or state whatsoever. And thus you see how the religion of the Gentiles was a part of their policy.

But where God himself, by supernatural revelation, planted religion; there he also made to himself a peculiar kingdom: and gave laws, not only of behaviour towards himself, but also towards one another; and thereby in the kingdom of God, the policy, and laws civil, are a part of religion; and therefore the distinction of temporal, and spiritual domination, hath there no place. It is true, that God is king of all the earth: yet may he be king of a peculiar, and chosen nation. For there is no more incongruity therein, than that he that hath the general command of the whole army, should have withal a peculiar regiment, or company of his own. God is king of all the earth by his power: but of his chosen people, he is king by covenant. But to speak more largely of the kingdom of God, both by nature, and covenant, I have in the following discourse assigned another place (chapter xxxv).

From the propagation of religion, it is not hard to understand the causes of the resolution of the same into its first seeds, or principles; which are only an opinion of a deity, and powers invisible, and supernatural; that can never be so abolished out of human nature, but that new religions may again be made to spring out of them, by the culture of such men, as for such purpose are in reputation.

For seeing all formed religion, is founded at first, upon the faith which a multitude hath in some one person, whom they believe not only to be a wise man, and to labour to procure their happiness, but also to be a holy man, to whom God himself vouchsafeth to declare his will supernaturally; it followeth necessarily, when they that have the government of religion, shall come to have either the wisdom of those men, their sincerity, or their love suspected; or when they shall be unable to show any probable token of divine revelation; that the religion which they desire to uphold, must be suspected likewise; and, without the fear of the civil sword, contradicted and rejected.

That which taketh away the reputation of wisdom, in him that formeth a religion, or addeth to it when it is already formed, is the enjoining of a belief of contradictories: for both parts of a contradiction cannot possibly be true: and therefore to enjoin the belief of them, is an argument of ignorance; which detects the author in that; and discredits him in all things else he shall propound as from revelation supernatural: which revelation a man may indeed have of many things above, but of nothing against natural reason.

That which taketh away the reputation of sincerity, is the doing or saying of such things, as appear to be signs, that what they require other men to believe, is not believed by themselves; all which doings, or sayings are therefore called scandalous, because they be stumbling blocks, that make men to fall in the way of religion; as injustice, cruelty, profaneness, avarice, and luxury. For who can believe, that he that doth ordinarily such actions as proceed from any of these roots, believeth there is any such invisible power to be feared, as he affrighteth other men withal, for lesser faults?

That which taketh away the reputation of love, is the being detected of private ends: as when the belief they require of others, conduceth or seemeth to conduce to the acquiring of dominion, riches, dignity, or secure pleasure, to themselves only, or specially. For that which men reap benefit by to themselves, they are thought to do for their own sakes, and not for love of others.

Lastly, the testimony that men can render of divine calling, can be no other, than the operation of miracles; or true prophecy, which also is a miracle; or extraordinary felicity. And therefore, to those points of religion, which have been received from them that did such miracles; those that are added by such, as approve not their calling by some miracle, obtain no greater belief, than what the custom and laws of the places, in which they be educated, have wrought into them. For as in natural things, men of judgment require natural signs, and arguments; so in supernatural things, they require signs supernatural, which are miracles before they consent inwardly, and from their hearts.

All which causes of the weakening of men's faith, do manifestly appear in the examples following. First, we have the example of the children of Israel: who when Moses, that had approved his calling to them by miracles, and by the happy conduct of them out of Egypt, was absent but forty days, revolted from the worship of the true God, recommended to them by him; and setting up (*Exod.* xxxiii. 1, 2) a golden calf for their god, relapsed into the idolatry of the Egyptians; from whom they had been so lately delivered. And again, after Moses, Aaron, Joshua, and that generation which had seen the great works of God in Israel, (*Judges* ii. 11) were dead; another generation arose, and served Baal. So that miracles failing, faith also failed.

Again, when the sons of Samuel, (1 *Sam.* viii. 3) being constituted by their father judges in Bersabee, received bribes, and judged unjustly, the people of Israel refused any more to have God to be their king, in other manner than he was king of other people; and therefore cried out to Samuel, to chose them a king after the manner of the nations. So that justice failing, faith also failed: insomuch, as they deposed their God, from reigning over them.

And whereas in the planting of Christian religion, the oracles ceased in all parts of the Roman empire, and the number of Christians increased wonderfully every day, and in every place, by the preaching of the Apostles, and Evangelists; a great part of that success, may reasonably be attributed, to the contempt, into which the priests of the Gentiles of that time, had brought themselves by their uncleanness, avarice, and juggling between princes. Also the religion of the church of Rome, was partly, for the same cause abolished in England, and many other parts of Christendom; insomuch, as the failing of virtue in the pastors, maketh faith fail in the people: and partly from bringing of the philosophy, and doctrine of Aristotle into religion, by the Schoolmen; from whence there arose so many contradictions, and absurdities, as brought the clergy into a reputation both of ignorance, and of fraudulent intention; and inclined people to revolt from them, either against the will of their own princes, as in France and Holland; or with their will, as in England.

Lastly, amongst the points by the church of Rome declared necessary for salvation, there be so many, manifestly to the advantage of the Pope, and of his spiritual subjects, residing in the territories of other Christian princes, that were it not for the mutual emulation of those princes, they might without war, or trouble, exclude all foreign authority, as easily as it has been excluded in England. For who is there that does not see, to whose benefit it conduceth, to have it believed, that a king hath not his authority from Christ, unless a bishop crown him? That a king, if he be a priest, cannot marry? That whether a prince be born in lawful marriage, or not, must be judged by authority from Rome? That subjects may be freed from their allegiance, if by the court of Rome, the king be judged an heretic? That a king, as Chilperic of France, may be deposed by a pope, as Pope Zachary, for no cause; and his kingdom given to one of his subjects? That the clergy and regulars, in what country soever, shall be exempt from the jurisdiction of their king in cases criminal? Or who does not see, to whose profit redound the fees of private masses, and vales of purgatory; with other signs of private interest, enough to mortify the most lively faith, if, as I said, the civil magistrate, and custom did not more sustain it, than any opinion they have of the sanctity, wisdom, or probity of their teachers? So that I may attribute all the changes of religion in the world, to one and the same cause; and that is, unpleasing priests; and those not only amongst Catholics, but even in that church that hath presumed most of reformation.

CHAPTER XIII

OF THE NATURAL CONDITION OF MANKIND AS CONCERNING THEIR FELICITY, AND MISERY

NATURE hath made men so equal, in the faculties of the body, and mind; as that though there be found one man sometimes manifestly stronger in body, or of quicker mind than another; yet when all is reckoned together, the difference between man, and man, is not so considerable, as that one man can thereupon claim to himself any benefit, to which another may not pretend, as well as he. For as to the strength of body, the weakest has strength enough to kill the strongest, either by secret machination, or by confederacy with others, that are in the same danger with himself.

And as to the faculties of the mind, setting aside the arts grounded upon words, and especially that skill of proceeding upon general, and infallible rules, called science; which very few have, and but in few things; as being not a native faculty, born with us; nor attained, as prudence, while we look after somewhat else, I find yet a greater equality amongst men, than that of strength. For prudence, is but experience; which equal time, equally bestows on all men, in those things they equally apply themselves unto. That which may perhaps make such equality incredible, is but a vain conceit of one's own wisdom, which almost all men think they have in a greater degree, than the vulgar; that is, than all men but themselves, and a few others, whom by fame, or for concurring with themselves, they approve. For such is the nature of men, that howsoever they may acknowledge many others to be more witty, or more eloquent, or more learned; yet they will hardly believe there be many so wise as themselves; for they see their own wit at hand, and other men's at a distance. But this proveth rather that men are in that point equal, tl.an unequal. For there is not ordinarily a greater sign of the equal distribution of any thing, than that every man is contented with his share.

From this equality of ability, ariseth equality of hope in the attaining of our ends. And therefore if any two men desire the same thing, which nevertheless they cannot both enjoy, they become enemies; and in the way to their end, which is principally their own conservation, and sometimes their delectation only, endeavour to destroy, or subdue one another. And from hence it comes to pass, that where an invader hath no more to fear, than another man's single power; if one plant, sow, build, or possess a convenient seat, others may probably be expected to come prepared with forces united, to dispossess, and deprive him, not only of the fruit of his labour, but also of his life, or liberty. And the invader again is in the like danger of another.

And from this diffidence of one another, there is no way for any man to secure himself, so reasonable, as anticipation; that is, by force, or wiles, to master the persons of all men he can, so long, till he see no other power great enough to endanger him: and this is no more than his own conservation requireth, and is generally allowed. Also because there be some, that taking pleasure in contemplating their own power in the acts of conquest, which they pursue farther than their security requires; if others, that otherwise would be glad to be at ease within modest bounds, should not by invasion increase their power, they would not be able, long time, by standing only on their defence, to subsist. And by consequence, such augmentation of dominion over men being necessary to a man's conservation, it ought to be allowed him.[1]

[1] Compare *Human Nature*, (M. IV, 85). "Seeing this right of protecting ourselves by our own discretion and force, proceedeth from danger, and that danger from the equality between men's forces, much more reason is there, that a man prevent such equality before the danger cometh, and before the necessity of battle. A man therefore that hath another man in his power to rule or govern, to do good to, or harm, hath right, by the advantage of this his present power, to take caution at his pleasure, for his security against that other in time to come. He therefore that hath already subdued his adversary, or gotten into his power any other, that either by infancy, or weakness, is unable to resist him, by right of nature may take the best caution, that such infant, or such feeble and subdued person can give him, of being ruled and governed by him for the time to come. For seeing we intend always our own safety and preservation, we manifestly

Again, men have no pleasure, but on the contrary a great deal of grief, in keeping company, where there is no power able to over-awe them all. For every man looketh that his companion should value him, at the same rate he sets upon himself: and upon all signs of contempt, or undervaluing, naturally endeavours, as far as he dares, (which amongst them that have no common power to keep them in quiet, is far enough to make them destroy each other), to extort a greater value from his contemners, by damage; and from others, by the example.

So that in the nature of man, we find three principal causes of quarrel. First, competition; second, diffidence; thirdly, glory.

The first, maketh men invade for gain; the second, for safety; and the third, for reputation. The first use violence, to make themselves masters of other men's persons, wives, children, and cattle; the second, to defend them; the third, for trifles, as a word, a smile, a different opinion, and any other sign of undervalue, either direct in their persons, or by reflection in their kindred, their friends, their nation, their profession, or their name.

Hereby it is manifest, that during the time men live without a common power to keep them all in awe, they are in that condition which is called war; and such a war, as is of every man, against every man. For WAR, consisteth not in battle only, or the act of fighting; but in a tract of time, wherein the will to contend by battle is sufficiently known: and therefore the notion of *time*, is to be considered in the nature of war; as it is in the nature of weather. For as the nature of foul weather,

contradict that our intention, if we willingly dismiss such a one, and suffer him at once to gather strength and be our enemy. Out of which may also be collected, that irresistible might, in the state of nature, is right."

lieth not in a shower or two of rain; but in an inclination thereto of many days together: so the nature of war, consisteth not in actual fighting; but in the known disposition thereto, during all the time there is no assurance to the contrary. All other time is PEACE.

Whatsoever therefore is consequent to a time of war, where every man is enemy to every man; the same is consequent to the time, wherein men live without other security, than what their own strength, and their own invention shall furnish them withal. In such condition, there is no place for industry; because the fruit thereof is uncertain: and consequently no culture of the earth; no navigation, nor use of the commodities that may be imported by sea; no commodious building; no instruments of moving, and removing, such things as require much force; no knowledge of the face of the earth; no account of time; no arts; no letters; no society; and which is worst of all, continual fear, and danger of violent death; and the life of man, solitary, poor, nasty, brutish, and short.

It may seem strange to some man, that has not well weighed these things; that nature should thus dissociate, and render men apt to invade, and destroy one another: and he may therefore, not trusting to this inference, made from the passions, desire perhaps to have the same confirmed by experience. Let him therefore consider with himself, when taking a journey, he arms himself, and seeks to go well accompanied; when going to sleep, he locks his doors; when even in his house he locks his chests; and this when he knows there be laws, and public officers, armed, to revenge all injuries shall be done him; what opinion he has of his fellow-subjects, when he rides armed; of his fellow citizens, when he locks his doors; and of his children, and servants, when he locks his chests. Does he not there as much accuse mankind

by his actions, as I do by my words? But neither of us
accuse man's nature in it. The desires, and other passions of man, are in themselves no sin. No more are the
actions, that proceed from those passions, till they know
a law that forbids them: which till laws be made they
cannot know: nor can any law be made, till they have
agreed upon the person that shall make it.[2]

---

[2] Compare *Leviathan* (M. III, 277). "A sin is not only a
transgression of a law, but also any contempt of the legislator. For such contempt, is a breach of all his laws at once.
And therefore may consist, not only in the *commission* of a
fact, or in speaking of words by the laws forbidden, or in the
omission of what the law commandeth, but also in the *intention*, or purpose to transgress. For the purpose to break the
law, is some degree of contempt of him, to whom it belongeth
to see it executed. To be delighted in the imagination only,
of being possessed of another man's goods, servants, or wife,
without any intention to take them from him by force or
fraud, is no breach of the law, that saith, *Thou shalt not covet*:
nor is the pleasure a man may have in imagining or dreaming
of the death of him, from whose life he expecteth nothing
but damage, and displeasure, a sin; but the resolving to put
some act in execution, that tendeth thereto. For to be pleased
in the fiction of that, which would please a man if it were
real, is a passion so adherent to the nature both of man, and
every other living creature, as to make it a sin, were to
make sin of being a man. The consideration of this, has made
me think them too severe, both to themselves, and others, that
maintain, that the first motions of the mind, though checked
with the fear of God, be sins. But I confess it is safer to
err on that hand, than on the other. A crime, is a sin, consisting in the committing, by deed or word, of that which the
law forbiddeth, or the omission of what it hath commanded.
So that every crime is a sin; but not every sin a crime. To
intend to steal, or kill, is a sin, though it never appear in
word, or fact: for God that seeth the thoughts of man, can
lay it to his charge: but till it appear by something done, or
said, by which the intention may be argued by a human judge,
it hath not the name of crime. * * * * From this relation
of sin to the law, and of crime to the civil law, may be inferred, first, that where law ceaseth, sin ceaseth. But because
the law of nature is eternal, violation of covenants, ingratitude, arrogance, and all facts contrary to any moral virtue,
can never cease to be sin. Secondly, that the civil law ceasing,
crimes cease: for there being no other law remaining, but that

It may peradventure be thought, there was never such a time, nor condition of war as this; and I believe it was never generally so, over all the world: but there are many places, where they live so now. For the savage people in many places of America, except the government of small families, the concord whereof dependeth on natural lust, have no government at all; and live at this day in that brutish manner, as I said before. Howsoever, it may be perceived what manner of life there would be, where there were no common power to fear,

---

of nature, there is no place for accusation; every man being his own judge, and accused only by his own conscience, and cleared by the uprightness of his own intention. When therefore his intention is right, his fact is no sin: if otherwise, his fact is sin; but not crime. Thirdly, that when the sovereign power ceaseth, crime also ceaseth; for where there is no such power, there is no protection to be had from the law; and therefore every one may protect himself by his own power: for no man in the institution of sovereign power can be supposed to give away the right of preserving his own body; for the safety whereof all sovereignty was ordained. But this is to be understood only of those, that have not themselves contributed to the taking away of the power that protected them; for that was a crime from the beginning." Also *Philosophical Rudiments*, (M. II, 152). "That is my sin indeed, which committing I do believe to be my sin; but what I believe to be another man's sin, I may sometimes do that without any sin of mine. For if I be commanded to do that which is a sin in him who commands me, if I do it, and he that commands me be by right lord over me, I sin not. For if I wage war at the commandment of my prince, conceiving the war to be unjustly undertaken, I do not therefore do unjustly; but rather if I refuse to do it, arrogating to myself the knowledge of what is just and unjust, which pertains only to my prince. They who observe not this distinction, will fall into a necessity of sinning, as oft as anything is commanded them which either is, or seems to be unlawful to them: for if they obey, they sin against their conscience; and if they obey not, against right. If they sin against their conscience, they declare that they fear not the pains of the world to come; if they sin against right, they do, as much as in them lies, abolish human society and the civil life of the present world."

by the manner of life, which men that have formerly
lived under a peaceful government, use to degenerate
into, in a civil war.

But though there had never been any time, wherein
particular men were in a condition of war one against
another; yet in all times, kings, and persons of sovereign
authority, because of their independency, are in continual jealousies, and in the state and posture of gladiators; having their weapons pointing, and their eyes
fixed on one another; that is, their forts, garrisons, and
guns upon the frontiers of their kingdoms; and continual spies upon their neighbours; which is a posture
of war. But because they uphold thereby, the industry
of their subjects; there does not follow from it, that
misery, which accompanies the liberty of particular men.

To this war of every man, against every man, this
also is consequent; that nothing can be unjust. The
notions of right and wrong, justice and injustice have
there no place. Where there is no common power, there
is no law: where no law, no injustice. Force, and fraud,
are in war the two cardinal virtues. Justice, and injustice are none of the faculties neither of the body, nor
mind. If they were, they might be in a man that were
alone in the world, as well as his senses, and passions.
They are qualities, that relate to men in society, not in
solitude.[3] It is consequent also to the same condition,
that there be no propriety, no dominion, no *mine* and
thine distinct; but only that to be every man's, that he
can get; and for so long, as he can keep it.[4] And thus

---

[3] See above Chapter VI n. 3. and compare below Chapter
XV.

[4] Compare *Philosophical Rudiments*, (M. II, 84 n.). "What
is objected by some, that the propriety of goods, even before
the constitution of cities, was found in fathers of families,
that objection is vain; because I have already declared, that
a family is a little city. For the sons of a family have a
propriety of their goods granted them by their father, dis-

much for the ill condition, which man by mere natu
is actually placed in; though with a possibility to con
out of it, consisting partly in the passions, partly in hi
reason.

The passions that incline men to peace, are fear of
death; desire of such things as are necessary to commodious living; and a hope by their industry to obtain
them. And reason suggesteth convenient articles of
peace, upon which men may be drawn to agreement.
These articles, are they, which otherwise are called the
Laws of Nature: whereof I shall speak more particularly, in the two following chapters.

PARALLEL CHAPTER FROM

PHILOSOPHICAL RUDIMENTS CONCERNING GOVERNMENT

CHAPTER I

OF THE STATE OF MEN WITHOUT CIVIL SOCIETY

THE faculties of human nature may be reduced unto
four kinds; bodily strength, experience, reason, passion.
Taking the beginning of this following doctrine from
these, we will declare, in the first place, what manner of
inclinations men who are endued with these faculties
bear towards each other, and whether, and by what
faculty they are born apt for society, and to preserve
themselves against mutual violence; then proceeding, we

tinguished indeed from the rest of the sons of the same
family, but not from the propriety of the father himself. But
the fathers of divers families, who are subject neither to any
common father nor lord, have a common right in all things."

will show what advice was necessary to be taken for
this business, and what are the conditions of society,
or of human peace; that is to say, (changing the words
only), what are the fundamental *laws of nature*.

2. The greatest part of those men who have written
aught concerning commonwealths, either suppose, or require us or beg of us to believe, that man is a creature
born fit * for society. The Greeks call him ζῶον
πολιτικόν; and on this foundation they so build up the
doctrine of civil society, as if for the preservation of
peace, and the government of mankind, there were nothing else necessary than that men should agree to make

---

*Born fit.] Since we now see actually a constituted society
among men, and none living out of it, since we discern all
desirous of congress and mutual correspondence, it may seem
a wonderful kind of stupidity, to lay in the very threshold
of this doctrine such a stumbling block before the reader, as
to deny *man to be born fit for society*. Therefore I must
more plainly say, that it is true indeed, that to man by nature, or as man, that is, as soon as he is born, solitude is an
enemy; for infants have need of others to help them to live,
and those of riper years to help them to live well. Wherefore I deny not that men (even nature compelling) desire to
come together. But civil societies are not mere meetings, but
bonds, to the making whereof faith and compacts are necessary; the virtue whereof to children and fools, and the profit
whereof to those who have not yet tasted the miseries which
accompany its defect, is altogether unknown; whence it happens, that those, because they know not what society is,
cannot enter into it; these, because ignorant of the benefit
it brings, care not for it. Manifest therefore it is, that all
men, because they are born in infancy, are born unapt for
society. Many also, perhaps most men, either through defect
of mind or want of education, remain unfit during the whole
course of their lives; yet have they, infants as well as those
of riper years, a human nature. Wherefore man is made fit
for society not by nature, but by education. Furthermore,
although man were born in such a condition as to desire it,
it follows not, that he therefore were born fit to enter into
it. For it is one thing to desire, another to be in capacity fit
for what we desire; for even they, who through their pride,
will not stoop to equal conditions, without which there can be
no society, do yet desire it.

certain covenants and conditions together, which themselves should then call laws. Which axiom, though received by most, is yet certainly false; and an error
proceeding from our too slight contemplation of human
nature. For they who shall more narrowly look into
the causes for which men come together, and delight
in each other's company, shall easily find that this happens not because naturally it could happen no otherwise,
but by accident. For if by nature one man should love
another, that is, as man, there could no reason be re-
turned why every man should not equally love every
man, as being equally man; or why he should rather
frequent those, whose society affords him honour or
profit. We do not therefore by nature seek society for
its own sake, but that we may receive some honour or
profit from it; these we desire primarily, that second-
arily. How, by what advice, men do meet, will be best
known by observing those things which they do when
they are met. For if they meet for traffic, it is plain
every man regards not his fellow, but his business; if
to discharge some office, a certain market-friendship is
begotten, which hath more of jealousy in it than true
love, and whence factions sometimes may arise, but good
will never; if for pleasure and recreation of mind, every
man is wont to please himself most with those things
which stir up laughter, whence he may, according to the
nature of that which is ridiculous, by comparison of
another man's defects and infirmities, pass the more cur-
rent in his own opinion. And although this be sometimes innocent and without offence, yet it is manifest
they are not so much delighted with the society, as their
own vain glory. But for the most part, in these kinds
of meeting we wound the absent; their whole life, sayings, actions are examined, judged, condemned. Nay,
it is very rare but some present receive a fling as soon

as they part; so as his reason was not ill, who was wont always at parting to go out last. And these are indeed the true delights of society, unto which we are carried by nature, that is, by those passions which are incident to all creatures, until either by sad experience or good precepts it so fall out, which in many it never happens, that the appetite of present matters be dulled with the memory of things past: without which the discourse of most quick and nimble men on this subject, is but cold and hungry.

But if it so happen, that being met they pass their time in relating some stories, and one of them begins to tell one which concerns himself; instantly every one of the rest most greedily desires to speak of himself too; if one relates some wonder, the rest will tell you miracles, if they have them; if not, they will feign them. Lastly, that I may say somewhat of them who pretend to be wiser than others: if they meet to talk of philosophy, look, how many men, so many would be esteemed masters, or else they not only love not their fellows, but even persecute them with hatred. So clear is it by experience to all men who a little more narrowly consider human affairs, that all free congress ariseth either from mutual poverty, or from vain glory, whence the parties met endeavour to carry with them either some benefit, or to leave behind them that same εὐδοχιμεῖν, some esteem an honour with those, with whom they have been conversant. The same is also collected by reason out of the definitions themselves of *will, good, honour, profitable*. For when we voluntarily contract society, in all manner of society we look after the object of the will, that is, that which everyone of those who gather together, propounds to himself for good. Now, whatsoever seems good, is pleasant, and relates either to the senses, or the mind. But all the mind's pleasure is either glory, (or to have a good opinion of one's self), or refers to glory in the end; the rest are sensual, or conducing to sensuality, which may be all comprehended under the word *conveniences*. All society therefore is either for gain, or for glory; that is, not so much for love of our fellows, as for the love of ourselves. But no society can be great or lasting, which begins from vain glory. Because that glory is like honour; if all men have it no man hath it, for they consist in comparison and precellence. Neither doth the society of others advance any whit the cause of my glorying in myself; for every man must account himself, such as he can make himself without the help of others. But though the benefits of this life may be much furthered by mutual help; since yet those may be better attained to by dominion than by the society of others, I hope no body will doubt, but that men would much more greedily be carried by nature, if all fear were removed, to obtain dominion, than to gain society. We must therefore resolve, that the original of all great and lasting societies consisted not in the mutual good will men had towards each other, but in the mutual fear * they had of each other.

* *The mutual fear.*] It is objected: it is so improbable that men should grow into civil societies out of fear, that if they had been afraid, they would not have endured each other's looks. They presume, I believe, that to fear is nothing else than to be affrighted. I comprehend in this word *fear*, a certain foresight of future evil; neither do I conceive flight the sole property of fear, but to distrust, suspect, take heed, provide so that they may not fear, is also incident to the fearful. They who go to sleep, shut their doors; they who travel, carry their swords with them, because they fear thieves. Kingdoms guard their coasts and frontiers with forts and castles; cities are compact with walls; and all for fear of neighbouring kingdoms and towns. Even the strongest armies, and most accomplished for fight, yet sometimes parley for peace, as fearing each other's power, and lest they might be overcome. It is through fear that men secure themselves by

3. The cause of mutual fear consists partly in the natural equality of men, partly in their mutual will of hurting: whence it comes to pass, that we can neither expect from others, nor promise to ourselves the least security. For if we look on men full-grown, and consider how brittle the frame of our human body is, which perishing, all its strength, vigour, and wisdom itself perisheth with it; and how easy a matter it is, even for the weakest man to kill the strongest: there is no reason why any man trusting to his own strength, should conceive himself made by nature above others. They are equals, who can do equal things one against the other; but they who can do the greatest things, namely, kill, can do equal things. All men therefore among themselves are by nature equal; the inequality we now discern, hath its spring from the civil law.

4. All men in the state of nature have a desire and will to hurt, but not proceeding from the same cause, neither equally to be condemned. For one man, according to that natural equality which is among us, permits as much to others as he assumes to himself; which is an argument of a temperate man, and one that rightly values his power. Another, supposing himself above others, will have a license to do what he lists, and challenges respect and honour, as due to him before others; which is an argument of a fiery spirit. This man's will to hurt ariseth from vain glory, and the false esteem he hath of his own strength; the other's from the necessity of defending himself, his liberty, and his goods, against this man's violence.

5. Furthermore, since the combat of wits is the

---

flight indeed, and in corners, if they think they cannot escape otherwise; but for the most part, by arms and defensive weapons; whence it happens, that daring to come forth they know each other's spirits. But then if they fight, civil society ariseth from the victory; if they agree, from their agreement.

fiercest, the greatest discords which are, must necessarily arise from this contention. For in this case it is not only odious to contend against, but also not to consent. For not to approve of what a man saith, is no less than tacitly to accuse him of an error in that thing which he speaketh: as in very many things to dissent, is as much as if you accounted him a fool whom you dissent from. Which may appear hence, that there are no wars so sharply waged as between sects of the same religion, and factions of the same commonweal, where the contestation is either concerning doctrines or politic prudence. And since all the pleasure and jollity of the mind consists in this, even to get some, with whom comparing, it may find somewhat wherein to triumph and vaunt itself; it is impossible but men must declare sometimes some mutual scorn and contempt, either by laughter, or by words, or by gesture, or some sign or other; than which there is no greater vexation of mind, and than from which there cannot possibly arise a greater desire to do hurt.

6. But the most frequent reason why men desire to hurt each other, ariseth hence, that many men at the same time have an appetite to the same thing; which yet very often they can neither enjoy in common, nor yet divide it; whence it follows that the strongest must have it, and who is strongest must be decided by the sword.

7. Among so many dangers therefore, as the natural lusts of men do daily threaten each other withal, to have a care of one's self is so far from being a matter scornfully to be looked upon, that one has neither the power nor wish to have done otherwise. For every man is desirous of what is good for him, and shuns what is evil, but chiefly the chiefest of natural evils, which is death; and this he doth by a certain impulsion of nature, no

less than that whereby a stone moves downward. It is therefore neither absurd nor reprehensible, neither against the dictates of true reason, for a man to use all his endeavours to preserve and defend his body and the members thereof from death and sorrows. But that which is not contrary to right reason, that all men account to be done justly, and with right. Neither by the word *right* is anything else signified, than that liberty which every man hath to make use of his natural faculties according to right reason. Therefore the first foundation of natural right is this, that *every man as much as in him lies endeavour to protect his life and members.*

8. But because it is in vain for a man to have a right to the end, if the right to the necessary means be denied him, it follows, that since every man hath a right to preserve himself, he must also be allowed a right *to use all the means, and do all the actions, without which he cannot preserve himself.*

9. Now whether the means which he is about to use, and the action he is performing, be necessary to the preservation of his life and members or not, he himself, by the right of nature, must be judge. For if it be contrary to right reason that I should judge of mine own peril, say, that another man is judge. Why now, because he judgeth of what concerns me, by the same reason, because we are equal by nature, will I judge also of things which do belong to him. Therefore it agrees with right reason, that is, it is the right of nature that I judge of his opinion, that is, whether it conduce to my preservation or not.

10. Nature hath given to *every one a right to all*; that is, it was lawful for every man, in the bare state of nature,* or before such time as men had engaged them-

* *In the bare state of nature.*] This is thus to be understood: what any man does in the bare state of nature, is

selves by any covenants or bonds, to do what he would, and against whom he thought fit, and to possess, use, and enjoy all what he would, or could get. Now because whatsoever a man would, it therefore seems good to him because he wills it, and either it really doth, or at least seems to him to contribute towards his preservation, (but we have already allowed him to be judge, in the foregoing article, whether it doth or not, insomuch as we are to hold all for necessary whatsoever he shall esteem so), and by the 7th article it appears that by the right of nature those things may be done, and must be had, which necessarily conduce to the protection of life and members, it follows, that in the state of nature,

---

injurious to no man; not that in such a state he cannot offend God, or break the laws of nature; for injustice against men presupposeth human laws, such as in the state of nature there are none. Now the truth of this proposition thus conceived, is sufficiently demonstrated to the mindful reader in the articles immediately foregoing; but because in certain cases the difficulty of the conclusion makes us forget the premises, I will contract this argument, and make it most evident to a single view. Every man hath right to protect himself, as appears by the seventh article. The same man therefore hath a right to use all the means which necessarily conduce to this end, by the eighth article. But those are the necessary means which he shall judge to be such, by the ninth article. He therefore hath a right to make use of, and to do all whatsoever he shall judge requisite for his preservation; wherefore by the judgment of him that doth it, the thing done is either right or wrong, and therefore right. True it is therefore in the bare state of nature, &c. But if any man pretend somewhat to tend necessarily to his preservation, which yet he himself doth not confidently believe so, he may offend against the laws of nature, as in the third chapter of this book is more at large declared. It hath been objected by some: if a son kill his father, doth he him no injury? I have answered, that a son cannot be understood to be at any time in the state of nature, as being under the power and command of them to whom he owes his protection as soon as ever he is born, namely, either his father's or his mother's, or him that nourished him; as is demonstrated in the ninth chapter.

to have all, and do all, is lawful for all. And this is that which is meant by that common saying, *nature hath given all to all.* From whence we understand likewise, that in the state of nature profit is the measure of right.

11. But it was the least benefit for men thus to have a common right to all things. For the effects of this right are the same, almost, as if there had been no right at all. For although any man might say of every thing, *this is mine,* yet could he not enjoy it, by reason of his neighbour, who having equal right and equal power, would pretend the same thing to be his.

12. If now to this natural proclivity of men, to hurt each other, which they derive from their passions, but chiefly from a vain esteem of themselves, you add, the right of all to all, wherewith one by right invades, the other by right resists, and whence arise perpetual jealousies and suspicions on all hands, and how hard a thing it is to provide against an enemy invading us with an intention to oppress and ruin, though he come with a small number, and no great provision; it cannot be denied but that the natural state of men, before they entered into society, was a mere war, and that not simply, but a war of all men against all men. For what is WAR, but that same time in which the will of contesting by force is fully declared, either by words or deeds? The time remaining is termed PEACE.

13. But it is easily judged how disagreeable a thing to the preservation either of mankind, or of each single man, a perpetual war is. But it is perpetual in its own nature; because in regard of the equality of those that strive, it cannot be ended by victory. For in this state the conqueror is subject to so much danger, as it were to be accounted a miracle, if any, even the most strong, should close up his life with many years and old age. They of America are examples hereof, even in this pres-

ent age: other nations have been in former ages; which
now indeed are become civil and flourishing, but were
then few, fierce, short-lived, poor, nasty, and deprived
of all that pleasure and beauty of life, which peace and
society are wont to bring with them. Whosoever therefore holds, that it had been best to have continued in
that state in which all things were lawful for all men,
he contradicts himself. For every man by natural necessity desires that which is good for him: nor is there
any that esteems a war of all against all, which necessarily adheres to such a state, to be good for him. And
so it happens, that through fear of each other we think
it fit to rid ourselves of this condition, and to get some
fellows; that if there needs must be war, it may not yet
be against all men, nor without some helps.

14. Fellows are gotten either by constraint, or by consent; by constraint, when after fight the conqueror
makes the conquered serve him, either through fear of
death, or by laying fetters on him: by consent, when
men enter into society to help each other, both parties
consenting without any constraint. But the conqueror
may by right compel the conquered, or the strongest the
weaker, (as a man in health may one that is sick, or he
that is of riper years a child), unless he will choose to
die, to give caution of his future obedience. For since
the right of protecting ourselves according to our own
wills, proceeded from our danger, and our danger from
our equality, it is more consonant to reason, and more
certain for our conservation, using the present advantage to secure ourselves by taking caution, than when
they shall be full grown and strong, and got out of our
power, to endeavour to recover that power again by
doubtful fight. And on the other side, nothing can be
thought more absurd, than by discharging whom you
already have weak in your power, to make him at once

both an enemy and a strong one. From whence we may understand likewise as a corollary in the natural state of men, that *a sure and irresistible power confers the right of dominion and ruling over those who cannot resist*; insomuch, as the right of all things that can be done, adheres essentially and immediately unto this omnipotence hence arising.

15. Yet cannot men expect any lasting preservation, continuing thus in the state of nature, that is, of war, by reason of that equality of power, and other human faculties they are endued withal. Wherefore to seek peace, where there is any hopes of obtaining it, and where there is none, to enquire out for auxiliaries of war, is the dictate of right reason, that is, the law of nature; as shall be showed in the next chapter.

CHAPTER XIV

OF THE FIRST AND SECOND NATURAL LAWS, AND OF CONTRACTS

THE RIGHT OF NATURE, which writers commonly call *jus naturale*, is the liberty each man hath, to use his own power, as he will himself, for the preservation of his own nature; that is to say, of his own life; and consequently, of doing anything, which in his own judgment, and reason, he shall conceive to be the aptest means thereunto.[1]

[1] Compare *Human Nature*, (M. IV, 83). "And forasmuch as necessity of nature maketh men to will and desire *bonum sibi*, that which is good for themselves, and to avoid that which is hurtful; but most of all, the terrible enemy of nature, death, from whom we expect both the loss of all power, and also the greatest of bodily pains in the losing; it is not against reason, that a man doth all he can to preserve his own body and limbs both from death and pain. And that which is not against reason, men call *right*, or *just*, or

By LIBERTY, is understood, according to the proper signification of the word, the absence of external impediments: which impediments, may oft take away part of a man's power to do what he would; but cannot hinder him from using the power left him, according as his judgment, and reason shall dictate to him.[2]

A LAW OF NATURE, *lex naturalis,* is a precept or general rule, found out by reason, by which a man is forbidden to do that, which is destructive of his life, or taketh away the means of preserving the same; and to omit that, by which he thinketh it may be best preserved. For though they that speak of this subject, use to confound *jus,* and *lex, right* and *law*: yet they ought to be distinguished; because RIGHT, consisteth in liberty to do, or to forbear; whereas LAW, determineth, and bindeth to one of them: so that law, and right, differ as much, as obligation, and liberty; which in one and the same matter are inconsistent.[3]

---

blameless liberty of using our own natural power and ability. It is therefore a right of nature, that every man may preserve his own life and limbs, with all the power he hath."

[2] Compare above chap. VI, n. 5.

[3] Compare *Philosophical Rudiments,* (M. II, 186). "Now *natural liberty* is a right not constituted, but allowed by the laws. For the *laws* being removed, our *liberty* is absolute. This is first restrained by the *natural* and *divine laws*; the residue is bounded by the *civil law*; and what remains, may again be restrained by the *constitutions* of particular towns and societies. There is great difference therefore between *law* and *right.* For law is *a fetter,* right is *freedom*; and they differ like contraries." Also *De Corpore Politico,* (M. IV, 87). "Reason is no less of the nature of man than passion, and is the same in all men, because all men agree in the will to be directed and governed in the way to that which they desire to attain, namely, their own good, which is the work of reason: there can therefore be no other law of nature than reason, nor no other precepts of *natural law,* than those which declare unto us the ways of peace, where the same may be obtained, and of defence where it may not."

And because the condition of man, as hath been declared in the precedent chapter, is a condition of war of every one against every one; in which case every one is governed by his own reason; and there is nothing he can make use of, that may not be a help unto him, in preserving his life against his enemies; it followeth, that in such a condition, every man has a right to every thing; even to one another's body. And therefore, as long as this natural right of every man to every thing endureth, there can be no security to any man, how strong or wise soever he be, of living out the time, which nature ordinarily alloweth men to live. And consequently it is a precept, or general rule of reason, *that every man, ought to endeavour peace, as far as he has hope of obtaining it; and when he cannot obtain it, that he may seek, and use, all helps, and advantages of war.* The first branch of which rule, containeth the first, and fundamental law of nature; which is, *to seek peace, and follow it.* The second, the sum of the right of nature; which is, *by all means we can, to defend ourselves.*

From this fundamental law of nature, by which men are commanded to endeavour peace, is derived this second law; *that a man be willing, when others are so too, as far forth, as for peace, and defence of himself he shall think it necessary, to lay down this right to all things; and be contented with so much liberty against other men, as he would allow other men against himself.* For as long as every man holdeth this right, of doing any thing he liketh; so long are all men in the condition of war. But if other men will not lay down their right, as well as he; then there is no reason for anyone, to divest himself of his: for that were to expose himself to prey, which no man is bound to, rather than to dispose himself to peace. This is that law of the Gospel;

*whatsoever you require that others should do to you,
that do ye to them.* And that law of all men, *quod tibi
fieri non vis, alteri ne feceris.*

To *lay down* a man's *right* to any thing, is to *divest*
himself of the *liberty*, of hindering another of the benefit
of his own right to the same. For he that renounceth,
or passeth away his right, giveth not to any other man a
right which he had not before; because there is nothing
to which every man had not right by nature: but only
standeth out of his way, that he may enjoy his own
original right, without hindrance from him; not without
hindrance from another. So that the effect which redoundeth to one man, by another man's defect of right,
is but so much diminution of impediments to the use of
his own right original.

Right is laid aside, either by simply renouncing it;
or by transferring it to another. By *simply* RENOUNC-
ING; when he cares not to whom the benefit thereof
redoundeth. By TRANSFERRING; when he intendeth the
benefit thereof to some certain person, or persons. And
when a man hath in either manner abandoned, or
granted away his right; then is he said to be OBLIGED,
or BOUND,[4] not to hinder those, to whom such right is
granted, or abandoned, from the benefit of it: and that
he *ought*, and it is his DUTY, not to make void that voluntary act of his own: and that such hindrance is INJUS-
TICE, and INJURY, as being *sine jure*; the right being
before renounced, or transferred. So that *injury*, or
injustice, in the controversies of the world, is somewhat
like to that, which in the disputations of scholars is
called *absurdity*. For as it is there called an absurdity,

[4] Compare *Philosophical Rudiments* (M. II, 110). "All obligation derives from contract." (M. II, 183). "To follow
what is prescribed by *law*, is *duty*; what by *counsel, is free
will.*"

to contradict what one maintained in the beginning: so in the world, it is called injustice, and injury, voluntarily to undo that, which from the beginning he had voluntarily done. The way by which a man either simply renounceth, or transferreth his right, is a declaration, or signification, by some voluntary and sufficient sign, or signs, that he doth so renounce, or transfer; or hath so renounced, or transferred the same, to him that accepteth it. And these signs are either words only, or actions only; or, as it happeneth most often, both words, and actions. And the same are the BONDS, by which men are bound, and obliged: bonds, that have their strength, not from their own nature, for nothing is more easily broken than a man's word, but from fear of some evil consequence upon the rupture.

Whensoever a man transferreth his right, or renounceth it; it is either in consideration of some right reciprocally transferred to himself; or for some other good he hopeth for thereby. For it is a voluntary act: and of the voluntary acts of every man, the object is some *good to himself*. And therefore there be some rights, which no man can be understood by any words, or other signs, to have abandoned, or transferred. As first a man cannot lay down the right of resisting them, that assault him by force, to take away his life; because he cannot be understood to aim thereby, at any good to himself. The same may be said of wounds, and chains, and imprisonment; both because there is no benefit consequent to such patience; as there is to the patience of suffering another to be wounded, or imprisoned: as also because a man cannot tell, when he seeth men proceed against him by violence, whether they intend his death or not. And lastly the motive, and end for which this renouncing, and transferring of right is introduced, is nothing else but the security of a man's person, in his life, and in the means of so preserving life, as not to be weary of it. And therefore if a man by words, or other signs, seem to despoil himself of the end, for which those signs were intended; he is not to be understood as if he meant it, or that it was his will; but that he was ignorant of how such words and actions were to be interpreted.[5]

The mutual transferring of right, is that which men call CONTRACT.

There is difference between transferring of right to the thing; and transferring, or tradition, that is delivery of the thing itself. For the thing may be delivered together with the translation of the right; as in buying and selling with ready-money; or exchange of goods, or lands: and it may be delivered some time after.

Again, one of the contractors, may deliver the thing

---

[5] Compare below p. 280. Also *Leviathan* (M. III, 297). "In the making of a commonwealth, every man giveth away the right of defending another; but not of defending himself. Also he obligeth himself, to assist him that hath the sovereignty, in the punishing of another; but of himself not. But to covenant to assist the sovereign, in doing hurt to another, unless he that so covenanteth have a right to do it himself, is not to give him a right to punish. It is manifest therefore that the right which the commonwealth, that is, he, or they that represent it, hath to punish, is not grounded on any concession, or gift of the subjects. But I have also showed formerly, that before the institution of commonwealth, every man had a right to every thing, and to do whatsoever he thought necessary to his own preservation; subduing, hurting, or killing any man in order thereunto. And this is the foundation of that right of punishing, which is exercised in every commonwealth. For the subjects did not give the sovereign that right; but only in laying down theirs, strengthened him to use his own, as he should think fit, for the preservation of them all: so that it was not given, but left to him, and to him only; and (excepting the limits set him by natural law) as entire, as in the condition of mere nature, and of war of every one against his neighbor."

contracted for on his part, and leave the other to perform his part at some determinate time after, and in the mean time be trusted; and then the contract on his part, is called PACT, or COVENANT: or both parts may contract now, to perform hereafter: in which cases, he that is to perform in time to come, being trusted, his performance is called *keeping of promise,* or faith; and the failing of performance, if it be voluntary, *violation of faith.*[6]

When the transferring of right, is not mutual: but one of the parties transferreth, in hope to gain thereby friendship, or service from another, or from his friends; or in hope to gain the reputation of charity, or magnanimity; or to deliver his mind from the pain of compassion; or in hope of reward in heaven; this is not contract, but GIFT, FREE-GIFT, GRACE: which words signify one and the same thing.

Signs of contract, are either *express,* or *by inference.* Express, are words spoken with understanding of what they signify: and such words are either of the time *present,* or *past*; as, *I give, I grant, I have given, I have granted, I will that this be yours:* or of the future; as, *I will give, I will grant:* which words of the future are called PROMISE.

Signs by inference, are sometimes the consequence of words; sometimes the consequence of silence; sometimes the consequence of actions; sometimes the consequence of forbearing an action: and generally a sign by inference, of any contract, is whatsoever sufficiently argues the will of the contractor.

[6] Compare *De Corpore Politico,* (M. IV, 221). "So that the difference between a covenant and a law, standeth thus: in simple covenant, the action to be done, or not done, is first limited and made known, and then followeth the promise to do or not do; but in a law, the obligation to do or not to do, precedeth, and the declaration what is to be done, or not done, followeth after."

Words alone, if they be of the time to come, and contain a bare promise, are an insufficient sign of a free-gift, and therefore not obligatory. For if they be of the time to come, as *to-morrow I will give,* they are a sign I have not given yet, and consequently that my right is not transferred, but remaineth till I transfer it by some other act. But if the words be of the time present, or past, as, *I have given,* or, *do give to be delivered to-morrow,* then is my to-morrow's right given away to-day; and that by the virtue of the words, though there were no other argument of my will. And there is a great difference in the signification of these words, *volo hoc tuum esse cras,* and *cras dabo;* that is, between *I will that this be thine to-morrow,* and, *I will give it thee to-morrow;* for the word *I will,* in the former manner of speech, signifies an act of the will present; but in the latter, it signifies a promise of an act of the will to come: and therefore the former words, being of the present, transfer a future right; the latter, that be of the future, transfer nothing. But if there be other signs of the will to transfer a right, besides words; then, though the gift be free, yet may the right be understood to pass by words of the future: as if a man propound a prize to him that comes first to the end of a race, the gift is free; and though the words be of the future, yet the right passeth: for if he would not have his words so be understood, he should not have let them run.

In contracts, the right passeth, not only where the words are of the time present, or past, but also where they are of the future: because all contract is mutual translation, or change of right; and therefore he that promiseth only, because he hath already received the benefit for which he promiseth, is to be understood as if he intended the right should pass: for unless he had been content to have his words so understood, the other would not have performed his part first. And for that cause, in buying, and selling, and other acts of contract, a promise is equivalent to a covenant; and therefore obligatory.

He that performeth first in the case of a contract, is said to MERIT that which he is to receive by the performance of the other; and he hath it as *due*. Also when a prize is propounded to many, which is to be given to him only that winneth; or money. is thrown amongst many, to be enjoyed by them that catch it; though this be a free gift; yet so to win, or so to catch, is to *merit*, and to have it as DUE. For the right is transferred in the propounding of the prize, and in throwing down the money; though it be not determined to whom, but by the event of the contention. But there is between these two sorts of merit, this difference, that in contract, I merit by virtue of my own power, and the contractor's need; but in this case of free gift, I am enabled to merit only by the benignity of the giver: in contract, I merit at the contractor's hand that he should part with his right; in this case of gift, I merit not that the giver should part with his right; but that when he has parted with it, it should be mine, rather than another's. And this I think to be the meaning of that distinction of the Schools, between *meritum congrui*, and *meritum condigni*. For God Almighty, having promised Paradise to those men, hoodwinked with carnal desires, that can walk through this world according to the precepts, and limits prescribed by him; they say, he that shall so walk, shall merit Paradise *ex congruo*. But because no man can demand a right to it, by his own righteousness, or any other power in himself, but by the free grace of God only; they say, no man can merit Paradise *ex condigno*. This I say, I think is the meaning of that distinction; but because disputers do not agree upon the signification of their own terms of art, longer than it serves their turn; I will not affirm any thing of their meaning: only this I say; when a gift is given indefinitely, as a prize to be contended for, he that winneth meriteth, and may claim the prize as due.

If a covenant be made, wherein neither of the parties perform presently, but trust one another; in the condition of mere nature, which is a condition of war of every man against every man, upon any reasonable suspicion, it is void: but if there be a common power set over them both, with right and force sufficient to compel performance, it is not void. For he that performeth first, has no assurance the other will perform after; because the bonds of words are too weak to bridle men's ambition, avarice, anger, and other passions, without the fear of some coercive power; which in the condition of mere nature, where all men are equal, and judges of the justness of their own fears, cannot possibly be supposed. And therefore he which performeth first, does but betray himself to his enemy; contrary to the right, he can never abandon, of defending his life, and means of living.

But in a civil estate, where there is a power set up to constrain those that would otherwise violate their faith, that fear is no more reasonable; and for that cause, he which by the covenant is to perform first, is obliged so to do.

The cause of fear, which maketh such a covenant invalid, must be always something arising after the covenant made; as some new fact, or other sign of the will not to perform: else it cannot make the covenant void. For that which could not hinder a man from promising, ought not to be admitted as a hindrance of performing.

He that transferreth any right, transferreth the means of enjoying it, as far as lieth in his power. As he that selleth land, is understood to transfer the herbage, and whatsoever grows upon it: nor can he that sells a mill turn away the stream that drives it. And they that give to a man the right of government in sovereignty, are understood to give him the right of levying money to maintain soldiers; and of appointing magistrates for the administration of justice.

To make covenants with brute beasts, is impossible; because not understanding our speech, they understand not, nor accept of any translation of right; nor can translate any right to another: and without mutual acceptation, there is no covenant.[7]

To make covenant with God, is impossible, but by mediation of such as God speaketh to, either by revelation supernatural, or by his lieutenants that govern under him, and in his name: for otherwise we know not whether our covenants be accepted, or not. And therefore they that vow anything contrary to any law of nature, vow in vain; as being a thing unjust to pay such

---

[7] Compare *Leviathan*, (M. III, 257). "Over natural fools, children, or madmen, there is no law, no more than over brute beasts; nor are they capable of the title of just, or unjust; because they had never power to make any covenant, or to understand the consequences thereof; and consequently never took upon them to authorize the actions of any sovereign, as they must do that make to themselves a commonwealth. And as those from whom nature or accident hath taken away the notice of all laws in general; so also every man, from whom any accident, not proceeding from his own default, hath taken away the means to take notice of any particular law, is excused, if he observe it not: and to speak properly, that law is no law to him."

vow. And if it be a thing commanded by the law of nature, it is not the vow, but the law that binds them.

The matter, or subject of a covenant, is always something that falleth under deliberation; for to covenant, is an act of the will; that is to say, an act, and the last act of deliberation; and is therefore always understood to be something to come; and which is judged possible for him that covenanteth, to perform.

And therefore, to promise that which is known to be impossible, is no covenant. But if that prove impossible afterwards, which before was thought possible, the covenant is valid, and bindeth, though not to the thing itself, yet to the value; or, if that also be impossible, to the unfeigned endeavour of performing as much as is possible: for to more no man can be obliged.

Men are freed of their covenants two ways; by performing; or by being forgiven. For performance, is the natural end of obligation; and forgiveness, the restitution of liberty; as being a retransferring of that right, in which the obligation consisted.

Covenants entered into by fear, in the condition of mere nature, are obligatory. For example, if I covenant to pay a ransom, or service, for my life, to an enemy; I am bound by it: for it is a contract, wherein one receiveth the benefit of life; the other is to receive money, or service for it; and consequently, where no other law, as in the condition of mere nature, forbiddeth the performance, the covenant is valid. Therefore prisoners of war, if trusted with the payment of their ransom, are obliged to pay it: and if a weaker prince, make a disadvantageous peace with a stronger, for fear; he is bound to keep it; unless, as hath been said before, there ariseth some new, and just cause of fear, to renew the war. And even in commonwealths, if I be forced to redeem myself from a thief by promising him money, I am bound to pay it, till the civil law discharge me. For whatsoever I may lawfully do without obligation, the same I may lawfully covenant to do through fear: and what I lawfully covenant, I cannot lawfully break.

A former covenant, makes void a later. For a man that hath passed away his right to one man to-day, hath it not to pass to-morrow to another: and therefore the later promise passeth no right, but is null.

A covenant not to defend myself from force, by force, is always void. For, as I have showed before, no man can transfer, or lay down his right to save himself from death, wounds, imprisonment, the avoiding whereof is the only end of laying down any right; and therefore the promise of not resisting force, in no covenant transferreth any right; nor is obliging. For though a man may covenant thus, *unless I do so, or so, kill me*; he cannot covenant thus, *unless I do so, or so, I will not resist you, when you come to kill me*. For man by nature chooseth the lesser evil, which is danger of death in resisting; rather than the greater, which is certain and present death in not resisting. And this is granted to be true by all men, in that they lead criminals to execution, and prison, with armed men, notwithstanding that such criminals have consented to the law, by which they are condemned.

A covenant to accuse oneself, without assurance of pardon, is likewise invalid. For in the condition of nature, where every man is judge, there is no place for accusation: and in the civil state, the accusation is followed with punishment; which being force, a man is not obliged not to resist. The same is also true, of the accusation of those, by whose condemnation a man falls into misery; as of a father, wife, or benefactor. For the testimony of such an accuser, if it be not willingly given, is presumed to be corrupted by nature; and therefore not to be received: and where a man's testimony is not to be credited, he is not bound to give it. Also accusations upon torture, are not to be reputed as testimonies. For torture is to be used but as means of conjecture, and light, in the further examination, and search of truth: and what is in that case confessed, tendeth to the ease of him that is tortured; not to the informing of the torturers: and therefore ought not to have the credit of a sufficient testimony: for whether he deliver himself by true, or false accusation, he does it by the right of preserving his own life.

The force of words, being, as I have formerly noted, too weak to hold men to the performance of their covenants; there are in man's nature, but two imaginable helps to strengthen it. And those are either a fear of the consequence of breaking their word; or a glory, or pride in appearing not to need to break it. This latter is a generosity too rarely found to be presumed on, especially in the pursuers of wealth, command, or sensual pleasure; which are the greatest part of mankind. The passion to be reckoned upon, is fear; whereof there be two very general objects: one, the power of spirits invisible; the other, the power of those men they shall therein offend. Of these two, though the former be the greater power, yet the fear of the latter is commonly the greater fear. The fear of the former is in every man, his own religion: which hath place in the nature of man before civil society. The latter hath not so; at least not place enough, to keep men to their promises; because in the condition of mere nature, the inequality of power is not discerned, but by the event of battle. So that before the time of civil society, or in the interruption thereof by war, there is nothing can strengthen a covenant of peace agreed on, against the temptations of avarice, ambition, lust, or other strong desire, but the fear of that invisible power, which they every one worship as God; and fear as a revenger of their perfidy. All therefore that can be done between two men not subject to civil power, is to put one another to swear by the God he feareth: which *swearing*, or OATH, is a *form of speech, added to a promise; by which he that promiseth, signifieth, that unless he perform, he renounceth the mercy of his God, or calleth to him for vengeance on himself.* Such was the heathen form, *Let* Jupiter *kill me else, as I kill this beast.* So is our form, *I shall do thus, and thus, so help me God.* And this, with the rites and ceremonies, which every one useth in his own religion, that the fear of breaking faith might be the greater.

By this it appears, that an oath taken according to any other form, or rite, than his, that sweareth, is in vain; and no oath: and that there is no swearing by any thing which the swearer thinks not God. For though men have sometimes used to swear by their kings, for fear, or flattery; yet they would have it thereby understood, they attributed to them divine honour. And that swearing unnecessarily by God, is but prophaning of his name: and swearing by other things, as men do in common discourse, is not swearing, but an impious custom, gotten by too much vehemence of talking.

It appears also, that the oath adds nothing to the obligation. For a covenant, if lawful, binds in the sight of God, without the oath, as much as with it: if unlawful, bindeth not at all; though it be confirmed with an oath.

PARALLEL CHAPTER FROM

PHILOSOPHICAL RUDIMENTS CONCERNING GOVERNMENT

CHAPTER II

OF THE LAW OF NATURE CONCERNING CONTRACTS

1. ALL authors agree not concerning the definition of *the natural law,* who notwithstanding do very often make use of this term in their writings. The method therefore wherein we begin from definitions and exclusion of all equivocation, is only proper to them who leave no place for contrary disputes. For the rest, if any man say that somewhat is done against the law of nature, one proves it hence; because it was done against the general agreement of all the most wise and learned nations: but this declares not who shall be the judge of the wisdom and learning of all nations. Another hence, that it was done against the general consent of all mankind; which definition is by no means to be admitted. For then it were impossible for any but children and fools, to offend against such a law; for sure, under the notion of mankind, they comprehend all men actually endued with reason. These therefore either do naught against it, or if they do aught, it is without their own consent, and therefore ought to be excused. But to receive the laws of nature from the consents of them who oftener break than observe them, is in truth unreasonable. Besides, men condemn the same things in others, which they approve in themselves;

on the other side, they publicly commend what they privately condemn; and they deliver their opinions more by hearsay, than any speculation of their own; and they accord more through hatred of some object, through fear, hope, love, or some other perturbation of mind, than true reason. And therefore it comes to pass, that whole bodies of people often do those things with the greatest unanimity and earnestness, which those writers most willingly acknowledge to be against the law of nature. But since all do grant, that is done by *right*, which is not done against reason, we ought to judge those actions only *wrong*, which are repugnant to right reason, that is, which contradict some certain truth collected by right reasoning from true principles. But that which is done *wrong*, we say it is done against some law. Therefore *true reason* is a certain *law*; which, since it is no less a part of human nature, than any other faculty or affection of the mind, is also termed natural. Therefore the *law of nature*, that I may define it, is the dictate of right reason,* conversant about those

* *Right reason.*] By right reason in the natural state of men, I understand not, as many do, an infallible faculty, but the act of reasoning, that is, the peculiar and true ratiocination of every man concerning those actions of his, which may either redound to the damage or benefit of his neighbours. I call it peculiar, because although in a civil government the reason of the supreme, that is, the civil law, is to be received by each single subject for the right; yet being without this civil government, in which state no man can know right reason from false, but by comparing it with his own, every man's own reason is to be accounted, not only the rule of his own actions, which are done at his own peril, but also for the measure of another man's reason, in such things as do concern him. I call it true, that is, concluding from true principles rightly framed, because that the whole breach of the laws of nature consists in the false reasoning, or rather folly of those men, who see not those duties they are necessarily to perform towards others in order to their own conservation. But the principles of right reasoning about such like duties, are those which are explained in the second,

things which are either to be done or omitted for the constant preservation of life and members, as much as in us lies.

2. But the first and fundamental law of nature is, *that peace is to be sought after, where it may be found; and where not, there to provide ourselves for helps of war.* For we showed in the last article of the foregoing chapter, that this precept is the dictate of right reason; but that the dictates of right reason are natural laws, that hath been newly proved above. But this is the first, because the rest are derived from this, and they direct the ways either to peace or self-defence.

3. But one of the natural laws derived from this fundamental one is this: *that the right of all men to all things ought not to be retained; but that some certain rights ought to be transferred or relinquished.* For if every one should retain his right to all things, it must necessarily follow, that some by right might invade, and others, by the same right, might defend themselves against them. For every man by natural necessity endeavours to defend his body, and the things which he judgeth necessary towards the protection of his body. Therefore war would follow. He therefore acts against the reason of peace, that is, against the law of nature, whosoever he be, that doth not part with his right to all things.

4. But he is said to part with his right, who either absolutely renounceth it, or conveys it to another. He absolutely renounceth it, who by some sufficient sign or meet tokens declares, that he is willing that it shall never be lawful for him to do that again, which before *by right* he might have done. But he conveys it to another, who by some sufficient sign or meet tokens declares to

_____

third, fourth, fifth, sixth, and seventh articles of the first chapter.

that other, that he is willing it should be unlawful for him to resist him, in going about to do somewhat in the performance whereof he might before *with right* have resisted him.   But that the conveyance of right consists merely in not resisting, is understood by this, that before it was conveyed, he to whom he conveyed it, had even then also a right to all; whence he could not give any new right; but the resisting right he had before he gave it, by reason whereof the other could not freely enjoy his rights, is utterly abolished.   Whosoever therefore acquires some right in the natural state of men, he only procures himself security and freedom from just molestation in the enjoyment of his primitive right.   As for example, if any man shall sell or give away a farm, he utterly deprives himself only from all right to this farm; but he does not so others also.

5. But in the conveyance of right, the will is requisite not only of him that conveys, but of him also that accepts it.   If either be wanting, the right remains.   For if I would have given what was mine to one who refused to accept of it, I have not therefore either simply renounced my right, or conveyed it to any man.   For the cause which moved me to part with it to this man, was in him only, not in others too.

6. But if there be no other token extant of our will either to quit or convey our right, but only words; those words must either relate to the present or time past; for if they be of the future only, they convey nothing.   For example, he that speaks thus of the time to come, *I will give to-morrow,* declares openly that yet he hath not given it.   So that all this day his right remains, and abides to-morrow too, unless in the interim he actually bestows it: for what is mine, remains mine till I have parted with it.   But if I shall speak of the time present, suppose thus; *I do give or have given you this to be*

received to-morrow: by these words is signified that I have already given it, and that his right to receive it to-morrow is conveyed to him by me to-day.

7. Nevertheless, although words alone are not sufficient tokens to declare the will; if yet to words relating to the future there shall some other signs be added, they may become as valid as if they had been spoken of the present. If therefore, as by reason of those other signs, it appear that he that speaks of the future, intends those words should be effectual toward the perfect transferring of his right, they ought to be valid. For the conveyance of right depends not on words, but, as hath been instanced in the fourth article, on the declaration of the will.

8. If any man convey some part of his right to another, and doth not this for some certain benefit received, or for some compact, a conveyance in this kind is called a gift or free donation. But in free donation, those words only oblige us, which signify the present or the time past; for if they respect the future, they oblige not as *words*, for the reason given in the foregoing article. It must needs therefore be, that the obligation arise from some other tokens of the will. But, because whatsoever is voluntarily done, is done for some good to him that wills it; there can no other token be assigned of the will to give it, except some benefit either already received, or to be acquired. But it is supposed that no such benefit is acquired, nor any compact in being; for if so, it would cease to be a free gift. It remains therefore, that a mutual good turn without agreement be expected. But no sign can be given, that he, who used future words toward him who was in no sort engaged to return a benefit, should desire to have his words so understood as to oblige himself thereby. Nor is it suitable to reason, that those who are easily

inclined to do well to others, should be obliged by every promise, testifying their present good affection. And for this cause, a promiser in this kind must be understood to have time to deliberate, and power to change that affection, as well as he to whom he made that promise, may alter his desert. But he that deliberates, is so far forth free, nor can be said to have already given. But if he promise often, and yet give seldom, he ought to be condemned of levity, and be called not a donor, but doson.

9. But the act of two, or more, mutually conveying their rights, is called a *contract*. But in every contract, either both parties instantly perform what they contract for, insomuch as there is no trust had from either to other; or the one performs, the other is trusted; or neither perform. Where both parties perform presently, there the contract is ended as soon as it is performed. But where there is credit given, either to one or both, there the party trusted promiseth after-performance; and this kind of promise is called a *covenant*.

10. But the covenant made by the party trusted with him who hath already performed, although the promise be made by words pointing at the future, doth no less transfer the right of future time, than if it had been made by words signifying the present or time past. For the other's performance is a most manifest sign that he so understood the speech of him whom he trusted, as that he would certainly make performance also at the appointed time; and by this sign the party trusted knew himself to be thus understood; which because he hindered not, was an evident token of his will to perform. The promises therefore which are made for some benefit received, which are also covenants, are tokens of the will; that is, as in the foregoing section hath been declared, of the last act of deliberating, whereby the

liberty of non-performance is abolished, and by consequence are obligatory. For where liberty ceaseth, there beginneth obligation.

11. But the covenants which are made in contract of mutual trust, neither party performing out of hand, if there arise * a just suspicion in either of them, are in the state of nature invalid. For he that first performs, by reason of the wicked disposition of the greatest part of men studying their own advantage either by right or wrong, exposeth himself to the perverse will of him with whom he hath contracted. For it suits not with reason, that any man should perform first, if it be not likely that the other will make good his promise after; which, whether it be probable or not, he that doubts it must be judge of, as hath been showed in the foregoing chapter in the ninth article. Thus, I say, things stand in the state of nature. But in a civil state, when there is a power which can compel both parties, he that hath contracted to perform first, must first perform; because, that since the other may be compelled, the cause which made him fear the other's non-performance, ceaseth.

12. But from this reason, that in all free gifts and compacts there is an acceptance of the conveyance of right required: it follows that no man can compact with him who doth not declare his acceptance. And therefore we cannot compact with beasts, neither can we give or take from them any manner of right, by reason of their want of speech and understanding. Neither can any man covenant with God, or be obliged to him by vow; except so far forth as it appears to him by Holy Scrip-

---

* *Arise.*] For, except there appear some new cause of fear, either from somewhat done, or some other token of the will not to perform from the other part, it cannot be judged to be a just fear; for the cause which was not sufficient to keep him from making compact, must not suffice to authorize the breach of it, being made.

tures, that he hath substituted certain men who have authority to accept of such-like vows and covenants, as being in God's stead.

13. Those therefore do vow in vain, who are in the state of nature, where they are not tied by any civil law, except, by most certain revelation, the will of God to accept their vow or pact, be made known to them. For if what they vow be contrary to the law of nature, they are not tied by their vow; for no man is tied to perform an unlawful act. But if what is vowed, be commanded by some law of nature, it is not their vow, but the law itself which ties them. But if he were free, before his vow, either to do it or not do it, his liberty remains; because that the openly declared will of the obligor is requisite to make an obligation by vow; which, in the case propounded, is supposed not to be. Now I call him the obligor, to whom any one is tied; and the obliged, him who is tied.

14. Covenants are made of such things only as fall under our deliberation. For it can be no covenant without the will of the contractor. But the will is the last act of him who deliberates; wherefore they only concern things *possible* and *to come*. No man, therefore, by his compact obligeth himself to an impossibility. But yet, though we often covenant to do such things as then seem possible when we promised them, which yet afterward appear to be impossible, are we not therefore freed from all obligation. The reason whereof is, that he who promiseth a future, in certainty receives a present benefit, on condition that he return another for it. For his will, who performs the present benefit, hath simply before it for its object a certain good, equally valuable with the thing promised; but the thing itself not simply, but with condition if it could be done. But if it should so happen, that even this should prove impossible, why

then he must perform as much as he can. Covenants, therefore, oblige us not to perform just the thing itself covenanted for, but our utmost endeavour; for this only is, the things themselves are not, in our power.

15. We are freed from covenants two ways, either by performing, or by being forgiven. By performing, for beyond that we obliged not ourselves. By being forgiven, because he whom we obliged ourselves to, by forgiving is conceived to return us that right which we passed over to him. For forgiving implies giving, that is, by the fourth article of this chapter, a conveyance of right to him to whom the gift is made.

16. It is a usual question, whether compacts extorted from us through fear, do oblige or not. For example, if, to redeem my life from the power of a robber, I promise to pay him 100*l.* next day, and that I will do no act whereby to apprehend and bring him to justice: whether I am tied to keep promise or not. But though such a promise must sometimes be judged to be of no effect, yet it is not to be accounted so because it proceedeth from fear. For then it would follow, that those promises which reduced men to a civil life, and by which laws were made, might likewise be of none effect; (for it proceeds from fear of mutual slaughter, that one man submits himself to the dominion of another); and he should play the fool finely, who should trust his captive covenanting with the price of his redemption. It holds universally true, that promises do oblige, when there is some benefit received, and when the promise, and the thing promised, be lawful. But it is lawful, for the redemption of my life, both to promise and to give what I will of mine own to any man, even to a thief. We are obliged, therefore, by promises proceeding from fear, except the civil law forbid them; by virtue whereof, that which is promised becomes unlawful.

17. Whosoever shall contract with one to do or omit somewhat, and shall after covenant the contrary with another, he maketh not the former, but the latter contract unlawful. For he hath no longer right to do or to omit aught, who by former contracts hath conveyed it to another. Wherefore he can convey no right by latter contracts, and what is promised is promised without right. He is therefore tied only to his first contract, to break which is unlawful.

18. No man is obliged by any contracts whatsoever not to resist him who shall offer to kill, wound, or any other way hurt his body. For there is in every man a certain high degree of fear, through which he apprehends that evil which is done to him to be the greatest; and therefore by natural necessity he shuns it all he can, and it is supposed he can do no otherwise. When a man is arrived to this degree of fear, we cannot expect but he will provide for himself either by flight or fight. Since therefore no man is tied to impossibilities, they who are threatened either with death, (which is the greatest evil to nature), or wounds, or some other bodily hurts, and are not stout enough to bear them, are not obliged to endure them. Furthermore, he that is tied by contract is trusted; for faith only is the bond of contracts; but they who are brought to punishment, either capital or more gentle, are fettered or strongly guarded; which is a most certain sign that they seemed not sufficiently bound from non-resistance by their contracts. It is one thing, if I promise thus: if I do it not at the day appointed, kill me. Another thing, if thus: if I do it not, though you should offer to kill me, I will not resist. All men, if need be, contract the first way, and there is need sometimes. This second way, none; neither is it ever needful. For in the mere state of nature, if you have a mind to kill, that state itself

affords you a right; insomuch as you need not first trust him, if for a breach of trust you will afterwards kill him. But in a civil state, where the right of life and death and of all corporal punishment is with the supreme, that same right of killing cannot be granted to any private person. Neither need the supreme himself contract with any man patiently to yield to his punishment; but only this, that no man offer to defend others from him. If in the state of nature, as between two realms, there should a contract be made on condition of killing if it were not performed, we must presuppose another contract of not killing before the appointed day. Wherefore on that day, if there be no performance, the right of war returns, that is a hostile state, in which all things are lawful, and therefore resistance also. Lastly, by the contract of not resisting, we are obliged, of two evils to make choice of that which seems the greater. For certain death is a greater evil than fighting. But of two evils it is impossible not to choose the least. By such a compact, therefore, we should be tied to impossibilities; which is contrary to the very nature of compacts.

19. Likewise no man is tied by any compacts whatsoever to accuse himself, or any other, by whose damage he is like to procure himself a bitter life. Wherefore neither is a father obliged to bear witness against his son, nor a husband against his wife, nor a son against his father, nor any man against any one by whose means he hath his subsistence; for in vain is that testimony which is presumed to be corrupted from nature. But although no man be tied to accuse himself by any compact, yet in a public trial he may by torture be forced to make answer. But such answers are no testimony of the fact, but helps for the searching out of truth; so that whether the party tortured his answer

be true or false, or whether he answer not at all, whatsoever he doth, he doth it by right.

20. Swearing is a speech joined to a promise, whereby the promisor declares his renouncing of God's mercy, unless he perform his word. Which definition is contained in the words themselves, which have in them the very essence of an oath, to wit, *so God help me*, or other equivalent, as with the Romans, *do thou Jupiter so destroy the deceiver, as I slay this same beast*. Neither is this any let, but that an oath may as well sometimes be affirmatory as promissory; for he that confirms his affirmation with an oath, promiseth that he speaks truth. But though in some places it was the fashion for subjects to swear by their kings, that custom took its original hence, that those kings took upon them divine honour. For oaths were therefore introduced, that by religion and consideration of the divine power, men might have a greater dread of breaking their faiths, than that wherewith they fear men, from whose eyes their actions may lie hid.

21. Whence it follows that an oath must be conceived in that form, which he useth who takes it; for in vain is any man brought to swear by a God whom he believes not, and therefore neither fears him. For though by the light of nature it may be known that there is a God, yet no man thinks he is to swear by him in any other fashion, or by any other name, than what is contained in the precepts of his own proper, that is (as he who swears imagines) the true religion.

22. By the definition of an oath, we may understand that a bare contract obligeth no less, than that to which we are sworn. For it is the contract which binds us; the oath relates to the divine punishment, which it could not provoke, if the breach of contract were not in itself unlawful; but it could not be unlawful, if the contract

were not obligatory. Furthermore, he that renounceth the mercy of God, obligeth himself not to any punishment; because it is ever lawful to deprecate the punishment, howsoever provoked, and to enjoy God's pardon if it be granted. The only effect therefore of an oath is this; to cause men, who are naturally inclined to break all manner of faith, through fear of punishment to make the more conscience of their words and actions.

23. To exact an oath where the breach of contract, if any be made, cannot but be known, and where the party compacted withal wants not power to punish, is to do somewhat more than is necessary unto self-defense, and shews a mind desirous not so much to benefit itself, as to prejudice another. For an oath, out of the very form of swearing, is taken in order to the provocation of God's anger, that is to say, of him that is omnipotent, against those who therefore violate their faith, because they think that by their own strength they can escape the punishment of men; and of him that is omniscient, against those who therefore usually break their trust, because they hope that no man shall see them.

CHAPTER XV

OF OTHER LAWS OF NATURE

FROM that law of nature, by which we are obliged to transfer to another, such rights, as being retained, hinder the peace of mankind, there followeth a third; which is this, *that men perform their covenants made*: without which, covenants are in vain, and but empty words; and the right of all men to all things remaining, we are still in the condition of war.

And in this law of nature, consisteth the fountain and original of JUSTICE. For where no covenant hath preceded, there hath no right been transferred, and every man has right to every thing; and consequently, no action can be unjust. But when a covenant is made, then to break it is *unjust*: and the definition of INJUSTICE, is no other than *the not performance of covenant*. And whatsoever is not unjust, is *just*.

But because covenants of mutual trust, where there is a fear of not performance on either part, as hath been said in the former chapter, are invalid; though the original of justice be the making of covenants; yet injustice actually there can be none, till the cause of such fear be taken away; which while men are in the natural condition of war, cannot be done. Therefore before the names of just, and unjust can have place, there must be some coercive power, to compel men equally to the performance of their covenants, by the terror of some punishment, greater than the benefit they expect by the breach of their covenant; and to make good that propriety, which by mutual contract men acquire, in recompense of the universal right they abandon: and such power there is none before the erection of a commonwealth.[1] And this is also to be

[1] Compare *De Corpore Politico*, (M. IV, 129). "Covenants agreed upon by every man assembled for the making of a commonwealth, and put in writing without erecting of a power of coercion, are no reasonable security for any of them that so covenant, nor are to be called laws, and leave men still in the estate of nature and hostility. For seeing the wills of most men are governed only by fear, and where there is no power of coercion, there is no fear, the wills of most men will follow their passions of covetousness, lust, anger, and the like, to the breaking of those covenants, whereby the rest, also, who otherwise would keep them, are set at liberty, and have no law, but from themselves. This power of coercion * * * * * consisteth in the transferring of every man's right of resistance against him, to whom he hath transferred the power of coercion. It followeth therefore, that no man in any commonwealth whatsoever, hath right to resist him, or them, to whom they have transferred this power coercive, or (as men use to call it) the sword of justice,

gathered out of the ordinary definition of justice in the Schools: for they say, that *justice is the constant will of giving to every man his own.* And therefore where there is no *own,* that is no propriety, there is no injustice; and where is no coercive power erected, that is, where there is no commonwealth, there is no propriety; all men having right to all things: therefore where there is no commonwealth, there nothing is unjust. So that the nature of justice, consisteth in keeping of valid covenants: but the validity of covenants begins not but with the constitution of a civil power, sufficient to compel men to keep them: and then it is also that propriety begins.

The fool hath said in his heart, there is no such thing as justice; and sometimes also with his tongue; seriously alleging, that every man's conservation, and contentment, being committed to his own care, there could be no reason, why every man might not do what he thought conduced thereunto: and therefore also to make, or not make; keep, or not keep covenants, was not against reason, when it conduced to one's benefit. He does not therein deny, that there be covenants; and that they are sometimes broken, sometimes kept; and that such breach of them may be called injustice, and the observance of them justice: but he questioneth, whether injustice, taking away the fear of God, for the same fool hath said in his heart there is no God, may not sometimes stand with that reason, which dictateth to every man his own good; and particularly then, when it conduceth to such a benefit, as shall put a man in a condition, to neglect not only the dispraise, and revilings, but also the power of other men. The kingdom of God is gotten by violence: but what if it could be gotten by

supposing the not-resistance possible." Also above p. 51 and below chap. XVII.

unjust violence? were it against reason so to get it,
when it is impossible to receive hurt by it? and if it be
not against reason, it is not against justice; or else
justice is not to be approved for good. From such
reasoning as this, successful wickedness hath obtained
the name of virtue: and some that in all other things
have disallowed the violation of faith; yet have allowed
it, when it is for the getting of a kingdom. And the
heathen that believed, that Saturn was deposed by his
son Jupiter, believed nevertheless the same Jupiter to
be the avenger of injustice: somewhat like to a piece
of law in Coke's *Commentaries on Littleton*; where he
says, if the right heir of the crown be attainted of
treason; yet the crown shall descend to him, and *eo
instante* the attainder be void: from which instances a
man will be very prone to infer; that when the heir apparent of a kingdom, shall kill him that is in possession,
though his father; you may call it injustice, or by what
other name you will; yet it can never be against reason,
seeing all the voluntary actions of men tend to the
benefit of themselves; and those actions are most reasonable, that conduce most to their ends. This specious
reasoning is nevertheless false.

For the question is not of promises mutual, where
there is no security of performance on either side; as
when there is no civil power erected over the parties
promising; for such promises are no covenants: but
either where one of the parties has performed already;
or where there is a power to make him perform; there
is the question whether it be against reason, that is,
against the benefit of the other to perform, or not. And
I say it is not against reason. For the manifestation
whereof, we are to consider; first, that when a man doth
a thing, which notwithstanding anything can be fore-
seen, and reckoned on, tendeth to his own destruction,

howsoever some accident which he could not expect, arriving may turn it to his benefit; yet such events do not make it reasonably or wisely done. Secondly, that in a condition of war, wherein every man to every man, for want of a common power to keep them all in awe, is an enemy, there is no man who can hope by his own strength, or wit, to defend himself from destruction, without the help of confederates; where everyone expects the same defence by the confederation, that any one else does: and therefore he which declares he thinks it reason to deceive those that help him, can in reason expect no other means of safety, than what can be had from his own single power. He therefore that breaketh his covenant, and consequently declareth that he thinks he may with reason do so, cannot be received into any society, that unite themselves for peace and defense, but by the error of them that receive him; nor when he is received, be retained in it, without seeing the danger of their error; which errors a man cannot reasonably reckon upon as the means of his security: and therefore if he be left, or cast out of society, he perisheth; and if he live in society, it is by the errors of other men, which he could not foresee, nor reckon upon; and consequently against the reason of his preservation; and so, as all men that contribute not to his destruction, forbear him only out of ignorance of what is good for themselves.

As for the instance of gaining the secure and perpetual felicity of heaven, by any way; it is frivolous: there being but one way imaginable; and that is not breaking, but keeping of covenant.

And for the other instance of attaining sovereignty by rebellion; it is manifest, that though the event follow, yet because it cannot reasonably be expected, but rather the contrary; and because by gaining it so, others are taught to gain the same in like manner, the attempt thereof is against reason. Justice therefore, that is to say, keeping of covenant, is a rule of reason, by which we are forbidden to do any thing destructive to our life; and consequently a law of nature.

There be some that proceed further; and will not have the law of nature, to be those rules which conduce to the preservation of man's life on earth; but to the attaining of an eternal felicity after death; to which they think the breach of covenant may conduce; and consequently be just and reasonable; such are they that think it a work of merit to kill, or depose, or rebel against, the sovereign power constituted over them by their own consent. But because there is no natural knowledge of man's estate after death; much less of the reward that is then to be given to breach of faith; but only a belief grounded upon other men's saying, that they know it supernaturally, or that they know those, that knew them, that knew others, that knew it supernaturally; breach of faith cannot be called a precept of reason, or nature.

Others, that allow for a law of nature, the keeping of faith, do nevertheless make exception of certain persons; as heretics, and such as use not to perform their covenant to others: and this also is against reason. For if any fault of a man, be sufficient to discharge our covenant made; the same ought in reason to have been sufficient to have hindered the making of it.

The names of just, and unjust, when they are attributed to men, signify one thing; and when they are attributed to actions, another. When they are attributed to men, they signify conformity, or inconformity of manners, to reason. But when they are attributed to actions, they signify the conformity, or inconformity to reason, not of manners, or manner of life, but of particular actions. A just man therefore, is he that taketh all the care he can, that his actions may be all just: and an unjust man, is he that neglecteth it. And such men are more often in our language styled by the names of righteous, and unrighteous; than just, and unjust; though the meaning be the same. Therefore a righteous man, does not lose that title, by one, or a few unjust actions, that proceed from sudden passion, or mistake of things, or persons: nor does an unrighteous man, lose his character, for such actions, as he does, or forbears to do, for fear: because his will is not framed by the justice, but by the apparent benefit of what he is to do. That which gives to human actions the relish of justice, is a certain nobleness or gallantness of courage, rarely found, by which a man scorns to be beholden for the contentment of his life, to fraud, or breach of promise. This justice of the manners, is that which is meant, where justice is called a virtue; and injustice a vice.

But the justice of actions denominates men, not just, but *guiltless*; and the injustice of the same, which is also called injury, gives them but the name of *guilty*.

Again, the injustice of manners, is the disposition, or aptitude to do injury; and is injustice before it proceed to act; and without supposing any individual person injured. But the injustice of an action, that is to say injury, supposeth an individual person injured; namely him, to whom the covenant was made: and therefore many times the injury is received by one man, when the damage redoundeth to another. As when the master commandeth his servant to give money to a stranger; if it be not done, the injury is done to the master, whom he had before covenanted to obey; but the damage redoundeth to the stranger, to whom he had no obligation; and therefore could not injure him. And so also in commonwealths, private men may remit to one an-

other their debts; but not robberies or other violences,
whereby they are endamaged; because the detaining of
debt, is an injury to themselves; but robbery and violence, are injuries to the person of the commonwealth.

Whatsoever is done to a man, conformable to his own
will signified to the doer, is no injury to him. For if
he that doeth it, hath not passed away his original right
to do what he please, by some antecedent covenant,
there is no breach of covenant; and therefore no injury
done him. And if he have; then his will to have it
done being signified, is a release of that covenant: and
so again there is no injury done him.

Justice of actions, is by writers divided into *commutative*, and *distributive*: and the former they say
consisteth in proportion arithmetical; the latter in proportion geometrical. Commutative therefore, they place
in the equality of value of the things contracted for;
and distributive, in the distribution of equal benefit, to
men of equal merit. As if it were injustice to sell
dearer than we buy; or to give more to a man than he
merits. The value of all things contracted for, is
measured by the appetite of the contractors: and therefore the just value, is that which they be contented to
give. And merit, besides that which is by covenant,
where the performance on one part, meriteth the performance of the other part, and falls under justice
commutative, not distributive, is not due by justice; but
is rewarded of grace only. And therefore this distinction, in the sense wherein it useth to be expounded, is
not right. To speak properly, commutative justice, is
the justice, of a contractor; that is, a performance of
covenant, in buying, and selling; hiring, and letting to
hire; lending, and borrowing; exchanging, bartering,
and other acts of contract.

And distributive justice, the justice of an arbitrator;

that is to say, the act of defining what is just. Wherein, being trusted by them that make him arbitrator, if he perform his trust, he is said to distribute to every man his own: and this is indeed just distribution, and may be called, though improperly, distributive justice; but more properly equity; which also is a law of nature, as shall be shown in due place.

As justice dependeth on antecedent covenant; so does GRATITUDE depend on antecedent grace; that is to say, antecedent free gift: and is the fourth law of nature; which may be conceived in this form, *that a man which receiveth benefit from another of mere grace, endeavour that he which giveth it, have no reasonable cause to repent him of his good will.* For no man giveth, but with intention of good to himself; because gift is voluntary; and of all voluntary acts, the object is to every man his own good; of which if men see they shall be frustrated, there will be no beginning of benevolence, or trust; nor consequently of mutual help; nor of reconciliation of one man to another; and therefore they are to remain still in the condition of *war*; which is contrary to the first and fundamental law of nature, which commandeth men to *seek peace.* The breach of this law, is called' *ingratitude*; and hath the same relation to grace, that injustice hath to obligation by covenant.

A fifth law of nature, is COMPLAISANCE; that is to say, *that every man strive to accommodate himself to the rest.* For the understanding whereof, we may consider, that there is in men's aptness to society, a diversity of nature, rising from their diversity of affections; not unlike to that we see in stones brought together for building of an edifice. For as that stone which by the asperity, and irregularity of figure, takes more room from others, than itself fills; and for the hardness, cannot be easily made plain, and thereby hindereth the building, is by the builders cast away as unprofitable, and troublesome: so also, a man that by asperity of nature, will strive to retain those things which to himself are superfluous, and to others necessary; and for the stubbornness of his passions, cannot be corrected, is to be left, or cast out of society, as cumbersome thereunto. For seeing every man, not only by right, but also by necessity of nature, is supposed to endeavour all he can, to obtain that which is necessary for his conservation; he that shall oppose himself against it, for things superfluous, is guilty of the war that thereupon is to follow; and therefore doth that, which is contrary to the fundamental law of nature, which commandeth *to seek peace*. The observers of this law, may be called SOCIABLE the Latins call them *commodi*; the contrary, *stubborn, insociable, froward, intractable*.

A sixth law of nature, is this, *that upon caution of the future time, a man ought to pardon the offences past of them that repenting, desire it*. For PARDON, is nothing but granting of peace; which though granted to them that persevere in their hostility, be not peace, but fear; yet not granted to them that give caution of the future time, is sign of an aversion to peace; and therefore contrary to the law of nature.

A seventh is, *that in revenges*, that is, retribution of evil for evil, *men look not at the greatness of the evil past, but the greatness of the good to follow*. Whereby we are forbidden to inflict punishment with any other design, than for correction of the offender, or direction of others. For this law is consequent to the next before it, that commandeth pardon, upon security of the future time. Besides, revenge without respect to the example, and profit to come, is a triumph, or glorying in the hurt of another, tending to no end; for the end is always somewhat to come; and glorying to no end, is vain-glory, and contrary to reason, and to hurt without reason, tendeth to the introduction of war; which is against the law of nature; and is commonly styled by the name of *cruelty*.

And because all signs of hatred, or contempt, provoke to fight; insomuch as most men choose rather to hazard their life, than not to be revenged; we may in the eighth place, for a law of nature, set down this precept, *that no man by deed, word, countenance, or gesture, declare hatred, or contempt of another*. The breach of which law, is commonly called *contumely*.

The question who is the better man, has no place in the condition of mere nature; where, as has been shewn before, all men are equal. The inequality that now is, has been introduced by the laws civil. I know that Aristotle in the first book of his *Politics*, for a foundation of his doctrine, maketh men by nature, some more worthy to command, meaning the wiser sort, such as he thought himself to be for his philosophy; others to serve, meaning those that had strong bodies, but were not philosophers as he; as if master and servant were not introduced by consent of men, but by difference of wit: which is not only against reason; but also against experience. For there are very few so foolish, that had not rather govern themselves, than be governed by others: nor when the wise in their own conceit, contend by force, with them who distrust their own wisdom, do they always, or often, or almost at any time, get the victory. If nature therefore have made men equal, that equality is to be acknowledged: or if nature have made men unequal; yet because men that think themselves equal, will not enter into conditions of peace, but upon equal terms, such equality must be admitted. And therefore for the ninth law of nature, I put this, *that*

every man acknowledge another for his equal by nature.
The breach of this precept is *pride.*

On this law, dependeth another, *that at the entrance
into conditions of peace, no man require to reserve to
himself any right, which he is not content should be
reserved to every one of the rest.* As it is necessary for
all men that seek peace, to lay down certain rights of
nature; that is to say, not to have liberty to do all they
list: so is it necessary for man's life, to retain some;
as right to govern their own bodies; enjoy air, water,
motion, ways to go from place to place; and all things
else, without which a man cannot live, or not live well.
If in this case, at the making of peace, men require for
themselves, that which they would not have to be granted
to others, they do contrary to the precedent law, that
commandeth the acknowledgment of natural equality,
and therefore also against the law of nature. The observers of this law, are those we call *modest,* and the
breakers *arrogant* men. The Greeks call the violation
of this law πλεονεξία; that is, a desire of more than
their share.[2]

Also if *a man be trusted to judge between man and
man*, it is a precept of the law of nature, *that he deal
equally between them.* For without that, the controversies of men cannot be determined but by war. He
therefore that is partial in judgment, doth what in him

---

[2] Compare *De Corpore Politico,* (M. IV, 103). "As it was
necessary that a man should not retain his right to every
thing, so also was it, that he should retain his right to some
things; to his own body, for example, the right of defending
whereof, he could not transfer; to the use of fire, water, free
air, and place to live in, and to all things necessary for life.
Nor doth the law of nature command any divesting of other
rights, than of those only which cannot be retained without
the loss of peace. Seeing then many rights are retained, when
we enter into peace one with another, reason and the law of
nature dictateth, *Whatsoever right any man requireth to retain,
he allow every other man to retain the same.*"

lies, to deter men from the use of judges, and arbitrators; and consequently, against the fundamental law of nature, is the cause of war.

The observance of this law, from the equal distribution to each man, of that which in reason belongeth to him, is called EQUITY, and, as I have said before, distributive justice: the violation, *acception of persons*, προσωποληψία.

And from this followeth another law, *that such things as cannot be divided, be enjoyed in common, if it can be; and if the quantity of the thing permit, without stint; otherwise proportionably to the number of them that have right.* For otherwise the distribution is unequal, and contrary to equity.

But some things there be, that can neither be divided, nor enjoyed in common. Then, the law of nature, which prescribeth equity, requireth, *that the entire right; or else, making the use alternate, the first possession, be determined by lot.* For equal distribution, is of the law of nature; and other means of equal distribution cannot be imagined.

Of *lots* there be two sorts, *arbitrary*, and *natural*. Arbitrary, is that which is agreed on by the competitors: natural, is either *primogeniture*, which the Greek calls κληρονομία, which signifies, *given by lot*; or *first seizure*.

And therefore those things which cannot be enjoyed in common, nor divided ought to be adjudged to the first possessor; and in some cases to the first born, as acquired by lot.

It is also a law of nature, *that all men that mediate peace, be allowed safe conduct.* For the law that commandeth peace, as the *end*, commandeth intercession, as the *means*; and to intercession the means is safe conduct.

And because, though men be never so willing to observe these laws, there may nevertheless arise questions concerning a man's action; first, whether it were done, or not done; secondly, if done, whether against the law, or not against the law; the former whereof, is called a question *of fact*; the latter a question *of right*, therefore unless the parties to the question, covenant mutually to stand to the sentence of another, they are as far from peace as ever. This other to whose sentence they submit is called an ARBITRATOR. And therefore it is of the law of nature, *that they that are at controversy, submit their right to the judgment of an arbitrator.*

And seeing every man is presumed to do all things in order to his own benefit, no man is a fit arbitrator in his own cause; and if he were never so fit; yet equity allowing to each party equal benefit, if one be admitted to be judge, the other is to be admitted also; and so the controversy, that is, the cause of war, remains, against the law of nature.

For the same reason no man in any cause ought to be received for arbitrator, to whom greater profit, or honour, or pleasure apparently ariseth out of the victory of one party, than of the other: for he hath taken, though an unavoidable bribe, yet a bribe; and no man can be obliged to trust him. And thus also the controversy, and the condition of war remaineth, contrary to the law of nature.

And in a controversy of *fact*, the judge being to give more credit to one, than to the other, if there be no other arguments, must give credit to a third; or to a third and fourth; or more: for else the question is undecided, and left to force, contrary to the law of nature.

These are the laws of nature, dictating peace, for a means of the conservation of men in multitudes; and which only concern the doctrine of civil society. There be other things tending to the destruction of particular men; as drunkenness, and all other parts of intemperance; which may therefore also be reckoned amongst those things which the law of nature hath forbidden; but are not necessary to be mentioned, nor are pertinent enough to this place.

And though this may seem too subtle a deduction of the laws of nature, to be taken notice of by all men; whereof the most part are too busy in getting food, and the rest too negligent to understand; yet to leave all men inexcusable, they have been contracted into one easy sum, intelligible even to the meanest capacity; and that is, *Do not that to another, which thou wouldst not have done to thyself*; which sheweth him, that he has no more to do in learning the laws of nature, but, when weighing the actions of other men with his own, they seem too heavy, to put them into the other part of the balance, and his own into their place, that his own passions, and self-love, may add nothing to the weight; and then there is none of these laws of nature that will not appear unto him very reasonable.

The laws of nature oblige *in foro interno*; that is to say, they bind to a desire they should take place: but *in foro externo*; that is, to the putting them in act, not always. For he that should be modest, and tractable, and perform all he promises, in such time, and place, where no man else should do so, should but make himself a prey to others, and procure his own certain ruin, contrary to the ground of all laws of nature, which tend to nature's preservation. And again, he that having sufficient security, that others shall observe the same laws towards him, observes them not himself, seeketh not peace, but war; and consequently the destruction of his nature by violence.

And whatsoever laws bind *in foro interno*, may be

broken, not only by a fact contrary to the law, but also by a fact according to it, in case a man think it contrary. For though his action in this case, be according to the law; yet his purpose was against the law; which, where the obligation is *in foro interno*, is a breach.

The laws of nature are immutable and eternal; for injustice, ingratitude, arrogance, pride, iniquity, acception of persons, and the rest, can never be made lawful. For it can never be that war shall preserve life, and peace destroy it.[3]

The same laws, because they oblige only to a desire, and endeavour, I mean an unfeigned and constant endeavour, are easy to be observed. For in that they require nothing but endeavour, he that endeavoureth their performance, fulfilleth them, and he that fulfilleth the law, is just.

And the science of them, is the true and only moral philosophy.[4] For moral philosophy is nothing else but the science of what is *good*, and *evil*, in the conversation, and society of mankind. *Good*, and *evil*, are names that signify our appetites, and aversions; which in different tempers, customs, and doctrines of men, are different: and divers men, differ not only in their judgment, on

---

[3] Compare *Philosophical Rudiments*, (M. II, 50). "The same law which is *natural* and *moral*, is also wont to be called *divine*, not undeservedly; as well because reason, which is the law of nature, is given by God to every man for the rule of his actions; as because the precepts of living which are thence derived, are the same with those which have been delivered from the divine Majesty for the *laws* of his heavenly kingdom, by our Lord Jesus Christ, and his holy prophets and apostles." And also p. 254, n. 2, and *De Corpore Politico*, (M. IV, 224). "The law of nature, which is also the moral law, is the law of the author of nature, God Almighty; and the law of God taught by our Saviour Christ, is the moral law."

[4] Compare above p. 189, n. 3.

the senses of what is pleasant, and unpleasant to the taste, smell, hearing, touch, and sight; but also of what is conformable, or disagreeable to reason, in the actions of common life. Nay, the same man, in divers times, differs from himself; and one time praiseth, that is, calleth good, what another time he dispraiseth, and calleth evil: from whence arise disputes, controversies, and at last war. And therefore so long as a man is in the condition of mere nature, which is a condition of war, his private appetite is the measure of good, and evil: and consequently all men agree on this, that peace is good, and therefore also the way, or means of peace, which, as I have shewed before, are *justice, gratitude, modesty, equity, mercy,* and the rest of the laws of nature, are good; that is to say; *moral virtues;* and their contrary *vices,* evil. Now the science of virtue and vice, is moral philosophy; and therefore the true doctrine of the laws of nature, is the true moral philosophy. But the writers of moral philosophy, though they acknowledge the same virtues and vices; yet not seeing wherein consisted their goodness; nor that they come to be praised, as the means of peaceable, sociable, and comfortable living, place them in a mediocrity of passions: as if not the cause, but the degree of daring, made fortitude; or not the cause, but the quantity of a gift, made liberality.

These dictates of reason, men used to call by the name of laws, but improperly: for they are but conclusions, or theorems concerning what conduceth to the conservation and defence of themselves; whereas law, properly, is the word of him, that by right hath command over others. But yet if we consider the same theorems, as delivered in the word of God, that by right commandeth all things; then are they properly called laws.

PHILOSOPHICAL RUDIMENTS CONCERNING GOVERNMENT

CHAPTER III

OF THE OTHER LAWS OF NATURE

1. ANOTHER of the laws of nature is, to *perform contracts*, or *to keep trust*. For it hath been showed in the foregoing chapter, that the law of nature commands every man, as a thing necessary, to obtain peace, to convey certain rights from each to other; and that this, as often as it shall happen to be done, is called a contract. But this is so far forth only conducible to peace, as we shall perform ourselves what we contract with others shall be done or omitted; and in vain would contracts be made, unless we stood to them. Because therefore to stand to our covenants, or to keep faith, is a thing necessary for the obtaining of peace; it will prove, by the second article of the second chapter, to be a precept of the natural law.

2. Neither is there in this matter any exception of the persons with whom we contract; as if they keep no faith with others, or hold that none ought to be kept, or are guilty of any other kind of vice. For he that contracts, in that he doth contract, denies that action to be in vain; and it is against reason for a knowing man to do a thing in vain; and if he think himself not bound to keep it, in thinking so he affirms the contract to be made in vain. He therefore who contracts with one with whom he thinks he is not bound to keep faith, he doth at once

think a contract to be a thing done in vain, and not in vain; which is absurd. Either therefore we must hold trust with all men, or else not bargain with them; that is, either there must be a declared war, or a sure and faithful peace.

3. The breaking of a bargain, as also the taking back of a gift, (which ever consists in some action or omission), is called an injury. But that action or omission is called unjust; insomuch as an injury, and an unjust action or omission, signify the same thing, and both are the same with breach of contract and trust. And it seems the word *injury* came to be given to any action or omission, because they were *without right*; he that acted or omitted, having before conveyed his right to some other. And there is some likeness between that which in the common course of life we call *injury*, and that which in the Schools is usually called *absurd*. For even as he who by arguments is driven to deny the assertion which he first maintained, is said to be brought to an absurdity; in like manner, he who through weakness of mind does or omits that which before he had by contract promised not to do or omit, commits an injury, and falls into no less contradiction than he who in the Schools is reduced to an absurdity. For by contracting for some future action, he wills it done; by not doing it, he wills it not done: which is to will a thing done and not done at the same time, which is a contradiction. An injury therefore is a kind of absurdity in conversation, as an absurdity is a kind of injury in disputation.

4. From these grounds it follows, that an injury can be done to no man * but him with whom we enter cove-

---

* *Injury can be done to no man, &c.*] The word *injustice* relates to some law: *injury*, to some person, as well as some law. For what is unjust, is unjust to all; but there may an injury be done, and yet not against me, nor thee, but some other; and sometimes against no private person, but the mag-

nant, or to whom somewhat is made over by deed of gift, or to whom somewhat is promised by way of bargain. And therefore damaging and injuring are often disjoined. For if a master command his servant, who hath promised to obey him, to pay a sum of money, or carry some present to a third man; the servant, if he do it not, hath indeed damaged this third party, but he injured his master only. So also in a civil government, if any man offend another with whom he hath made no contract, he damages him to whom the evil is done; but he injures none but him to whom the power of government belongs. For if he who receives the hurt should expostulate the mischief, he that did it should answer thus: *what art thou to me; why should I rather do according to your than mine own will, since I do not hinder but you may do your own, and not my mind?* In which speech, where there hath no manner of pre-contract passed, I see not, I confess, what is reprehensible.

5. These words, *just* and *unjust*, as also *justice* and *injustice*, are equivocal; for they signify one thing when they are attributed to persons, another when to actions. When they are attributed to actions, *just* signifies as much as what is done with right, and *unjust*, as what is done with injury. He who hath done some just thing, is not therefore said to be a *just* person, but *guiltless*; and he that hath done some unjust thing, we do not

---

istrate only; sometimes also neither against the magistrate, nor any private man, but only against God. For through contract and conveyance of right, we say, that an injury is done against this or that man. Hence it is, which we see in all kind of government, that what private men contract between themselves by word or writing, is released again at the will of the obligor. But those mischiefs which are done against the laws of the land, as theft, homicide, and the like, are punished, not as he wills to whom the hurt is done, but according to the will of the magistrate; that is, the constituted laws.

therefore say he is an *unjust*, but *guilty* man. But when
the words are applied to persons, *to be just* signifies as
much as to be delighted in just dealing, to study how to
do righteousness, or to endeavour in all things to do
that which is just; and *to be unjust* is to neglect righteous dealing, or to think it is to be measured not
according to my contract, but some present benefit. So
as the justice or injustice of the mind, the intention,
or the man, is one thing, that of an action or omission
another; and innumerable actions of a just man may
be unjust, and of an unjust man, just. But that man
is to be accounted just, who doth just things because
the law commands it, unjust things only by reason of
his infirmity; and he is properly said to be unjust, who
doth righteousness for fear of the punishment annexed
unto the law, and unrighteousness by reason of the
iniquity of his mind.

6. The justice of actions is commonly distinguished
into two kinds, commutative and distributive; the former
whereof, they say, consists in arithmetical, the latter in
geometrical proportion; and that is conversant in exchanging, in buying, selling, borrowing, lending, loca-
tion and conduction, and other acts whatsoever belonging
to contractors; where, if there be an equal return made,
hence, they say, springs a commutative justice: but this
is busied about the dignity and merits of men; so as if
there be rendered to every man χατὰ τὴν ἀξίαν, more to
him who is more worthy, and less to him that deserves
less, and that proportionably; hence, they say, ariseth
distributive justice. I acknowledge here some certain
distinction of equality: to wit, that one is an equality
simply so called; as when two things of equal value are
compared together, as a pound of silver with twelve
ounces of the same silver: the other is an equality
secundum quod; as when a thousand pounds is to be

divided to a hundred men, six hundred pounds are given to sixty men, and four hundred to forty, where there is no equality between six hundred and four hundred; but when it happens that there is the same inequality in the number of them to whom it is distributed, every one of them shall take an equal part, whence it is called an equal distribution. But such like equality is the same thing with geometrical proportion. But what is all this to justice? For neither if I sell my goods for as much as I can get for them, do I injure the buyer, who sought and desired them of me; neither if I divide more of what is mine to him who deserves less, so long as I give the other what I have agreed for, do I wrong to either. Which truth our Saviour himself, being God, testifies in the Gospel. This therefore is no distinction of justice, but of equality. Yet perhaps it cannot be denied but that justice is a certain equality, as consisting in this only; that since we are all equal by nature, one should not arrogate more right to himself than he grants to another, unless he have fairly gotten it by compact. And let this suffice to be spoken against this distinction of justice, although now almost generally received by all; lest any man should conceive an injury to be somewhat else than the breach of faith or contract, as hath been defined above.

7. It is an old saying, *volenti non fit injuria*, the willing man receives no injury; yet the truth of it may be derived from our principles. For grant that a man be willing that that should be done which he conceives to be an injury to him; why then, that is done by his will, which by contract was not lawful to be done. But he being willing that should be done which was not lawful by contract, the contract itself (by the fifteenth article of the foregoing chapter) becomes void. The

right therefore of doing it returns; therefore it is done by right; wherefore it is no injury.

8. The third precept of the natural law is, *that you suffer not him to be the worse for you, who, out of the confidence he had in you, first did you a good turn; or that you accept not a gift, but with a mind to endeavour that the giver shall have no just occasion to repent him of his gift.* For without this, he should act without reason, that would confer a benefit where he sees it would be lost; and by this means all beneficence and trust, together with all kind of benevolence, would be taken from among men, neither would there be aught of mutual assistance among them, nor any commencement of gaining grace and favour; by reason whereof the state of war would necessarily remain, contrary to the fundamental law of nature. But because the breach of this law is not a breach of trust or contract, (for we suppose no contracts to have passed among them), therefore is it not usually termed an injury; but because good turns and thanks have a mutual eye to each other, it is called *ingratitude.*

9. The fourth precept of nature is, *that every man render himself useful unto others*: which that we may rightly understand, we must remember that there is in men a diversity of dispositions to enter into society, arising from the diversity of their affections, not unlike that which is found in stones, brought together in the building, by reason of the diversity of their matter and figure. For as a stone, which in regard of its sharp and angular form takes up more room from other stones than it fills up itself, neither because of the hardness of its matter can it well be pressed together, or easily cut, and would hinder the building from being fitly compacted, is cast away, as not fit for use: so a man, for the harshness of his disposition in retaining superfluities for him-

self, and detaining of necessaries from others, and being
incorrigible by reason of the stubborness of his affections, is commonly said to be useless and troublesome
unto others. Now, because each one not by right only,
but even by natural necessity, is supposed with all his
main might to intend the procurement of those things
which are necessary to his own preservation; if any man
will contend on the other side for superfluities, by his
default there will arise a war; because that on him alone
there lay no necessity of contending; he therefore acts
against the fundamental law of nature. Whence it follows, (which we were to show), that it is a precept of
nature, that every man accommodate himself to others.
But he who breaks this law, may be called *useless* and
troublesome. Yet Cicero opposeth *inhumanity* to this
usefulness, as having regard to this very law.

10. The fifth precept of the law of nature is, *that
we must forgive him who repents and asks pardon for
what is past, having first taken caution for the time to
come.* The pardon of what is past, or the remission of
an offence, is nothing else but the granting of peace to
him that asketh it, after he hath warred against us, and
now is become penitent. But peace granted to him that
repents not, that is, to him that retains a hostile mind,
or that gives not caution for the future, that is, seeks not
peace, but opportunity; is not properly peace, but fear,
and therefore is not commanded by nature. Now to him
that will not pardon the penitent that gives future caution, peace itself it seems is not pleasing: which is contrary to the natural law.

11. The sixth precept of the natural law is, *that in
revenge and punishments we must have our eye not at
the evil past, but the future good*: that is, it is not lawful
to inflict punishment for any other end, but that the
offender may be corrected, or that others warned by his

punishment may become better. But this is confirmed chiefly from hence, that each man is bound by the law of nature to forgive one another, provided he give caution for the future, as hath been showed in the foregoing article. Furthermore, because revenge, if the time past be only considered, is nothing else but a certain triumph and glory of mind, which points at no end; for it contemplates only what is past, but the end is a thing to come; but that which is directed to no end, is vain: that revenge therefore which regards not the future, proceeds from vain glory, and is therefore without reason. But to hurt another without reason, introduces a war, and is contrary to the fundamental law of nature. It is therefore a precept of the law of nature, that in revenge we look not backwards, but forward. Now the breach of this law is commonly called *cruelty*.

12. But because all signs of hatred and contempt provoke most of all to brawling and fighting, insomuch as most men would rather lose their lives (that I say not, their peace) than suffer slander; it follows in the seventh place, that it is prescribed by the law of nature, that no man, either by deeds or words, countenance or laughter, *do declare himself to hate or scorn another*. The breach of which law is called *reproach*. But although nothing be more frequent than the scoffs and jeers of the powerful against the weak, and namely, of judges against guilty persons, which neither relate to the offense of the guilty, nor the duty of the judges; yet these kind of men do act against the law of nature, and are to be esteemed for contumelious.

13. The question whether of two men be the more worthy, belongs not to the natural, but civil state. For it hath been showed before (chap. 1, art. 3) that all men by nature are equal; and therefore the inequality which now is, suppose from riches, power, nobility of

kindred, is come from the civil law. I know that Aristotle, in his first book of *Politics,* affirms as a foundation of the whole political science, that some men by nature are made worthy to command, others only to serve; as if lord and servant were distinguished not by consent of men, but by an aptness, that is, a certain kind of natural knowledge or ignorance. Which foundation is not only against reason, (as but now hath been showed), but also against experience. For neither almost is any man so dull of understanding as not to judge it better to be ruled by himself, than to yield himself to the government of another; neither if the wiser and stronger do contest, have these always or often the upper hand of those. Whether therefore men be equal by nature, the equality is to be acknowledged; or whether unequal, because they are like to contest for dominion, it is necessary for the obtaining of peace, *that they be esteemed as equal*; and therefore it is in the eighth place a precept of the law of nature, *that every man be accounted by nature equal to another*; the contrary to which law is *pride.*

14. As it was necessary to the conservation of each man that he should part with some of his rights, so it is no less necessary to the same conservation that he retain some others, to wit, the right of bodily protection, of free enjoyment of air, water, and all necessaries for life. Since therefore many common rights are retained by those who enter into a peaceable state, and that many peculiar ones are also acquired, hence ariseth this ninth dictate of the natural law, to wit, that what rights soever any man challenges to himself, he also grant the same as due to all the rest; otherwise he frustrates the equality acknowledged in the former article. For what is it else to acknowledge an equality of persons in the making up of society, but to attribute equal right and power

to those whom no reason would else engage to enter into society? But to ascribe *equal things* to *equals*, is the same with giving things *proportional* to *proportionals*. The observation of this law is called *meekness*, the violation πλεονεξία; the breakers by the Latins are styled *immodici et immodesti*.

15. In the tenth place it is commanded by the law of nature, *that every man in dividing right to others, shew himself equal to either party.* By the foregoing law we are forbidden to assume more right by nature to ourselves, than we grant to others. We may take less if we will; for that sometimes is an argument of modesty. But if at any time matter of right be to be divided by us unto others, we are forbidden by this law to favour one more or less than another. For he that by favouring one before another observes not this natural equality, reproaches him whom he thus undervalues: but it is declared above, that a reproach is against the laws of nature. The observance of this precept is called *equity*; the breach, *respect of persons*. The Greeks in one word term it προσωποληψία.

16. From the foregoing law is collected this eleventh, *those things which cannot be divided, must be used in common if they can, and if the quantity of the matter permit, every man as much as he lists; but if the quantity permit not, then with limitation, and proportionally to the number of the users.* For otherwise that equality can by no means be observed, which we have showed in the foregoing article to be commanded by the law of nature.

17. Also what cannot be divided nor had in common, it is provided by the law of nature, which may be the twelfth precept, *that the use of that thing be either by turns, or adjudged to one only by lot; and that in the using it by turns, it be also decided by lot, who shall*

have the first use of it. For here also regard is to be had unto equality: but no other can be found but that of lot.

18. But all lot is twofold, *arbitrary* or *natural*. *Arbitrary* is that which is cast by the consent of the contenders, and it consists in mere chance, as they say, or fortune. *Natural* is primogeniture, in Greek, κληρονομία, as it were, given by lot; or first possession. Therefore the things which can neither be divided nor had in common, must be granted to the first possessor; as also those things which belonged to the father are due to the son, unless the father himself have formerly conveyed away that right to some other. Let this therefore stand for the thirteenth law of nature.

19. The fourteenth precept of the law of nature is, *that safety must be assured to the mediators for peace.* For the reason which commands the end, commands also the means necessary to the end. But the first dictate of reason is peace; all the rest are means to obtain it, and without which peace cannot be had. But neither can peace be had without mediation, nor mediation without safety. It is therefore a dictate of reason, that is, a law of nature, that we must give all security to the mediators for peace.

20. Furthermore because, although men should agree to make all these and whatsoever other laws of nature, and should endeavour to keep them, yet doubts and controversies would daily arise concerning the application of them unto their actions, to wit, whether what was done were against the law or not, which we call the question of right; whence will follow a fight between parties, either-sides supposing themselves wronged: it is therefore necessary to the preservation of peace, because in this case no other fit remedy can possibly be thought on, that both the disagreeing parties refer the

matter unto some third, and oblige themselves by mutual
compacts to stand to his judgment in deciding the
controversy. And he to whom they thus refer themselves, is called an arbiter. It is therefore the fifteenth
precept of the natural law, *that both parties disputing
concerning the matter of right, submit themselves unto
the opinion and judgment of some third.*

21. But from this ground, that an arbiter or judge
is chosen by the differing parties to determine the controversy, we gather that the arbiter must not be one of
the parties. For every man is presumed to seek what
is good for himself naturally, and what is just only for
peace sake and accidentally; and therefore cannot observe that same equality commanded by the law of
nature, so exactly as a third man would do. It is
therefore in the sixteenth place contained in the law of
nature, *that no man must be judge or arbiter in his own
cause.*

22. From the same ground follows in the seventeenth
place, *that no man must be judge, who propounds unto
himself any hope of profit or glory from the victory of
either part*: for the like reason sways here, as in the
foregoing law.

23. But when there is some controversy of the fact
itself, to wit, whether that be done or not which is said
to be done, the natural law wills that the arbiter trust
both parties alike, that is, because they affirm contradictories, that he believe neither. He must therefore give
credit to a third, or a third and fourth, or more, that
he may be able to give judgment of the fact, as often
as by other signs he cannot come to the knowledge of
it. The eighteenth law of nature therefore enjoins
arbiters and judges of fact, *that where firm and certain
signs of the fact appear not, there they rule their sen-*

*tence by such witnesses as seem to be indifferent to
both parts.*

24. From the above declared definition of an arbiter
may be furthermore understood, *that no contract or
promise must pass between him and the parties whose
judge he is appointed, by virtue whereof he may be engaged to speak in favour of either part, nay, or be
obliged to judge according to equity, or to pronounce
such sentence as he shall truly judge to be equal.* The
judge is indeed bound to give such sentence as he shall
judge to be equal, by the law of nature recounted in the
15th article: to the obligation of which law nothing can
be added by way of compact. Such compact therefore
would be in vain. Besides, if giving wrong judgment
he should contend for the equity of it, except such compact be of no force, the controversy would remain after
judgment given: which is contrary to the constitution of
an arbiter, who is so chosen, as both parties have obliged
themselves to stand to the judgment which he should
pronounce. The law of nature therefore commands the
judge to be disengaged, which is its nineteenth precept.

25. Furthermore, forasmuch as the laws of nature
are nought else but the dictates of reason; so as, unless
a man endeavour to preserve the faculty of right reasoning, he cannot observe the laws of nature; it is manifest,
that he who knowingly or willingly doth aught whereby
the rational faculty may be destroyed or weakened, he
knowingly and willingly breaks the law of nature. For
there is no difference between a man who performs not
his duty, and him who does such things willingly as
make it impossible for him to do it. But they destroy
and weaken the reasoning faculty, who do that which
disturbs the mind from its natural state; that which
most manifestly happens to drunkards, and gluttons.

We therefore sin, in the twentieth place, against the law of nature by drunkenness.

26. Perhaps some man, who sees all these precepts of nature derived by a certain artifice from the single dictate of reason advising us to look to the preservation and safeguard of ourselves, will say that the deduction of these laws is so hard, that it is not to be expected they will be vulgarly known, and therefore neither will they prove obliging: for laws, if they be not known, oblige not, nay indeed, are not laws. To this I answer, it is true, that hope, fear, anger, ambition, covetousness, vain glory, and other perturbations of mind, do hinder a man, so as he cannot attain to the knowledge of these laws whilst those passions prevail in him: but there is no man who is not sometimes in a quiet mind. At that time therefore there is nothing easier for him to know, though he be never so rude and unlearned, than this only rule, that when he doubts whether what he is now doing to another may be done by the law of nature or not, he conceive himself to be in that other's stead. Here instantly those perturbations which persuaded him to the fact, being now cast into the other scale, dissuade him as much. And this rule is not only easy, but is anciently celebrated in these words, *quod tibi fieri non vis, alteri ne feceris*: *do not that to others, you would not have done to yourself*.

27. But because most men, by reason of their perverse desire of present profit, are very unapt to observe these laws, although acknowledged by them; if perhaps some, more humble than the rest, should exercise that equity and usefulness which reason dictates, the others not practicing the same, surely they would not follow reason in so doing: nor would they hereby procure themselves peace, but a more certain quick destruction, and the keepers of the law become a mere prey to the

breakers of it. It is not therefore to be imagined, that by nature, that is, by reason, men are obliged to the exercise of all these laws * in that state of men wherein they are not practiced by others. We are obliged yet, in the interim, to a readiness of mind to observe them, whensoever their observation shall seem to conduce to the end for which they were ordained. We must therefore conclude, that the law of nature doth always and everywhere oblige in the internal court, or that of conscience; but not always in the external court, but then only when it may be done with safety.

28. But the laws which oblige conscience, may be broken by an act not only contrary to them, but also agreeable with them; if so be that he who does it, be of another opinion. For though the act itself be answerable to the laws, yet his conscience is against them.

29. *The laws of nature are immutable and eternal*: what they forbid, can never be lawful; what they command, can never be unlawful. For *pride, ingratitude, breach of contracts* (or *injury*), *inhumanity, contumely,*

---

* *The exercise of all these laws.*] Nay, among these laws some things there are, the omission whereof, provided it be done for peace or self-preservation, seems rather to be the fulfilling, than breach of the natural law. For he that doth all things against those that do all things, and plunders plunderers, doth equity. But on the contrary, to do that which in peace is a handsome action, and becoming an honest man, is dejectedness and poorness of spirit, and a betraying of one's self, in the time of war. But there are certain natural laws, whose exercise ceaseth not even in the time of war itself. For I cannot understand what drunkenness or cruelty, that is, revenge which respects not the future good, can advance toward peace, or the preservation of any man. Briefly, in the state of nature, what is just and unjust, is not to be esteemed by the actions but by the counsel and conscience of the actor. That which is done out of necessity, out of endeavour for peace, for the preservation of ourselves, is done with right, otherwise every damage done to a man would be a breach of the natural law, and an injury against God.

will never be lawful, nor the contrary virtues to these ever unlawful, as we take them for dispositions of the mind, that is, as they are considered in the court of conscience, where only they oblige and are laws. Yet actions may be so diversified by circumstances and the civil law, that what is done with equity at one time, is guilty of iniquity at another; and what suits with reason at one time, is contrary to it another. Yet reason is still the same, and changeth not her end, which is peace and defence, nor the means to attain them, to wit, those virtues of the mind which we have declared above, and which cannot be abrogated by any custom or law whatsoever.

30. It is evident by what hath hitherto been said, how easily the laws of nature are to be observed, because they require the endeavour only, (but that must be true and constant); which whoso shall perform, we may rightly call him *just*. For he who tends to this with his whole might, namely, that his actions be squared according to the precepts of nature, he shows clearly that he hath a mind to fulfil all those laws; which is all we are obliged to by rational nature. Now he that hath done all he is obliged to, is a just man.

31. All writers do agree, that the natural law is the same with the moral. Let us see wherefore this is true. We must know, therefore, that good and evil are names given to things to signify the inclination or aversion of them, by whom they were given. But the inclinations of men are diverse, according to their diverse constitutions, customs, opinions; as we may see in those things we apprehend by sense, as by tasting, touching, smelling; but much more in those which pertain to the common actions of life, where what this man commends, that is to say, calls *good*, the other undervalues, as being evil. Nay, very often the same man at diverse times praises

and dispraises the same thing. Whilst thus they do, necessary it is there should be discord and strife. They are, therefore, so long in the state of war, as by reason of the diversity of the present appetite, they mete good and evil by diverse measures. All men easily acknowledge this state, as long as they are in it, to be evil, and by consequence that peace is good. They therefore who could not agree concerning a present, do agree concerning a future good; which indeed is a work of reason; for things present are obvious to the sense, things to come to our reason only. Reason declaring peace to be good, it follows by the same reason, that all the necessary means to peace be good also; and therefore that modesty, equity, trust, humanity, mercy, (which we have demonstrated to be necessary to peace), are good manners or habits, that is, virtues. The law therefore, in the means to peace, commands also good manners, or the practice of virtue; and therefore it is called *moral*.

32. But because men cannot put off this same irrational appetite, whereby they greedily prefer the present good (to which, by strict consequence, many unforseen evils do adhere) before the future; it happens, that though all men do agree in the commendation of the foresaid virtues, yet they disagree still concerning their nature, to wit, in what each of them doth consist. For as oft as another's good action displeaseth any man, that action hath the name given of some neighbouring vice; likewise the bad actions which please them, are ever entitled to some virtue. Whence it comes to pass that the same action is praised by these, and called virtue, and dispraised by those, and termed vice. Neither is there as yet any remedy found by philosophers for this matter. For since they could not observe the goodness of actions to consist in this, that it was in

order to peace, and the evil in this, that it related to discord, they built a moral philosophy wholly estranged from the moral law, and unconstant to itself. For they would have the nature of virtues seated in a certain kind of mediocrity between two extremes, and the vices in the extremes themselves; which is apparently false. For *to dare* is commended, and, under the name of *fortitude* is taken for a virtue, although it be an extreme, if the cause be approved. Also the quantity of a thing given, whether it be great or little, or between both, makes not liberality, but the cause of giving it. Neither is it injustice, if I give any man more of what is mine own than I owe him. The laws of nature, therefore, are the sum of *moral* philosophy; whereof I have only delivered such precepts in this place, as appertain to the preservation of ourselves against those dangers which arise from discord. But there are other precepts of *rational* nature, from whence spring other virtues; for temperance, also, is a precept of reason, because intemperance tends to sickness and death. And so fortitude too, that is, that same faculty of resisting stoutly in present dangers, and which are more hardly declined than overcome; because it is a means tending to the preservation of him that resists.

33. But those which we call the laws of nature, (since they are nothing else but certain conclusions, understood by reason, of things to be done and omitted; but a law, to speak properly and accurately, is the speech of him who by right commands somewhat to others to be done or omitted), are not in propriety of speech laws, as they proceed from nature. Yet, as they are delivered by God in holy Scriptures, as we shall see in the chapter following, they are most properly called by the name of laws. For the sacred Scripture is the speech of God commanding over all things by greatest right.

CHAPTER XVI

OF PERSONS, AUTHORS, AND THINGS PERSONATED

A PERSON, is he, *whose words or actions are considered, either as his own, or as representing the words or actions of another man, or of any other thing, to whom they are attributed, whether truly or by fiction.*

When they are considered as his own, then is he called a *natural person*: and when they are considered as representing the words and actions of another, then is he a *feigned* or *artificial person*.

The word person is Latin: instead whereof the Greeks have πρόσωπον, which signifies the *face*, as *persona* in Latin signifies the *disguise*, or *outward appearance* of a man, counterfeited on the stage; and sometimes more particularly that part of it, which disguiseth the face, as a mask or vizard: and from the stage, hath been translated to any representer of speech and action, as well in tribunals, as theatres. So that a *person*, is the same that an *actor* is, both on the stage and in common conversation; and to *personate*, is to *act*, or *represent* himself, or another; and he that acteth another, is said to bear his person, or act in his name; in which sense Cicero useth it where he says, *Unus sustineo tres personas; mei, adversarii, et judicis*: I bear three persons; my own, my adversary's, and the judge's; and is called in divers occasions, diversely; as a *representer*, or *representative*, a *lieutenant*, a *vicar*, an *attorney*, a *deputy*, a *procurator*, an *actor*, and the like.

Of persons artificial, some have their words and actions *owned* by those whom they represent. And then the person is the *actor*; and he that owneth his words

and actions, is the AUTHOR: in which case the actor
acteth by authority. For that which in speaking of
goods and possessions, is called an *owner*, and in Latin
dominus, in Greek κύριος, speaking of actions, is called
author. And as the right of possession, is called dominion; so the right of doing any action, is called AUTHORITY.
So that by authority, is always understood a right of
doing any act; and *done by authority*, done by commission, or licence from him whose right it is.

From hence it followeth, that when the actor maketh
a covenant by authority, he bindeth thereby the author,
no less than if he had made it himself; and no less subjecteth him to all the consequences of the same. And
therefore all that hath been said formerly, (chap. xiv)
of the nature of covenants between man and man in
their natural capacity, is true also when they are made
by their actors, representers, or procurators, that have
authority from them, so far forth as is in their commission, but no further.

And therefore he that maketh a covenant with the
actor, or representer, not knowing the authority he hath,
doth it at his own peril. For no man is obliged by a
covenant, whereof he is not author; nor consequently by
a covenant made against, or beside the authority he gave.

When the actor doth anything against the law of
nature by command of the author, if he be obliged by
former covenant to obey him, not he, but the author
breaketh the law of nature; for though the action be
against the law of nature; yet it is not his: but contrarily, to refuse to do it, is against the law of nature,
that forbiddeth breach of covenant.

And he that maketh a covenant with the author, by
mediation of the actor, not knowing what authority he
hath, but only takes his word; in case such authority be
not made manifest unto him upon demand, is no longer

obliged: for the covenant made with the author, is not valid, without his counter-assurance. But if he that so covenanteth, knew beforehand he was to expect no other assurance, than the actor's word; then is the covenant valid; because the actor in this case maketh himself the author. And therefore, as when the authority is evident, the covenant obligeth the author, not the actor; so when the authority is feigned, it obligeth the actor only; there being no author but himself.

There are few things, that are incapable of being represented by fiction. Inanimate things, as a church, an hospital, a bridge, may be personated by a rector, master, or overseer. But things inanimate, cannot be authors, nor therefore give authority to their actors: yet the actors may have authority to procure their maintenance, given them by those that are owners, or governors of those things. And therefore, such things cannot be personated, before there be some state of civil government.

Likewise children, fools, and madmen that have no use of reason, may be personated by guardians, or curators; but can be no authors, during that time, of any action done by them, longer than, when they shall recover the use of reason, they shall judge the same reasonable. Yet during the folly, he that hath right of governing them, may give authority to the guardian. But this again has no place but in a state civil, because before such estate, there is no dominion of persons.

An idol, or mere figment of the brain, may be personated; as were the gods of the heathen: which by such officers as the state appointed, were personated, and held possessions, and other goods, and rights, which men from time to time dedicated, and consecrated unto them. But idols cannot be authors: for an idol is nothing. The authority proceeded from the state: and therefore before introduction of civil government, the gods of the heathen could not be personated.

The true God may be personated. As he was; first, by Moses; who governed the Israelites, that were not his, but God's people, not in his own name, with *hoc dicit Moses*; but in God's name, with *hoc dicit Dominus*. Secondly, by the Son of man, his own Son, our blessed Saviour Jesus Christ, that came to reduce the Jews, and induce all nations into the kingdom of his father; not as of himself, but as sent from his father. And thirdly, by the Holy Ghost, or Comforter, speaking, and working in the Apostles: which Holy Ghost, was a Comforter that came not of himself; but was sent, and proceeded from them both.

A multitude of men are made *one* person, when they are by one man, or one person, represented; so that it be done with the consent of every one of that multitude in particular. For it is the *unity* of the representer, not the *unity* of the represented, that maketh the person *one*. And it is the representer that beareth the person, and but one person: and *unity*, cannot otherwise be understood in multitude.

And because the multitude naturally is not *one*, but *many*; they cannot be understood for one; but many authors, of every thing their representative saith, or doth in their name; every man giving their common representer, authority from himself in particular; and owning all the actions the representer doth, in case they give him authority without stint: otherwise, when they limit him in what, and how far he shall represent them, none of them owneth more than they gave him commission to act.

And if the representative consist of many men, the voice of the greater number, must be considered as the voice of them all. For if the lesser number pronounce, for example, in the affirmative, and the greater in the negative, there will be negatives more than enough to destroy the affirmatives; and thereby the excess of negatives, standing uncontradicted, are the only voice the representative hath.

And a representative of even number, especially when the number is not great, whereby the contradictory voices are oftentimes equal, is therefore oftentimes mute, and incapable of action. Yet in some cases contradictory voices equal in number, may determine a question; as in condemning, or absolving, equality of votes, even in that they condemn not, do absolve; but not on the contrary condemn, in that they absolve not. For when a cause is heard; not to condemn, is to absolve: but on the contrary, to say that not absolving, is condemning, is not true. The like it is in a deliberation of executing presently, or deferring till another time: for when the voices are equal, the not decreeing execution, is a decree of dilation.

Or if the number be odd, as three, or more, men or assemblies; whereof every one has by a negative voice, authority to take away the effect of all the affirmative voices of the rest, this number is no representative; because by the diversity of opinions, and interests of men, it becomes oftentimes, and in cases of the greatest consequence, a mute person, and unapt, as for many things else, so for the government of a multitude, especially in time of war.

Of authors there be two sorts. The first simply so called; which I have before defined to be him, that owneth the action of another simply. The second is he, that owneth an action, or covenant of another conditionally; that is to say, he undertaketh to do it, if the other doth it not, at, or before a certain time. And these authors conditional, are generally called SURETIES, in Latin, *fidejussores*, and *sponsores*; and particularly for debt, *praedes*; and for appearance before a judge, or magistrate, *vades*.

Part II

OF COMMONWEALTH

CHAPTER XVII

OF THE CAUSES, GENERATION, AND DEFINITION OF A COMMONWEALTH

THE final cause, end, or design of men, who naturally love liberty, and dominion over others, in the introduction of that restraint upon themselves, in which we see them live in commonwealths, is the foresight of their own preservation, and of a more contented life thereby; that is to say, of getting themselves out from that miserable condition of war, which is necessarily consequent, as hath been shown in chapter xiii, to the natural passions of men, when there is no visible power to keep them in awe, and tie them by fear of punishment to the performance of their covenants, and observation of those laws of nature set down in the fourteenth and fifteenth chapters.

For the laws of nature, as *justice, equity, modesty, mercy,* and, in sum, *doing to others, as we would be done to,* of themselves, without the terror of some power, to cause them to be observed, are contrary to our natural passions, that carry us to partiality, pride, revenge, and the like. And covenants, without the sword, are but words, and of no strength to secure a man at all. Therefore notwithstanding the laws of nature, which every one hath then kept, when he has the will to keep them, when

he can do it safely, if there be no power erected, or not
great enough for our security; every man will, and may
lawfully rely on his own strength and art, for caution
against all other men.   And in all places, where men
have lived by small families, to rob and spoil one another, has been a trade, and so far from being reputed
against the law of nature, that the greater spoils they
gained, the greater was their honour; and men observed
no other laws therein, but the laws of honour; that is,
to abstain from cruelty, leaving to men their lives, and
instruments of husbandry.   And as small families did
then; so now do cities and kingdoms which are but
greater families, for their own security, enlarge their
dominions, upon all pretences of danger, and fear of
invasion, or assistance that may be given to invaders,
and endeavour as much as they can, to subdue, or weaken
their neighbours, by open force, and secret arts, for
want of other caution, justly; and are remembered for it
in after ages with honour.

Nor is it the joining together of a small number of
men, that gives them this security; because in small
numbers, small additions on the one side or the other,
make the advantage of strength so great, as is sufficient
to carry the victory; and therefore gives encouragement
to an invasion.   The multitude sufficient to confide in for
our security, is not determined by any certain number,
but by comparison with the enemy we fear; and is then
sufficient, when the odds of the enemy is not of so visible
and conspicuous moment, to determine the event of war,
as to move him to attempt.

And be there never so great a multitude; yet if
their actions be directed according to their particular
judgments, and particular appetites, they can expect
thereby no defence, nor protection, neither against a
common enemy, nor against the injuries of one another.

For being distracted in opinions concerning the best use
and application of their strength, they do not help but
hinder one another; and reduce their strength by mutual
opposition to nothing: whereby they are easily, not only
subdued by a very few that agree together; but also
when there is no common enemy, they make war upon
each other, for their particular interests. For if we
could suppose a great multitude of men to consent in
the observation of justice, and other laws of nature,
without a common power to keep them all in awe; we
might as well suppose all mankind to do the same; and
then there neither would be, nor need to be any civil
government, or commonwealth at all; because there
would be peace without subjection.

Nor is it enough for the security, which men desire
should last all the time of their life, that they be
governed, and directed by one judgment, for a limited
time; as in one battle, or one war. For though they
obtain a victory by their unanimous endeavour against
a foreign enemy; yet afterwards, when either they have
no common enemy, or he that by one part is held for
an enemy, is by another part held for a friend, they
must needs by the difference of their interests dissolve,
and fall again into a war amongst themselves.

It is true, that certain living creatures, as bees, and
ants, live sociably one with another, which are therefore
by Aristotle numbered amongst political creatures; and
yet have no other direction, than their particular judgments and appetites; nor speech, whereby one of them
can signify to another, what he thinks expedient for the
common benefit: and therefore some man may perhaps
desire to know, why mankind cannot do the same. To
which I answer,

First, that men are continually in competition for
honour and dignity, which these creatures are not; and

consequently amongst men there ariseth on that ground, envy and hatred, and finally war; but amongst these not so.

Secondly, that amongst these creatures, the common good differeth not from the private; and being by nature inclined to their private, they procure thereby the common benefit. But man, whose joy consisteth in comparing himself with other men, can relish nothing but what is eminent.

Thirdly, that these creatures, having not, as man, the use of reason, do not see, nor think they see any fault, in the administration of their common business; whereas amongst men, there are very many, that think themselves wiser, and able to govern the public, better than the rest; and these strive to reform and innovate, one this way, another that way; and thereby bring it into distraction and civil war.

Fourthly, that these creatures, though they have some use of voice, in making known to one another their desires, and other affections; yet they want that art of words, by which some men can represent to others, that which is good, in the likeness of evil; and evil, in the likeness of good; and augment, or diminish the apparent greatness of good and evil; discontenting men, and troubling their peace at their pleasure.

Fifthly, irrational creatures cannot distinguish between *injury*, and *damage*; and therefore as long as they be at ease, they are not offended with their fellows: whereas man is then most troublesome, when he is most at ease: for then it is that he loves to shew his wisdom, and control the actions of them that govern the commonwealth.

Lastly, the agreement of these creatures is natural; that of men, is by covenant only, which is artificial: and therefore it is no wonder if there be somewhat else required, besides covenant, to make their agreement constant and lasting; which is a common power, to keep them in awe, and to direct their actions to the common benefit.

The only way to erect such a common power, as may be able to defend them from the invasion of foreigners, and the injuries of one another, and thereby to secure them in such sort, as that by their own industry, and by the fruits of the earth, they may nourish themselves and live contentedly; is, to confer all their power and strength upon one man, or upon one assembly of men, that may reduce all their wills, by plurality of voices, unto one will: which is as much as to say, to appoint one man, or assembly of men, to bear their person; and every one to own, and acknowledge himself to be author of whatsoever he that so beareth their person, shall act, or cause to be acted, in those things which concern the common peace and safety; and therein to submit their wills, every one to his will, and their judgments, to his judgment. This is more than consent, or concord; it is a real unity of them all, in one and the same person, made by covenant of every man with every man, in such manner, as if every man should say to every man, *I authorize and give up my right of governing myself, to this man, or to this assembly of men, on this condition, that thou give up thy right to him, and authorize all his actions in like manner.* This done, the multitude so united in one person, is called a COMMONWEALTH, in Latin CIVITAS. This is the generation of that great LEVIATHAN, or rather, to speak more reverently, of that *mortal god*, to which we owe under the *immortal God*, our peace and defence. For by this authority, given him by every particular man in the commonwealth, he hath the use of so much power and strength conferred on him, that by terror thereof, he is enabled to perform the wills of them all, to peace at home, and mutual aid against their enemies abroad. And in him consisteth the essence of the commonwealth; which, to define it, is *one person, of whose acts a great multitude, by mutual covenants one with another, have made themselves every one the author, to the end he may use the strength and means of them all, as he shall think expedient, for their peace and common defence.*

And he that carrieth this person, is called SOVEREIGN, and said to have *sovereign power*; and every one besides, his SUBJECT.

The attaining to this sovereign power, is by two ways. One, by natural force; as when a man maketh his children, to submit themselves, and their children, to his government, as being able to destroy them if they refuse; or by war subdueth his enemies to his will, giving them their lives on that condition. The other, is when men agree amongst themselves, to submit to some man, or assembly of men, voluntarily, on confidence to be protected by him against all others. This latter, may be called a political commonwealth, or commonwealth by *institution*; and the former, a commonwealth by *acquisition*. And first, I shall speak of a commonwealth by institution.

CHAPTER XVIII

OF THE RIGHTS OF SOVEREIGNS BY INSTITUTION

A *commonwealth* is said to be *instituted*, when a *multitude* of men do agree, and *covenant, every one, with every one*, that to whatsoever *man*, or *assembly of men*, shall be given by the major part, the *right* to *present* the person of them all, that is to say, to be their *representative*; every one, as well he that *voted for it*, as he that *voted against it*, shall *authorize* all the actions and judgments, of that man, or assembly of men, in the same manner, as if they were his own, to the end, to live peaceably amongst themselves, and be protected against other men.

From this institution of a commonwealth are derived all the *rights*, and *faculties* of him, or them, on whom sovereign power is conferred by the consent of the people assembled.

First, because they covenant, it is to be understood, they are not obliged by former covenant to anything repugnant hereunto. And consequently they that have already instituted a commonwealth, being thereby bound by covenant, to own the actions, and judgments of one, cannot lawfully make a new covenant, amongst themselves, to be obedient to any other, in any thing whatsoever, without his permission. And therefore, they that are subject to a monarch, cannot without his leave cast off monarchy, and return to the confusion of a disunited multitude; nor transfer their person from him that beareth it, to another man, or other assembly of men: for they are bound, every man to every man, to own, and be reputed author of all, that he that already is their sovereign, shall do, and judge fit to be done: so that any one man dissenting, all the rest should break their covenant made to that man, which is injustice: and they have also every man given the sovereignty to him that beareth their person; and therefore if they depose him, they take from him that which is his own, and so again it is injustice. Besides, if he that attempteth to depose his sovereign, be killed, or punished by him for such attempt, he is author of his own punishment, as

being by the institution, author of all his sovereign shall
do: and because it is injustice for a man to do anything,
for which he may be punished by his own authority, he
is also upon that title, unjust. And whereas some men
have pretended for their disobedience to their sovereign,
a new covenant, made, not with men, but with God;
this also is unjust: for there is no covenant with God,
but by mediation of somebody that representeth God's
person; which none doth but God's lieutenant, who hath
the sovereignty under God. But this pretence of covenant with God, is so evident a lie, even in the pretenders'
own consciences, that it is not only an act of an unjust,
but also of a vile and unmanly disposition.[1]

[1] Compare *Philosophical Rudiments*, (M. II, 106). "We
have seen how subjects, nature dictating, have obliged themselves by mutual compacts to obey the supreme power. We
will see now by what means it comes to pass, that they are
released from these bonds of obedience. And first of all,
this happens by *rejection*, namely, if a man cast off or forsake,
but convey not the *right of his command* on some other.
For what is thus rejected, is openly exposed to all alike,
catch who catch can; whence again, by the right of nature,
every subject may heed the preservation of himself according
to his own judgment. In the second place, if the kingdom
fall into the power of the enemy, so as there can no more
opposition be made against them, we must understand that
he who before had the supreme authority, hath now lost it:
for when the subjects have done their full endeavour to
prevent their falling into the enemy's hands, they have ful-
filled those contracts of obedience which they made each with
other; and what, being conquered, they promise afterwards to
avoid death, they must with no less endeavour labour to perform. Thirdly, in a monarchy, (for a democracy and aristocracy cannot fail), if there be no successor, all the subjects
are discharged from their obligations; for no man is supposed to be tied he knows not to whom; for in such a case
it were impossible to perform aught. And by these three
ways, all subjects are restored from their civil subjection to
that liberty which all men have to all things; to wit, natural
and savage; for the natural state hath the same proportion
to the civil, (I mean, liberty to subjection), which passion

Secondly, because the right of bearing the person of them all, is given to him they make sovereign, by covenant only of one to another, and not of him to any of them; there can happen no breach of covenant on the part of the sovereign; and consequently none of his subjects, by any pretence of forfeiture, can be freed from his subjection. That he which is made sovereign maketh no covenant with his subjects beforehand, is manifest; because either he must make it with the whole multitude, as one party to the covenant; or he must make a several covenant with every man. With the whole, as one party, it is impossible; because as yet they are not one person: and if he make so many several covenants as there be men, those covenants after he hath the sovereignty are void; because what act soever can be pretended by any one of them for breach thereof, is the act both of himself, and of all the rest, because done in the person, and by the right of every one of them in particular. Besides, if any one, or more of them, pretend a breach of the covenant made by the sovereign at his institution; and others, or one other of his subjects, or himself alone, pretend there was no such breach, there is in this case, no judge to decide the controversy; it returns therefore to the sword again; and every man recovereth the right of protecting himself by his own strength, contrary to the design they had in the institution. It is therefore in vain to grant

---

hath to reason, or a beast to a man. Furthermore, each subject may lawfully be freed from his subjection by the will of him who hath the supreme power, namely, if he change his soil; which may be done two days, either by permission, as he who gets license to dwell in another country; or command, as he who is banished. In both cases, he is free from the laws of his former country; because he is tied to observe those of the latter." Also below, p. 380.

sovereignty by way of precedent covenant. The opinion
that any monarch receiveth his power by covenant, that
is to say, on condition, proceedeth from want of understanding this easy truth, that covenants being but words
and breath, have no force to oblige, contain, constrain,
or protect any man, but what it has from the public
sword; that is, from the untied hands of that man, or
assembly of men that hath the sovereignty, and whose
actions are avouched by them all, and performed by
the strength of them all, in him united. But when an
assembly of men is made sovereign; then no man
imagineth any such covenant to have passed in the
institution; for no man is so dull as to say, for example,
the people of Rome made a covenant with the Romans,
to hold the sovereignty on such or such conditions;
which not performed, the Romans might lawfully depose
the Roman people. That men see not the reason to
be alike in a monarchy, and in a popular government,
proceedeth from the ambition of some, that are kinder
to the government of an assembly, whereof they may
hope to participate, than of monarchy, which they
despair to enjoy.[2]

[2] Compare *Philosophical Rudiments*, (M. II, 89). "Forasmuch as the supreme command is constituted by virtue of the
compacts which each single citizen or subject mutually makes
with the other; but all contracts, as they receive their force
from the contractors, so by their consent they lose it again
and are broken: perhaps some may infer hence, that by the
consent of all the subjects together the supreme authority
may be wholly taken away. Which inference, if it were true,
I cannot discern what danger would thence by right arise to
the supreme commanders. For since it is supposed that each
one hath obliged himself to each other; if any one of them
shall refuse, whatsoever the rest shall agree to do, he is bound
notwithstanding. Neither can any man without injury to
me, do that which by contract made with me he hath obliged
himself not to do. But it is not to be imagined that ever it

Thirdly, because the major part hath by consenting voices declared a sovereign; he that dissented must now consent with the rest; that is, be contented to avow all the actions he shall do, or else justly be destroyed by

---

will happen, that all the subjects together, not so much as one excepted, will combine against the supreme power. Wherefore there is no fear for rulers in chief, that by any right they can be despoiled of their authority. If, notwithstanding, it were granted that their right depended only on that contract which each man makes with his fellow-citizen, it might very easily happen that they might be robbed of that dominion under pretence of right. For subjects being called either by the command of the city, or seditiously flocking together, most men think that the consents of all are contained in the votes of the greater part; which in truth is false. For it is not from nature that the consent of the major part should be received for the consent of all, neither is it true in tumults; but it proceeds from civil institution: and is then only true, when that man or court which hath the supreme power, assembling his subjects, by reason of the greatness of their number allows those that are elected a power of speaking for those who elected them; and will have the major part of voices, in such matters as are by him propounded to be discussed, to be as effectual as the whole. But we cannot imagine that he who is chief, ever convened his subjects with intention that they should dispute his right; unless weary of the burthen of his charge, he declared in plain terms that he renounces and abandons his government. Now because most men through ignorance esteem not the consent of the major part of citizens only, but even of a very few, provided they be of their opinion, for the consent of the whole city; it may very well seem to them, that the supreme authority may by right be abrogated, so it be done in some great assembly of citizens by the votes of the greater number. But though a government be constituted by the contracts of particular men with particulars, yet its right depends not on that obligation only; there is another tie also towards him who commands. For each citizen compacting with his fellow, says thus: *I convey my right on this party, upon condition that you pass yours to the same*: by which means, that right which every man had before to use his faculties to his own advantage, is now wholly translated on some certain man or council for the common benefit. Wherefore what by the mutual contracts each one hath made with the other, what by

the rest. For if he voluntarily entered into the congregation of them that were assembled, he sufficiently
declared thereby his will, and therefore tacitly covenanted, to stand to what the major part should ordain:
and therefore if he refuse to stand thereto, or make
protestation against any of their decrees, he does contrary to his covenant, and therefore unjustly. And
whether he be of the congregation, or not; and whether
his consent be asked, or not, he must either submit to
their decrees, or be left in the condition of war he was
in before; wherein he might without injustice be destroyed by any man whatsoever.

Fourthly, because every subject is by this institution
author of all the actions, and judgments of the sovereign
instituted; it follows, that whatsoever he doth, it can be
no injury to any of his subjects; nor ought he to be by
any of them accused of injustice. For he that doth anything by authority from another, doth therein no injury
to him by whose authority he acteth: but by this institution of a commonwealth, every particular man is
author of all the sovereign doth: and consequently he
that complaineth of injury from his sovereign, complaineth of that whereof he himself is author; and therefore ought not to accuse any man but himself; no nor
himself of injury; because to do injury to one's self,

---

the donation of right which every man is bound to ratify to
him that commands, the government is upheld by a double
obligation from the citizens; first, that which is due to their
fellow-citizens; next, that which they owe to their prince.
Wherefore no subjects, how many soever they be, can with
any right despoil him who bears the chief rule of his authority, without his own consent." The Molesworth edition
reads, "even without his own consent." This makes the final
sentence of the extract meaningless, and is evidently the result
of a mistranslation of the words of the *De Cive*: "Non ergo
cives, quotcunque fuerint, sine consensu etiam ipsius im-
perantis, eum spoliare imperio jure possunt."

is impossible. It is true that they that have sovereign power may commit iniquity, but not injustice, or injury in the proper signification.[3]

Fifthly, and consequently to that which was said last, no man that hath sovereign power can justly be put to death, or otherwise in any manner by his subjects punished. For seeing every subject is author of the actions

---

[3] Compare *Philosophical Rudiments*, (M. II, 101). "Because * * * * they who have gotten the *supreme command*, are by no compacts obliged to any man, it necessarily follows, that they can do no *injury* to the subjects. For *injury* * * * * is nothing else but a breach of contract; and therefore where no contracts have part, there can be no injury. Yet the people, the nobles, and the monarch may diverse ways transgress against the other laws of nature, as by cruelty, iniquity, contumely, and other like vices, which come not under this strict and exact notion of *injury*. But if the subject yield not obedience to the supreme, he will in propriety of speech be said to be *injurious*, as well to his fellow-subjects, because each man hath compacted with the other to obey; as to his *chief ruler*, in resuming that right which he hath given him, without his consent. And in a *democracy* or *aristocracy*, if anything be decreed against any *law of nature*, the city itself, that is, the civil person sins not, but those subjects only by whose votes it was decreed; for sin is a consequence of the natural express will, not of the political, which is artificial. For if it were otherwise, they would be guilty by whom the decree was absolutely disliked. But in a *monarchy*, if the *monarch* make any decree against the *laws of nature*, he sins himself; because in him the civil will and the natural are all one." Also *De Corpore Politico*, (M. IV, 140). "How unjust soever the action be, that this sovereign *demus* shall do, is done by the will of every particular man subject to him, who are therefore guilty of the same. If therefore they style it *injury*, they but accuse themselves. And it is against reason for the same man, both to do and complain; implying this contradiction, that whereas he first ratified the people's acts in general, he now disalloweth the same of them in particular. It is therefore said truly, *volenti non fit injuria*. Nevertheless nothing doth hinder, but that divers actions done by the people, may be unjust before God Almighty, as breaches of the laws of nature."

of his sovereign; he punisheth another for the actions committed by himself.[4]

[4] Compare *Philosophical Rudiments*, (M. II, 153). "A city can neither be bound to itself, nor to any subject; not to itself, because no man can be obliged except it be to another; not to any subject, because the single wills of the subjects are contained in the will of the city; insomuch that if the city will be free from all such obligation, the subjects will so too; and by consequence she is so. But that which holds true in a city, that must be supposed to be true in a man, or an assembly of men who have the supreme authority; for they make a city, which hath no being but by their supreme power. Now that this opinion cannot consist with the very being of government, is evident from hence; that by it the knowledge of what is *good* and *evil*, that is to say, the definition of what is, and what is not against the laws, would return to each single person. Obedience therefore will cease, as oft as anything seems to be commanded contrary to the civil laws, and together with it all coercive jurisdiction; which cannot possibly be without the destruction of the very essence of government. Yet this error hath great props, Aristotle and others; who, by reason of human infirmity, suppose the supreme power to be committed with most security to the laws only. But they seem to have looked very shallowly into the nature of government, who thought that the constraining power, the interpretation of laws, and the making of laws, all which are powers necessarily belonging to government, should be left wholly to the laws themselves. Now although particular subjects may sometimes contend in judgment, and go to law with the supreme magistrate; yet this is only then, when the question is not what the magistrate may, but what by a certain rule he hath declared he would do. As, when by any law the judges sit upon the life of a subject, the question is not whether the magistrate could by his absolute right deprive him of his life; but whether by that law his will was that he should be deprived of it. But his will was, he should, if he brake the law; else his will was, he should not. This therefore, that a subject may have an action of law against his supreme magistrate, is not strength of argument sufficient to prove, that he is tied to his own laws. On the contrary, it is evident that he is not tied to his own laws; because no man is bound to himself. Laws therefore are set for Titius and Caius, not for the ruler. However, by the ambition of lawyers it is so ordered, that the laws to unskilful men seem not to depend on the authority of the magistrate, but their prudence." Also *Leviathan*, (M. III, 312). An "opinion repugnant to the nature of a commonwealth, is this, *that he*

And because the end of this institution, is the peace and defence of them all· and whosoever has right to the end, has right to the means; it belongeth of right, to whatsoever man, or assembly that hath the sovereignty, to be judge both of the means of peace and defence, and also of the hindrances, and disturbances of the same; and to do whatsoever he shall think necessary to be done, both beforehand, for the preserving of peace and security, by prevention of discord at home, and hostility from abroad; and, when peace and security are lost, for the recovery of the same. And therefore,

Sixthly, it is annexed to the sovereignty, to be judge of what opinions and doctrines are averse, and what conducing to peace; and consequently, on what occasions, how far, and what men are to be trusted withal, in speaking to multitudes of people; and who shall examine the doctrines of all books before they be published. For the actions of men proceed from their opinions; and in the well-governing of opinions, consisteth the well-governing of men's actions, in order to their peace, and concord. And though in matter of doctrine, nothing ought to be regarded but the truth; yet this is not repugnant to regulating the same by peace. For doctrine repugnant to peace, can no more

---

that hath the sovereign power is subject to the civil laws. It is true, that sovereigns are all subject to the laws of nature; because such laws be divine, and cannot by any man, or commonwealth be abrogated. But to those laws which the sovereign himself, that is, which the commonwealth maketh, he is not subject. For to be subject to laws, is to be subject to the commonwealth, that is to the sovereign representative, that is to himself; which is not subjection, but freedom from the laws. Which error, because it setteth the laws above the sovereign, setteth also a judge above him, and a power to punish him; which is to make a new sovereign; and again for the same reason a third, to punish the second; and so continually without end, to the confusion, and dissolution of the commonwealth."

be true, than peace and concord can be against the law
of nature. It is true, that in a commonwealth, where
by the negligence, or unskilfulness of governors, and
teachers, false doctrines are by time generally received;
the contrary truths may be generally offensive. Yet
the most sudden, and rough bursting in of a new truth,
that can be, does never break the peace, but only sometimes awake the war. For those men that are so
remissly governed, that they dare take up arms to
defend, or introduce an opinion, are still in war; and
their condition not peace, but only a cessation of arms
for fear of one another; and they live, as it were, in
the precincts of battle continually. It belongeth therefore to him that hath the sovereign power, to be judge,
or constitute all judges of opinions and doctrines, as a
thing necessary to peace; thereby to prevent discord
and civil war.

Seventhly, is annexed to the sovereignty, the whole
power of prescribing the rules, whereby every man may
know, what goods he may enjoy, and what actions he
may do, without being molested by any of his fellow-
subjects; and this is it men call *propriety*. For before
constitution of sovereign power, as hath already been
shown, all men had right to all things; which necessarily
causeth war: and therefore this propriety, being necessary to peace, and depending on sovereign power, is the
act of that power, in order to the public peace. These
rules of propriety, or *meum* and *tuum*, and of *good,
evil, lawful*, and *unlawful* in the actions of subjects,
are the civil laws; that is to say, the laws of each commonwealth in particular; though the name of civil law
be now restrained to the ancient civil laws of the city
of Rome; which being the head of a great part of the
world, her laws at that time were in these parts the
civil law.

Eighthly, is annexed to the sovereignty, the right of judicature; that is to say, of hearing and deciding all controversies, which may arise concerning law, either civil, or natural; or concerning fact. For without the decision of controversies, there is no protection of one subject, against the injuries of another; the laws concerning *meum* and *tuum* are in vain; and to every man remaineth, from the natural and necessary appetite of his own conservation, the right of protecting himself by his private strength, which is the condition of war, and contrary to the end for which every commonwealth is instituted.

Ninthly, is annexed to the sovereignty, the right of making war and peace with other nations, and commonwealths; that is to say, of judging when it is for the public good, and how great forces are to be assembled, armed, and paid for that end; and to levy money upon the subjects, to defray the expenses thereof. For the power by which the people are to be defended, consisteth in their armies; and the strength of an army, in the union of their strength under one command; which command the sovereign instituted, therefore hath; because the command of the *militia*, without other institution, maketh him that hath it sovereign. And therefore whosoever is made general of an army, he that hath the sovereign power is always generalissimo.

Tenthly, is annexed to the sovereignty, the choosing of all counsellors, ministers, magistrates, and officers, both in peace and war. For seeing the sovereign is charged with the end, which is the common peace and defense, he is understood to have power to use such means, as he shall think most fit for his discharge.

Eleventhly, to the sovereign is committed the power of rewarding with riches, or honour, and of punishing with corporal or pecuniary punishment, or with ignominy, every subject according to the law he hath formerly made; or if there be no law made, according as he shall judge most to conduce to the encouraging of men to serve the commonwealth, or deterring of them from doing disservice to the same.

Lastly, considering what value men are naturally apt to set upon themselves; what respect they look for from others; and how little they value other men; from whence continually arise amongst them, emulation, quarrels, factions, and at last war, to the destroying of one another, and diminution of their strength against a common enemy; it is necessary that there be laws of honour, and a public rate of the worth of such men as have deserved, or are able to deserve well of the commonwealth; and that there be force in the hands of some or other, to put those laws in execution. But it hath already been shown, that not only the whole *militia*, or forces of the commonwealth; but also the judicature of all controversies, is annexed to the sovereignty. To the sovereign therefore it belongeth also to give titles of honour; and to appoint what order of place, and dignity, each man shall hold; and what signs of respect, in public or private meetings, they shall give to one another.

These are the rights, which make the essence of sovereignty; and which are the marks, whereby a man may discern in what man, or assembly of men, the sovereign power is placed, and resideth. For these are incommunicable, and inseparable. The power to coin money; to dispose of the estate and persons of infant heirs; to have præemption in markets; and all other statute prerogatives, may be transferred by the sovereign; and yet the power to protect his subjects be retained. But if he transfer the *militia*, he retains the judicature in vain, for want of execution of the laws: or if he grant away the power of raising money; the *militia* is in vain; or if he give away the government of doctrines, men will be frighted into rebellion with the fear of spirits. And so if we consider any one of the said rights, we shall presently see, that the holding of all the rest will produce no effect, in the conservation of peace and justice, the end for which all commonwealths are instituted. And this division is it, whereof it is said, a *kingdom divided in itself cannot stand*: for unless this division precede, division into opposite armies can never happen. If there had not first been an opinion received of the greatest part of England, that these powers were divided between the King, and the Lords, and the House of Commons, the people had never been divided and fallen into this civil war; first between those that disagreed in politics; and after between the dissenters about the liberty of religion; which have so instructed men in this point of sovereign right, and there be few now in England that do not see, that these rights are inseparable, and will be so generally acknowledged at the next return of peace; and so continue, till their miseries are forgotten; and no longer, except the vulgar be better taught than they have hitherto been.

And because they are essential and inseparable rights, it follows necessarily, that in whatsoever words any of them seem to be granted away, yet if the sovereign power itself be not in direct terms renounced, and the name of sovereign no more given by the grantees to him that grants them, the grant is void: for when he has granted all he can, if we grant back the sovereignty, all is restored, as inseparably annexed thereunto.

This great authority being indivisible, and inseparably annexed to the sovereignty, there is little ground for the opinion of them, that say of sovereign kings, though they be *singulis majores*, of greater power than every one of their subjects, yet they be *universis minores*, of less power than them all together. For if by *all together*, they mean not the collective body as one person, then *all together*, and *every one*, signify the same; and the speech is absurd. But if by *all together*, they understand them as one person, which person the sovereign bears, then the power of all together, is the same with the sovereign's power; and so again the speech is absurd: which absurdity they see well enough, when the sovereignty is in an assembly of the people; but in a monarch they see it not; and yet the power of sovereignty is the same in whomsoever it be placed.[5]

[5] Compare *Philosophical Rudiments*, (M. II, 80 n.). "A popular state openly challengeth absolute dominion, and the citizens oppose it not. For, in the gathering together of many men, they acknowledge the face of a city; and even the unskilful understand, that matters there are ruled by council. Yet monarchy is no less a city than democracy; and absolute kings have their counsellors, from whom they will take advice, and suffer their power. in matters of greater consequence, to be guided but not recalled. But it appears not to most men, how a city is contained in the person of a king. And therefore they object against absolute command: first, that if any man had such a right, the condition of the citizens would be miserable. For thus they think; he will take all, spoil all, kill all; and every man counts it his only happiness, that he is not already spoiled and killed. But why should he do thus? Not because he can; for unless he have mind to it, he will not do it. Will he, to please one or some few, spoil all the rest? First, though by right, that is, without injury to them, he may do it, yet can he not do it justly, that is, without breach of the natural laws and injury against God. And therefore there is some security for subjects in the oaths which princes take. Next, if he could justly do it, or that he made no account of his oath, yet appears there no reason why he should desire it, since he finds no good in it. But it cannot be denied, but a prince may sometimes have an inclination to do wickedly. But grant then, that thou hadst given him a power which were not absolute, but so much only as sufficed to defend thee from the injuries of others; which, if thou wilt be safe, is necessary for thee to give; are not all the same things to be feared? For he that hath strength enough to protect all, wants not sufficiency to op-

And as the power, so also the honour of the sovereign, ought to be greater, than that of any, or all the subjects. For in the sovereignty is the fountain of honour. The dignities of lord, earl, duke, and prince are his creatures. As in the presence of the master, the servants are equal, and without any honour at all; so are the subjects, in the presence of the sovereign. And though they shine some more, some less, when they are out of his sight; yet in his presence, they shine no more than the stars in the presence of the sun.

---

press all. Here is no other difficulty then, but that human affairs cannot be without some inconvenience. And this inconvenience itself is in the citizens, not in the government. For if men could rule themselves, every man by his own command, that is to say, could they live according to the laws of nature, there would be no need at all of a city, nor of a common coercive power. Secondly, they object, that there is no dominion in the Christian world absolute. Which, indeed, is not true; for all monarchies, and all other states, are so. For although they who have the chief command, do not all those things they would, and what they know profitable to the city; the reason of that is, not the defect of right in them, but the consideration of their citizens, who busied about their private interest, and careless of what tends to the public, cannot sometimes be drawn to perform their duties without the hazard of the city. Wherefore princes sometimes forbear the exercise of their right; and prudently remit somewhat of the act, but nothing of their right." On the rights of sovereignty by acquisition compare *Leviathan*, (M. III, 186). "But the rights, and consequences of sovereignty, are the same in both. His power cannot, without his consent, be transferred to another: he cannot forfeit it: he cannot be accused by any of his subjects, of injury: he cannot be punished by them: he is judge of what is necessary for peace; and judge of doctrines: he is sole legislator; and supreme judge of controversies; and of the times, and occasions of war, and peace: to him it belongeth to choose magistrates, counsellors, commanders, and all other officers, and ministers; and to determine of rewards, and punishments, honour, and order. The reasons whereof, are the same which are alleged in the precedent chapter, for the same rights and consequences of sovereignty by institution."

But a man may here object, that the condition of subjects is very miserable; as being obnoxious to the lusts, and other irregular passions of him, or them that have so unlimited a power in their hands. And commonly they that live under a monarch, think it the fault of monarchy; and they that live under the government of democracy, or other sovereign assembly, attribute all the inconvenience to that form of commonwealth; whereas the power in all forms, if they be perfect enough to protect them, is the same: not considering that the state of man can never be without some incommodity or other; and that the greatest, that in any form of government can possibly happen to the people in general, is scarce sensible, in respect to the miseries, and horrible calamities, that accompany a civil war, or that dissolute condition of masterless men, without subjection to laws, and a coercive power to tie their hands from rapine and revenge: nor considering that the greatest pressure of sovereign governors, proceedeth not from any delight, or profit they can expect in the damage or weakening of their subjects, in whose vigour, consisteth their own strength and glory; but in the restiveness of themselves, that unwillingly contributing to their own defence, make it necessary for their governors to draw from them what they can in time of peace, that they may have means on any emergent occasion, or sudden need, to resist, or take advantage on their enemies. For all men are by nature provided of notable multiplying glasses, that is their passions and self-love, through which, every little payment appeareth a great grievance; but are destitute of those prospective glasses, namely moral and civil science, to see afar off the miseries that hang over them, and cannot without such payment be avoided.

CHAPTER XIX

OF THE SEVERAL KINDS OF COMMON-WEALTH BY INSTITUTION, AND OF SUCCESSION TO THE SOVEREIGN POWER

THE difference of commonwealths, consisteth in the difference of the sovereign, or the person representative of all and every one of the multitude. And because the sovereignty is either in one man, or in an assembly of more than one; and into that assembly either every man hath right to enter, or not every one, but certain men distinguished from the rest; it is manifest, there can be but three kinds of commonwealth. For the representative must needs be one man, or more: and if more, then it is the assembly of all, or but of a part. When the representative is one man, then is the commonwealth a MONARCHY: when an assembly of all that will come together, then it is a DEMOCRACY, or popular commonwealth: when an assembly of a part only, then it is called an ARISTOCRACY. Other kind of commonwealth there can be none: for either one, or more, or all, must have the sovereign power, which I have shown to be indivisible, entire.

There be other names of government, in the histories, and books of policy; as *tyranny*, and *oligarchy*: but they are not the names of other forms of government, but of the same forms misliked. For they that are discontented under *monarchy*, call it *tyranny*; and they that are displeased with *aristocracy*, call it *oligarchy*: so also, they which find themselves grieved under a *democracy*, call it *anarchy*, which signifies want of government; and yet I think no man believes, that want of government, is any new kind of government: nor by the same reason ought they to believe, that the government is of one kind, when they like it, and other, when they mislike it, or are oppressed by the governors.

It is manifest, that men who are in absolute liberty, may, if they please, give authority to one man, to represent them every one; as well as give such authority to any assembly of men whatsoever; and consequently may subject themselves, if they think good, to a monarch, as absolutely, as to any other representative. Therefore, where there is already erected a sovereign power, there can be no other representative of the same people, but only to certain particular ends, by the sovereign limited. For that were to erect two sovereigns; and every man to have his person represented by two actors, that by opposing one another, must needs divide that power, which, if men will live in peace, is indivisible; and thereby reduce the multitude into the condition of war, contrary to the end for which all sovereignty is instituted. And therefore as it is absurd, to think that a sovereign assembly, inviting the people of their dominion, to send up their deputies, with power to make known their advice, or desires, should therefore hold such deputies, rather than themselves, for the absolute representatives of the people: so it is absurd also, to think the same in a monarchy. And I know not how this so manifest a truth, should of late be so little observed; that in a monarchy, he that had the sovereignty from a descent of six hundred years, was alone called sovereign, had the title of Majesty from every one of his subjects, and was unquestionably taken by them for their king, was notwithstanding never considered as their representative; the name with contradiction passing for the title of those men, which at his command were sent up by the people to carry their petitions, and give him, if he permitted it, their advice. Which may serve as an admonition, for those that are the true, and absolute representative of a people, to instruct men in the nature of that office, and to take heed how they admit of any other general representation upon any occasion whatsoever, if they mean to discharge the trust committed to them.

The difference between these three kinds of commonwealth, consisteth not in the difference of power; but in the difference of convenience, or aptitude to produce the peace, and security of the people; for which end they were instituted. And to compare monarchy with the other two, we may observe; first, that whosoever beareth the person of the people, or is one of that assembly that bears it, beareth also his own natural person. And though he be careful in his politic person to procure the common interest; yet he is more, or no less careful to procure the private good of himself, his family, kindred and friends; and for the most part, if the public interest chance to cross the private, he prefers the private: for the passions of men, are commonly more potent than their reason. From whence it follows, that where the public and private interest are most closely united, there is the public most advanced. Now in monarchy, the private interest is the same with the public. The riches, power, and honour of a monarch arise only from the riches, strength and reputation of his subjects. For no king can be rich, nor glorious, nor secure, whose subjects are either poor, or contemptible, or too weak through want or dissension, to maintain a war against their enemies: whereas in a democracy, or aristocracy, the public prosperity confers not so much to the private fortune of one that is corrupt, or ambitious, as doth many times a perfidious advice, a treacherous action, or a civil war.

Secondly, that a monarch receiveth counsel of whom, when, and where he pleaseth; and consequently may hear the opinion of men versed in the matter about which he deliberates, of what rank or quality soever, and as long before the time of action, and with as much secrecy, as he will. But when a sovereign assembly has need of counsel, none are admitted but such as have a right thereto from the beginning; which for the most part are of those who have been versed more in the acquisition of wealth than of knowledge; and are to give their advice in long discourses, which may, and do commonly excite men to action, but not govern them in it. For the *understanding* is by the flame of the passions, never enlightened, but dazzled. Nor is there any place, or time, wherein an assembly can receive counsel with secrecy, because of their own multitude.

Thirdly, that the resolutions of a monarch, are subject to no other inconstancy, than that of human nature; but in assemblies, besides that of nature, there ariseth an inconstancy from the number. For the absence of a few, that would have the resolution once taken, continue firm, which may happen by security, negligence, or private impediments, or the diligent appearance of a few of the contrary opinion, undoes to-day, all that was concluded yesterday.

Fourthly, that a monarch cannot disagree with himself, out of envy, or interest; but an assembly may; and that to such a height, as may produce a civil war.

Fifthly, that in monarchy there is this inconvenience; that any subject, by the power of one man, for the enriching of a favourite or flatterer, may be deprived of all he possesseth; which I confess is a great and inevitable inconvenience. But the same may as well happen, where the sovereign power is in an assembly: for their power is the same; and they are as subject to evil counsel, and to be seduced by orators, as a monarch by flatterers; and becoming one another's flatterers, serve one another's covetousness and ambition by turns. And whereas the favourites of monarchs, are few, and they have none else to advance but their own kindred; the favourites of an assembly, are many; and the kindred much more numerous, than of any monarch. Besides, there is no favourite of a monarch, which cannot as well succour his friends, as hurt his enemies: but orators, that is to say, favourites of sovereign assemblies, though they have great power to hurt, have little to save. For to accuse, requires less eloquence, such is man's nature, than to excuse; and condemnation, than absolution more resembles justice.

Sixthly, that it is an inconvenience in monarchy, that the sovereignty may descend upon an infant, or one that cannot discern between good and evil: and consisteth in this, that the use of his power, must be in the hand of another man, or of some assembly of men, which are to govern by his right, and in his name; as curators, and protectors of his person, and authority. But to say there is inconvenience, in putting the use of the sovereign power, into the hand of a man, or an assembly of men; is to say that all government is more inconvenient, than confusion, and civil war. And therefore all the danger that can be pretended, must arise from the contention of those, that for an office of so great honour, and profit, may become competitors. To make it appear, that this inconvenience, proceedeth not from that form of government we call monarchy, we are to consider, that the precedent monarch hath appointed who shall have the tuition of his infant successor, either expressly by testament, or tacitly, by not controlling the custom in that case received: and then such inconvenience, if it happen, is to be attributed, not to the monarchy, but to the ambition, and injustice of the subjects; which in all kinds of government, where the people are not well instructed in their duty, and the rights of sovereignty, is the same. Or else the precedent monarch hath not at all taken order for such tuition; and then the law of nature hath provided this sufficient rule, that the tuition shall be in him, that hath by nature most interest in the preservation of the authority of the infant, and to whom least benefit can accrue by his death, or diminution. For seeing every man by nature seeketh his own benefit, and promotion; to put an infant into the power of those, that can promote themselves by his destruction, or damage, is not tuition, but treachery. So that sufficient provision being taken, against all just quarrel, about the government under a child, if any contention arise to the disturbance of the public peace, it is not to be attributed to the form of monarchy, but to the ambition of subjects, and ignorance of their duty. On the other side, there is no great commonwealth, the sovereignty whereof is in a great assembly, which is not, as to consultations of peace, and war, and making of laws, in the same condition, as if the government were in a child. For as a child wants the judgment to dissent from counsel given him, and is thereby necessitated to take the advice of them, or him, to whom he is committed: so an assembly wanteth the liberty, to dissent from the counsel of the major part, be it good, or bad. And as a child has need of a tutor, or protector, to preserve his person and authority: so also, in great commonwealths, the sovereign assembly, in all great dangers and troubles, have need of *custodes libertatis*; that is of dictators, or protectors of their authority; which are as much as temporary monarchs, to whom for a time, they may commit the entire exercise of their power; and have, at the end of that time, been oftener deprived thereof, than infant kings, by their protectors, regents, or any other tutors.

Though the kinds of sovereignty be, as I have now shown, but three; that is to say, monarchy, where one man has it; or democracy, where the general assembly of subjects hath it; or aristocracy, where it is in an assembly of certain persons nominated, or otherwise distinguished from the rest; yet he that shall consider the particular commonwealths that have been, and are in the world, will not perhaps easily reduce them to three, and may thereby be inclined to think there be other forms, arising from these mingled together. As for example, elective kingdoms; where kings have the sovereign power put into their hands for a time; or kingdoms, wherein the king hath a power limited: which governments, are nevertheless by most writers called monarchy. Likewise if a popular, or aristocratical commonwealth, subdue an enemy's country, and govern the same, by a president, procurator, or other magistrate; this may seem perhaps at first sight, to be a democratical, or aristocratical government. But it is not so. For elective kings, are not sovereigns, but ministers of the sovereign; nor limited kings, sovereigns, but ministers of them that have the sovereign power; nor are those provinces which are in subjection to a democracy, or aristocracy of another commonwealth, democratically or aristocratically governed, but monarchically.

And first, concerning an elective king, whose power is limited to his life, as it is in many places of Christendom at this day; or to certain years or months, as the dictator's power amongst the Romans; if he have right to appoint his successor, he is no more elective but hereditary. But if he have no power to elect his successor, then there is some other man, or assembly known, which after his decease may elect anew, or else the commonwealth dieth, and dissolveth with him, and returneth to the condition of war. If it be known who have the power to give the sovereignty after his death, it is known also that the sovereignty was in them before: for none have right to give that which they have not right to possess, and keep to themselves, if they think good. But if there be none that can give the sovereignty, after the decease of him that was first elected; then has he power, nay he is obliged by the law of nature, to provide, by establishing his successor, to keep those that had trusted him with the government, from relapsing into the miserable condition of civil war. And consequently he was, when elected, a sovereign absolute.

Secondly, that king whose power is limited, is not superior to him, or them that have the power to limit it; and he that is not superior, is not supreme; that is to say not sovereign. The sovereignty therefore was always in that assembly which had the right to limit him; and by consequence the government not monarchy, but either democracy, or aristocracy; as of old time in Sparta; where the kings had a privilege to lead their armies; but the sovereignty was in the Ephori.

Thirdly, whereas heretofore the Roman people governed the land of Judea, for example, by a president; yet was not Judea therefore a democracy; because they were not governed by any assembly, into the which, any of them had right to enter; nor an aristocracy; because they were not governed by any assembly, into which, any man could enter by their election: but they were governed by one person, which, though as to the people of Rome, was an assembly of the people, or democracy; yet as to the people of Judea, which had no right at all of participating in the government, was a monarch. For though where the people are governed by an assembly, chosen by themselves out of their own number, the government is called a democracy, or aristocracy; yet when they are governed by an assembly, not of their own choosing, it is a monarchy; not of *one* man, over another man; but of one people, over another people.

Of all these forms of government, the matter being mortal, so that not only monarchs, but also whole assemblies die, it is necessary for the conservation of the peace of men, that as there was order taken for an artificial man, so there be order also taken, for an artificial eternity of life; without which, men that are governed by an assembly, should return into the condition of war in every age; and they that are governed by one man, as soon as their governor dieth. This artificial eternity, is that which men call the right of *succession*.

There is no perfect form of government, where the disposing of the succession is not in the present sovereign. For if it be in any other particular man, or private assembly, it is in a person subject, and may be assumed by the sovereign at his pleasure; and consequently the right is in himself. And if it be in no particular man, but left to a new choice; then is the commonwealth dissolved; and the right is in him that can get it; contrary to the intention of them that did institute the commonwealth, for their perpetual, and not temporary security.

In a democracy, the whole assembly cannot fail, unless the multitude that are to be governed fail. And therefore questions of the right of succession, have in that form of government no place at all.

In an aristocracy, when any of the assembly dieth, the election of another into his room belongeth to the assembly, as the sovereign, to whom belongeth the choosing of all counsellors and officers. For that which the representative doth, as actor, every one of the subjects doth, as author. And though the sovereign assembly may give power to others, to elect new men, for supply of their court; yet it is still by their authority, that the election is made; and by the same it may, when the public shall require it, be recalled.

The greatest difficulty about the right of succession, is in monarchy: and the difficulty ariseth from this, that at first sight, it is not manifest who is to appoint the successor; nor many times, who it is whom he hath appointed. For in both these cases, there is required a more exact ratiocination, than every man is accustomed to use. As to the question, who shall appoint the successor, of a monarch that hath the sovereign authority; that is to say, who shall determine of the right of inheritance, (for elective kings and princes have not the sovereign power in propriety, but in use only), we are to consider, that either he that is in possession, has right to dispose of the succession, or else that right is again in the dissolved multitude. For the death of him that hath the sovereign power in propriety, leaves the multitude without any sovereign at all; that is, without any representative in whom they should be united, and be capable of doing any one action at all: and therefore they are incapable of election of any new monarch; every man having equal right to submit himself to such as he thinks best able to protect him; or if he can, protect himself by his own sword; which is a return to confusion, and to the condition of a war of every man against every man, contrary to the end for which monarchy had its first institution. Therefore it is manifest, that by the institution of monarchy, the disposing of the successor, is always left to the judgment and will of the present possessor.

And for the question, which may arise sometimes, who

it is that the monarch in possession, hath designed to the succession and inheritance of his power; it is determined by his express words, and testament; or by other tacit signs sufficient.

By express words, or testament, when it is declared by him in his lifetime, *viva voce*, or by writing; as the first emperors of Rome declared who should be their heirs. For the word heir does not of itself imply the children, or nearest kindred of a man; but whomsoever a man shall any way declare, he would have to succeed him in his estate. If therefore a monarch declare expressly, that such a man shall be his heir, either by word or writing, then is that man immediately after the decease of his predecessor, invested in the right of being monarch.

But where testament, and express words are wanting, other natural signs of the will are to be followed: whereof the one is custom. And therefore where the custom is, that the next of kindred absolutely succeedeth, there also the next of kindred hath right to the succession; for that, if the will of him that was in possession had been otherwise, he might easily have declared the same in his lifetime. And likewise where the custom is, that the next of the male kindred succeedeth, there also the right of succession is in the next of the kindred male, for the same reason. And so it is if the custom were to advance the female. For whatsoever custom a man may by a word control, and does not, it is a natural sign he would have that custom stand.

But where neither custom, nor testament hath preceded, there it is to be understood, first, that a monarch's will is, that the government remain monarchical; because he hath approved that government in himself. Secondly, that a child of his own, male, or female, be preferred before any other; because men are presumed

to be more inclined by nature, to advance their own
children, than the children of other men; and of their
own, rather a male than a female; because men, are
naturally fitter than women, for actions of labour and
danger. Thirdly, where his own issue faileth, rather a
brother than a stranger; and so still the nearer in blood,
rather than the more remote; because it is always presumed that the nearer of kin, is the nearer in affection;
and it is evident that a man receives always, by reflection, the most honour from the greatness of his nearest
kindred.

But if it be lawful for a monarch to dispose of the
succession by words of contract, or testament, men may
perhaps object a great inconvenience: for he may sell,
or give his right of governing to a stranger; which,
because strangers, that is, men not used to live under
the same government, nor speaking the same language,
do commonly undervalue one another, may turn to the
oppression of his subjects; which is indeed a great inconvenience: but it proceedeth not necessarily from the
subjection to a stranger's government, but from the unskilfulness of the governors, ignorant of the true rules
of politics. And therefore the Romans when they had
subdued many nations, to make their government
digestible, were wont to take away that grievance, as
much as they thought necessary, by giving sometimes
to whole nations, and sometimes to principal men of
every nation they conquered, not only the privileges,
but also the name of Romans; and took many of them
into the senate, and offices of charge, even in the Roman
city. And this was it our most wise king, king James,
aimed at, in endeavouring the union of his two realms
of England and Scotland. Which if he could have obtained, had in all likelihood prevented the civil wars,
which make both those kingdoms, at this present, miser-

able. It is not therefore any injury to the people, for a monarch to dispose of the succession by will; though by the fault of many princes, it hath been sometimes found inconvenient. Of the lawfulness of it, this also is an argument, that whatsoever inconvenience can arrive by giving a kingdom to a stranger, may arrive also by so marrying with strangers, as the right of succession may descend upon them: yet this by all men is accounted lawful.

CHAPTER XXI

OF THE LIBERTY OF SUBJECTS

LIBERTY, OR FREEDOM, signifieth, properly, the absence of opposition; by opposition, I mean external impediments of motion; and may be applied no less to irrational, and inanimate creatures, than to rational. For whatsoever is so tied, or environed, as it cannot move but within a certain space, which space is determined by the opposition of some external body, we say it hath not liberty to go further. And so of all living creatures, whilst they are imprisoned, or restrained, with walls, or chains; and of the water whilst it is kept in by banks, or vessels, that otherwise would spread itself into a larger space, we use to say, they are not at liberty, to move in such manner, as without those external impediments they would. But when the impediment of motion, is in the constitution of the thing itself, we use not to say; it wants the liberty; but the power to move; as when a stone lieth still, or a man is fastened to his bed by sickness.

And according to this proper, and generally received meaning of the word, a FREEMAN, *is he, that in those things, which by his strength and wit he is able to do, is not hindered to do what he has a will to.* But when the words *free,* and *liberty,* are applied to any thing but bodies, they are abused; for that which is not subject to motion is not subject to impediment: and therefore, when it is said, for example, the way is free, no liberty of the way is signified, but of those that walk in it without stop. And when we say a gift is free, there is not meant any liberty of the gift, but of the giver, that was not bound by any law or covenant to give it. So when we *speak freely,* it is not the liberty of voice, or pronunciation, but of the man, whom no law hath obliged to speak otherwise than he did. Lastly, from the use of the word *free-will,* no liberty can be inferred of the will, desire, or inclination, but the liberty of the man; which consisteth in this, that he finds no stop, in doing what he has the will, desire, or inclination to do.

Fear and liberty are consistent; as when a man throweth his goods into the sea for *fear* the ship should sink, he doth it nevertheless very willingly, and may refuse to do it if he will; it is therefore the action of one that was *free:* so a man sometimes pays his debt, only for *fear* of imprisonment, which because nobody hindered him from detaining, was the action of a man at *liberty.* And generally all actions which men do in commonwealths, for *fear* of the law, are actions, which the doers had *liberty* to omit.

Liberty, and *necessity* are consistent: as in the water, that hath not only *liberty,* but a *necessity* of descending by the channel; so likewise in the actions which men voluntarily do: which, because they proceed from their will, proceed from *liberty*; and yet, because every act of man's will, and every desire, and inclination proceedeth from some cause, and that from another cause, in a continual chain, whose first link is in the hand of

God the first of all causes, proceed from *necessity*. So that to him that could see the connexion of those causes, the *necessity* of all men's voluntary actions, would appear manifest. And therefore God, that seeth, and disposeth all things, seeth also that the liberty of man in doing what he will, is accompanied with the *necessity* of doing that which God will, and no more, nor less. For though men may do many things, which God does not command, nor is therefore author of them; yet they can have no passion, nor appetite to anything, of which appetite God's will is not the cause. And did not his will assure the *necessity* of man's will, and consequently of all that on man's will dependeth, the *liberty* of men would be a contradiction, and impediment to the omnipotence and *liberty* of God. And this shall suffice, as to the matter in hand, of that natural *liberty*, which only is properly called *liberty*.

But as men, for the attaining of peace, and conservation of themselves thereby, have made an artificial man, which we call a commonwealth; so also have they made artificial chains, called *civil laws*, which they themselves, by mutual covenants, have fastened at one end, to the lips of that man, or assembly, to whom they have given the sovereign power; and at the other end to their own ears. These bonds, in their own nature but weak, may nevertheless be made to hold, by the danger, though not by the difficulty of breaking them.

In relation to these bonds only it is, that I am to speak now, of the *liberty* of *subjects*. For seeing there is no commonwealth in the world, wherein there be rules enough set down, for the regulating of all the actions, and words of men; as being a thing impossible: it followeth necessarily, that in all kinds of actions by the laws praetermitted, men have the liberty, of doing what their own reasons shall suggest, for the most profitable to themselves. For if we take liberty in the proper sense, for corporal liberty; that is to say, freedom from chains and prison; it were very absurd for men to clamour as they do, for the liberty they so manifestly enjoy. Again, if we take liberty, for an exemption from laws, it is no less absurd, for men to demand as they do, that liberty, by which all other men may be masters of their lives. And yet, as absurd as it is, this is it they demand; not knowing that the laws are of no power to protect them, without a sword in the hands of a man, or men, to cause those laws to be put in execution. The liberty of a subject, lieth therefore only in those things, which in regulating their actions, the sovereign hath praetermitted: such as is the liberty to buy, and sell, and otherwise contract with one another; to choose their own abode, their own diet, their own trade of life, and institute their children as they themselves think fit; and the like.

Nevertheless we are not to understand, that by such liberty, the sovereign power of life and death, is either abolished, or limited. For it has been already shown, that nothing the sovereign representative can do to a subject, on what pretence soever, can properly be called injustice, or injury; because every subject is author of every act the sovereign doth; so that he never wanteth right to anything, otherwise, than as he himself is the subject of God, and bound thereby to observe the laws of nature. And therefore it may, and doth often happen in commonwealths, that a subject may be put to death, by the command of the sovereign power; and yet neither do the other wrong; as when Jephtha caused his daughter to be sacrificed: in which, and the like cases, he that so dieth, had liberty to do the action, for which he is nevertheless, without injury put to death. And the same holdeth also in a sovereign prince, that putteth to death an innocent subject. For though the action be against the law of nature, as being contrary to equity, as was the killing of Uriah, by David; yet it was not an injury to Uriah, but to God. Not to Uriah, because the right to do what he pleased was given him by Uriah himself: and yet to God, because David was God's subject, and prohibited all iniquity by the law of nature: which distinction, David himself, when he repented the fact, evidently confirmed, saying, *To thee only have I sinned.* In the same manner, the people of Athens, when they banished the most potent of their commonwealth for ten years, thought they committed no injustice; and yet they never questioned what crime he had done; but what hurt he would do: nay they commanded the banishment of they knew not whom; and every citizen bringing his oystershell into the market place, written with the name of him he desired should be banished, without actually accusing him, sometimes banished an Aristides, for his reputation of justice; and sometimes a scurrilous jester, as Hyperbolus, to make a jest of it. And yet a man cannot say, the sovereign people of Athens wanted right to banish them; or an Athenian the liberty to jest, or to be just.

The liberty, whereof there is so frequent and honourable mention, in the histories, and philosophy of the ancient Greeks, and Romans, and in the writings, and discourse of those that from them have received all their learning in the politics, is not the liberty of particular men; but the liberty of the commonwealth: which is the same with that which every man then should have, if there were no civil laws, nor commonwealth at all. And the effects of it also be the same. For as amongst masterless men, there is perpetual war, of every man against his neighbor; no inheritance, to transmit to the son, nor to expect from the father; no propriety of goods, or lands; no security; but a full and absolute liberty in every particular man: so in states, and commonwealths not dependent on one another, every commonwealth, not every man, has an absolute liberty, to do what it shall judge, that is to say, what that man, or assembly that representeth it, shall judge most conducing to their benefit. But withal, they live in the condition of a perpetual war, and upon the confines of battle, with their frontiers armed, and cannons planted against their neighbours round about. The Athenians, and Romans were free; that is, free commonwealths: not that any particular men had the liberty to resist their own representative; but that their representative had the liberty to resist, or invade other people. There is written on the turrets of the city of Lucca in great characters at this day, the word LIBERTAS; yet no man can thence infer, that a particular man has more liberty, or immunity from the service of the commonwealth there, than in Constantinople. Whether a commonwealth be monarchical, or popular, the freedom is still the same.

But it is an easy thing, for men to be deceived, by the specious name of liberty; and for want of judgment to distinguish, mistake that for their private inheritance, and birth-right, which is the right of the public only. And when the same error is confirmed by the authority of men in reputation for their writings on this subject, it is no wonder if it produce sedition, and change of government. In these western parts of the world, we are made to receive our opinions concerning the institution, and rights of commonwealths, from Aristotle, Cicero, and other men, Greeks and Romans, that living under popular states, derived those rights, not from the principles of nature, but transcribed them into their books, out of the practice of their own com-

monwealths, which were popular; as the grammarians
describe the rules of language, out of the practice of
the time; or the rules of poetry, out of the poems of
Homer and Virgil. And because the Athenians were
taught, to keep them from desire of changing their
government, that they were freemen, and all that lived
under monarchy were slaves; therefore Aristotle puts
it down in his *Politics,* (*lib.* 6. *cap.* ii.) *In democracy,*
LIBERTY *is to be supposed: for it is commonly held,*
that no man is FREE *in any other government.* And as
Aristotle; so Cicero, and other writers have grounded
their civil doctrine, on the opinions of the Romans, who
were taught to hate monarchy, at first, by them that
having deposed their sovereign, shared amongst them
the sovereignty of Rome; and afterwards by their successors. And by reading of these Greek, and Latin
authors, men from their childhood have gotten a habit,
under a false show of liberty, of favouring tumults, and
of licentious controlling the actions of their sovereigns,
and again of controlling those controllers; with the
effusion of so much blood, as I think I may truly say,
there was never any thing so dearly bought, as these
western parts have bought the learning of the Greek
and Latin tongues.

To come now to the particulars of the true liberty
of a subject; that is to say, what are the things, which
though commanded by the sovereign, he may nevertheless, without injustice, refuse to do; we are to consider,
what rights we pass away, when we make a commonwealth; or, which is all one, what liberty we deny
ourselves, by owning all the actions, without exception,
of the man, or assembly, we make our sovereign. For
in the act of our *submission,* consisteth both our *obliga-*
tion, and our *liberty;* which must therefore be inferred
by arguments taken from thence; there being no obliga-

tion on any man, which ariseth not from some act of his own; for all men equally, are by nature free. And because such arguments, must either be drawn from the express words, *I authorize all his actions*, or from the intention of him that submitteth himself to his power, which intention is to be understood by the end for which he so submitteth; the obligation, and liberty of the subject, is to be derived, either from those words, or others equivalent; or else from the end of the institution of sovereignty, namely, the peace of the subjects within themselves, and their defence against a common enemy.

First therefore, seeing sovereignty by institution, is by covenant of every one to every one; and sovereignty by acquisition, by covenants of the vanquished to the victor, or child to the parent; it is manifest, that every subject has liberty in all those things, the right whereof cannot by covenant be transferred. I have shewn before in the 14th chapter, that covenants, not to defend a man's own body, are void. Therefore,

If the sovereign command a man, though justly condemned, to kill, wound, or maim himself; or not to resist those that assault him; or to abstain from the use of food, air, medicine, or any other thing, without which he cannot live; yet hath that man the liberty to disobey.

If a man be interrogated by the sovereign, or his authority, concerning a crime done by himself, he is not bound, without assurance of pardon, to confess it; because no man, as I have shown in the same chapter, can be obliged by covenant to accuse himself.

Again, the consent of a subject to sovereign power, is contained in these words, *I authorize, or take upon me, all his actions;* in which there is no restriction at all, of his own former natural liberty: for by allowing him to *kill me,* I am not bound to kill myself when he commands me. It is one thing to say, *kill me, or my fellow, if you please;* another thing to say, *I will kill myself, or my fellow.* It followeth therefore, that

No man is bound by the words themselves, either to kill himself, or any other man; and consequently, that the obligation a man may sometimes have, upon the command of the sovereign to execute any dangerous, or dishonourable office, dependeth not on the words of our submission; but on the intention, which is to be understood by the end thereof. When therefore our refusal to obey, frustrates the end for which the sovereignty was ordained; then there is no liberty to refuse: otherwise there is.

Upon this ground, a man that is commanded as a soldier to fight against the enemy, though his sovereign have right enough to punish his refusal with death, may nevertheless in many cases refuse, without injustice; as when he substituteth a sufficient soldier in his place: for in this case he deserteth not the service of the commonwealth. And there is allowance to be made for natural timorousness; not only to women, of whom no such dangerous duty is expected, but also to men of feminine courage. When armies fight, there is on one side, or both, a running away; yet when they do it not out of treachery, but fear, they are not esteemed to do it unjustly, but dishonourably. For the same reason, to avoid battle, is not injustice, but cowardice. But he that inrolleth himself a soldier, or taketh imprest money, taketh away the excuse of a timorous nature; and is obliged, not only to go to the battle, but also not to run from it, without his captain's leave. And when the defence of the commonwealth, requireth at once the help of all that are able to bear arms, every one is obliged; because otherwise the institution of the commonwealth, which they have not the purpose, or courage to preserve, was in vain.

To resist the sword of the commonwealth, in defence of another man, guilty, or innocent, no man hath liberty; because such liberty, takes away from the sovereign, the means of protecting us; and is therefore destructive of the very essence of government. But in case a great many men together, have already resisted the sovereign power unjustly, or committed some capital crime, for which every one of them expecteth death, whether have they not the liberty then to join together, and assist, and defend one another? Certainly they have: for they but defend their lives, which the guilty man may as well do, as the innocent. There was indeed injustice in the first breach of their duty; their bearing of arms subsequent to it, though it be to maintain what they have done, is no new unjust act. And if it be only to defend their persons, it is not unjust at all. But the offer of pardon taketh from them, to whom it is offered, the plea of self-defence, and maketh their perseverance in assisting, or defending the rest, unlawful.

As for other liberties, they depend on the silence of the law. In cases where the sovereign has prescribed no rule, there the subject hath the liberty to do, or forbear, according to his own discretion. And therefore such liberty is in some places more, and in some less; and in some times more, in other times less, according as they that have the sovereignty shall think most convenient. As for example, there was a time, when in England a man might enter into his own land, and dispossess such as wrongfully possessed it, by force. But in after times, that liberty of forcible entry, was taken away by a statute made, by the king, in parliament. And in some places of the world, men have the liberty of many wives: in other places, such liberty is not allowed.

If a subject have a controversy with his sovereign, of debt, or of right of possession of lands or goods, or concerning any service required at his hands, or concerning any penalty, corporal, or pecuniary, grounded on a precedent law; he hath the same liberty to sue for his right, as if it were against a subject; and before such judges, as are appointed by the sovereign. For seeing the sovereign demandeth by force of a former law, and not by virtue of his power; he declareth thereby, that he requireth no more, than shall appear to be due by that law. The suit therefore is not contrary to the will of the sovereign; and consequently the subject hath the liberty to demand the hearing of his cause; and sentence, according to that law. But if he demand, or take anything by pretence of his power; there lieth, in that case, no action of law; for all that is done by him in virtue of his power, is done by the authority of every subject, and consequently he that brings an action against the sovereign, brings it against himself.

If a monarch, or sovereign assembly, grant a liberty to all, or any of his subjects, which grant standing, he is disabled to provide for their safety, the grant is void; unless he directly renounce, or transfer the sovereignty to another. For in that he might openly, if it had been his will, and in plain terms, have renounced, or transferred it, and did not; it is to be understood it was not his will, but that the grant proceeded from ignorance of the repugnancy between such a liberty and the sovereign power; and therefore the sovereignty is still retained; and consequently all those powers, which are necessary to the exercising thereof; such as are the power of war, and peace, of judicature, of appointing officers, and councillors, of levying money, and the rest named in the 18th chapter.

The obligation of subjects to the sovereign, is understood to last as long, and no longer, than the power lasteth, by which he is able to protect them. For the right men have by nature to protect themselves, when none else can protect them, can by no covenant be relinquished. The sovereignty is the soul of the commonwealth; which once departed from the body, the members do no more receive their motion from it. The end of obedience is protection; which, wheresoever a man seeth it, either in his own, or in another's sword, nature applieth his obedience to it, and his endeavour to maintain it. And though sovereignty, in the intention of them that make it, be immortal; yet it is in its own nature, not only subject to violent death, by foreign war; but also through the ignorance, and passions of men, it hath in it, from the very institution, many seeds of a natural mortality, by intestine discord.

If a subject be taken prisoner in war; or his person or his means of life be within the guards of the enemy, and hath his life and corporal liberty given him, on condition to be subject to the victor, he hath liberty to accept the condition; and having accepted it, is the subject of him that took him; because he had no other way to preserve himself. The case is the same, if he be detained on the same terms, in a foreign country. But if a man be held in prison, or bonds, or is not trusted with the liberty of his body; he cannot be understood to be bound by covenant to subjection; and therefore may, if he can, make his escape by any means whatsoever.

If a monarch shall relinquish the sovereignty, both for himself, and his heirs; his subjects return to the absolute liberty of nature; because, though nature may declare who are his sons, and who are the nearest of his kin; yet it dependeth on his own will, as hath been said in the precedent chapter, who shall be his heir. If therefore he will have no heir, there is no sovereignty, nor subjection. The case is the same, if he die without known kindred, and without declaration of his heir. For then there can no heir be known, and consequently no subjection be due.

If the sovereign banish his subject; during the banishment, he is not subject. But he that is sent on a message, or hath leave to travel, is still subject; but it is, by contract between sovereigns, not by virtue of the covenant of subjection. For whosoever entereth into another's dominion, is subject to all the laws thereof; unless he have a privilege of the amity of the sovereigns, or by special licence.

If a monarch subdued by war, render himself subject to the victor; his subjects are delivered from their former obligation, and become obliged to the victor. If he be held prisoner, or have not the liberty of his own body; he is not understood to have given away the right of sovereignty; and therefore his subjects are obliged to yield obedience to the magistrates formerly placed, governing not in their own name, but in his. For, his right remaining, the question is only of the administration; that is to say, of the magistrates and officers; which, if he have not means to name, he is supposed to approve those, which he himself had formerly appointed.

CHAPTER XXXI

OF THE KINGDOM OF GOD BY NATURE

THAT the condition of mere nature, that is to say, of absolute liberty, such as is theirs, that neither are sovereigns, nor subjects, is anarchy, and the condition of war: that the precepts, by which men are guided to avoid that condition, are the laws of nature: that a commonwealth, without sovereign power, is but a word without substance, and cannot stand: that subjects owe to sovereigns, simple obedience, in all things wherein their obedience is not repugnant to the laws of God, I have sufficiently proved, in that which I have already written. There wants only, for the entire knowledge of civil duty, to know what are those laws of God. For without that, a man knows not, when he is commanded any thing by the civil power, whether it be contrary to the law of God, or not: and so, either by too much civil obedience, offends the Divine Majesty; or through fear of offending God, transgresses the commandments of the commonwealth. To avoid both these rocks, it is necessary to know what are the laws divine. And seeing the knowledge of all law, dependeth on the knowledge of the sovereign power, I shall say something in that which followeth, of the KINGDOM OF GOD.

God is king, let the earth rejoice, saith the psalmist. (xcvii. 1). And again, (*Psalm* xcix. 1), *God is king, though the nations be angry; and he that sitteth on the cherubims, though the earth be moved.* Whether men will or not, they must be subject always to the divine power. By denying the existence, or providence of God, men may shake off their ease, but not their yoke. But to call this power of God, which extendeth itself not only to man, but also to beasts, and plants, and bodies inanimate, by the name of kingdom, is but a metaphorical use of the word. For he only is properly said to reign, that governs his subjects by his word, and by promise of rewards to those that obey it, and by threatening them with punishment that obey it not. Subjects therefore in the kingdom of God, are not

bodies inanimate, nor creatures irrational; because they
understand no precepts as his: nor atheists, nor they
that believe not that God has any care of the actions of
mankind; because they acknowledge no word for his,
nor have hope of his rewards or fear of his threatenings.
They therefore that believe there is a God that governeth the world, and hath given precepts, and propounded rewards, and punishments to mankind, are
God's subjects; all the rest, are to be understood as
enemies.

To rule by words, requires that such words be manifestly made known; for else they are no laws: for to the
nature of laws belongeth a sufficient, and clear promulgation, such as may take away the excuse of ignorance;
which in the laws of men is but of one only kind, and
that is, proclamation, or promulgation by the voice of
man. But God declareth his laws three ways; by the
dictates of *natural reason*, by *revelation*, and by the
voice of some *man*, to whom by the operation of miracles,
he procureth credit with the rest. From hence there
ariseth a triple word of God, *rational, sensible,* and
prophetic: to which correspondeth a triple hearing;
right reason, sense supernatural, and *faith.* As for
sense supernatural, which consisteth in revelation or inspiration, there have not been any universal laws so
given, because God speaketh not in that manner but to
particular persons, and to divers men divers things.

From the difference between the other two kinds of
God's word, *rational*, and *prophetic*, there may be attributed to God, a twofold kingdom, *natural*, and *prophetic*:
natural, wherein he governeth as many of mankind as
acknowledge his providence, by the natural dictates of
right reason; and prophetic, wherein having chosen out
one peculiar nation, the Jews, for his subjects, he governed them, and none but them, not only by natural

reason, but by positive laws, which he gave them by the mouths of his holy prophets. Of the natural kingdom of God I intend to speak in this chapter.

The right of nature, whereby God reigneth over men, and punisheth those that break his laws, is to be derived, not from his creating them, as if he required obedience as of gratitude for his benefits; but from his *irresistible power*. I have formerly shown how the sovereign right ariseth from pact: to show how the same right may arise from nature, requires no more; but to show in what case it is never taken away. Seeing all men by nature had right to all things, they had right every one to reign over all the rest. But because this right could not be obtained by force, it concerned the safety of every one, laying by that right, to set up men, with sovereign authority, by common consent, to rule and defend them: whereas if there had been any man of power irresistible, there had been no reason, why he should not by that power have ruled and defended both himself, and them, according to his own discretion. To those therefore whose power is irresistible, the dominion of all men adhereth naturally by their excellence of power; and consequently it is from that power, that the kingdom over men, and the right of afflicting men at his pleasure, belongeth naturally to God Almighty; not as Creator, and gracious; but as omnipotent. And though punishment be due for sin only, because by that word is understood affliction for sin; yet the right of afflicting, is not always derived from men's sin, but from God's power.

This question, *why evil men often prosper, and good men suffer adversity*, has been much disputed by the ancient, and is the same with this of ours, *by what right God dispenseth the prosperities and adversities of this life*; and is of that difficulty, as it hath shaken the faith, not only of the vulgar, but of philosophers, and which is more, of the Saints, concerning the Divine Providence. *How good,* saith David, (*Psalm* lxxiii. 1, 2, 3) *is the God of Israel to those that are upright in heart; and yet my feet were almost gone, my treadings had well-nigh slipt; for I was grieved at the wicked, when I saw the ungodly in such prosperity.* And Job, how earnestly does he expostulate with God, for the many afflictions he suffered, notwithstanding his righteousness. This question in the case of Job, is decided by God himself, not by arguments derived from Job's sin, but his own power. For whereas the friends of Job drew their arguments from his affliction to his sin, and he defended himself by the conscience of his innocence, God himself taketh up the matter, and having justified the affliction by arguments drawn from his power, such as this, (*Job* xxxviii. 4) *Where wast thou, when I laid the foundations of the earth?* and the like, both approved Job's innocence, and reproved the erroneous doctrine of his friends. Conformable to this doctrine is the sentence of our Saviour, concerning the man that was born blind, in these words, *Neither hath this man sinned, nor his fathers; but that the works of God might be made manifest in him.* And though it be said, *that death entered into the world by sin,* (by which is meant, that if Adam had never sinned, he had never died, that is, never suffered any separation of his soul from his body), it follows not thence, that God could not justly have afflicted him, though he had not sinned, as well as he afflicteth other living creatures, that cannot sin.

Having spoken of the right of God's sovereignty, as grounded only on nature; we are to consider next, what are the Divine laws, or dictates of natural reason; which laws concern either the natural duties of one man to another, or the honour naturally due to our Divine Sovereign. The first are the same laws of nature, of which

I have spoken already in the fourteenth and fifteenth chapters of this treatise; namely, equity, justice, mercy, humility, and the rest of the moral virtues. It remaineth therefore that we consider, what precepts are dictated to men, by their natural reason only, without other word of God, touching the honour and worship of the Divine Majesty.

Honour consisteth in the inward thought, and opinion of the power, and goodness of another; and therefore to honour God, is to think as highly of his power and goodness, as is possible. And of that opinion, the external signs appearing in the words and actions of men, are called *worship*; which is one part of that which the Latins understand by the word *cultus*. For *cultus* signifieth properly, and constantly, that labour which a man bestows on anything, with a purpose to make benefit by it. Now those things whereof we make benefit, are either subject to us, and the profit they yield, followeth the labour we bestow upon them, as a natural effect; or they are not subject to us, but answer our labour, according to their own wills. In the first sense the labour bestowed on the earth, is called *culture*; and the education of children, a *culture* of their minds. In the second sense, where men's wills are to be wrought to our purpose, not by force, but by complaisance, it signifieth as much as courting, that is, a winning of favour by good offices; as by praises, by acknowledging their power, and by whatsoever is pleasing to them from whom we look for any benefit. And this is properly *worship*: in which sense *Publicola*, is understod for a worshipper of the people; and *cultus Dei*, for the worship of God.

From internal honour, consisting in the opinion of power and goodness, arise three passions; *love*, which hath reference to goodness; and *hope*, and *fear*, that relate to power: and three parts of external worship; *praise*, *magnifying*, and *blessing*: the subject of praise, being goodness; the subject of magnifying and blessing, being power, and the effect thereof felicity. Praise, and magnifying are signified both by words, and actions: by words, when we say a man is good, or great: by actions, when we thank him for his bounty, and obey his power. The opinion of the happiness of another, can only be expressed by words.

There be some signs of honour, both in attributes and actions, that be naturally so; as amongst attributes, *good*, *just*, *liberal*, and the like; and amongst actions, *prayers*, *thanks*, and *obedience*. Others are so by institution, or custom of men; and in some times and places are honourable; in others, dishonourable; in others, indifferent: such as are the gestures in salutation, prayer, and thanksgiving, in different times and places, differently used. The former is *natural*; the latter *arbitrary* worship.

And of arbitrary worship, there be two differences: for sometimes it is a *commanded*, sometimes *voluntary* worship: commanded, when it is such as he requireth, who is worshipped: free, when it is such as the worshipper thinks fit. When it is commanded, not the words, or gesture, but the obedience is the worship. But when free, the worship consists in the opinion of the beholders: for if to them the words, or actions by which we intend honour, seem ridiculous, and tending to contumely, they are no worship, because no signs of honour; and no signs of honour, because a sign is not a sign to him that giveth it, but to him to whom it is made, that is, to the spectator.

Again, there is a *public*, and a *private* worship. Public, is the worship that a commonwealth performeth, as one person. Private, is that which a private person exhibiteth. Public, in respect to the whole common-wealth, is free; but in respect to particular men, it is not so. Private, is in secret free; but in the sight of the multitude, it is never without some restraint, either from the laws, or from the opinion of men; which is contrary to the nature of liberty.

The end of worship amongst men, is power. For where a man seeth another worshipped, he supposeth him powerful, and is the readier to obey him; which makes his power greater. But God has no ends: the worship we do him, proceeds from our duty, and is directed according to our capacity, by those rules of honour, that reason dictateth to be done by the weak to the more potent men, in hope of benefit, for fear of damage, or in thankfulness for good already received from them.

That we may know what worship of God is taught us by the light of nature, I will begin with his attributes. Where, first, it is manifest, we ought to attribute to him *existence*. For no man can have the will to honour that, which he thinks not to have any being.

Secondly, that those philosophers, who said the world, or the soul of the world was God, spake unworthily of him; and denied his existence. For by God, is under-stood the cause of the world; and to say the world is God, is to say there is no cause of it, that is, no God.

Thirdly, to say the world was not created, but eternal, seeing that which is eternal has no cause, is to deny there is a God.

Fourthly, that they who attributing, as they think, ease to God, take from him the care of mankind; take from him his honour: for it takes away men's love, and fear of him; which is the root of honour.

Fifthly, in those things that signify greatness, and power; to say he is *finite*, is not to honour him: for it is not a sign of the will to honour God, to attribute to him less than we can; and finite, is less than we can; because to finite, it is easy to add more.

Therefore to attribute *figure* to him, is not honour; for all figure is finite:

Nor to say we conceive, and imagine, or have an *idea* of him, in our mind: for whatsoever we conceive is finite:

Nor to attribute to him *parts*, or *totality*; which are the attributes only of things finite:

Nor to say he is in this, or that *place*: for whatsoever is in place, is bounded, and finite:

Nor that he is *moved*, or *resteth*: for both these attributes ascribe to him place:

Nor that there be more Gods than one; because it implies them all finite: for there cannot be more than one infinite:

Nor to ascribe to him, (unless metaphorically, meaning not the passion but the effect), passions that partake of grief; as *repentance, anger, mercy*: or of want; as *appetite, hope, desire*; or of any passive faculty; for passion, is power limited by somewhat else.

And therefore when we ascribe to God a *will*, it is not to be understood, as that of man, for a *rational appetite*; but as the power, by which he affecteth every thing.

Likewise when we attribute to him *sight*, and other acts of sense; as also *knowledge*, and *understanding*; which in us is nothing else, but a tumult of the mind, raised by external things that press the organical parts of man's body: for there is no such thing in God; and being things that depend on natural causes, cannot be attributed to him.

He that will attribute to God, nothing but what is warranted by natural reason, must either use such negative attributes, as *infinite, eternal, incomprehensible*; or superlatives, as *most high, most great,* and the like; or indefinite, as *good, just, holy, creator,* and in such sense, as if he meant not to declare what he is, (for that were to circumscribe him within the limits of our fancy), but how much we admire him, and how ready we would be to obey him; which is a sign of humility, and of a will to honour him as much as we can. For there is but one name to signify our conception of his nature, and that is, I AM: and but one name of his relation to us, and that is, *God*; in which is contained Father, King, and Lord.

Concerning the actions of divine worship, it is a most general precept of reason, that they be signs of the intention to honour God; such as are, first, *prayers*. For not the carvers, when they made images, were thought to make them gods; but the people that *prayed* to them.

Secondly, *thanksgiving*; which differeth from prayer in divine worship, no otherwise, than that prayers precede, and thanks succeed the benefit; the end, both of the one and the other, being to acknowledge God, for author of all benefits, as well past, as future.

Thirdly, *gifts*, that is to say, *sacrifices* and *oblations*, if they be of the best, are signs of honour: for they are thanksgivings.

Fourthly, *not to swear by any but God*, is naturally a sign of honour: for it is a confession that God only knoweth the heart; and that no man's wit or strength can protect a man against God's vengeance on the perjured.

Fifthly, it is a part of rational worship, to speak considerately of God; for it argues a fear of him, and fear is a confession of his power. Hence followeth, that the name of God is not to be used rashly, and to no purpose; for that is as much, as in vain: and it is to no

purpose, unless it be by way of oath, and by order of
the commonwealth, to make judgments certain; or between commonwealths, to avoid war. And that disputing of God's nature is contrary to his honour: for
it is supposed, that in this natural kingdom of God,
there is no other way to know anything, but by natural
reason, that is, from the principles of natural science;
which are so far from teaching us anything of God's
nature, as they cannot teach us our own nature, nor
the nature of the smallest creature living. And therefore, when men out of the principles of natural reason,
dispute of the attributes of God, they but dishonour
him: for in the attributes which we give to God, we
are not to consider the signification of philosophical
truth; but the signification of pious intention, to do him
the greatest honour we are able. From the want of
which consideration, have proceeded the volumes of disputation about the nature of God, that tend not to his
honour, but to the honour of our own wits and learning;
and are nothing else but inconsiderate and vain abuses
of his sacred name.

Sixthly, in *prayers, thanksgivings, offerings,* and
sacrifices, it is a dictate of natural reason, that they be
every one in his kind the best, and most significant of
honour. As for example, that prayers and thanksgiving, be made in words and phrases, not sudden, nor
light, nor plebeian; but beautiful, and well composed.
For else we do not God as much honour as we can.
And therefore the heathens did absurdly, to worship
images for gods: but their doing it in verse, and with
music, both of voice and instruments, was reasonable.
Also that the beasts they offered in sacrifice, and the
gifts they offered, and their actions in worshipping, were
full of submission, and commemorative of benefits re-

ceived, was according to reason, as proceeding from an intention to honour him.

Seventhly, reason directeth not only to worship God in secret; but also, and especially, in public, and in the sight of men. For without that, that which in honour is most acceptable, the procuring others to honour him, is lost.

Lastly, obedience to his laws, that is, in this case to the laws of nature, is the greatest worship of all. For as obedience is more acceptable to God than sacrifice; so also to set light by his commandments, is the greatest of all contumelies. And these are the laws of that divine worship, which natural reason dictateth to private men.

But seeing a commonwealth is but one person, it ought also to exhibit to God but one worship; which then it doth, when it commandeth it to be exhibited by private men, publicly. And this is public worship; the property whereof, is to be *uniform*: for those actions that are done differently, by different men, cannot be said to be a public worship. And therefore, where many sorts of worship be allowed, proceeding from different religions of private men, it cannot be said there is any public worship, nor that the commonwealth is of any religion at all.

And because words, and consequently the attributes of God, have their signification by agreement and constitution of men, those attributes are to be held significative of honour, that men intend shall so be; and whatsoever may be done by the wills of particular men, where there is no law but reason, may be done by the will of the commonwealth, by laws civil. And because a commonwealth hath no will, nor makes no laws, but those that are made by the will of him, or them that have the sovereign power; it followeth that those attributes which the sovereign ordaineth, in the worship of

God, for signs of honour, ought to be taken and used for such, by private men in their public worship.

But because not all actions are signs by constitution, but some are naturally signs of honour, others of contumely; these latter, which are those that men are ashamed to do in the sight of them they reverence, cannot be made by human power a part of Divine worship; nor the former, such as are decent, modest, humble behaviour, ever be separated from it. But whereas there be an infinite number of actions and gestures of an indifferent nature; such of them as the commonwealth shall ordain to be publicly and universally in use, as signs of honour, and part of God's worship, are to be taken and used for such by the subjects. And that which is said in the Scripture, *It is better to obey God than man,* hath place in the kingdom of God by pact, and not by nature.

Having thus briefly spoken of the natural kingdom of God, and his natural laws, I will add only to this chapter a short declaration of his natural punishments. There is no action of man in this life, that is not the beginning of so long a chain of consequences, as no human providence is high enough, to give a man a prospect to the end. And in this chain, there are linked together both pleasing and unpleasing events; in such manner, as he that will do anything for his pleasure, must engage himself to suffer all the pains annexed to it; and these pains, are the natural punishments of those actions, which are the beginning of more harm than good. And hereby it comes to pass, that intemperance is naturally punished with diseases; rashness, with mischances; injustice, with the violence of enemies; pride, with ruin; cowardice, with oppression; negligent government of princes, with rebellion; and rebellion, with

slaughter. For seeing punishments are consequent to
the breach of laws; natural punishments must be naturally consequent to the breach of the laws of nature;
and therefore follow them as their natural, not arbitrary
effects.

And thus far concerning the constitution, nature, and
right of sovereigns, and concerning the duty of subjects, derived from the principles of natural reason.
And now, considering how different this doctrine is,
from the practice of the greatest part of the world,
especially of these western parts, that have received
their moral learning from Rome and Athens; and how
much depth of moral philosophy is required, in them
that have the administration of the sovereign power; I
am at the point of believing this my labour, as useless,
as the commonwealth of Plato. For he also is of opinion
that it is impossible for the disorders of state, and
change of governments by civil war, ever to be taken
away, till sovereigns be philosophers. But when I consider again, that the science of natural justice, is the
only science necessary for sovereigns and their principal ministers; and that they need not be charged with
the sciences mathematical, as by Plato they are, farther
than by good laws to encourage men to the study of
them; and that neither Plato, nor any other philosopher
hitherto, hath put into order, and sufficiently or probably proved all the theorems of moral doctrine, that
men may learn thereby, both how to govern, and how
to obey; I recover some hope, that one time or other,
this writing of mine may fall into the hands of a sovereign, who will consider it himself, (for it is short,
and I think clear), without the help of any interested,
or envious interpreter; and by the exercise of entire
sovereignty, in protecting the public teaching of it,

convert this truth of speculation, into the utility of practice.

Part III

OF A CHRISTIAN COMMONWEALTH

CHAPTER XLIII

OF WHAT IS NECESSARY FOR A MAN'S RECEPTION INTO THE KINGDOM OF HEAVEN

THE most frequent pretext of sedition, and civil war, in Christian commonwealths, hath a long time proceeded from a difficulty, not yet sufficiently resolved, of obeying at once both God and man, then when their commandments are one contrary to the other. It is manifest enough, that when a man receiveth two contrary commands, and knows that one of them is God's, he ought to obey that, and not the other, though it be the command even of his lawful sovereign, (whether a monarch, or a sovereign assembly), or the command of his father. The difficulty therefore consisteth in this, that men, when they are commanded in the name of God, know not in divers cases, whether the command be from God, or whether he that commandeth do but abuse God's name for some private ends of his own. For as there were in the Church of the Jews, many false prophets, that sought reputation with the people, by feigned dreams and visions; so there have been in all times in the Church of Christ, false teachers, that seek reputation with the people, by fantastical and false doctrines; and by such reputation, (as is the nature of ambition), to govern them for their private benefit.

But this difficulty of obeying both God and the civil sovereign on earth, to those that can distinguish between what is *necessary*, and what is not *necessary for their reception into the kingdom of God*, is of no moment. For if the command of the civil sovereign be such, as that it may be obeyed without the forfeiture of life eternal; not to obey it is unjust; and the precept of the apostle takes place: *Servants obey your masters in all things*; and *Children obey your parents in all things*; and the precept of our Saviour, *The Scribes and Pharisees sit in Moses' chair; all therefore they shall say, that observe and do.* But if the command be such as cannot be obeyed, without being damned to eternal death; then it were madness to obey it, and the council of our Saviour takes place, (*Matth.* x. 28), *Fear not those that kill the body, but cannot kill the soul.* All men therefore that would avoid, both the punishments that are to be in this world inflicted, for disobedience to their earthly sovereign, and those that shall be inflicted in the world to come, for disobedience to God, have need be taught to distinguish well between what is, and what is not necessary to eternal salvation.

All that is NECESSARY *to salvation*, is contained in two virtues, *faith in Christ*, and *obedience to laws*. The latter of these, if it were perfect, were enough to us. But because we are all guilty of disobedience to God's law, not only originally in Adam, but also actually by our own transgressions, there is required at our hands now, not only *obedience* for the rest of our time, but also a *remission of sins* for the time past; which remission is the reward of our faith in Christ. That nothing else is necessarily required to salvation, is manifest from this, that the kingdom of heaven is shut to none but to sinners; that is to say, to the disobedient, or transgressors of the law; nor to them, in case they repent, and believe all the articles of Christian faith necessary to salvation.

The obedience required at our hands by God, that accepteth in all our actions the will for the deed, is a serious endeavour to obey him; and is called also by all such names as signify that endeavour. And therefore obedience is sometimes called by the names of *charity* and *love,* because they imply a will to obey; and our Saviour himself maketh our love to God, and to one another, a fulfilling of the whole law: and sometimes by the name of *righteousness*; for righteousness is but the will to give to every one his own; that is to say, the will to obey the laws: and sometimes by the name of *repentance*; because to repent, implieth a turning away from sin, which is the same with the return of the will to obedience. Whosoever therefore unfeignedly desireth to fulfill the commandments of God, or re-penteth him truly of his transgressions, or that loveth God with all his heart, and his neighbour as himself, hath all the obedience necessary to his reception into the kingdom of God. For if God should require perfect innocence, there could no flesh be saved.

But what commandments are those that God hath given us? Are all those laws which were given to the Jews by the hand of Moses, the commandments of God? If they be, why are not Christians taught to obey them? If they be not, what others are so, besides the law of nature? For our Saviour Christ hath not given us new laws, but counsel to observe those we are subject to; that is to say, the laws of nature, and the laws of our several sovereigns: nor did he make any new law to the Jews in his sermon on the Mount, but only expounded the law of Moses, to which they were subject before. The laws of God therefore are none but the laws of nature, whereof the principal is, that we should not violate our faith, that is, a commandment to obey our civil sovereigns, which we constituted over us by mutual pact one with another. And this law of God, that commandeth obedience to the law civil, commandeth by consequence obedience to all the precepts of the Bible; which, as I have proved in the precedent chapter, is there only law, where the civil sovereign hath made it so; and in other places, but counsel; which a man at his own peril may without injustice refuse to obey.

Knowing now what is the obedience necessary to salvation, and to whom it is due; we are to consider next concerning faith, whom, and why we believe; and what are the articles, or points necessary to be believed by them that shall be saved. And first, for the person whom we believe, because it is impossible to believe any person, before we know what he saith, it is necessary he be one that we have heard speak. The person, therefore, whom Abraham, Isaac, Jacob, Moses, and the prophets, believed, was God himself, that spake unto them supernaturally: and the person, whom the apostles and disciples that conversed with Christ believed, was our Saviour himself. But of them, to whom neither God the father, nor our Saviour, ever spake, it cannot be said that the person whom they believed, was God. They believed the apostles, and after them the pastors and doctors of the Church, that recommended to their faith the history of the Old and New Testament: so that the faith of Christians ever since our Saviour's time, hath had for foundation, first, the reputation of their pastors, and afterward, the authority of those that made the Old and New Testament to be received for the rule of faith; which none could do but Christian sovereigns; who are therefore the supreme pastors, and the only persons whom Christians now hear speak from God; except such as God speaketh to in these days supernaturally. But because there be many false prophets *gone out into the world,* other men are to examine such spirits, as St. John adviseth us, (1st Eipstle iv. 1), *whether they be of God, or not.* And therefore, seeing the examination of doctrines belongeth to the supreme pastor, the person, which all they that have no special revelation are to believe, is, in every commonwealth, the supreme pastor, that is to say, the civil sovereign.

The causes why men believe any Christian doctrine, are various. For faith is the gift of God; and he worketh it in each several man, by such ways as it seemeth good unto himself. The most ordinary immediate cause of our belief, concerning any point of Christian faith, is, that we believe the Bible to be the word of God. But why we believe the Bible to be the word of God, is much disputed, as all questions must needs be, that are not well stated. For they make not the question to be, *why we believe it,* but, *how we know it;* as if *believing* and *knowing* were all one. And thence while one side ground their knowledge upon the infallibility of the Church, the other side, on the testimony of the private spirit, neither side concludeth what it pretends. For how shall a man know the infallibility of the Church, but by knowing first the infallibility of the Scripture? Or how shall a man know his own private spirit to be other than a belief, grounded upon the authority and arguments of his teachers, or upon a presumption of his own gifts? Besides, there is nothing in the Scripture, from which can be inferred the infallibility of the Church; much less, of any particular Church; and least of all, the infallibility of any particular man.

It is manifest therefore, that Christian men do not know, but only believe the Scripture to be the word of God; and that the means of making them believe, which

God is pleased to afford men ordinarily, is according to the way of nature, that is to say, from their teachers. It is the doctrine of St. Paul concerning Christian faith in general (*Rom.* x. 17), *Faith cometh by hearing*, that is, by hearing our lawful pastors. He saith also, (verses 14, 15, of the same chapter), *How shall they believe in him of whom they have not heard? and how shall they hear without a preacher? and how shall they preach, except they be sent?* Whereby it is evident, that the ordinary cause of believing that the Scriptures are the word of God, is the same with the cause of the believing of all other articles of our faith, namely, the hearing of those that are by the law allowed and appointed to teach us, as our parents in their houses, and our pastors in the churches. Which also is made more manifest by experience. For what other cause can there be assigned, why in Christian commonwealths all men either believe, or at least profess the Scripture to be the word of God, and in other commonwealths scarce any; but that in Christian commonwealths they are taught it from their infancy; and in other places they are taught otherwise?

But if teaching be the cause of faith, why do not all believe? It is certain therefore that faith is the gift of God, and he giveth it to whom he will. Nevertheless, because to them to whom he giveth it, he giveth it by the means of teachers, the immediate cause of faith is hearing. In a school, where many are taught, and some profit, others profit not, the cause of learning in them that profit, is the master; yet it cannot be thence inferred, that learning is not the gift of God. All good things proceed from God; yet cannot all that have them, say they are inspired; for that implies a gift supernatural, and the immediate hand of God; which he that pretends to, pretends to be a prophet, and is subject to the examination of the Church.

But whether men *know*, or *believe*, or *grant* the Scriptures to be the word of God; if out of such places of them, as are without obscurity, I shall show what articles of faith are necessary, and only necessary for salvation, those men must needs *know, believe,* or *grant* the same.

The *unum necessarium,* only article of faith, which the Scripture maketh simply necessary to salvation, is this, that JESUS IS THE CHRIST. By the name of *Christ* is understood the king, which God had before promised by the prophets of the Old Testament, to send into the world, to reign, (over the Jews, and over such of other nations as should believe in him), under himself eternally; and to give them that eternal life, which was lost by the sin of Adam. Which when I have proved out of Scripture, I will further show when, and in what sense, some other articles may be also called *necessary.*

*　　*　　*　　*　　*　　*　　*　　*　　*

But a man may here ask, whether it be not as necessary to salvation, to believe, that God is omnipotent; Creator of the world; that Jesus Christ is risen; and that all men else shall rise again from the dead at the last day; as to believe that *Jesus is the Christ.* To which I answer, they are; and so are many more articles: but they are such, as are contained in this one, and may be deduced from it, with more or less difficulty. For who is there that does not see, that they who believe Jesus to be the Son of the God of Israel, and that the Israelites had for God the Omnipotent Creator of all things, do therein also believe, that God is the Omnipotent Creator of all things? Or how can a man believe, that Jesus is the king that shall reign eternally, unless he believe him also risen again from the dead?

For a dead man cannot exercise the office of a king. In sum, he that holdeth this foundation, *Jesus is the Christ,* holdeth expressly all that he seeth rightly deduced from it, and implicitly all that is consequent thereunto, though he have not skill enough to discern the consequence. And therefore it holdeth still good, that the belief of this one article is sufficient faith to obtain remission of sins to the *penitent,* and consequently to bring them into the kingdom of heaven.

* * * * * * * * *

Seeing then it is necessary that faith and obedience, implied in the word repentance, do both concur to our salvation; the question by which of the two we are justified, is impertinently disputed. Nevertheless, it will not be impertinent, to make manifest in what manner each of them contributes thereunto; and in what sense it is said, that we are to be justified by the one, and by the other. And first, if by righteousness be understood the justice of the works themselves, there is no man that can be saved; for there is none that hath not transgressed the law of God. And therefore when we are said to be justified by works, it is to be understood of the will, which God doth always accept for the work itself, as well in good, as in evil men. And in this sense only it is, that a man is called *just,* or *unjust;* and that his justice justifies him, that is, gives him the title, in God's acceptation, of *just;* and renders him capable of *living by his faith,* which before he was not. So that justice justifies in that sense, in which to *justify,* is the same as that to *denominate a man just;* and not in the signification of discharging the law; whereby the punishment of his sins should be unjust.

But a man is then also said to be justified, when his

plea, though in itself insufficient, is accepted; as when we plead our will, our endeavour to fulfil the law, and repent us of our failings, and God accepteth it for the performance itself. And because God accepteth not the will for the deed, but only in the faithful; it is therefore faith that makes good our plea; and in this sense it is, that faith only justifies. So that *faith* and *obedience* are both necessary to salvation; yet in several senses each of them is said to justify.

Having thus shown what is necessary to salvation; it is not hard to reconcile our obedience to God, with our obedience to the civil sovereign; who is either Christian, or infidel. If he be a Christian, he alloweth the belief of this article, that *Jesus is the Christ*; and of all the articles that are contained in, or are by evident consequence deduced from it: which is all the faith necessary to salvation. And because he is a sovereign, he requireth obedience to all his own, that is, to all the civil laws; in which also are contained all the laws of nature, that is all the laws of God: for besides the laws of nature, and the laws of the Church, which are part of the civil law, (for the Church that can make laws is the commonwealth), there be no other laws divine. Whosoever therefore obeyeth his Christian sovereign, is not thereby hindered, neither from believing, nor from obeying God. But suppose that a Christian king should from this foundation *Jesus is the Christ*, draw some false consequences, that is to say, make some superstructions of hay or stubble, and command the teaching of the same; yet seeing St. Paul says he shall be saved; much more shall he be saved, that teacheth them by his command; and much more yet, he that teaches not, but only believes his lawful teacher. And in case a subject be forbidden by the civil sovereign to

profess some of those his opinions, upon what just
ground can he disobey? Christian kings may err in
deducing a consequence, but who shall judge? Shall
a private man judge, when the question is of his own
obedience? Or shall any man judge but he that is appointed thereto by the Church, that is, by the civil sovereign that representeth it? Or if the pope, or an
apostle judge, may he not err in deducing of a consequence? Did not one of the two, St. Peter or St. Paul,
err in a superstructure, when St. Paul withstood St.
Peter to his face? There can therefore be no contradiction between the laws of God, and the laws of a
Christian commonwealth.

And when the civil sovereign is an infidel, every one
of his own subjects that resisteth him, sinneth against
the laws of God, (for such are the laws of nature), and
rejecteth the counsel of the apostles, that admonisheth
all Christians to obey their princes, and all children and
servants to obey their parents and masters in all things.
And for their *faith*, it is internal, and invisible; they
have the license that Naaman had, and need not put
themselves into danger for it. But if they do, they
ought to expect their reward in heaven, and not complain of their lawful sovereign; much less make war
upon him. For he that is not glad of any just occasion
of martyrdom, has not the faith he professeth, but pretends it only, to set some colour upon his own contumacy. But what infidel king is so unreasonable, as
knowing he has a subject, that waiteth for the second
coming of Christ, after the present world shall be burnt,
and intendeth then to obey him, (which is the intent of
believing that Jesus is the Christ), and in the mean
time thinketh himself bound to obey the laws of that
infidel king, (which all Christians are obliged in con-

science to do), to put to death or to persecute such a subject? [1]

And thus much shall suffice, concerning the kingdom of God, and policy ecclesiastical. Wherein I pretend not to advance any position of my own, but only to show what are the consequences that seem to me deducible

[1] Compare *Philosophical Rudiments*, (M. II, 314). "By what hath been said hitherto, it will be easy to discern what the duty of Christian subjects is towards their sovereigns; who, as long as they profess themselves Christians, cannot command their subjects to deny Christ, or to offer him any contumely: for if they should command this, they would profess themselves to be no Christians. For seeing we have showed, both by natural reason and out of holy Scriptures, that subjects ought in all things to obey their princes and governors, excepting those which are contrary to the command of God; and that the commands of God, in a Christian city, concerning *temporal affairs*, that is to say, those which are to be discussed by human reason, are the laws and sentence of the city, delivered from those who have received authority from the city to make laws and judge of controversies; but concerning spiritual matters, that is to say, those which are to be defined by the holy Scripture, are the laws and sentences of the city, that is to say, the Church, (for a Christian city and a Church * * * * are the same thing), delivered by pastors lawfully ordained, and who have to that end authority given them by the city; it manifestly follows, that in a Christian commonweal obedience is due to the sovereign in all things, as well *spiritual* as *temporal*. And that the same obedience, even from a Christian subject, is due in all *temporal matters* to those princes who are no Christians, is without any controversy; but in *matters spiritual*, that is to say, those things which concern God's worship, some Christian Church is to be followed. For it is an hypothesis of the Christian faith, that God speaks not in things supernatural but by the way of Christian interpreters of holy Scriptures. But what? Must we resist princes, when we cannot obey them? Truly, no; for this is contrary to our civil covenant. What must we do then? Go to Christ by martyrdom; which if it seem to any man to be a hard saying, most certain it is that he believes not with his whole heart, *that Jesus is the Christ, the son of the living God*; for he would then desire to be dissolved, and to be with Christ; but he would by a feigned Christian faith elude that obedience, which he hath contracted to yield unto the city."

from the principles of Christian politics, (which are the holy Scriptures), in confirmation of the power of civil sovereigns, and the duty of their subjects. And in the allegation of Scripture, I have endeavoured to avoid such texts as are of obscure or controverted interpretation; and to allege none, but in such sense as is most plain, and agreeable to the harmony and scope of the whole Bible; which was written for the re-establishment of the kingdom of God in Christ. For it is not the bare words, but the scope of the writer, that giveth the true light, by which any writing is to be interpreted; and they that insist upon single texts, without considering the main design, can derive nothing from them clearly; but rather by casting atoms of Scripture, as dust before men's eyes, make every thing more obscure than it is; an ordinary artifice of those that seek not the truth, but their own advantage.

A REVIEW AND CONCLUSION

FROM the contrariety of some of the natural faculties of the mind, one to another, as also of one passion to another, and from their reference to conversation, there has been an argument taken, to infer an impossibility that any one man should be sufficiently disposed to all sorts of civil duty. The severity of judgment, they say, makes men censorious, and unapt to pardon the errors and infirmities of other men: and on the other side, celerity of fancy, makes the thoughts less steady than is necessary, to discern exactly between right and wrong. Again, in all deliberations, and in all pleadings, the faculty of solid reasoning is necessary: for without it, the resolutions of men are rash, and their sentences unjust: and yet if there be not powerful eloquence, which procureth attention and consent, the effect of reason

will be little. But these are contrary faculties; the
former being grounded upon principles of truth; the
other upon opinions already received, true or false; and
upon the passions and interests of men, which are different, and mutable.

And amongst the passions, *courage,* (by which I mean
the contempt of wounds, and violent death), inclineth
men to private revenges, and sometimes to endeavour
the unsettling of the public peace: and *timorousness,*
many times disposeth to the desertion of the public
defence. Both these, they say, cannot stand together in
the same person.

And to consider the contrariety of men's opinions, and
manners, in general, it is, they say, impossible to entertain a constant civil amity with all those, with whom
the business of the world constrains us to converse:
which business consisteth almost in nothing else but a
perpetual contention for honour, riches, and authority.

To which I answer, that these are indeed great difficulties, but not impossibilities: for by education, and
discipline, they may be, and are sometimes reconciled.
Judgment and fancy may have place in the same man;
but by turns; as the end which he aimeth at requireth.
As the Israelites in Egypt, were sometimes fastened to
their labour of making bricks, and other times were
ranging abroad to gather straw: so also may the judgment sometimes be fixed upon one certain consideration,
and the fancy at another time wandering about the
world. So also reason, and eloquence, though not perhaps in the natural sciences, yet, in the moral, may
stand very well together. For wheresoever there is
place for adorning and preferring of error, there is
much more place for adorning and preferring of truth,
if they have it to adorn. Nor is there any repugnancy
between fearing the laws, and not fearing a public

enemy; nor between abstaining from injury, and pardoning it in others. There is therefore no such inconsistence of human nature, with civil duties, as some think. I have known clearness of judgment, and largeness of fancy; strength of reason, and graceful elocution; a courage for the war, and a fear for the laws, and all eminently in one man; and that was my most noble and honoured friend, Mr. Sidney Godolphin; who hating no man, nor hated of any, was unfortunately slain in the beginning of the late civil war, in the public quarrel, by an undiscerned and an undiscerning hand.

To the Laws of Nature, declared in Chapter xv. I would have this added, *that every man is bound by nature, as much as in him lieth, to protect in war the authority, by which he is himself protected in time of peace.* For he that pretendeth a right of nature to preserve his own body, cannot pretend a right of nature to destroy him, by whose strength he is preserved: it is a manifest contradiction of himself. And though this law may be drawn by consequence, from some of those that are there already mentioned; yet the times require to have it inculcated, and remembered.

And because I find by divers English books lately printed, that the civil wars have not yet sufficiently taught men in what point of time it is, that a subject becomes obliged to the conqueror; nor what is conquest; nor how it comes about, that it obliges men to obey his laws: therefore for further satisfaction of men therein, I say, the point of time, wherein a man becomes subject to a conqueror, is that point, wherein having liberty to submit to him, he consenteth, either by express words, or by other sufficient sign, to be his subject. When it is that a man hath the liberty to submit, I have showed before in the end of Chapter xxi.; namely, that for him that hath no obligation to his former sovereign but that of an ordinary subject, it is then, when the means of his life are within the guards and garrisons of the enemy; for it is then, that he hath no longer protection from him, but is protected by the adverse party for his contribution. Seeing therefore such contribution is every where, as a thing inevitable, notwithstanding it be an assistance to the enemy, esteemed lawful; a total submission, which is but an assistance to the enemy, cannot be esteemed unlawful. Besides, if a man consider that they who submit, assist the enemy but with part of their estates, whereas they that refuse, assist him with the whole, there is no reason to call their submission, or composition, an assistance; but rather a detriment to the enemy. But if a man, besides the obligation of a subject, hath taken upon him a new obligation of a soldier, then he hath not the liberty to submit to a new power, as long as the old one keeps the field, and giveth him means of subsistence, either in his armies, or garrisons: for in this case, he cannot complain of want of protection, and means to live as a soldier. But when that also fails, a soldier also may seek his protection wheresoever he has most hope to have it; and may lawfully submit himself to his new master. And so much for the time when he may do it lawfully, if he will. If therefore he do it, he is undoubtedly bound to be a true subject: for a contract lawfully made, cannot lawfully be broken.

By this also a man may understand, when it is, that men may be said to be conquered; and in what the nature of conquest, and the right of a conqueror consisteth: for this submission in itself implieth them all. Conquest, is not the victory itself; but the acquisition, by victory, of a right over the persons of men. He therefore that is slain, is overcome, but not conquered: he that is taken, and put into prison, or chains, is not conquered, though overcome; for he is still an enemy, and may save himself if he can: but he that upon promise of obedience, hath his life and liberty allowed him, is then conquered, and a subject; and not before. The Romans used to say, that their general had *pacified* such a *province*, that is to say, in English, *conquered* it; and that the country was *pacified* by victory, when the people of it had promised *imperata facere*, that is, *to do what the Roman people commanded them:* this was to be conquered. But this promise may be either express, or tacit: express, by promise: tacit, by other signs. As for example, a man that hath not been called to make such an express promise, because he is one whose power perhaps is not considerable; yet if he live under their protection openly, he is understood to submit himself to the government: but if he live there secretly, he is liable to anything that may be done to a spy, and enemy of the state. I say not, he does any injustice; for acts of open hostility bear not that name; but that he may be justly put to death. Likewise, if a man, when his country is conquered, be out of it, he is not conquered, nor subject: but if at his return, he submit to the government, he is bound to obey it. So that *conquest*, to define it, is the acquiring of the right of sovereignty by victory. Which right, is acquired in the people's submission, by which they contract with the victor, promising obedience for life and liberty.

In Chapter xxix, I have set down for one of the causes of the dissolutions of commonwealths, their imperfect generation, consisting in the want of an absolute and arbitrary legislative power; for want whereof, the civil sovereign is fain to handle the sword of justice unconstantly, and as if it were too hot for him to hold. One reason whereof, which I have not there mentioned, is this, that they will all of them justify the war, by which their power was at first gotten, and whereon, as they think, their right dependeth, and not on the possession. As if, for example, the right of the kings of England did depend on the goodness of the cause of William the Conqueror, and upon their lineal, and directest descent from him; by which means, there would perhaps be no tie of the subjects' obedience to their sovereign at this day in all the world: wherein whilst they needlessly think to justify themselves, they justify all the successful rebellions that ambition shall at any time raise against them, and their successors. Therefore I put down for one of the most effectual seeds of the death of any state, that the conquerors require not only a submission of men's actions to them for the future, but also an approbation of all their actions past; when there is scarce a commonwealth in the world, whose beginnings can in conscience be justified.

And because the name of tyranny, signifieth nothing more, nor less, than the name of sovereignty, be it in one, or many men, saving that they that use the former word, are understood to be angry with them they call tyrants; I think the toleration of a professed hatred of tyranny, is a toleration of hatred to commonwealth in general, and another evil seed, not differing much from the former. For to the justification of the cause of a conqueror, the reproach of the cause of the conquered, is for the most part necessary: but neither of them necessary for the obligation of the conquered. And thus much I have thought fit to say upon the review of the first and second part of this discourse.

In Chapter xxxv, I have sufficiently declared out of the Scripture, that in the commonwealth of the Jews, God himself was made the sovereign, by pact with the people; who were therefore called his *peculiar people*, to distinguish them from the rest of the world, over whom God reigned not by their consent, but by his own power: and that in this kingdom Moses was God's lieutenant on earth; and that it was he that told them what laws God appointed them to be ruled by. But I have omitted to set down who were the officers appointed to do execution; especially in capital punishments; not then thinking it a matter of so necessary consideration, as I find it since. We know that generally in all commonwealths, the execution of corporal punishments, was either put upon the guards, or other soldiers of the sovereign power; or given to those, in whom want of means, contempt of honour, and hardness of heart, concurred, to make them sue for such an office. But amongst the Israelites it was a positive law of God their sovereign, that he that was convicted of a capital crime, should be stoned to death by the people; and that the witnesses should cast the first stone, and after the witnesses, then the rest of the people. This was a law that designed who were to be the executioners; but not that any one should throw a stone at him before conviction and sentence, where the congregation was judge. The witnesses were nevertheless to be heard before they proceeded to execution, unless the fact were committed in the presence of the congregation itself, or in sight of the lawful judges; for then there needed no other witnesses but the judges themselves. Nevertheless, this manner of proceeding being not thoroughly understood, hath given occasion to a dangerous opinion, that any man may kill another, in some cases, by a right of zeal; as if the executions done upon offenders in the kingdom of God in old time, proceeded not from the sovereign command, but from the authority of private zeal: which, if we consider the texts that seem to favour it, is quite contrary.

First, where the Levites fell upon the people, that had

made and worshipped the Golden Calf, and slew three
thousand of them; it was by the commandment of Moses,
from the mouth of God; as is manifest, *Exod.* xxxii. 27.
And when the son of a woman of Israel had blasphemed
God, they that heard it, did not kill him, but brought
him before Moses, who put him under custody, till God
should give sentence against him; as appears, *Levit.*
xxiv. 11, 12. Again, (*Numb.* xxv. 6, 7), when Phinehas
killed Zimri and Cosbi, it was not by right of private
zeal: their crime was committed in the sight of the
assembly; there needed no witness; the law was known,
and he the heir-apparent to the sovereignty; and, which
is the principal point, the lawfulness of his act depended
wholly upon a subsequent ratification by Moses, whereof
he had no cause to doubt. And this presumption of a
future ratification, is sometimes necessary to the safety
of a commonwealth; as in a sudden rebellion, any man
that can suppress it by his own power in the country
where it begins, without express law or commission,
may lawfully do it, and provide to have it ratified, or
pardoned, whilst it is in doing, or after it is done. Also
Numb. xxxv. 30, it is expressly said, *Whosoever shall
kill the murderer, shall kill him upon the word of witnesses:* but witnesses suppose a formal judicature, and
consequently condemn that pretence of *jus zelotarum.*
The law of Moses concerning him that enticeth to
idolatry, that is to say, in the kingdom of God to a
renouncing of his allegiance, (*Deut.* xiii. 8, 9), forbids
to conceal him, and commands the accuser to cause him
to be put to death, and to cast the first stone at him;
but not to kill him before he be condemned. And (*Deut.*
xvii. 4, 5, 6, 7), the process against idolatry is exactly
set down: for God there speaketh to the people, as
judge, and commandeth them, when a man is accused
of idolatry, to enquire diligently of the fact, and find-

ing it true, then to stone him; but still the hand of the witness throweth the first stone. This is not private zeal, but public condemnation. In like manner when a father hath a rebellious son, the law is, (*Deut.* xxi. 18-21), that he shall bring him before the judges of the town, and all the people of the town shall stone him. Lastly, by pretence of these laws it was, that St. Stephen was stoned, and not by pretence of private zeal: for before he was carried away to execution, he had pleaded his cause before the high-priest. There is nothing in all this, nor in any other part of the Bible, to countenance executions by private zeal; which being oftentimes but a conjunction of ignorance and passion, is against both the justice and peace of a commonwealth.

In Chapter xxxvi, I have said, that it is not declared in what manner God spake supernaturally to Moses: nor that he spake not to him sometimes by dreams and visions, and by a supernatural voice, as to other prophets: for the manner how he spake unto him from the mercy-seat, is expressly set down, *Numbers* vii. 89, in these words, *From that time forward, when Moses entered into the Tabernacle of the congregation to speak with God, he heard a voice which spake unto him from over the mercy-seat, which is over the Ark of the testimony; from between the cherubims he spake unto him.* But it is not declared in what consisteth the preeminence of the manner of God's speaking to Moses, above that of his speaking to other prophets, as to Samuel, and to Abraham, to whom he also spake by a voice, (that is, by vision), unless the difference consist in the clearness of the vision. For *face to face*, and *mouth to mouth*, cannot be literally understood of the infiniteness, and incomprehensibility of the Divine nature.

And as to the whole doctrine, I see not yet, but the principles of it are true and proper; and the ratiocination solid. For I ground the civil right of sovereigns, and both the duty and liberty of subjects, upon the known natural inclinations of mankind, and upon the articles of the law of nature; of which no man, that pretends but reason enough to govern his private family, ought to be ignorant. And for the power ecclesiastical of the same sovereigns, I ground it on such texts, as are both evident in themselves, and consonant to the scope of the whole Scripture. And therefore am persuaded, that he that shall read it with a purpose only to be informed, shall be informed by it. But for those that by writing, or public discourse, or by their eminent actions, have already engaged themselves to the maintaining of contrary opinions, they will not be so easily satisfied. For in such cases, it is natural for men, at one and the same time, both to proceed in reading, and to lose their attention, in the search of objections to that they had read before. Of which in a time wherein the interests of men are changed, (seeing much of that doctrine, which serveth to the establishing of a new government, must needs be contrary to that which conduced to the dissolution of the old), there cannot choose but be very many.

In that part which treateth of a Christian commonwealth, there are some new doctrines, which, it may be, in a state where the contrary were already fully determined, were a fault for a subject without leave to divulge, as being an usurpation of the place of a teacher. But in this time, that men call not only for peace, but also for truth, to offer such doctrines as I think true, and that manifestly tend to peace and loyalty, to the consideration of those that are yet in deliberation, is no more, but to offer new wine, to be put into new casks, that both may be preserved together. And I suppose, that then, when novelty can breed no trouble nor disorder in a state, men are not generally so much inclined to the reverence of antiquity, as to prefer ancient errors, before new and well-proved truth.

There is nothing I distrust more than my elocution, which nevertheless I am confident, excepting the mischances of the press, is not obscure. That I have neglected the ornament of quoting ancient poets, orators, and philosophers, contrary to the custom of late time, whether I have done well or ill in it, proceedeth from my judgment, grounded on many reasons. For first, all truth of doctrine dependeth either upon *reason*, or upon *Scripture*; both which give credit to many, but never receive it from any writer. Secondly, the matters in question are not of *fact*, but of *right*, wherein there is no place for *witnesses*. There is scarce any of those old writers, that contradicteth not sometimes both himself and others; which makes their testimonies insufficient. Fourthly, such opinions as are taken only upon credit of antiquity, are not intrinsically the judgment of those that cite them, but words that pass, like gaping, from mouth to mouth. Fifthly, it is many times with a fraudulent design that men stick their corrupt doctrine with the cloves of other men's wit. Sixthly, I find not that the ancients they cite, took it for an ornament, to do the like with those that wrote before them. Seventhly, it is an argument of indigestion, when Greek and Latin sentences unchewed come up again, as they used to do, unchanged. Lastly, though I reverence those men of ancient time, that either have written truth perspicuously, or set us in a better way to find it out ourselves; yet to the antiquity itself I think nothing due. For if we will reverence the age, the present is the oldest. If the antiquity of the writer, I am not sure, that generally they to whom such honour is given, were more ancient when they wrote, than I am that am writing. But if it be well considered, the praise of ancient authors, proceeds not from the reverence of the dead, but from the competition, and mutual envy of the living.

To conclude, there is nothing in this whole discourse, nor in that I writ before of the same subject in Latin, as far as I can perceive, contrary either to the Word of God, or to good manners; or to the disturbance of the public tranquillity. Therefore I think it may be profitably printed, and more profitably taught in the Universities, in case they also think so, to whom the judgment of the same belongeth. For seeing the Universities are the fountains of civil and moral doctrine, from whence the preachers, and the gentry, drawing such water as they find, use to sprinkle the same, (both from the pulpit and in their conversation), upon the people, there ought certainly to be great care taken, to have it pure, both from the venom of heathen politicians, and from the incantation of deceiving spirits. And by that means the most men, knowing their duties, will be the less subject to serve the ambition of a few discontented persons, in their purposes against the state; and be the less grieved with the contributions necessary for their peace, and defence; and the governors themselves have the less cause, to maintain at the common charge any greater army, than is necessary to make good the public liberty, against the invasions and encroachments of foreign enemies.

And thus I have brought to an end my Discourse of Civil and Ecclesiastical Government, occasioned by the disorders of the present time, without partiality, without application, and without other design than to set before men's eyes the mutual relation between protection and obedience; of which the condition of human nature, and the laws divine, both natural and positive, require an inviolable observation. And though in the revolution of states, there can be no very good constellation for truths of this nature to be born under, (as having an angry aspect from the dissolvers of an old government, and seeing but the backs of them that erect a new), yet I cannot think it will be condemned at this time, either by the public judge of doctrine, or by any that desires the continuance of public peace. And in this hope I return to my interrupted speculation of bodies natural; wherein, if God give me health to finish it, I hope the novelty will as much please, as in the doctrine of this artificial body it useth to offend. For such truth, as opposeth no man's profit, nor pleasure, is to all men welcome.